T0234032

Communications
in Computer and Information Science   1204

More information about this series at http://www.springer.com/series/7899

Vladimir Sukhomlin · Elena Zubareva (Eds.)

Modern Information Technology and IT Education

12th International Conference, SITITO 2017
Moscow, Russia, November 24–26, 2017
Revised Selected Papers

 Springer

Editors
Vladimir Sukhomlin ⓘ
Moscow State University
Moscow, Russia

Elena Zubareva ⓘ
Moscow State University
Moscow, Russia

ISSN 1865-0929   ISSN 1865-0937 (electronic)
Communications in Computer and Information Science
ISBN 978-3-030-78272-6   ISBN 978-3-030-78273-3 (eBook)
https://doi.org/10.1007/978-3-030-78273-3

This Springer imprint is published by the registered company Springer Nature Switzerland AG
The registered company address is: Gewerbestrasse 11, 6330 Cham, Switzerland

Preface

This CCIS volume, published by Springer, contains the proceedings of the 12th International Conference on Modern Information Technology and IT Education (SITITO 2017), which took place during November 24–26, 2017, at the Faculty of Computational Mathematics and Cybernetics, Lomonosov Moscow State University. The Lomonosov Moscow State University was founded in 1755 and was the first university in Russia. It currently hosts more than 50,000 students. The Lomonosov Moscow State University is one of the major traditional educational institutions in Russia, offering training in almost all branches of modern science and humanities. By providing up-to-date infrastructure and convenient logistics, as well as historical and natural attractions, the venue allowed for the successful organization of SITITO 2017.

The conference series is now more than ten years old, having taken place regularly since 2005, and has contributed significantly to the advancement of the new educational direction "Information Technology", which was created in 2002 upon an initiative of the Faculty of Computational Mathematics and Cybernetics, Lomonosov Moscow State University. Later this educational direction was renamed "The Fundamental Informatics and Information Technologies".

The SITITO conference series has gathered a rich collection of scientific works from conference participants that reflect the history of the development of IT and the IT education system. This volume contains 30 contributed papers selected from 126 full paper submissions. Each submission was reviewed by at least three Program Committee members, with the help of external reviewers, and the final decisions took into account the feedback from a rebuttal phase. We wish to thank all the authors who submitted their papers to SITITO 2017, the Program Committee members, and the external reviewers.

The relevance and timeliness of the conference was emphasized by the fact that the Government of the Russian Federation approved the program "Digital Economy of the Russian Federation" just before the conference (Order of the Government of the Russian Federation of July 28, 2017 No. 1632- p). This program is aimed at "creating conditions for the development of the knowledge society in the Russian Federation, improving the welfare and quality of life of our country's citizens by improving access and quality of goods and services produced in the digital economy using modern digital technologies, raising awareness and digital literacy, improving the availability and quality of public services for citizens, as well as security, both within and outside the country".

A plenary report on "Contours of Digital Reality" was delivered by Georgy Malinetsky, Professor of the Keldysh Institute of Applied Mathematics, Russia, who examined the main features of the global economy in its current state, as well as the main trends associated with total digitalization of the social-economic sphere in the information society.

A second plenary report entitled "Scientific and Methodological Aspects of the Problem of Technology Integration" was given by Konstantin Kolin, Professor of the Federal Research Center "Computer Science and Control" of the Russian Academy of Sciences, Russia, who presented a general methodological view on the integration and convergence of technologies and justified the urgency of creating a new scientific discipline, with the technologies themselves, their classification, integration methods, and performance criteria, as its subject matter.

The third plenary report entitled "Modern Didactics of Mass Electronic Education" was delivered by Mikhail Karpenko, Professor and President of the Modern University for the Humanities (MUH), Russia, who predicted the structure of higher education based on an analysis of new opportunities provided by modern high-tech applications. He emphasized the consideration of the advantages of electronic educational technologies in comparison with the traditional campus education. The report proposed a structure for the organizational and technological methodology of a robotic educational process, identified the composition and functionality of the robotic educational components, and considered the automation tools for the administration of the educational process developed at the MUH.

Boris Slavin, Academic Advisor of the Faculty of Applied Mathematics and Information Technologies, Financial University under the Government of the Russian Federation, Russia, devoted his report to a critical analysis of the Digital Economy (DE) program. Specific coverage was given to the programs that are directly related to the teaching staff and education for DE. The forecasts of the characteristics and indicators of the Future University were presented.

SITITO 2017 was attended by about 400 people. The Program Committee reviewed 224 submissions and accepted 154 as full papers, 34 as short papers, 2 as posters, and 2 as demos; 32 submissions were rejected. According to the conference program, these 150 oral presentations (of the full and short papers) were structured into eight sessions, including IT Education: Methodology, Methodological Support, E-learning and IT in Education; Educational Resources and Best Practices of IT Education; Research and Development in the Field of New IT and their Applications; Scientific Software in Education and Science; School Education in Computer Science and ICT; and Economic Informatics, Innovative Information and Pedagogical Technologies in IT Education.

Besides the above, the conference also hosted the following satellite events: a meeting summing up the results of the 7th International Internet-Conference-Competition "Innovative Information and Pedagogical Technologies in IT Education" (IP-2017); a workshop containing four presentations; an open workshop "Digital Economy: the Concept of Digital Skills and the Training System of Highly Demanded Personnel", including three round tables with discussions on business models and mobile technologies; two master classes entitled "Gamification in Education" and "Training in Network Security Technologies"; video conferences under the title "Modern Training Courses and Manuals"; and round table discussions on topical issues of IT Education.

The conference was attended by leading experts and teams from research centers, universities, the IT industry, institutes of the Russian Academy of Sciences, Russian high-tech companies, and from countries abroad.

SITITO 2017 was further supported by the following associations and societies:

- Federal Educational-Methodical Association in higher education for the enlarged group of specialties and areas of training 02.00.00 Computer and Information Sciences;
- Fund for Promotion of Internet Media, IT Education, Human Development League Internet Media;
- Federal Research Center "Computer Science and Control' of the Russian Academy of Sciences;
- Russian Transport Academy;
- Samsung Research Center;
- D-Link Corporation;
- BaseALT.

March 2020

Vladimir Sukhomlin
Elena Zubareva

Organization

General Chair

Evgeny Moiseev — Russian Academy of Sciences and Lomonosov Moscow State University, Russia

Program Chair

Igor Sokolov — Federal Research Center "Computer Science and Control" of the Russian Academy of Sciences, Russia

Vladimir Sukhomlin — Lomonosov Moscow State University, Russia

Organization Chair

Evgeny Moiseev — Russian Academy of Sciences and Lomonosov Moscow State University, Russia

Vladimir Sukhomin — Lomonosov Moscow State University, Russia

Organizing Committee

Leonid Dmitriev — Lomonosov Moscow State University, Russia
Mikhail Fedotov — Lomonosov Moscow State University, Russia
Dmitry Gouriev — Lomonosov Moscow State University, Russia
Evgeniy Ilyushin — Lomonosov Moscow State University, Russia
Sergey Lozhkin — Lomonosov Moscow State University, Russia
Mikhail Lugachyov — Lomonosov Moscow State University, Russia
Vassily Lyubetsky — Kharkevich Institute for Information Transmission Problems, Russian Academy of Sciences, and Lomonosov Moscow State University, Russia
Evgeniy Morkovin — Lomonosov Moscow State University, Russia
Dmitry Namiot — Lomonosov Moscow State University, Russia
Mikhail Posypkin — Federal Research Center "Computer Science and Control" of the Russian Academy of Sciences and Lomonosov Moscow State University, Russia
Alexander Razgulin — Lomonosov Moscow State University, Russia
Vasiliy Tikhomirov — Lomonosov Moscow State University, Russia
Alexander Tomilin — Lomonosov Moscow State University, Russia
Evgeniy Zakharov — Lomonosov Moscow State University, Russia
Elena Zubareva — Lomonosov Moscow State University, Russia

Program Committee

Sergei Andrianov	Saint Petersburg State University, Russia
Sergei Avdonin	University of Alaska Fairbanks, USA
Esen Bidaibekov	Abai Kazakh National Pedagogical University, Kazakhstan
Yousef Daradkeh	Prince Sattam bin Abdulaziz University, Saudi Arabia
Alekzander Emelianov	National Research University - Moscow Power Engineering Institute, Russia
Yuri Evtushenko	Federal Research Center "Computer Science and Control" of the Russian Academy of Sciences, Russia
Victor Gergel	Lobachevsky State University of Nizhni Novgorod, Russia
Luis Gouveia	University Fernando Pessoa, Portugal
Sava Grozdev	VUZF University, Bulgaria
Tatyana Gubina	BaseALT, Russia
Dmitry Izmestiev	LANIT Group of Companies, Russia
Evgeniy Khenner	Russian Academy of Education and Perm State National Research University, Russia
Alekzander Kim	The Institute of Electronic Control Computers, Russia
Alexander Klimov	Russian University of Transport (MIIT), Russia
Vladimir Korenkov	Joint Institute for Nuclear Research, Russia
Sergey Kramarov	Surgut State University, Russia
Tok Ling	National University of Singapore, Singapore
Alexander Misharin	Russian Railways and Russian University of Transport (MIIT), Russia
Valentin Nechaev	MIREA - Russian Technological University, Russia
Diethard Pallaschke	Karlsruhe Institute of Technology, Germany
Oleg Pokusaev	Russian University of Transport (MIIT), Russia
Gennady Ryabov	Russian Academy of Sciences and Lomonosov Moscow State University, Russia
Konstantin Samouylov	Peoples Friendship University of Russia, Russia
Manfred Sneps-Sneppe	Ventspils University College, Latvia
Alexey Smirnov	BaseALT, Russia
Leonid Sokolinsky	South Ural State University, Russia
Margarita Sotnikova	Saint Petersburg State University, Russia
Vladimir Sukhomlin	Lomonosov Moscow State University, Russia
Dmitry Tarkhov	Peter the Great St. Petersburg Polytechnic University, Russia
Mourat Tchoshanov	University of Texas at El Paso, USA
Andrey Terekhov	Saint Petersburg State University, Russia
Alexander Vasilyev	Peter the Great St. Petersburg Polytechnic University, Russia
Evgeny Veremey	Saint Petersburg State University, Russia

Contents

Research and Development in the Field of New IT and Their Applications

Scientific Software in Education and Science

Economic Informatics

IT-Education: Methodology, Methodological Support

Multiplatform System of Digital Talents Development "Academy of OIT"

Vladimir Sukhomlin⬚, Elena Zubareva(✉) ⬚, and Dmitry Namiot⬚

Moscow State University, Leninskie gory, 1, GSP-1, 119991 Moscow, Russia
e.zubareva@cs.msu.ru

Abstract. This article presents the principles of constructing the system of supplementary and master's education entitled "Академия ОИТ" ("Academy of OIT"). The Academy will provide training of highly qualified specialists, innovative and scientific personnel in the field of information technologies and their applications. As a basis for the methodical support of the Academy, the concept of digital skills was used. The information-technological part of this system was created as an aggregate of interconnected problem-oriented platforms providing a wide range of opportunities for students to solve tasks of targeted training and implementation of their educational and career paths. The Academy focuses on programs of supplementary vocational training of a sectoral focus, developed and implemented by the M.V. Lomonosov Moscow State University (the Laboratory of Open Information Technologies) together with leading IT industry companies, as well as on the practice-oriented nature of scientific research within the framework of master's degree theses directly related to the development of actual applied problems of the digital economy.

Keywords: Digital skills · Model of skills representation · Digital talents · "Academy of OIT" · Platform

1 Introduction

Modern society enters a new stage of world economic development, known as the "digital economy", which is characterized by comprehensive and in-depth informatization and digitization of all aspects of human activity. At the same time, both industrial and social spheres are subjects to digital transformation, including science and education.

It is convenient to consider the Cancún Ministerial Conference held on June 22–23, 2016, where the Declaration of Ministers "On the Digital Economy: Innovation, Growth and Social Well-being" [1] was adopted as the starting point for a systemic, purposeful movement towards the digital economy on a global scale.

The Declaration emphasizes that the world economy is becoming increasingly digital, that the growing use and investments in digital and knowledge-based capital are causing a profound transformation of our society and that the digital economy is a powerful catalyst for innovation, growth and social well-being. It outlines the main tasks of the digital economy development, one of which determines the need for efforts to ensure

V. Sukhomlin and E. Zubareva (Eds.): SITITO 2017, CCIS 1204, pp. 3–13, 2021.
https://doi.org/10.1007/978-3-030-78273-3_1

that all people have the skills necessary to participate in the digital economy and digital society to develop the potential of educational and training systems aimed at identifying the demand for general and specialized digital skills, to develop skills through complementary education, through continuing education and on-the-job training, and also contributing to the increase in the digital literacy rate, the effectiveness of the use of information and communication technologies in education and training.

For Russia, which has also embarked upon the path of building a digital economy [2], one of the central issues is the personnel with the necessary skills and the educational technologies aimed at identification of the demand for marketable general and specialized digital skills and teaching these skills.

The domestic system of vocational education has a significant potential for solving the problem of training much-needed personnel for the digital economy. However, exploiting this potential in relation to the current tasks requires new solutions, both in the development of new basic training directions and updating the existing ones, and especially it requires the development of new forms of supplementary education and lifelong learning. Moreover, the effectiveness of solutions on this path will largely depend on the success of the integration of the efforts of the education system and the community of prospective employers.

The article deals with the principles of building the system of supplementary and master's education the "Academy of OIT" (Academy), specializing in training highly qualified specialists, innovative and scientific personnel in the field of information technologies and their applications. As a basis for the methodical support of the Academy, the concept of digital skills was used. The information-technological part of this system was created as an aggregate of interconnected problem-oriented platforms providing a wide range of opportunities for students to solve tasks of targeted training and implementation of their educational and career paths. The Academy focuses on programs of supplementary vocational training of a sectoral focus, developed and implemented by the M.V. Lomonosov Moscow State University (the Laboratory of Open Information Technologies) together with leading IT industry companies, as well as on the practice-oriented nature of scientific research within the framework of master's degree theses directly related to the development of actual applied problems of the digital economy.

2   Digital Skills: Definition, Taxonomy, Description Tools

Let us first consider the methodological aspects of the concept of digital skills used in this project - their role in the digital economy, definition, properties, classification, and ways to describe such skills. We will take as a basis the methodical solutions proposed in [3], which will be briefly considered below.

It is obvious that for the accelerated development of all sectors of the digital, essentially innovative economy, it is urgent to provide it with personnel with the marketable skills at specific workplaces and at a particular time. In practice, therefore, not only diplomas and certificates of education are in demand, but the final results of educational, training, and training processes, namely, professional skills. It should be noted that in the digital economy a large part of skills is totally digital. Therefore, *digital skills* and *digital literacy* play a crucial role in the digital age.

By the digital literacy needed for all the cohabitants of the digital world [4] we mean the ability to be confident in using IT tools, as well as the ability to assess information obtained from several sources, to evaluate its reliability and usefulness with the help of self-established criteria, and the ability to solve tasks that involve finding the information related to an unfamiliar context, if there is ambiguity and absence of explicit instructions.

According to the [3], skills should be considered an ability of a particular or abstract worker in the performance of some specific professional activity or part of it in a specific work position and at a particular time. Thus, skills are purely dynamic entities associated with a specific context or ecosystem of professional activity (workplace).

Essentially, a skill is understood as a certain system of *professional skills (processes, procedures, labor functions)*, embodied with the help of **target** or **operational** skills. An important role in this system belongs to the **basic skills** (fundamental and instrumental), which constitutes the foundation upon which operational skills are formed.

The following classes of digital skills are defined in the cited work.

1. **Generic IT skills** enabling workers of a wide range of professions to use IT in their daily work.
2. **Professional IT skills** required by professionals in the IT areas for the production of IT products, services and resources.
3. **Problem-oriented digital skills – the skills of specialists developing and using specialized problem-oriented platforms, applications, software packages, computer-aided design systems, etc.**
4. **Complementary skills** – the skills of using the capabilities of the ecosystem to perform specific tasks related to the application of IT in the workplace.
5. **Skills in the use of digital economy services** – the skills in the use of various specialized services and processes implemented on the basis of the Internet of Things infrastructure and functional components of the digital economy.

The creation of a skill building system must take into account their main features. In the first place, such characteristics include:

1. Dynamism, i.e. variability in time.
2. The dependence on the workplace ecosystem, i.e. context of a particular workplace.
3. The constant renewal of complementary and service digital skills, due to the rapid development of technological and information equipment of the workplace ecosystem.
4. The interdisciplinary nature of skills that can potentially cover several different convergent subject areas.
5. Mobility and competitiveness of skills, their ability to unite in a virtual space to solve common problems, bypassing administrative and international borders.
6. The growing importance of knowledge and ability to apply international standards.

From the tasks of personnel management point of view, planning and organization of training of professional personnel in the IT industry and its applications we are not only interested in the digital skills in general, but in the skill sets corresponding to the specific occupational positions of the employees, i.e. sets of digital skills determining

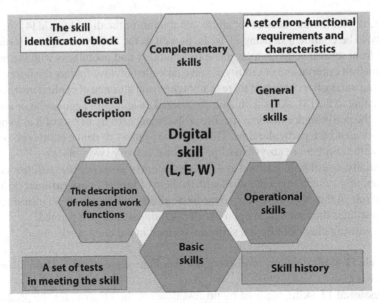

Fig. 1. The digital skill model.

the content of the profession, specialty, specialization, and finally, the workplace. Such a set of digital skills needed for a specific professional position will be called a **digital skills profile** or a **digital workplace skill**. Further in the text, if this is clear from the context, instead of the digital skill of the workplace, we will simply use "the skill".

In order to describe the digital skills the [3] proposes a metamodel, presented in Fig. 1, reflecting both the composition of the sections of the skill specification, and the multidimensionality of this concept and its dynamic essence. In general, the profile of digital skills is given by a set of descriptions of the skills that make up it. Such a set can include both descriptions of already defined skills, and descriptions of basic skills. At the moment, as shown in the [5], the most comprehensive system of basic skills is the SFIA system claiming international standard [6]. The sixth version of the SFIA specifications defines 97 basic ICT skills. Combinations of these skills can describe the absolute majority of skills corresponding to the possible work positions in the IT industry.

The skill model includes the following components:

- **The skill identification block** including the name of the skill (possibly composite) and its code in the chosen qualification system.
- **General description**-definition of the scope, purpose and general description of the functional skills.
- **The description of roles and work functions**- a definition of the most characteristic roles performed by a specialist with this skill, as well as a description of labor functions, processes and procedures corresponding to roles.

- **Operational skills** directly related to the performance of targeted (labor) functions and, as a rule, requiring constant updating and development throughout the target skill life cycle.
- **Basic skills**-basic knowledge and skills required for professional development and use of operational skills.
- **Complementary skills**-digital ecosystem skills that might cause new opportunities when using them in the workplace.
- **General IT skills**-the ability to use general-purpose IT-tools in the workplace.
- **A set of non-functional requirements and characteristics**-determines the additional attributes associated with this skill (salary level for an employee with this skill, work experience, educational qualification, grade of access to classified information, etc.).
- **A set of tests in meeting the skill**-a set of descriptions of typical tasks for the application of basic labor functions to verify the fulfillment of the professional criteria by the candidate.
- **Skill history**-the information base that stores the history of skill changes throughout its life cycle.

As sated, an important property of this model is that it reflects the multidimensionality and dynamics of the digital skill concept. Both the skill itself (the basic functional skill plan) and its constituent parts have additional dimensions, the advancement of which might change all or parts of the skill specification.

Additional dimensions of the skill are:

1. L – a career level or a level of responsibility for the realization of the skill;
2. S – a scale of events in the life cycle of the skill, causing a change in its status, by which the version of the skill is determined;
3. W – a space of requirements specifications for the workplace (the space of employers' organizations with their requirement specifications for the workplace with this skill), determining the additional conditions for the skill realization.

The examined above descriptive apparatus of digital skills plays an important role in building a system of professional skills development, providing the possibility for creating databases with descriptions of skills required for different contexts of application and using them for designing appropriate educational and training technologies for training personnel with the required skills.

3   Creating a Digital Skills Development System

The issues of forming digital skills are considered as national policies strategic tasks. Thus, virtually all developed countries are working to create a dynamic, flexible and high-quality skill building system that would provide students with the knowledge and skills necessary for full participation in the economic activities of society, as well as active living in digital world.

In the present case, the objective was to develop an educational system that implements supplementary education programs and master's degree programs in order to train highly qualified, innovative and scientific IT staff with marketable IT skills. It should be noted that in an innovative economy, a significant part of the IT industry lacks such personnel, known as **"digital talents"** or simply **talents** [7].

In view of the above and the fact that the initiator and developer of the project to create the digital skills development system was the staff of the Laboratory of Open Information Technologies of the Faculty of Computational Mathematics and Cybernetics, Lomonosov Moscow State University, this system was called the "Academy of OIT".

Let us formulate general provisions or trends that have influenced the choice of the approach to the implementation of this project.

1. The central paradigm of modern education is the student-centric approach taken as a basis in the Bologna process, considering the student as an active subject of the educational process, at the center of which there is the cognitive activity of the student.
2. In the student-centric paradigm, the education system is seen as a flexible environment (the student's ecosystem) functionally saturated with educational technologies, resources and services, supporting the student's educational activity and providing him/her with ample opportunities for fulfillment of their scientific, educational and career plans on the basis of the choice of forms of education, educational technologies, resources and services.
3. Platformness of ecosystems is a modern trend, in which the most important functional components of ecosystems are problem-oriented information-digital platforms providing to a wide range of users online services, including the resources and real-world processes management.
4. The high rates of digital transformation of the economy and the introduction of innovations require the acceleration of the processes of preparing relevant skills for solving urgent business tasks; this stimulates the development of partnership between industry organizations and educational institutions in the formation of popular digital skills, including joint development and implementation of industry-specific training programs.
5. The knowledge-based innovative nature of the digital economy's instrumental base seeks to create mechanisms and resources for involving teaching staff and students in research and innovation activities, to encourage their interaction with the scientific world and the world of high technologies among the most urgent tasks of the education system.
6. The urgency of targeted development of information resources of general use of scientific and educational nature (scientific libraries, advanced pedagogical experience, best educational practices, innovative solutions, student projects, etc.) and the introduction of all this into the ecosystem of education.
7. Development of the concept of mass courses of open online learning (MCOOL), on the basis of which many universities around the world have created public libraries of quality teaching and methodological complexes in various disciplines, which can significantly accelerate the development of new curricula using the educational resources already created within the MCOOL concept.

Taking into account the general trends noted above, a multi-platform approach was chosen to create information technology support for the target system, i.e. the system was created as a set of interrelated platforms and services complementing the student's ecosystem.

The composition of the basic platforms of the Academy is shown in Fig. 2.

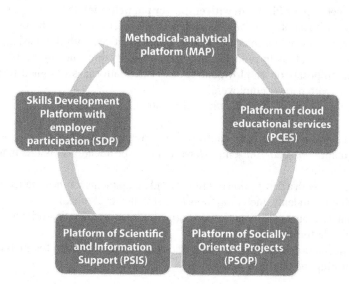

Fig.2. The composition of the basic platforms of "the Academy of OIT".

Let us consider the purpose and the functions of the basic platforms of the Academy.

1. **Methodical-analytical platform (MAP)** - is an integration platform designed to perform research and analytical work for development of educational and methodological support and educational standards in the field of IT education; it operates on the basis of a consortium process, covering universities, companies, public organizations, experts, students; includes - portals, websites, Internet resources and thematic blogs of social media (the prototype of the platform was the portal "IT Education in Russia" - http://it-edu.ru/).

2. **Platform of cloud educational services (PCES)** - a set of cloud educational resources and services to support and implement educational processes. The main emphasis in the development of this platform is placed on the development and implementation of training programs for supplementary education in industry orientation in partnership with the leading companies of the IT industry (the group of companies LANIT, Samsung, D-link, etc.). Currently, priority programs for training are the programs aimed at developing skills for developing large-scale Web applications and Internet of Things applications [8–10].

This platform also includes two more important components:

- the cloud configurable computational polygon to support modeling and computing scientific experiments, accomplished through the grid technologies [11];
- a cloud-based service that automatically checks maturity of professional digital skills [12, 13].

3. **Skills Development Platform with employer participation (SDP)** is a platform for interaction with employers' organizations; it designed to create databases of popular skills, to support online internships and online practices with the participation of employers, as well as to promote information about companies in the IT industry and their proposals on employment issues. This platform is designed to manage interaction with partner employers.
   This platform supports the following information:

   - a register of partner organizations with information about partners;
   - information base of the employer-provided specifications of the marketable digital skills;
   - a database with a description of projects and assignments for the practice-oriented training of students, including tools to assess the level of skills development;
   - personal accounts of students undertaking internship or practice-oriented training on this platform;
   - the information base of history and statistics for the subsystem for analyzing and monitoring the platform functioning.

   The main subsystems of this platform are:

   - the subsystem of interaction with partners;
   - the subsystem of interaction with students;
   - the subsystem of implementing online internships and online practices involving employers;
   - the subsystem of information base management of digital skills specifications;
   - the subsystem of analysis of monitoring, statistics and audit;
   - the subsystem of access to the platform information platform control;
   - the subsystem of information policy and advertising support.

4. **Platform of Scientific and Information Support (PSIS)** – it is a system of information and technological support for scientific periodicals (journals), scientific events (forums, thematic conferences and symposia), information resources of scientific and educational nature (archives of journals, libraries of best educational practices and innovative pedagogical decisions, archives of student projects etc.).

Scientific periodicals and highly rated scientific conferences directly related to the system of advanced staff training in science-intensive areas with significant innovative potential serve as an effective tool for involving students and teaching staff in research and innovation activities, facilitate the integration of efforts and the exchange of experience in promising fields of science and technology, education, and generally lead to improved quality of educational processes.

As part of the activities of "the Academy OIT", the following scientific journals serve as the basic solutions fulfilling the purpose and functionality of this platform:

- Online international scientific journal "International Journal of Open Information Technologies" (INJOIT), included in the list of VAK of the Ministry of Education and Science of the Russian Federation. Official website of the publication http://injoit.ru.
- International scientific journal "Modern Information Technologies and IT Education", included in the list of VAK of the Ministry of Education and Science of the Russian Federation. Official website of the publication http://sitito.cs.msu.ru.

And also the following scientific conferences:

- Annual International Scientific Conference "Convergent Cognitive-Information Technologies" http://it-edu.oit.cmc.msu.ru/index.php/convergent/convergent2017;
- Annual International Scientific and Practical Conference "Modern Information Technologies and IT Education" http://it-edu.oit.cmc.msu.ru/index.php/SITITO/sitito 2017;
- Annual International Conference-Competition "Innovative Information and Pedagogical Technologies in the IT Education System" http://it-edu.oit.cmc.msu.ru/index.php/IP/IP-2017.

The tasks and profiles of these conferences are coordinated with the tasks and profiles of the above-mentioned scientific journals, where accounts of the proceedings of these conferences are published.

4   Platform of Socially-Oriented Projects (PSOP)

One of the components of this platform is the educational cloud ОИТ_ВМК – РОИ_СТРАТЕГИЯ - a virtual university for the development of digital skills of people with disabilities [14]. A central feature of the project is that it seeks not only to increase the "information literacy" of people with disabilities, but it was intended to select the students who are inclined and capable of professional work in the field of IT, and to train them for work in IT companies. Currently, the basis of the teaching process is a specialized educational portal/cloud "Strategy" (http://www.ooi.ru) offering an extensive range of courses and corresponding educational and methodical complexes (EMC). At the same time, the offered courses are characterized by easy adaptation for listeners of different training levels, due to structuring them according to the levels of complexity. For convenience purposes and for improving the effectiveness of the training material, EMC include some video courses. Education for people with disabilities is free. This educational technology is developed and supported by the specialists of the Laboratory of Open Information Technologies of the Faculty of Computational Mathematics and Cybernetics, Lomonosov Moscow State University.

5 Conclusion

The article describes principles of creation of the additional and master's education system "Academy OIT" specializing on the training of highly skilled professionals, innovative and scientific staff (digital talents) in the field of information technology and its various applications. Methodological supply kit for the Academy was developed on the basis of the digital skills concept, as well as the language of skills description in the ICT field of SFIA. The information-technological part of this system was created as an aggregate of interconnected problem-oriented platforms providing a wide range of opportunities for students to solve tasks of targeted training and implementation of their educational and career paths. The Academy focuses on programs of supplementary vocational training of a sectoral focus, developed and implemented by the M.V. Lomonosov Moscow State University (the Laboratory of Open Information Technologies) together with leading IT industry companies, as well as on the practice-oriented nature of scientific research within the framework of master's degree theses directly related to the development of actual applied problems of the digital economy. The educational system under consideration is characterized by a well-developed platform for supporting the research and innovation activities of students and teaching staff, which includes top-rated periodicals and a series of international conferences on topical areas of the IT field and its applications. Also, the system includes a socially-oriented platform devoted to develop digital skills of people with disabilities.

References

1. Ministerial Declaration on the Digital Economy: Innovation, Growth and Social Prosperity ("Cancuán Declaration"). http://www.oecd.org/sti/ieconomy/Digital-Economy-Ministerial-Declaration-2016.pdf.
2. Message from the President to the Federal Assembly of the Russian Federation, 1 December 2016. http://www.kremlin.ru/events/president/news/53379. (in Russian)
3. Sukhomlin, V.A., Zubareva, E.V., Yakushin, A.V.: Methodological aspects osf the digital skills concept. Mod. Inf. Technol. IT-Educ. **13**(2), 146–152 (2017). https://doi.org/10.25559/SITITO.2017.2.253. (in Russaian)
4. Kolin, K.K., Ursul, A.D.: Information and culture. In: Introduction to Information Culture. Publishing Strategy Priorities, Moscow (2015)
5. Drozhzhinov, V.I.: SFIA – the system of it professional standards for the digital economy. Mod. Inf. Technol. IT-Educ. **13**(1), 132–143 (2017). https://doi.org/10.25559/SITITO.2017.1.466. (in Russaian)
6. The Skills Framework for the Information Age (SFIA). https://www.sfia-online.org/en
7. Menshikova, E.: "Digital Talents": how a new generation of specialists changes the way companies work. ITMO.NEWS, 22 June (2017). http://news.ifmo.ru/en/startups_and_business/initiative/news/6755/
8. Namiot, D.: On internet of things and smart cities educational courses. Int. J. Open Inf. Technol. **4**(5), 26–38 (2016). (in Russian)
9. Namiot, D., Sneps-Sneppe, M., Daradkeh, Y.: On internet of things education. In: Proceedings of the FRUCT 2020. Saint-Petersburg Electrotechnical University "LETI" and Technopark of ITMO University, Saint-Petersburg, Russia, pp. 309-315 (2017)
10. Namiot, D., Sneps-Sneppe, M.: On internet of things and big data in university courses. Int. J. Embed. Real-Time Commun. Syst. (IJERTCS). **8**(1), 18–30 (2017)

11. Posypkin, M.A., Sukhomlin, V.A., Khrapov, N.P.: Combined distributed infrastructures in science and education. Mod. Inf. Technol. IT-Educ. **11**(1), 31–36 (2015). (in Russian)
12. Yakushin, A.V., Gladkikh, Y.I.: Selection of automated testing solutions programming tasks. Int. J. Open Inf. Technol. **4**(6), 38–43 (2016). (in Russian)
13. Yakushin, A.V., Gladkikh, I.Y.: System of automated testing programs in learning environment. Mod. Prob. Sci. Educ. **3**, 326–336 (2016). (in Russian)
14. Krupennikov, V.A., Sukhomlin, V.A., Yakushin, A.V.: Socialization of people with disabilities in the electronic educational space. Mod. Inf. Technol. IT-Educ. **7**, 1028–1032 (2011). (in Russian)

Manifestation Technology of Non-linear Dynamics Synergetic Effects of Schwartz Cylinder's Areas

Sveltlana Dvoryatkina[1]([✉]) [ID], Eugeny Smirnov[2] [ID], and Artem Uvarov[2] [ID]

[1] Bunin Yelets State University, Kommunarov Str. 28, 399770 Yelets, Russia
sobdvor@yelets.lipetsk.ru
[2] Yaroslavl State Pedagogical University named after K.D.Ushinsky, Respublikanskya Str. 108/1, 150000 Yaroslavl, Russia
e.smirnov@yspu.org

Abstract. In the present article "problem zone" of school mathematics by means of computer and mathematical modeling simulation is investigated. The problem of variables measurement of major generalized designs concerning the analysis and an entity of "problem zone" by means of the construction and adaptation to present conditions of school knowledge is solved. The second stage of developed technology of synergetic effects manifestation on the example of complex concept of surface area development is described in details. So in school mathematical education it is defined only at the visual level (according to Comenius Y.) by means of understanding surface area formulas of three-dimensional objects such as: sphere, cone, cylinder. In a research the functional parameters, technological constructs and regularities of approximation of a lateral surface of Schwarz's cylinder on the basis of its triangulations at the regular and irregular limiting refinement are manifested by stratified polyhedral complexes with using of computer and mathematical modeling. Pedagogical experience allowed to record significant raise of students' educational motivation and understanding of school mathematics and IT by means of modern scientific achievements adaptation.

Keywords: Mathematical education of students · Technology of visual and mathematical modeling · Computer design · Schwartz's cylinder · Surface area

1 Introduction

Synergy as a science explores the phenomena, processes and content structures in open and non-equilibrium systems in various manifestations of their organization with the transition to higher degrees of development. The reference points for the study of systems are the functional characteristics of order parameters transitions from chaos to the equilibrium of systems (fractal objects and processes, turbulence and lasers, nonlinear dynamics, etc.). It is quite significant that the transition from chaos to order (and vice versa) occur through the universal mechanisms of the system complexity. An example is the deployment tree of M. Feigenbaum with the passage through the cascade of

V. Sukhomlin and E. Zubareva (Eds.): SITITO 2017, CCIS 1204, pp. 14–25, 2021.
https://doi.org/10.1007/978-3-030-78273-3_2

period-doubling bifurcations and implementation under Verhulst's scenario. The main resource means the analysis and research of chaotic processes by computer and mathematical modeling. Moreover, in modern science there is the strengthening of integrating role of mathematics, the apparatus and methods of which can be used in the study of qualitatively different fragments of reality. This is possible, first of all, because there is an objectively a commonality, connection, unity between different areas of real world, which can be described using the same equations, scenarios and procedures. The most important component is the identification of the essence of complex mathematical knowledge, scenarios and procedures in the context of building hierarchies, plurality of goal setting and analysis of side solutions, search for bifurcation transitions and attraction basins in the studied processes, coordination of information flows in the emergence of new product. At the same time, the implementation of the process of the efficiency of educational systems improving is possible on the basis of the actualization of synergetic principles and approaches in the development of educational activities of students in a rich information and educational environment and support of their creative independence, including on the basis of computer modeling. At the same time, first of all, there is a growing need for updating the generalized structures and relations of modern scientific knowledge (complex problems) and their subsequent adaptation to the mathematical content of schools and vocational education as mechanisms and foundations for the creation of bifurcation and fluctuation transitions to higher stages of universal educational activities of and the development of intellectual operations of students in the course of research activities and dialogue of cultures. As noted by S. L. Rubinstein with this approach,"...the generalization of relations of subject content acts then and is realized as the generalization of operations made over generalized subject content; generalization and fixing in the individual of these generalized operations lead to formation at the individual of corresponding abilities" [1]. The need to address complex knowledge appears in the process of updating the "problem zones" in school (or university) mathematics, when the available formalization of mathematical structures does not allow the student to understand the essence of mathematical objects and actions. After all, the essence, as a rule, is "hidden" and can be manifested in the design and adaptation to the educational activities of generalized structures of complex knowledge, mastering which the student with the help of a teacher builds the hierarchies and threshold transitions of the formation of this essence of objects, processes and phenomena. This article examines the "problem zones" of school mathematics, which consider the problem of values measurement through the construction and adaptation to current state of school knowledge as the most important generalized structures relating to the analysis and the essence of "problem zones". A complex concept of surface area will be investigated, the development of formulas of three-dimensional body's areas: sphere, cone and cylinder. So, this concept remains inaccessible to the students (as the limit areas of multi-faceted complexes of tangent planes fragments on the crumbling of surface triangulations). At the same time, the formation of synergetic effects of self – organization, self-actualization and self–development in the study process of the surface area concept, communications and personal students development during the second technological stage (content–technological) by means of computer and mathematical modeling (a full number of stages is presented in the works of E. I. Smirnov [2, 3]: preparatory, content–technological, evaluation-correction, generalized-transforming) will be characterized. In particular, the authors identify the functional parameters of patterns approximation and research the square layered polyhedral complexes of Schwartz cylinder surface.

2 Methodology and Methods

Mathematics education has a huge potential of self-organization and positive manifestation of synergetic effects: personal development and education, the orderliness of the content and structure of cognitive experiences on the basis of cultures dialogue. While students' research activity acts as an essential attribute of an effective system of self-regulation of personality traits of the students (F. Maslow, K. Rogers, V. M. Monakhov V.D. Shadrikov et al. [4–6]). Synergy of mathematical education will be considered by us as a symbiosis of the effects of self-organization and self-development of the individual in the process of nonlinearity development of complex mathematical objects and procedures by means of knowledge integration and step-by-step coordination of actions of different factors and beginnings. This approach is particularly important and sensitive for mathematics education, where naturally occurring multi-stage abstraction of the subject substance to create the conditions for such generalizations. Note that the content of mathematical education in schools and universities should undoubtedly reflect the following trends and features of self-movement of the content of mathematics in the modern period:

- deep formalization of mathematical apparatus in professional and practical problems solving (Dirac's δ-function as generalized function: point pulse, movement of the tacks; fuzzy logics; theory of wavelets, etc.);
- deepening of mathematical knowledge structure: axiomatic theory (set theory, non-Euclidean geometry, Gödel's incompleteness theorem, ets.); Frechet derivative (number, vector, matrix, linear operator as a linear approximation); Lebesgue integral (generalized solutions of differential equations; category theory, etc.);
- integration of mathematical knowledge in development dynamics (fractal geometry (dimension and self-similarity as an effective mechanism for storage of information, natural, social or economic phenomena and processes computer modeling, Lorenz strange attractors, computer graphics); variation methods (generalized solutions of differential equations, isoperimetric problems, etc.); discrete mathematics (theory of graphs, cellular automata, coding, integer programming, etc.);
- improved means of information coding (fuzzy sets (microchips with fuzzy-logic control algorithms, intelligent expert systems); coding theory (protection and compression of information, cryptographic algorithms, encryption, electronic signature, etc.); stochastic systems (Brownian motion, Lotka–Volterra equation (predator–prey), strange Lorentz attractor, etc.).

As an example of research "problem zones" in school mathematics will consider the measure problem—surface area of revolution bodies by constructing and adaptation to current state of school mathematics the most important generalized knowledge structures concerning with analysis and substance of solved problem. The experimental bases of teaching mathematics were secondary schools and lyceums of Yaroslavl and Kostroma cities. The sample was made by students of the eleventh grade of natural science education profile.

3   Results

The paper [3] presents in details the technological constructs of mathematical education synergy at the preparatory stage of reflection and the adaptation of components and functional parameters of generalized design of scientific knowledge to the studying of «problem zone» of school mathematics following the procedure:

1. **Definition and actualization of "problem zone" of school mathematics by means of search and study of generalized construct of scientific knowledge, followed by adaptation to current level of school knowledge and methods.** Such of that, for example, may be learned the problem of quantities measurement – the surface area in three-dimensional space.
   Motivational field. Visual modeling (video clips, presentations, business games) of motivational and applied situations of «new» interpretation of length and area concepts (straight curve, generalized curve, fractal curve, dimension of the curve):

   - Movement of tacks from point A to point B along the narrowing water corridor (trajectory analysis, discontinuity of the curve length function);
   - Koch snowflake (construction, calculation of length and area, variations and natural effects);
   - Van der Waerden function (construction, calculation of length and area of iterative figures, continuity and absence of derivative, natural analogs).

2. **Multiple Goal-Setting in the Study of Serpinsky "napkins" (SP):**

   - To define the iterative process of SP construction for an equilateral (versatile) triangle;
   - To visual modeling the SP by chaos method in several ways;
   - To build the SP method is broken, alternately replacing the previous three-tier broken links, changing the direction; to identify the topological and Hausdorff – Besikovitch dimensions; find the area of limiting object; develop and implement a computer program of broken line visualization;
   - To reveal the multiracial characteristics of SP construction; to develop and implement computer programs for visualization of iterations and variability of probabilistic bases.

3. **Updating in Small Groups the Attributes of Synergy (Bifurcation, Attractors, Fluctuation, Basins of Attraction) in Adaptation Process of Sierpinsky "napkin" for School Mathematics.**
   The tasks for analysts groups: to find the area and perimeter of triangles emitted; to find the ultimate objects and their characteristics, to explain and forecast the numerical result; to reveal the fractal structure of the object to determine its topological

dimension and the dimension of Hausdorff – Besicovitch; consolidate the scheme and the steps to solve for an arbitrary triangle; to draw up an integration table of concepts and theorems in school of mathematics required for the study; to explore geometrically self-similar continued fractions and "Golden section".

The tasks for programming and computer design groups: to put the starting point as inside and outside the triangle; to develop and implement a computer program to build the SP by chaos method (regular and multiracial variant); compile Pascal's triangle and a computer program rendering it SP; derive the formula for sum of binomial coefficients.

4. **Forecast and "by-Products" of the Study (Video Clips, Project Methods, Presentations):**

   – Historiogenesis, construction, computer design, mathematics of "Menger's sponges"; origami construction of "Menger's sponge" first iterations; topological and fractal dimension and properties of "Menger's sponge"; natural and production effects similar to "Menger's sponge" (fractal sculptures and architectural masterpieces); dynamic sections of "Menger's sponge" (video clip);
   – Minkowsky curve and "dragon" Harter: genesis of history, construction, computer graphics, topological and fractal dimension, natural analogs and computational modeling, generators, circuit of the "dragon" with a variable angle;
   – Stochastic fractals and modeling of natural phenomena and processes: the image of planets, satellites, clouds and mountain ranges; random movement of midpoint method; modifications of fractals with different generators;

At the same time, the duration of preparatory stage depends from the level of students training and can make up the academic year and also provides the following forms, means and technologies:

– *Forms* (project activities; laboratory and design classes; video clips);
– *Tools* (statistical packages and office editors; Web–support systems; pedagogical software products; systems of dynamic geometry and computer algebra (GeoGebra, Autograph, Maple, Mathematica);
– Technologies (web-quest; visual modeling; training technologies; founding of personal experience; computer modeling and design, programming and design of pedagogical products).

The second content-technological stage of mathematical education synergy is aimed at the development of adaptation stages of generalized design of "problem zone" of school mathematics to current state of mathematical knowledge and methods of student's educational activity with development and study of technological parameters of system functioning for adaptation and obtaining new results. In our case, generalized construct of scientific knowledge is the concept of surface area, which is indirectly actualized through computer and mathematical modeling of research processes of Schwartz cylinder lateral surface "area" (Table 1).

Technological constructs of second stage realization

Table 1. Technological parameters and characteristics of teacher and student activity support in mathematical education synergy (content-technological stage)

2 stage Content-technological (reflection of technological order parameters of system functioning)

Student	Teacher
– multiple goal-setting of tools, tasks, methods, procedures and algorithms based on cultures dialogue in effective solution of transition problem from chaos to order; – visual modeling of processes and development of meaningful constructs on the basis of generalized constructs search essence and visualization of objects and procedures; – development of student's divergent thinking against the background of integrative constructs revealing, taking into account the probable and incredible circumstances, design content, stages, basic and variable characteristics of object design; – construction of guidelines and plan for problem solving based on the identification of bifurcation zones, conceptual, subject, information and mathematical models, analysis of the possibilities of ICT support tools, the formation of the integrity of procedure decision; – updating the plurality of solutions based on the uniqueness of data, search of bifurcation points and self-organized structures, state and order parameters; – intuition and prediction of results, search and solution algorithm, insight, fixation and verification of procedures and algorithms, presentation of results; – theoretical and empirical generalization of knowledge and methods, integration of knowledge and methods against the background of obtaining a new quality of interaction, updating and becoming in "zones of nearest development" of personal experience	– construction of founding spirals and clusters by type: theoretical and empirical generalization of knowledge and methods, integration of knowledge and methods against the background of obtaining a new quality of interaction, actualization and formation in "zones of nearest development" of personal experience; – historical and genetic equipment of spirals and clusters of knowledge founding; – ability to adapt and develop in social communications; – development of divergent thinking against the background of development of integrative constructs; – creating the situations of choice and uncertainty, decision making with high degree of responsibility; – personal experience of creativity and formation of individual style of pedagogical activity; – visual modeling based on visualization of objects and processes; – updating the plurality of solutions based on the uniqueness of data; – intuition and prediction of results, search and solution algorithm, insight, fixation and verification of procedures and algorithms, presentation of results; – creation of creative environment in educational institution (stimulation of success situation; work in research groups; tolerance to uncertainty; – readiness for discussions and multiplicity of solutions to the problem; identification and popularization of patterns of creative behavior and its results)

1. Components, actualization and organization of adaptation processes of "problem zone" of school mathematics to the content of scientific knowledge generalized

structure (variability of definitions and conditions of the existence, verification of analogies and associations of generalized construct, computer and mathematical modeling of specific manifestations of generalized construct essence, contradictions and availability of mathematical apparatus and methods, search for stable clusters of empirical generalizations).

Motivational field: visual modeling of motivational and applied situations of "new" interpretation of surface area concept (area of multi-faceted surfaces, impossibility of scanning the sphere, surface of the cavity, regular of Schwartz cylinder (uniform division of the base into sectors and height into layers), surface area of sphere, cylinder, cone, torus by method of G. Minkowsky [7]).

Forms: lesson-lecture, laboratory and calculation classes, resource classes, business games, scientific conferences and seminars.

Tools: computer modeling, dynamic geometry systems (GeoGebra), small information tools (ClassPad400), pedagogical software products, presentations, video clips.

Technologies: "warming up" mode, project activity, experimental mathematics [8].

Tasks for actualization of "problem zone" for small groups of students:

1.1. Computer and mathematical modeling of area finding of polyhedral surfaces;

1.2. Existence and finding the surface area of smooth curves rotation around the axis; impossibility of sphere sweep;

1.3. Finding the "area" of Schwartz cylinder surface in regular case ($m < n^2$, $m = n^2$, $m > n^2$);

The form of: laboratory design and resource lessons (4–6 classes) [9].

2. Multiple goal-setting of research processes of scientific knowledge generalized construct (example: actualization of surface area concept by research methods of Schwartz cylinder "area" (containing aspect): pathological properties of lateral surface cylinder "area" are well studied in so-called "regular" case [10, 11]. This occurs when its height H is divided into m equal parts (according to the layers of the cylinder), and the circle lying at the base is divided into n equal parts, followed by a shift φ on each layer on $\frac{\pi}{n}$. With such lateral surface triangulation of the cylinder, the formula for calculating its "area" by means of resulting polyhedral is as follows:

$$S_q = 2\pi R \sqrt{R^2 \frac{\pi^4}{4} q^2 + H^2}, \qquad q = \lim_{m,n \to \infty} \frac{m}{n^2} \tag{1}$$

Thus, the "area" of lateral surface Sq of regular Schwartz cylinder of height H and radius R (if this limit exists – finite or infinite) is completely determined by the limit (1). B. Mandelbrot in [12] showed that for $m = n^k$ the area of polyhedral surface grows as $n^k (k \neq 2)$. Thus, to calculate the "area" of lateral surface of regular Schwartz cylinder at sufficiently large values instead of the formula (1), you can use the formula:

$$S_q = R^2 \pi^3 q \tag{2}$$

Consider the part of Schwartz cylinder layer of radius R = 1 and height H = 1. In the works of E. I. Smirnov and A. D. Uvarov [13, 14] the behavior of function (1) and the angle α between triangulation triangles with a common base is studied, if and $m = f^n(a_0) \cdot n^2$, $m, n \to \infty$ where $f(a_0) = xa_0(1 - a_0)$—logistic map adequate to the scenario of P. Verhulst [15]. The authors obtained the following bifurcation diagram (Fig. 1) using information technology (Qt Creator environment).

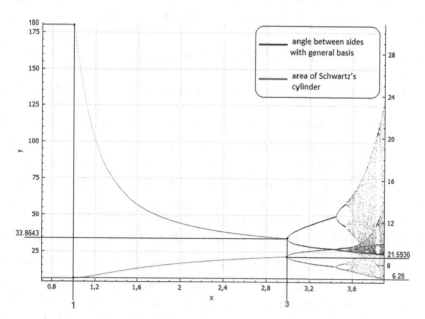

Fig.1. Bifurcation diagram of the area and angle between triangle faces

Figure 1 shows two bifurcation diagrams for which $0.7 \leq x \leq 3.9$ and $a_0 = 0.2$. On the left vertical axis, the values of the angle α between the sides with general basis calculated by the formula are postponed: $\alpha = 2 \cdot \arctan(\frac{1}{1-\cos\frac{\pi}{n}} \cdot m)$ and on the right axis the values of the "area" of Schwartz cylinder calculated by the formula (1) are postponed taking into account that $R = H = 1$, so n changes from 500 till 1000.

There are hierarchies of issues solved by means of computer and mathematical modeling of research activities in small groups of students in remote environment [16] or in the form of multi-stage mathematical and information tasks research [17, 18]:

(a) What is the dynamics and patterns of changes in the "area" of the cylinder, when we consider the constancy of the angles α at the vertices of triangles triangulation; the upper face of the angles at the vertices of triangles at the fineness of the partitions tends to $\beta < 180°$; and it is also required to find β;

(b) what is the dynamics and patterns of changes in the "area" of the cylinder, when considered the constancy of the angles γ at the bases of triangles triangulation; the upper face of the angles at the bases of triangles in the grinding of partitions tends to $\delta < 180°$; and also required to find δ;

(c) What is the dynamics and patterns of changes in the "area" of the cylinder, when considered the shift of the layers at an angle $0 < \varphi < \pi/n$; investigate the situation when different shifts of the layers at the angles φ_m for $n, m \to \infty$;

(d) What is the dynamics and regularities of the growth of the "area" of the cylinder, the height of Schwartz cylinder is divided, different from the regular (i.e. uniform as the shifts of the partitions of layers and the divisions of circumferences). Such a partitioning will be called irregular. Research of the following problems:

- Let $\{a_i\}$—limited positive sequence such that $\sum_{i=1}^{\infty} a_i = +\infty$. If height H of Schwartz cylinder divided on m parts so it construct the sequence $\left\{ H \frac{\sum_{i=1}^{i=k} a_i}{S_m} \right\}$ of heights H_k, where $S_m = \sum_{i=1}^{m} a_i$, $k = 1, 2, 3, ..., m$, so we should find by means of computer and mathematical modeling the values q, then the "areas" of regular or irregular Schwartz cylinder have at the same trend. If $R(q) = \lim_{n \to \infty} \left| \left\{ S'(q) - S(q) \right\} \right|$—function expressing the difference between the "area" of the regular and irregular cylinder with $q = n^{k-2}$, so it is necessary to investigate values of function R(q);
- let $H = R = 1$. The height of the cylinder is divided into layers by the sequence $\left\{ \frac{a_i}{S_m} \right\}$, where $\{a_i\} = \{\frac{1}{\sqrt{i}}\}$ и $\sum_{i=1}^{\infty} a_i = \sum_{i=1}^{\infty} \frac{1}{\sqrt{i}}$ — generalized harmonic series. To study the dependence of the distance function between the "area" S_q of regular cylinder and "area" of irregular cylinder S' at sufficiently large n and considering the parameter q, defined by equality (1). To draw by means of computer modeling the graphic $r(k) = \left| S(200^{K-2}) - S'(200^{k-2}) \right|$ according to the module of difference of cylinders "squares" when $k \in [0.8; 3.2]$. To show that the distance between the areas of the cylinders is not zero at any $q = n^{k-2}$, moreover for $k \neq 2$ and sufficiently large n this distance still tends to zero.
   д) What is the dynamics and regularities of cylinder "area" growth, when considered the height of Schwartz cylinder splits different from the regular and uneven shifts φ_m of lowers, when φ_m committed to $\frac{\pi}{n}$ for $n, m \to \infty$;

(e) What value of the angle γ between the faces with the same base of the regular Schwartz cylinder there is the first bifurcation of the "area" if $m = f''(a_0) \cdot n^2$ and $m, n \to \infty$s, where $f(a_0) = xa_0(1 - a_0)$ - logistic mapping; to investigate the cascade of sub harmonic bifurcations of Schwartz cylinder "area" at $1 < x < 3.57$ and values of corresponding angles γ; using the information technologies (MathLab, MathCad, ClassPad400, Maple so on) show $m = f''(a_0) \cdot n^2 = \infty$., so $m \to \infty$ for $n \to \infty$.

3. Actualization of synergy attributes (bifurcations, attractors, fluctuations, attraction pools) in study course (adaptation of surface area to school mathematics when students are working in small groups with variations of Schwartz cylinder "area"):

Forms: distance learning of project teams, laboratory and design lessons, multistep mathematical and information sessions, conferences and workshops, networking and panel discussions, work in small groups.

Tools: mathematical and computer modeling, Qt Creator is a cross-platform free IDE for C++ development, pedagogical software products, small information tools - Classpad400, WebQuest–as a means of integration of Web–technologies with academic subjects, Wiki-sites, Messenger, Skype.

Technologies: graphs matching of mathematical knowledge and procedures, WebQuest – the technology of self-organization in collective creativity, project method, Wiki technology, visual modeling, founding of personal experience.

Analysis groups (main activity–mathematical modeling of new structures) consist of 8–12 performers, which are divided into 3–4 research mini-projects. Tasks: to reveal the genesis of history and mathematical substantiation of identified parameters and characteristics of the problem; to identify the limit objects and their characteristics depending on the changes in initial conditions by means of mathematical modeling; to give an explanation and forecast of numerical and functional results; to reveal the fractal structure of the object and determine its topological and Minkowsky or Hausdorff–Besicovitch dimension; identifying points (functions, procedures) that marks the transition to new level of dependency; to generalize the scheme and the steps to solve for a source other mathematical objects; to write the integration table of the concepts and mathematics theorems in school relationships and hierarchies required for the study; to explore geometrically self-similar mathematical objects and procedures;

The groups of programming and computer design (the main activity of which is computer modeling and design) are divided into 3–4 research mini – projects. Tasks: to develop and implement a computer program for visualization of basic iterations, fluctuations and patterns in the context of the problem; to study the dependence on the variation of information environment parameters near the bifurcation points; to determine the comparative power of computational procedures and to make a forecast for limit values of variable parameters; to determine the visual interpretation of computer design of attraction pools of identified attractors and the possibility to obtain side-effects, including artistic creativity; to implement laboratory and computational studies on integrative problems of computational procedures;

Groups of integration of knowledge and methods (the main activity of which is network communication with research groups on the identification and description of synergy thesaurus and the construction of coordination graphs of educational elements of school mathematics and mathematical objects of the problem to be solved) are divided into 2–3 mini–projects. Job: to construct graphs of the negotiation of mathematical apparatus and procedures for the construction of generalized construct of scientific knowledge and training elements and procedures of school mathematics; to describe and concretize the synergy thesaurus of mathematical problem research, to consider patterns of synergetic effects in real life phenomena and processes, science achievements, computer and mathematical modeling; to organize and accompany network interaction of research groups on the development of new educational elements (genesis of history, content, variability of approaches, visualization, formalization, applications).

At the end of the second stage of modern achievements adaptation to school mathematics education a series of resource lessons with presentations, discussion, forecasts for further research activities of small groups are held (in our example, the results of the study of Schwartz cylinder "area" are discussed). Thus, the tasks of research groups are outlined for the third–evaluation and correction stage of innovative technology.

4　Conclusion

Thus, generalized constructions in science adaptation to school mathematics education with manifestation of synergetic effects are identified and characterized. The technology of the essence revealing of school mathematics "problem zones" is concretized on example. So, surface area in dynamics details of lateral surface triangulations of Schwartz cylinder or "boot" by means of computer and mathematical modeling are presented. Bifurcation points, attraction pools, computational procedures and fluctuations of state parameters, computer design and side results of the "area" of lateral surface of regular and irregular Schwartz cylinder are identified and characterized. Hierarchies of research activity of students are built: resource and laboratory-calculation lessons, complexes of multi-stage mathematical and information tasks, project methods and network interaction, technology of visual modeling of mathematical problem, patterns of synergetic effects and artistic creativity of students are involved in mathematical education, use of Qt Creator-cross-platform free IDE for development in C+ + , pedagogical software products as a means of Web-technologies integration with academic subjects and Wiki-sites.

The quality of mathematical education of students depends on implementation of rich information and educational environment. This is possible with the identification of complex objects essence by means of computer and mathematical modeling with the reflection of synergy procedures attributes. At the same time, self – determination, self-actualization, self-organization and self-development of personal reflection on complexity and non-equilibrium of mathematical content are constructs and developed using technology of implemented nonlinear dynamics of lateral surface of Schwartz cylinder. Pedagogical experience shows a significant increase in educational motivation of students and improving the quality of school mathematics and computer science development on the base of modern achievements in science adaptation.

Acknowledgements. The research was supported by Russian Scientific Foundation (project No. 16-18-10304)

References

1. Rubinshtein, S.L.: Ability problems and questions of psychological theory. Voprosy Psychologii. **3**, 12–23 (1960). (in Russian)
2. Smirnov, E.I., Smirnov, N.E., Uvarov, A.D.: Stages of Technological Support of the Process of Self-Organization in the Future Teacher's Mathematical Training. Yaroslavl Pedagog. Bull. **3**, 102–111 (2017). (in Russian)

3. Smirnov, E.I.: Technology of mathematics teaching with synergetic effects in 'problem zones" using information technologies. In: XIV International Scientific Conference. Oder analysis and related problems of mathematical modeling, RNO-A, Tzey, pp. 209–210 (2017). https:// elibrary.ru/item.asp?id=32511807. (in Russian)

4. Shadrikov, V.D.: From individual to individual. Institute of Psychology of RAS, Moscow (2009).(in Russian)

5. Monakhov, V.M., Tikhomirov, S.A.: A Systemological Approach to Methodical Disclosure of the Second Generation FSES Prognostic Potential. Yaroslavl Pedagog. Bull. **6**, 117–126 (2016). (in Russian)

6. Ostashkov, V.N., Smirnov, E.I., Belonogova, E.A.: Education Sinergy in Research of Attractors and Basins of Nonlinear Mapping Attraction. Yaroslavl Pedagog. Bull. **6**, 146–157 (2016). (in Russian)

7. Dubrovsky, V.N.. : In Search of Determination of Surface Area. Quantum. **6**, 31–34 (1978). (in Russian)

8. Dvoryatkina, S., Smirnov, E., Lopukhin, A.: New opportunities of computer assessment of knowledge based on fractal modeling. In: Proceedings of the 3rd international conference on higher education advances, HEAd 2017, Valensia, Universitat Politecnica de Valencia, pp. 854–864 (2017)

9. Smirnov, E.I.: Activity and development of student's intellectual operation in intersection physics and mathematics. Bull. Sci. Educ. Develop. **4**, 25–50 (2013). (in Russian)

10. Fikhtengolts, G.M.: Course of differential and integral calculus. Manual. Fismatlit, Moscow, vol. 1 (2001). (in Russian)

11. Schwarz, H.A.: Sur une définition erronée de l'aire d'une surface courbe: Gesammelte Mathematische Abhandlungen. No. **1**, 309–311 (1890)

12. Mandelbrot, B.B.: The Fractal Geometry of Nature, 2nd edn. Times Books, New York City (1982)

13. Smirnov, E.I., Bogun, V.V., Uvarov, A.D.: Synergy of the Teacher's Mathematical Education: Introduction to Analysis. Kantsler Publishing House, Yaroslavl (2016).(in Russian)

14. Smirnov, E.I., Sekovanov, V.S., Uvarov, A.D.: Synergetic effects of Schwartz Cylin-der's computer design in mathematics education. In: Proceedings of the International Conference on Applied Mathematics & Computational Science (ICAMCS.NET), pp. 56–70. Budapest, Hungary (2018)

15. Kronover, R.M.: Fractals and chaos in dynamic systems. Theory bases. Postmarket, Moscow (2000). (in Russian)

16. Smirnov, E.I.: Founding in Professional Training and Innovative Activity of a Teacher. Kantsler publishing house, Yaroslavl (2012). (in Russian)

17. Sekovanov, V.S.: Elements of the Theory of Discrete Dynamical Systems. Lan, Saint Petersburg (2016). (in Russian)

18. Dvoryatkina, S.N., Melnikov, R.A., Smirnov, E.I.: Technology of Synergy Manifestation in the Research of Solution's Stability of Differential Equations System. Eur. J. Contemp. Educ. **6**(4), 684–699 (2017). https://doi.org/10.13187/ejced.2017.4.684

How the Education System Should Respond to the Technological Development and Informatization of the Society

Esen Bidaibekov[1]([✉]) [iD] and Vadim Grinshkun[2] [iD]

[1] Abai Kazakh National Pedagogical University, Dostyk Ave. 13, 050010 Almaty, Kazakhstan
[2] Moscow City Teacher Training University, 2nd Selskohoziajstvenny proezd 4, 129226 Moscow, Russia

Abstract. The education system always reflects technological changes taking place in society. On the one hand, education reacts to such changes, on the other hand, in the bowels of the education system new members of the society that affect technologicalization are trained. Currently, about half of the world's population is of an age characterized by the widespread use of information technology. For this part of global society, the use of modern technology in education is natural. This article discusses the process of technological societal development, characterized by a sequence of industrial revolutions. It shows that, arising from the development of informatization tools, information revolutions are superimposed on such revolutions. The characteristic features of the taking place right now fourth industrial revolution, which are significant from the point of view of the educational system development, are discussed. A well-reasoned forecasting of a new information revolution related to the emergence of automated translation systems is carried out. For each of the aspects of such revolutions, the set of proposed recommendations for improving the content, methods, tools and other components of educational systems is described. The article also considers the negative consequences for society and its educational system that can entail new information and industrial revolutions. The approaches by which the education system can reduce the negative aspects of the transition of society to a new informational and technological stage of its development are discussed.

Keywords: Industrial development · Informatization of education · Globalization · Information technology · Computer technologies

1 Introduction

Education is a special area of human activity in terms of the impact of technological progress on it. On the one hand, technological innovations are fundamentally changing human activities in almost all areas, including education, but only education plays a decisive role in preparing people for life in the environment of informatization of society, only education prepares new members of such a society. Due to this, the processes

V. Sukhomlin and E. Zubareva (Eds.): SITITO 2017, CCIS 1204, pp. 26–33, 2021.
https://doi.org/10.1007/978-3-030-78273-3_3

of training and education not only absorb the latest achievements of science and technology, but also through training, have a decisive influence on the course and intensity of technological progress. It should be noted that these factors are emphasized in modern economic and technological development projects adopted in most CIS countries. As an example, we can highlight the priority project "Digital Economy" discussed in Russia or approaches to the modernization of education in the Republic of Kazakhstan, defined in the context of a new model of economic growth reflected in the directions of the Third Modernization [1, 2].

Under these conditions, the relevance of issues related to the search for possible trajectories of the development of the education system operating in the conditions of informatization and provides training for members of the information society, is inevitable. The search for such trajectories can be based on the study of the features of the information and technological development of society.

First of all, it should be noted that the activity of the main participants involved in the educational process (a teacher and a student) is based on information processing. The so-called information revolution described in the works of Rakitov, Ursula and many other specialists involved in the social aspects of informatization has a key influence on the education system, as well as on the development of society [3, 4]. As a rule, six information revolutions are reflected in scientific works and studies. The fundamental difference between one information revolution and another is the emergence and mass introduction of such information technologies that bring radically new possibilities for interacting with information and using information. Among the information revolutions, the following are traditionally distinguished: the emergence of human speech (the emergence of the possibility of information communication between people located at a short distance), writing (information storage technologies), the replication of books and newspapers (the ability to make information accessible to the masses), electric and electronic communications including gramophone recording, telegraph, telephony and broadcasting (technologies and tools for prompt and mass information delivery, in which a person is deprived of the opportunity to choose the information that he receives), computer technology (a universal tool for operating the information that is capable of performing various actions with information of various types), global telecommunications (the possibility of mass and targeted provision of information with the simultaneous ability to select and find the required information). Until now, the issue of technology that could be the basis of the seventh information revolution has remained unresolved. The authors of the article may suggest that the new revolution may be due to the emergence and improvement of technologies and automation tools for translation from one human language to another. These revolutionary technological transformations provide opportunities for the final elimination of the boundaries of information exchange between states and peoples; information becomes a single global resource accessible to every person, regardless of language and place of residence. Many people today actively use such technologies at home and at work. The quality of electronic translators is growing steadily.

For an adequate and timely response of the education system to the emergence of a new information revolution, it is necessary to:

– take into account the need to form an adequate attitude to information, critical thinking, the need to use and study information not only from domestic, but also from global sources when teaching all disciplines in all educational organizations, regardless of their level;
– improve the content of training, applied tasks, tasks, models and other means, taking into account the fact that world sources of information have become available;
– develop the personality qualities of students and schoolchildren due to the need for an adequate attitude to other cultures and views of life, to have tolerance and other similar qualities;
– prepare all teachers for further training, the selection and retrieval of information, to expand and improve the list of areas of training in the vocational education system, based on training in the search, use and protection of information, the creation of electronic tools for global telecommunication networks [5];
– increase the cross-border nature of education due to additional opportunities for exchanges of students, scientists and teachers, taking into account the gradual elimination of linguistic barriers, expand the mobility of participants in the educational process in a virtual environment [6].

It was important to bear in mind that the development of information revolutions is superimposed on the revolutionary nature of industrial and technological development. Such development and the widespread introduction of technology is also traditionally described using a series of industrial or industrial revolutions. The first of them, based on the massive use of "mechanical" energy, has almost fallen into desuetude. In that period of time, various tools and instruments based on water or steam made it possible to significantly mechanize production, revolutionizing its efficiency.

The second industrial revolution was associated with the development of technologies based on electricity and electric instruments of production. These new for that time tools and technologies led to a new level of mass production and the prevalence of industry. The third of its kind industrial revolution is distinguished by researchers on the basis of the development of electronic devices, computers and everything to do with them. The global telecommunication networks and services built around the Internet are usually referred to the same revolution. Informatization in its modern sense and industrial electronics form the basis for the third industrial revolution, most of the technologies of which are massive and relevant today.

At the same time, the scientific literature and many public speeches of scientists, politicians and managers more and more often put forward the thesis that at present the fourth wave of transformations, the fourth industrial revolution, is replacing the third industrial revolution [7–9]. The presence of this stage of technological development was discussed in detail at the Davos Economic Forum 2016 [7].

It should be emphasized that so far there is no clear and unambiguous criterion for separating this technological revolution from the previous revolutions. Different authors use different characteristics and different indicators.

According to some sources, such a revolution can be determined by fixing the fact of combining technologies, eliminating borders and differences between the biological, physical and digital spheres [8].

Under this discussion, I would not want to strengthen discussion on the appropriateness or inappropriateness of highlighting this new industrial revolution, and how it should be differentiated from previous revolutionary transformations of industry and society. It is important that new technologies and tools attributed to the fourth industrial revolution are developing. Their presence entails an inevitable reflection on the society life and on its members, necessitates the search for recommendations on improving organizational, substantive and methodological approaches to training and education.

The fourth industrial revolution is characterized by specific means and technologies, just as it was with the third industrial revolution, based on the introduction of electronic devices and computer networks. The new revolution is linked to the emergence of large amounts of digital data, the Internet of Things approach, robotics interacting with a computer, augmented and virtual reality tools, printing on 3D printers, and computing on quantum computers. All these tools and the peculiarities of their implementation in real public life and manufacturing make us think about the need to search for ways of improving educational systems in accordance with the challenges of the modern stage of the technical development of society.

The emergence and widespread use of large amounts of digital data will naturally have an impact on the completion of methodological systems for teaching school and university subjects. The content and teaching methods, relevant teaching materials should be promptly adjusted in order to include those innovations that would help students develop critical thinking, the correct attitude to the information, the search for it, selection and systematization. Teachers need training and retraining for working with big data and learning to find information, which requires the development of the relevant components of teacher education. A similar improvement is appropriate for training systems in educational institutions of secondary and higher professional education for specialties related to modern resources and tools for the protection, selection and transformation of information.

The technologies' proliferation called the Internet of Things makes it possible to transform interactions between things, make such communications more independent, and partially or completely turn a person off from the activity of exchanging information between things. Within this technology, things themselves identify each other, reveal the states of other things. All this also indicates the feasibility of seeking updated approaches to the development of education. With such a development of methodological training systems for different disciplines, it will certainly require additional emphasis for students on the nature and characteristics of object orientation in terms of the specifics of identifying objects and inter-object relationships. There is a need to reorient engineering, technological and design training within universities and colleges towards the creation of technologies, tools and tools that have the ability to independently exchange data between them and, most likely, the opening of new areas of training related to the described technological aspects. In this regard, partnership with manufacturing firms will be an important factor in the development of such educational organizations. Due to such a partnership, training systems without constant purchases can be provided with relevant and modern models of technology.

The appropriateness of revising training within the engineering specialties at the secondary or higher vocational education level is indicated by the appearance of the next stages in the development and functionality of robotics, due to interaction with computer equipment and telecommunications. Not so obvious, but no less important is the problem of the universally available training of teachers for conducting basic and additional classes in robotics and mechatronics in schools, colleges and universities. The education system has a clear need for educators who have a high level of relevant teaching methods. It is important to develop teacher training systems for teaching robotics, which should be taken into account in the process of developing teacher education [10]. As with the "Internet of Things" approach, all kinds of partnership support for educational organizations and manufacturers is advisable to provide the educational system with the latest models of robots and other similar equipment.

Evolving volume printing technologies, augmented and virtual reality should be included in the training in computer science and related disciplines. In this case, such technologies and tools should be considered as objects to study. At the same time, the use of these and other tools should already be reflected in the development and implementation of new tools that can provide teachers and students with the opportunity to interact with objects and processes at a different level. Thus some of these tools were not previously available for most educational organizations.

In the meantime, it is advisable to form a system for training professionals, within which volumetric printing, augmented and virtual reality will be taught, considering the appropriate tools to increase the effectiveness of the work of specialists.

The cooperation of educational organizations with manufacturers organized for the delivery of equipment samples, as proposed above, should be expanded through the use of 3D printing technologies to develop real learning tools. This will make a significant contribution to saturating the education system not only with fashionable virtual models, but also with traditional material models and samples. At different levels of the vocational education system, it is important to take into account the need for specialties, including the training of our own specialists in the field of 3D modeling. The presence of such professionals plays a decisive role in the development and dissemination of 3D printing technology, virtual and augmented reality.

Currently, quantum technologies and quantum elements of computer technology, based on the transfer, processing and storage of information at the level of photons and atoms, are under development and testing. The educational system has a real opportunity to be proactive by including in the development plans the creation of new specialties related to the mathematical and physical foundations of quantum information processing, as well as engineering specialties for training professionals who develop, maintain and operate such new computers. Along with this, the expanding training of information security specialists is becoming particularly relevant. To solve these and other problems, as equipment becomes available, it is necessary to timely equip educational organizations with specific tools enabling the storage, transmission and processing of information based on physical systems. Despite the presence of the recommendations presented above, which are due to the emergence of specific technologies of the new industrial revolution, it is possible to formulate a set of relatively general recipes related to the prospective development of education systems. The point is, that schoolchildren and students, whose training is currently underway, will have to work in conditions of even newer means, resources and technologies. Many of them are to be created and implemented in the future. With this in mind, the education system should focus on the future and rely in development not only on the fourth industrial revolution, which is characteristic of the present, but on fundamentally new technological approaches of the next decades.

One can distinguish relatively universal recommendations that affect the degree of invariance of specialist training regarding technological progress. As an example of such a recommendation, the feasibility of increasing the fundamental nature of education should be considered, since the fundamental aspects and principles of the development of science and technology at all times remain the most inherited and durable [11, 12].

So, for example, for the system of higher education, this means focusing students on time-invariant principles for improving engineering and technology rather than learning the specifics of the design and functioning of individual technological innovations. It is advisable to update the content of fundamental in nature disciplines and their simultaneous addition of a set of practical exercises, the inclusion in the content of training of approaches to determining the prospects for the development of technological progress, the close interaction of scientists conducting basic research and teachers involved in the creation of fundamental training systems for students. It is advisable to update the content of fundamental in nature disciplines and their simultaneous addition of a set of practical exercises, the inclusion in the content of training of approaches to determining the prospects for the development of technological progress, the close interaction of scientists conducting basic research and teachers involved in the creation of fundamental training systems for students. For secondary vocational colleges, it is recommended that students be taught general methods of performing technological procedures based on the use of specific samples of modern technology, rather than considering individual technical devices as the final goal. It is necessary to set a course for the combination of increasing the volumes of classical and fundamental components of students' training with their practical classes, conducted on the basis of modern existing industries.

Recently, much has been said about attracting representatives of employers to implement vocational education programs. This is particularly relevant in light of the adaptation of educational programs to the needs of new industrial and information revolutions. It is necessary to strengthen links between schools, colleges, universities and technologically updated enterprises in the following areas:

- employers of enterprises with modern equipment are involved in the implementation of programs in educational organizations;
- employees of scientific organizations involved in the creation and implementation of new information and other technologies take part in the development of student training programs;
- improvement of educational programs is carried out taking into account the feedback received from fresh graduates working at technologically equipped enterprises;
- the procedures for the final certification and employment of graduates include the participation of representatives of employing enterprises;
- constantly changing modern equipment of educational organizations is provided on the basis of close interaction with employers;
- students' on-the-job training is ensured by their activities at modern enterprises using real industrial equipment;

– specialists with significant practical experience in the technological field receive teacher education through training in master's programs at pedagogical universities; in the future, such specialists participate in the implementation of educational programs.

Among other things, one should take into account the existing and arising negative aspects of the emergence of new information and industrial revolutions, including new forms of social stratification, the impact on the stability of existing political systems, changes in the economy and its greater transparency, strengthening creative and intellectual components, as well as a reducing percentage of routine labor in the professional activities of most people. While modernizing and developing educational systems, it is necessary to take these and other factors into account when we improve the content and methods of training economists, media specialists, and sociologists.

2 Conclusion

An informatics course with updated content should be introduced for students of these specialties. Specialized universities and colleges should receive appropriate technological equipment. The system of teacher education should be improved in regard of preparing all teachers to participate in the collective minimization of the negative social aspects of new information and industrial revolutions. And, finally, the education system can play a significant role, including obtaining new specialties by members of society who are left without permanent employment due to the emergence of new technologies and industrial changes.

References

1. The President of Kazakhstan: Nursultan Nazarbayev's Address to the Nation of Kazakhstan, 31 January 2017. https://www.akorda.kz/en/addresses/addresses_of_president/the-president-of-kazakhstan-nursultan-nazarbayevs-address-to-the-nation-of-kazakhstan-january-31-2017
2. Abishev, N.K., Dalinger, V.A., Bidaibekov, Y.Y., Knyazyev, O.V.: Higher education in Russia and Kazakhstan in modern condition. Rupkatha J. Interdiscip. Stud. Hum. **8**(2), 117–127 (2016). https://doi.org/10.21659/rupkatha.v8n2.14
3. Rakitov, A.I.: Philosophy of Computer Revolution. Politicheskaja Literatura, Moscow (1990). (in Russian)
4. Ursul, A.D.: Informatization of Society: Introduction to Social Informatics. Moscow (1990). (in Russian)
5. Bakhtibaeva, S.A., Grinshkun, V.V., Berkimbaev, K.M., Turmambekov, T.A.: Use of information technology in teaching semiconductors physics. Indian J. Sci. Technol. **9**(19), 1–6 (2016). https://doi.org/10.17485/ijst/2016/v9i19/93892
6. Filippov, V.M., Krasnova, G.A., Grinshkun, V.V.: Cross-border education. Paid Educ. **6**, 36–38 (2008). (in Russian)
7. Extreme automation and connectivity: The global, regional, and investment implications of the Fourth Industrial Revolution. In: UBS White Paper for the World Economic Forum Annual Meeting. River, 36 (2016)
8. Schwab, K.: The Fourth Industrial Revolution. Crown Business, New York (2017)

9. Komissarov, A.: The Fourth Industrial Revolution. Vedomosti, vol. 3938, 13 October 2015. https://www.vedomosti.ru/opinion/articles/2015/10/14/612719-promishlennaya-revolyutsiya. (in Russian)

10. Onalbek, Z., Grinshkun, V.V., Omarov, B.S., Abuseytov, B.Z., Makhanbet, E.T., Kendzhaeva, B.B.: The main systems and types of forming of future teacher-trainers' professional competence. Life Sci. J. **10**(4), 2397–2400 (2013). https://doi.org/10.7537/marslsj100413.320

11. Bidaibekov, E., Kamalova, G., Bostanov, B., Umbetbaev, K.: Information technology in teaching mathematical heritage of Al-Farabi. In: CEUR Workshop Proceedings, vol. **1761**, pp. 426–439 (2016). http://ceur-ws.org/Vol-1761/paper54.pdf. (in Russian)

12. Bidaibekov, E., Kamalova, G., Bostanov, B., Salgozha, I.: Development of Information Competency in Students during Training in Al-Farabi's Geometric Heritage within the Framework of Supplementary School Education. Eur. J. Contemp. Educ. **6**(3), 479–496 (2017). https://doi.org/10.13187/ejced.2017.3.479

Aspects of Requirements Elaboration to Basic Competences of a Personality in the Digital Economy Environment

Lubov Kurzaeva⬤, Galina Chusavitina⬤, Natalia Zerkina⬤,
Liliya Davletkireeva$^{(\boxtimes)}$⬤, and Liliia Votchel⬤

Nosov Magnitogorsk State Technical University, Lenin Street 38, 455000 Magnitogorsk, Russia

Abstract. The rapid development of digital economy influences the society in general and ordinary life of a human particularly. Rapid changes are challenges for the system of education. They course the problem of elaborating the system for basic competences of a personality that would provide person with a possibility of fast adaptation to social and economic changes and also their successful socialization, professionalization and well-being under the conditions of digital economy. The article focuses on methods that allow constructing of a possible relevant model of requirements to basic competences of a personality in the environment of digital economy in the system of the adaptive control of professional education quality – the educational framework of qualifications. The proposed methods for determining the content and levels of competencies have been successfully tested in the development of requirements and evaluation of the results of formal education. The article is aimed at researchers who are dealing with the problem of adaptive control of the quality of human resources and with results of formal and informal training.

Keywords: Competence of the digital economy; education (learning) outcomes · Expert information · Ontological model

1 Introduction

Development of digital technologies changes not only conceptual diagrams of economic, production, legal relations but also everyday life of an ordinary person.

The authors of the program "Digital Economy of the Russian Federation" consider digital economy as a system that consists of three tightly interacting levels which influence on life of citizens and society in general. The following ones are underlined:

- markets and branches of economy (field of activity) where interaction of specific subjects is carried out (suppliers and customers of goods, activities and services);
- platforms and technologies where competences for market development and branches of economy development (fields of activity) are created;

V. Sukhomlin and E. Zubareva (Eds.): SITITO 2017, CCIS 1204, pp. 34–44, 2021.
https://doi.org/10.1007/978-3-030-78273-3_4

- the environment which creates conditions for platforms and technologies development and effective interaction of markets subjects and branches of economy (fields of activity) and covers normative regulation, information infrastructure, personnel and information security.

Undoubtedly, the development of each level is connected with a solution of the problem of human resource quality improvement. This problem has multi discipline consideration and is viewed from different scientific directions and aspects that are connected with it:

- administrative aspect – the study of the considered research object from the point of view of adaptive control theory;
- professional environment aspect – development of relevant methods and means of control of the human resource according to the modern requirements and unicity of branch market labor;
- professional and pedagogical aspect – development of pedagogical models and techniques of result quality management of training with the advancing accounting of perspective requirements to them that are connected with the development of science and technology;
- personal acmiologic aspect – a study and accounting of a motivational and valuable directivity of a personality and also elaboration of methods of potential competitive advantages development in the professional environment;
- normative and methodical aspect – coordination of decisions on implementation of the adaptive control by results quality training that takes into account requirements of educational standards, frames of qualifications and competences of different levels and also professional standards.
- aspect of quality – guaranteeing quality of training results on the basis of proposed solutions.
- innovative and technological aspect – technological support of development of the rest aspects due to implementation of methods and means of intellectual support of decision-making and knowledge engineering.

Among the listed aspects the last one is the least worked upt, at the same time in the modern conditions and volumes of the accumulated knowledge of a research problem it is necessary for carrying out both theoretical scientific researches, and development of application-oriented evidence-based decisions on quality management of results of the formal and informal education.

For system consideration of the professional education quality management problem that is based of competence approach, the attention was focused on the theory of adaptive management and knowledge engineering.

The elaboration of the general concept of adaptive quality management of professional training that is based on competence approach, was developed on considering the "adaptability" as an educational system ability to meet requirements of the labor market in employees with appropriate level of qualification on the one hand and to respond to the needs of the personality with taking into account his/her motivational and valuable orientations in their achievement of professional competitiveness and ensuring prospect of further professional and personal development.

While considering adaptive management of professional education quality system based on competence approach as the system of the theory of adaptive management the object of management, a final set of inputs and outputs (corresponding to educational levels/steps), the operating subsystem (including the bank of results of references of personality training models and a subsystem of monitoring) were defined.

One of such models is the qualifications framework. The qualifications framework is the systematized and level-structured description of the recognized qualifications.

In fact, it contains a formalized description of the requirements for basic competencies in terms of knowledge, skills and qualities of personality.

The aim of the article is to demonstrate the complex of processing expert information methods which were used for elaboration of educational qualifications framework. While working in Tempus project "Development of the frame of qualifications for the system of the higher education of the Ural region.

"Educational" means that the qualifications framework is developed in terminology of an education system and its further application is assumed in the context of professional training management in educational institutions, at the same time both requirement of labor market and educational community have to be considered.

The elaborated educational qualifications framework represents the result description of training in the two-dimensional system: "level – descriptor".

As descriptors were originally allocated:

Initially the following factors were accepted for descriptors:

1. Basic general background. (Basic knowledge in various areas)
2. Basic professional background. (Professional knowledge)
3. Information and analytical skills (ability to the analysis and synthesis; elementary computer-user skills; information management skills: ability to find and analyze information from various sources).
4. Projective skills (ability to organizing and planning, problem solving and decision-making).
5. Communicative skills (written and oral communication skills in the native language; knowledge of the second (foreign) language).
6. Motivational and axiological orientations (adherence to ethical values; to legal and ethical standards).
7. Reflexive qualities (ability to criticism and self-criticism; team – working ability; interpersonal communicative skills; ability to cross-disciplinary team working; ability to communicate with experts from other areas; leadership; aspiration to success).
8. Culturological qualities (ability to understanding cross-cultural distinctions; understanding of cultures and customs of other countries; ability to work in international environment
9. Basic individual qualities (ability to work independently; ability to generate new ideas, to be creative)
10. Adaptive and developing qualities (ability to adapt to new conditions; to be initiative and show entrepreneurial spirit; ability to training, increasing your level of educational).

There are distinguished eight qualification levels which are corresponded to levels of formal training.

For educational qualifications framework elaboration, the expert data was analyzed and collected while questioning the Heads and representatives of professional educational institutions of different level (149 professional educational institutions of Chelyabinsk region) and also the Heads and representatives of various enterprises (33 enterprises) were questioned concerning training results requirements (graduates' and enterprises employees" knowledge, skills and competences).

The analysis of the results that were received from interviewing was carried out both concerning the expert assessment of requirements to the level of training results formation according to the underlined descriptors, and concerning the specification of the descriptors system and formalization of its' training results description.

For definition characteristic of the training results at each educational level respondents were offered to correlate the assessment of training results to a metric scale from 0 to 5.

This scale was chosen for several reasons. Firstly, it is common for experts in the form of its analog - the five-level school scale that is traditionally applied to estimate knowledge.

Secondly, it is rather simple to receive its interpretation in compliance with Blum's taxonomy which has six levels on a cognitive component (knowledge, understanding, application, analysis, synthesis, creation of new).

Thirdly, working with a such scale of measurements allows to estimate «distances of nearness» between requirements (that is impossible to carry out in a mark system) and to use data processing methods for quantitative signs.

According to the results of expert estimation the average tendency of representatives' evaluation was formed. Representatives were of different educational institutions levels. The average tendency (Fig. 1) forms a certain "portrait" of formal education levels.

Studying the results showed the existence of anomalies (see a descriptor "Basic professional background " and "motivational and axiological orientations" to Fig. 1) that is a consequence of lapses which can be treated as isolated cases excessive understating or overestimating of experts' estimation to training results requirements.

For their localization such superstructure as Microsoft Excel AtteStat was used because it contains several methods of the task solution.

In compliance with the characteristic and the volume of selection that was received after stratification on qualification levels, two methods were chosen: Thompson's Rule (Rosher's criterion) and Dickson criterion.

Dickson's criterion is developed especially for small selections processing ($n < 30$). The both criteria showed the similar results, however preference was given to Thompson's Rule (mostly because Dickson's criterion allowed to localize only single lapses).

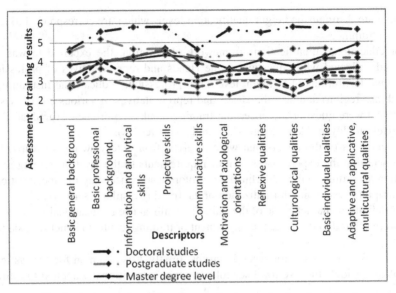

Fig. 1. Average values of quality standard on each educational level

In Thompson's Rule the statistics is used:

$$t_i = \frac{|x_i - \bar{x}|}{S},$$

where $x_i = x_1, x_2, \ldots, x_n$ – results of n observations; $\bar{x}$ – selective average value; S – selective standard deviation, root square of selective dispersion.

The size of criterion statistics is compared to critical value which precise distribution is set by a formula:

$$T = \sqrt{\frac{(n-1)t^2_{(1-\frac{\alpha}{2}),(n-2)}}{n-2+t^2_{(1-\frac{\alpha}{2}),(n-2)}}},$$

where $t^2_{(1-\frac{\alpha}{2}),(n-2)}$ – value of the inverse function of t-distribution with parameters $1 - \frac{a}{2}$ and $n-2$, α – the given significance level, is normal 0.05.

When the size of statistics is larger than critical value the observation is excluded. The procedure repeats for each observation.

Considering that anomalies have to be explained, the average tendencies of training results estimates of the next levels were presented for discussion to experts of secondary professional and higher education levels.

The specified average values of training results levels which are presented in Fig. 2 allowed to obtain the corrected data on expert estimates.

After localization of lapses and specification of estimation s from experts, a transferring of all available values of estimates in the qualitative analogs having six levels

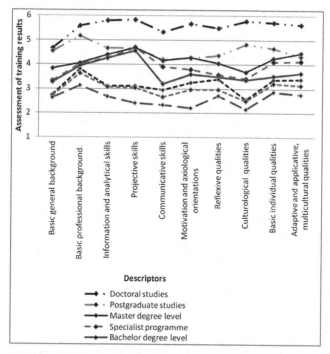

Fig. 2. The specified average values of estimation on each educational level.

$(k = 6$ (from 1 to 6)) on a formula was done:

$$k_{ij} = \frac{(x_{ij} - x_{i\,\min})(k-1)}{(x_{i\,\max} - x_{i\,\min})} + 1,$$

where k_{ij} – is qualitative value of i descriptor at the j-level; x_{ij} – value i descriptor at the j-level; $x_{i\,\min}$– minimum value of i descriptor on all levels; $x_{i\,\max}$– the maximal value of i descriptor on all levels.

The choice of this scale is bound to a possibility of its correlation with a cognitive component of Blum taxonomy. The approach will help further with substantial interpretation of received estimations.

The dispersion of general average at the level of 95% according to the quantitative data without lapses, and also the frequency analysis on qualitative analogs (it is given in [6, 8]) allowed to estimate requirements to training results of different formal education levels (see Table 1).

Table 1. Assessment of training results.

Descriptors	Levels of education							
	Primary professional	Secondary professional (basic level)	Secondary professional (advanced level)	Bachelor degree level	Specialist programme	Master degree level	Postgraduate study	Doctoral studies
Basic general background	2–3	2–3	3	3–4	4	4–5	5	5
Basic professional background	3	3	4	4	4–5	4–5	4–5	5–6
Information and analytical skills	2–3	3	3	4	4–5	5	5–6	6
Projective skills	2	3	3	3–4	4–5	5	5	6
Communicative skills	2–3	2–3	3	3	4	4–5	5	5–6
Motivation and axiological orientations	2	2–3	3	3–4	3–4	4	4–5	5–6
Reflexive qualities	2–3	3	3	3–4	4	4–5	5	6
Culturological qualities	2	2–3	2–3	3–4	4	4–5	4–5	5–6
Basic individual qualities	2–3	3	3	3	4	4	5	6
Adaptive and developing qualities	2–3	3	3–4	4	4–5	5	5	6

The above table shows that on levels of the higher education the requirements to training results of the bachelor degree level, the level of a specialist programme and magistracy, the master degree level regarding the knowledge and abilities coincided.

The explanation may be connected with the fact that when elaborating curricula for a bachelor degree and a magistracy higher education institutions initially try to keep the available methodical and resource base while accepting the two-level education system. It can be the cause that representatives of the graduate training divisions can't accurately differentiate the requirement.

After interviewing and studying the respondents' opinion separate descriptors were changed.

Thus, the name of a descriptor "motivational and valuable orientations" was changed to "motivation"; "the adaptive and developing qualities" was changed on "adaptive and ampliative, menticultural qualities".

Such descriptors as "reflexive qualities" and "basic personal qualities" were united in the general descriptor "reflexive qualities", "Communicative skills" and "Culturological qualities" were united in "communicativeness".

The final version of descriptors formed the basis for elaboration of oncologic model, which is presented in Fig. 3.

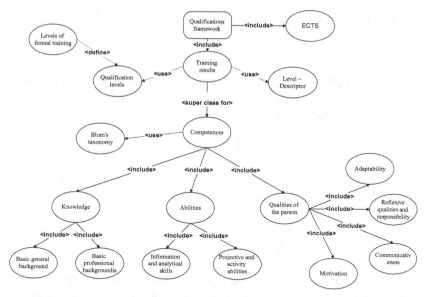

Fig. 3. Ontologic model of educational qualifications framework.

It is consisted of:

1. Basic general background – declarative and procedural knowledge in relation to the scientific worldview. Such knowledge can be gained by an empirical way from practical or educational professional experience, and mainly by formal training.
2. Basic professional background is a set of knowledge about work structure, ways of applying professional activity. The knowledge that is received in the course of training. This knowledge is mainly procedural.
3. Projective and activity abilities. The result fulfilling the actions of a goal-setting, problem statement; organizing, activity planning.
4. Information and analytical skills are the mastered methods of search performing, selecting, analyzing, synthezing, comparing information and the ways of task solving.
5. Motivation is a system of the internal and external factors causing and directing the behavior of an individual which is focused on the goal achievement.
6. Communicativeness is the ability to communicate. It is shown in the sphere of educational and professional and scientific interaction
7. Reflexive qualities and responsibility are a complex of abilities to your own actions judgment, criticism, self-criticism, leadership and a measure of your responsibility for them.
8. Adaptability, an ability to development that is a complex of abilities, promoting adaptation in new conditions of activity, to training, self-training, increase your educational, professional or scientific level.

Taking into account experts' opinions there were made basic notionally multiple models for the description knowledge content, abilities and competences.

Thus, knowledge is described by attributes of the following tuple:

$$Kn = \left\{ W, L^{kn} \right\},$$

where W - the width characterizing the coverage of the available representations, i.e. declarative aspect; L^{kn} - the level of proficiency representing procedural aspect.

Abilities, are described by attributes of the following tuple:

$$Sk = \left\{ C^{sk}, R, L^{sk} \right\},$$

where C^{sk} – context filling of abilities; R – the role that defines the degree an individual activity; L^{sk} – level of complexity of the tasks.

Qualities of the person, are described by attributes of the following tuple:

$$Ch = \left\{ C^{Ch}, Kontext, L^{Ch} \right\},$$

where C^{Ch} – substantial filling of the person quality; *Kontext*– the context that defines the frame (area) in which there is implementation of the considered quality; L^{Ch} – manifestations of the considered the person quality.

The-level component of knowledge, abilities and qualities of the person forms a set $L = \left\{ L^{kn}, L^{sk}, L^{Ch} \right\}$, which elements are defined by correlation of these Table 2 from a cognitive component of taxonomy of Blum.

The undertaken complex of methods that formed the elaboration basis of the substantial description of requirements to training results, at the same time the continuity on the marked levels of the formal training was potentially provided.

The fragment of qualifications framework is presented in Table 2.

The research is focused on use of both its results, and experience of their receiving in the projects devoted to development of qualification system of the Russian Federation, and also quality management of professional education and process of professional training on the basis of the harmonized requirements of employers and educational community to results of training in the form of a qualifications framework.

Table 2. Educational qualifications framework (fragment).

Descriptors	Bachelors	Masters
Basic general background	Systematic evidence\facts which contribute to a holistic understanding of the scientific world view	Knowledge of the scientific world view at the level of its use to solve the problems of the research
Basic professional background	Generalized theoretical and practical knowledge at the level of a comprehension of the organization substance and processes control operating within the educational professional activity and collective activity	The scientific knowledge used for processes optimization within educational and professional by means of introduction of innovations
Projective skills	One organizes one's own activities and/or group work to solve complex tasks consisting of a large number of operations of different contents and scale within industrial practice activity	One organizes work of group to solve complex and nonstandard tasks, one carries out scientific searching in the field of educational professional activity under the scientific tutor management
Information and analytical skills	One carries out independent search, selection and assessment of information for statement and solution of complex educational and professional tasks	One independently carries out generalization, the analysis and synthesis of information that was obtained from any sources for taking organizational and administrative decisions in unusual situations
Motivation	One seeks for recognition in the professional environment as qualified specialist	One seeks for recognition of his/her professional activity results while elaborating and implementing socially important projects
Communicative skills	One uses oral and written speech in the state language as a means of business communication and presentation of the educational and professional activity results, has some initial training for intercultural communication	One states accurately and clearly the point of view on a research problem, takes part in public statements, has basic preparation for work in the international professional environment
Reflexive qualities and responsibility	Under the conditions of science and technology development one is capable to critical revaluation of the accumulated experience, to estimate efficiency of the formulated idea and to bear personal responsibility for consequences from its introduction. One is able to give the full written account on the performed work	One takes decisions in situations of high risk and bears personal responsibility for them, generates the new ideas and fulfills them in research and professional activity, forms the analytical report
Adaptability, an ability to development	One organizes one's own activities in the conditions of updating of the purposes, contents, change of technologies in the professional environment, chooses the perspective directions of personal and professional development taking into account his own vision and requirements, one is engaged in self-education	One organizes one's own activities in the conditions of updating of the purposes, contents, change of technologies in the professional and scientific environments, builds his own promotion program on the basis of the nearest aims achievement

2 Conclusion

The described approach can be successfully realized during formalization of requirements to basic competences of digital economy.

The considered complex of methods and the ontological model constructed thus can be used at the level of obtaining new scientific results during development of new methods and models of knowledge control, the general and particular pedagogical concepts of adaptive control of quality of training results and the human resources (including target reference points and theoretic-informative filling).

It also can be useful at the level of practical application of scientific results during development of educational and professional standards, frames of competences and qualifications, educational programs of formal and informal education (such as [5, 7]), creation of certification systems and certification of students and practicing experts (such as [4]), creation of personal educational and career paths, development of intellectual information systems of decision-making support in case of design, the organization and implementation of quality management of results of training in the conditions of formal and informal education.

References

1. Anderson, L.W., Krathwohl, D. (eds.): A Taxonomy for Learning, Teaching and Assessing A Revision of Bloom's Taxonomy of Educational Objectives, pp. 1–54. Longman, New York (2001)
2. Batrova, O.F.: National qualifications framework of the Russian Federation: recommendations. Federal Institute for Educational Development, Moscow (2008, in Russian)
3. Bloom, S.: Taxonomy of Educational Objectives, Book 1 Cognitive Domain. Longman Publishing, New York (1975)
4. Chusavitin, M.O., Chusavitina, G.N., Kurzaeva, L.V.: Development models of competence information security for the future teachers computer science and ICT. Fundam. Res. **10–13**, 2991–2995 (2013). (in Russian)
5. Kurzaeva, L.V., Ovchinnikova I.G., Slepuhina G.V.: Adaptive management of vocational education quality on the basis of competence approach (for example, the IT Industry): methodological bases, models and basic tools on installation of requirements for learning results. Magnitogorsk State University, Magnitogorsk (2013, in Russian)
6. Masalimova, A.R., Ovchinnikova, I.G., Kurzaeva, L.V., Samarokova, I.V.: Experience of the development of a regional qualification framework for the system of vocational education. Int. J. Environ. Sci. Educ. **11**(6), 979–987 (2016). https://doi.org/10.12973/ijese.2016.356a
7. Ovchinnikova, I.G., Kurzaeva, L.V., Zakharova, T.V., Mironova, A.A.: Development of basic education programs through the use of modular competence approach: methodic recommendations. Magnitogorsk State University, Magnitogorsk (2013, in Russian)
8. Ovchinnikova, I.G., et al.: Elaboration of a frame model for intensification and managing requirements to learning outcomes in regional systems of continuing professional education. Int. Rev. Manag. Market. **6**(S2), 190–197.(2016). https://pdfs.semanticscholar.org/c9ae/69f38d6306d9fec67b6dd43d9cde73a9e1d1.pdf

E-learning and IT in Education

Application of Tools to Increase Learning Efficiency in the Remote Learning System QNET+

Kirill Yesalov$^{(\boxtimes)}$, Anton Belov , and Anton Zarubin

The Bonch-Bruevich Saint-Petersburg State University of Telecommunication, Bol'shevikov Avenue 22, k. 1, 193232 Saint-Petersburg, Russia
yk@bonch-ikt.ru

Abstract. This article discusses the basic principles of the QNet+ distance learning system; it also reveals the fundamental ideas of the platform and tools designed to increase the effectiveness of the learning process. The first part of the article tells about the approaches used in organizing virtual laboratories on the basis of heterogeneous model networks for a laboratory workshop on various courses in the field of information and communication. The second part presents the developed subsystem to assess knowledge, which is to perform comprehensive verification of the students' actions when working with network equipment during laboratory work. The third part emphasizes the effectiveness of the no less important intellectual subsystem of student interaction with the equipment of model networks; the conceptual idea of smart access as an abstract interaction interface is revealed and three key aspects of the concept are considered. The article describes in more detail the use of flexible control commands through a system of aliases and behavior patterns. It provides examples and statistics on the use of the platform in real laboratory work.

Keywords: E-Learning · Interactive programs · Telecommunications · Virtual labs · IT education

1 Introduction

The QNet+ distance learning system is used on the basis of the Research Center for Studying the Problems of Infocommunication Technologies and Protocols at the Bonch-Bruevich Saint Petersburg State University of Telecommunications. It provides access to various courses on infocommunications [1]. Unlike many similar systems, the implementation of a model training ground in this system implies the interaction of students with virtualized or real equipment, and not its emulation [2]. The strong point of the solution is that to evaluate students' knowledge, program verification modules turn to the devices and elements of the model network used in the course of laboratory work.

V. Sukhomlin and E. Zubareva (Eds.): SITITO 2017, CCIS 1204, pp. 47–54, 2021.
https://doi.org/10.1007/978-3-030-78273-3_5

1.1 Working Principle of the Distance Learning System QNet+

In the process of training, model networks are distributed individually to learners, so that users cannot interfere with each other. As a rule, the number of workplaces in educational institutions varies from 10 to 15 personal computers in the audience. A single module is created taking into account this indicator. The stack of model networks is combined into a virtual laboratory. Thus, we can say that a virtual laboratory is a set of network devices configured in a certain way and providing access to a group of students in parallel.

The list of possible virtual laboratories with model networks:

- small home network and corporate office (SOHO Network) on Linux and Mikrotik (Router OS);
- provider core networks, MPLS in particular;
- network providing access to the services of the provider (Access Network), including cost accounting technologies;
- VoIP Telephony Services Network (NGN);
- virtual environment stand, including virtualization platform, containers and virtual switches;
- IoT Lab, a study of Internet-of-things techniques.

The presence of virtual laboratories allows us to develop teaching materials for training courses on information and communication educational disciplines. For course training one or more virtual laboratories may be used. Laboratory workshops on telecommunication equipment are performed in the terminal web-emulator panel in a single workspace for the student. The terminal emulator completely repeats the work in the console, as if it is actually connected to the equipment. The choice of network devices for connection is carried out on an interactive stand. An interactive stand displays and monitors changes in network conditions and provides an interface to the menu of smart access of devices on a model training ground, depending on the discipline being studied.

The course contains a number of laboratory works and exercises, structured according to the increasing complexity of the taught material. The choice of exercises and model stand is carried out through a self-explanatory navigation panel. The training material includes a theoretical explanatory note. The user starts working after reading this explanatory note. The course of work displays the sequence of actions corresponding to the educational option assigned to the student. If you repeatedly access the same set of actions in the QNet+ system, it is possible to save such sets in the knowledge base. The QNet+ system provides the ability to save sets of actions that a student can reuse.

The knowledge base interface is built around network devices through smart access. We will describe below the prerequisites for the appearance of this toolkit. An extended feature of such procedures is integration with third-party software. Additionally, installed services on the platform allow us to deepen the study of IT technology. The use of such programs additionally allows analyzing the client-server exchange of protocol units, It becomes possible to study the headers of datagrams and packets, to identify errors in distorted information [3].

2 Application of Software Tools for Verifying Completed Tasks

The practical task is a crowning event in the knowledge assessment system. In general terms, the process of performing a typical laboratory work is as follows. The work is set, the data of the first task and the next task are loaded. These data contain theoretical material, the order of execution and the statement of the problem. The necessary hardware resources are allocated and a model training ground is prepared, which, as a rule, is a certain network or network segment. The student performs each task of the laboratory work and performs some actions of manipulating equipment on a model stand. Based on the results of these actions, verification tasks are offered. Answers to these tasks can be filled out by students in the following options:

- without data entry;
- input field for arbitrary text information;
- several input fields for arbitrary text information;
- selection of one answer from the list of provided;
- a selection from a plural list of answer options.

The information entered by the student is transmitted to the server of the QNet+ system. Verification scripts are initiated on the server that access network devices of the model polygon. The information received from the scripts is compared with the information entered by the student. Depending on the matches, a score is given.

The verification script is implemented as a utility in C++, managed using the "config" file. For course developers, there is no need to write any code, all the necessary settings are filled in the configuration file. Working principle of such a script is that after entering the data and sending it for verification, the verification program is activated. It also contains the "config" file and startup parameters. Startup parameters include information about which device to connect to, host IP address, username and password, option, etc.

The parameters in the "config" file describe the launch command, parameters of its invocation, parameters of parsing the file with the output file of the command entered on the device, additional keys, such as evaluation criteria on the 100th scale and comparing the response entered by the user with what the program parsed. If no matches are found in the parsed file, no points will be awarded for the task. Another situation: if several fields are presented and if no information was found in the parsed file that matches the one recorded in the first response field by the user, then the system does not stop checking, but just does not accrue points for this answer and proceeds to analyze the next one.

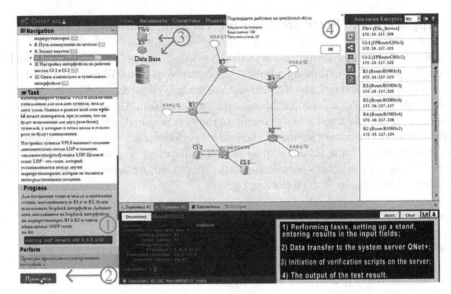

Fig. 1. Qnet+ system. The principle of the knowledge assessment module.

The information received from the scripts is compared with the information entered by the student. Depending on the matches, a score is given. If a complex check structure is used with several questions, each question will be evaluated individually, each has its own weight, and in total, the total score for the task will be displayed. With the correct solution of all tasks, the work is considered to be 100% complete. If there are gaps in the answers, the value decreases. The threshold of passage is set by the course curator, by default it is 60% (Fig. 1).

Assessment of knowledge is calculated as the product of the value of complexity and completeness. Difficulty is indicated by the course curator at the time of filling the system on a 100-point scale. Estimated results of users are accumulated and stored in a database. At any time when using the training system, you can refer to viewing current results through the corresponding interface element.

An integral part of modern teaching systems is the presence of interactive interaction between the course curator and students. The curator monitors the state of the model networks on which the group of students takes classes and identifies problem areas when this or that task is performed by individual students [4, 5]. Aggregate statistics for all students assigned to it helps to identify laggards and fine-tune the group learning process.

A distance learning system for integrating into the educational process on the basis of the Open Education Platform in 2016 [7]. At the moment, classes are being held on two courses "Infocommunication Protocols" and "Mobile and Converged Systems". Based on the results of one of the courses, the following statistics were obtained on the average number of attempts at each individual task (Fig. 2):

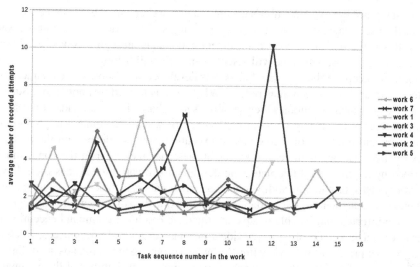

Fig. 2. Statistics on the average number of attempts during each individual task of a group of laboratory works.

3 Using the Mechanism of Smart Access to Network Devices

Analysis of statistics showed that some tasks caused certain difficulties for students. It was found that, as a rule, these were tasks requiring significant manipulation of the web terminal. In addition, entire groups of errors were revealed that were not related in any way to the learning context. For example, this is a series of commands necessary to remove traffic from some network interface and upload the received *.pcap* file to the server for further work with it. This sequence of actions is not only superfluous, but also reveals some technical details of the system mechanisms to the ordinary user. There are definitely side effects in evaluating the results of the work done. And the lack of careful control over the commands executed in the terminal increases the risk of rendering the model network inoperative. In order to solve these problems and, as a result, to improve the quality of laboratory work, the concept of smart access to the equipment of model networks was developed.

Smart access is an abstract interface for interacting with the equipment of model networks both from the side of the user (student, moderator of the course or network administrator), and from the software components of the platform. A proper level of abstraction is achieved through the implementation of three key aspects of the concept. Firstly, it hides the mechanism of remote access to the device and maintain a communication session with it. When the client of the system wants to get the configuration of the device's network interfaces, he is not interested in the protocol used to connect (whether it is SSH, Telnet or SNMP), the operating system, model or equipment vendor (Linux, Mikrotik, Cisco, etc.), whether it is physical or virtual (e.g. based on Open vSwitch). There is polymorphism: one function works with different types of data, but has its own interface and returns a result that satisfies a certain general contract. Secondly, it is n smart web terminal as a shell customizable for different contexts. "Smart" here means "thinking over" the user's actions when working with the command line and this is achieved by means of auto-completion, prompts and restriction of authority. And thirdly, this is the use of flexible management commands through a system of aliases and behavior patterns, which we will discuss in more detail below.

So, the concept of the command alias was developed as a short name characterizing the command action. An alias reflects WHAT needs to be done, not HOW. Such a declarative approach encourages the use of the same aliases for commands of the same type, and their number may be unlimited. In addition, if the command implies some parameters, and the logic of the command execution does not depend on the particular executable instance with certain values of these parameters, then the command is described by a generalized template. The developed software module has the following priority tasks: provide the ability to use custom variables in the command templates, attributes of the elements of the available model network, data of the current work option, other meta-information; be able to save intermediate results of command execution in order to organize a chain of calls; provide a mechanism for restricting access to commands by user profile, as well as by time; provide a grouping of commands according to various criteria of use and a mechanism for managing the availability of the command depending on the environment; variability of processing the result of the executed command. Possible commands were divided into three conditional groups: a group executed on the equipment of the model network (such as ifconfig, uname, reboot, etc.), a group executed on the platform server, usually with respect to the target device (ping, traceroute), use of an external resource (following the link, opening the necessary third-party software in the work) [6].

On the technical side, the command's life cycle is as follows: providing a command alias with a description of its actions on the client side forming a request from the client with user parameters and specifying identifiers of the model network, device and the command itself; determining the template of the executable command according to the request parameters and the environment (user session and other settings), converting the template to the final instance of the command, ready for execution. The execution module is responsible for remote access to the requested equipment with the choice of control protocol and control of the communication session.

Now let's give some examples of the use of smart commands in laboratory work. Figure 3 shows a screenshot of a model network with an open panel for quick access to smart commands on a specific device using ICMP Echo Request in laboratory work:

A complicated example of using the *tshark* traffic analyzer program and saving a *.pcap* file to a dedicated server is shown in Fig. 3. The last step in this chain is the opening of the saved file on the file server through a third-party editor application, which was extremely difficult before the introduction of the smart access system. As you can see, the difficult commands of the terminal are now represented by three corresponding buttons associated with the target device.

Smart access opens up new opportunities for configuring model networks for new laboratory works. Figure 5 shows two options for organizing a model network with a controller and virtual switches.

In the first case, control of the latter is proxied through the controller by a chain of commands at a low level, thereby raising the question of the advisability of the presence

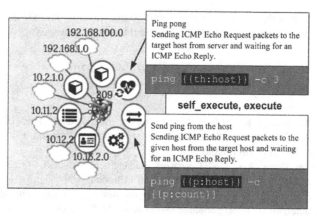

Fig. 3. Examples of using smart commands to send an ICMP Echo Request message (with command templates).

of the controller on the circuit. In the second case, the commands are executed on the controller itself, and the target virtual switch is set using parameters (Fig. 4).

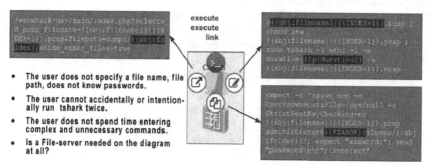

Fig. 4. Using smart commands to control traffic on the device's network interface.

Fig. 5. Using smart access to organize a model network based on Open v Switch (controller and virtual switches).

4 Conclusion

These developed software tools for testing knowledge and the smart access system significantly increased the quality of the laboratory work: from the material presentation and the preparation of the model training ground to the students' knowledge assessment. At present, options are being considered for using the system as a network administration tool.

References

1. Yermakov, A.V., Yesalov, K.E., Fitsov, V.V.: Using the distributed structure of the SOTSBI-U training complex for the study of telecommunication protocols. Proc. Int. High. Educ. Acad. Sci. **56**(2), 94–98 (2011). (in Russian)
2. Loskutova, A.A., Belov, A.S.: QNET Network management system. T-Comm. **10**(2), 48–52 (2016). https://elibrary.ru/item.asp?id=25612016 (in Russian)
3. Goikhman, V.U., Yesalov, K.E., Sokolov, N.A.: Application of specialized computer systems to study the characteristics of telecommunication networks. In: Proceeding of the 18th Conference of FRUCT Association, Saint-Petersburg, pp. 456–462 (2016)
4. Goikhman, V.U, Yermakov, A.V., Yesalov, K.E., Yakovlev, V.V.: Modeling of communication networks. Visualization of graphs. Inf. Space (4), 71–74 (2016, in Russian). https://elibrary.ru/item.asp?id=27656720
5. Goikhman, V.U., Yermakov, A.V., Yesalov, K.E., Yakovlev, V.V.: Modeling of communication networks. Visualization of unconnected graphs. Inf. Space. (1), 84–91 (2017, in Russian). https://elibrary.ru/item.asp?id=28875025
6. Yesalov, K.E., Pavlenko, M.E.: Technicians of social engineering in information environments and the analysis of methods of protection against them. Actual problems of Infotelecommunications in Science and Education, Saint-Petersburg, pp. 358–363 (2016, in Russian). https://elibrary.ru/item.asp?id=27296331
7. National Open Education Platform. http://openedu.ru (in Russian)

Educational Resources and Best Practices of IT-Education

The Ecosystem of Training the Future Leaders of the Digital World: Results of the Inclusion of "Internet Entrepreneurship" in the Educational Program of the University of Economics

Natalia Altukhova and Elena Vasilieva(✉)

Financial University Under the Government of the Russian Federation, Leningradsky Prospekt 49, GSP-3, 125993 Moscow, Russia
{nfaltuhova,evvasileva}@fa.ru

Abstract. The article discusses the features of teaching the course "Internet entrepreneurship", supported by the Foundation for development of Internet initiatives in universities in Russia, Belarus, Kazakhstan. The Department of "Business Informatics" of the Financial University has been teaching students and postgraduates the basics of entrepreneurship on the Internet since 2015. The authors highlight the problems of teaching students technological entrepreneurship. The key participants in the process of training specialists whose competencies can be in demand in the digital world are identified. Recommendations for improving the effectiveness of the learning process are given. An important advantage of the approach to teaching the course" Internet entrepreneurship" is the integration of Lean Startup methodology and Design thinking. The authors developed cases and practical recommendations for the creation of digital services based on the Human-Centered Design. The article also describes the developed business game "Your profession in the field of IT". The tasks of the business game describe necessary personal qualities and competencies of 8 popular IT professions: Consultant, Presales, Product Manager, Software Developer, Support Engineer, Tester, Project Manager, System Administrator. A portrait of a typical representative of the profession, the type of behaviour in a conflict situation, behavioural characteristics is constructed. The game uses psychological tests, checks subject area knowledge, identification of communication skills, logic. The result of the game is a set of competencies inherent to the IT profession competency, as well as a roadmap for learning and the pattern of career development.

Keywords: IT education · New educational technologies · Personnel training · Technological entrepreneurship · Digital markets · Design thinking · Gamification

1 Introduction

When a list of demand in the future competences of specialists is brought up on conferences, the emphasis is mostly made on the importance of creativity, enterprise, ability to

© Springer Nature Switzerland AG 2021
V. Sukhomlin and E. Zubareva (Eds.): SITITO 2017, CCIS 1204, pp. 57–66, 2021.
https://doi.org/10.1007/978-3-030-78273-3_6

process information quickly and to find a solution outside of templates and the standard framework. The speakers emphasize the importance of team skills development and lifelong personal development. Soft skills are necessary for large companies, who find it most challenging to adapt the control mechanisms and technological platform to the requirements of the digital future. The labour market today demands ambitions and enterprising. The companies introduce the position of Chief Digital Officer (CDO) because they understand the importance of digital process management and digital transformation activity. However, how to improve the effectiveness of training of future leaders of the digital world?

In 2015, the Financial University under the Government of the Russian Federation signed an agreement with the Foundation for development of Internet initiatives (IIDF) about the inclusion of the course "Internet entrepreneurship" in the educational programs of the bachelor's and master's degree in the field of "Business Informatics". Over the past two years, IIDF has been actively promoting the idea of introducing this course in more than 100 universities in Russia, as well as in Kazakhstan and Belarus.

However, we are facing a problem that is likely to be relevant for many economic universities. Ideas offered by students in the classroom on the course "Internet entrepreneurship", do not reach the stage of implementation in the Internet service or mobile application. Our students, who have good training in business engineering, management, are not confident enough in application development. As a result, for two years of teaching students the basics of Internet entrepreneurship, we have accumulated a sufficient base of unrealized useful ideas. This would not have happened if our University or other universities had a developed ecosystem of training support for Internet entrepreneurs.

2   Ecosystem of the Course "Internet-Entrepreneurship"

Participants in such ecosystem (Fig. 1) should not only be teachers and students of one University, but also some include support from the University management. The course itself and the new forms that we use in training and for which the IIDF highly rated us by giving us the title of laureate twice. It all could not be realized without the participation of the Vice-Rector for educational and methodical work, the head of this educational program. Now we are promoting the idea of Internet entrepreneurship, organizing various sessions of design research, hackathons, business games within the framework of scientific conferences and events at the Financial University, and also we are holding elective classes, including courses for teachers and administrative staff. Now the course "Internet entrepreneurship" has become mandatory in the direction of 38.04.05 "Business Informatics", master's program "Strategic Management of Information Technologies in Business". The developed cases are applied in the academic disciplines "Management", "Marketing", "Business Models in Digital Markets", "Internet Marketing", "Business Planning", "Business Communication", "Innovation", "Integrated Marketing Communications", "Information Business", "Commercial Activity", "Methods of Decision-Making", etc.

We also believe that it is essential to develop Inter-University relations when students from different faculties or areas of training of different universities can be involved in the project, which will ensure the interdisciplinary approach to the project.

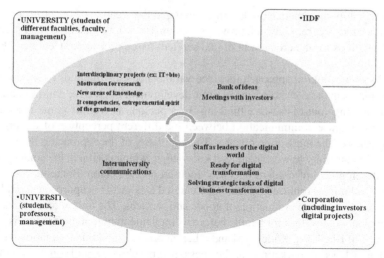

Fig. 1. Ecosystem of the course "Internet entrepreneurship".

IIDF, as the main inspirer of the course, takes on tasks such as communication and organisational activities, as well as the interaction between the authors of the best projects and investors.

Besides, an important role is given to IT companies, which will receive not only exciting design solutions but also their potential employees prepared to work in the digital markets. No need to say that, for example, the introduction of Design Thinking principles among main partners is one of the key areas of the SAP technology leader. For advanced companies, it is essential to be able to identify key customers' needs in order to develop new customer-centred services in the context of digitalising society and to ensure the use of innovative techniques and tools. Design Thinking is now implemented in IBM, General Electric, Procter & Gamble, Philips Electronics, Airbnb [9–11, 14, 16]. In Russia, Design sessions are held in Sberbank, Raiffeisenbank.

In the ecosystem of training future leaders of the digital world University enrollees also became important participants. Career guidance work should be carried out with students for the profession to receive dedicated specialists.

3   Methodology and Approach of Design Thinking

Note that a significant advantage of our strategy in teaching the course "Internet Business" is to integrate the Lean Startup methodology [5, 6, 20] with the stages of Design Thinking, according to d.school, as follows: Empathise, Define (the problem), Ideate (Generation and Voice), Prototype, and Test. This allowed us to solve the problem arising in practice at many universities, testing this course in the educational process, with the formation of new ideas, customer research at the stage of Customer Development, testing hypotheses with the participation of representatives of the target audience.

The team of authors of the Department "Business Informatics "Together with The Internet Initiatives Development Fund (IIDF) developed a textbook" Internet

Entrepreneurship: the practice of Design Thinking in the creation of the project (bachelor's and master's degree)", which provides Design Thinking tools, cases and practical recommendations for the creation of digital services based on Human-Centered Design process).

The Design Thinking approach included various heuristic methods of solving nontrivial problems in the context of uncertainty, development of creative abilities and nonstandard thinking (out-of-the-box thinking) of a person, as well as game mechanics, allowing to organise communication between the different perception of the problem by participants of the innovation process. The popularity of the approach is determined, first of all, by its ability to work with tacit knowledge, which is vital in the context of the trend of development of modern business, focused on the person. Sometimes the term "Design Thinking" is replaced by Human-Centered Design. This approach should now become the basis for the production of goods and services. The importance of studying the value of any innovation for people before its implementation in the product is stated in the works of Blank [6], Kotler [15] and other theorists. Brand image creation requires knowledge of laws of marketing and business, and psychology, anthropology, cultural studies. Moreover, empathy, which is the basis of most Design Thinking techniques is, first of all, understanding the experience of the consumers, their feelings and thoughts, which is aimed to further filling the developed innovative product understandable to the consumers' emotions.

The undoubted advantage of Design Thinking is the change in the approach to the study of the problem. It is based on the search for an answer to the question "how to do?" instead of "what to do?" [24, 25]. Also, most importantly - a process that works on an unexpected result, the generation of a new one.

How to implement Design Thinking in the processes of the company that has chosen the strategy of digital transformation? The answer to this question depends on the purpose of the company. It could be a solution to the problems of monitoring changes in customer requests or problem areas in customer service, finding ways to transform old approaches in doing business, training staff to make decisions in unusual situations. Session duration is possible from 8 h to 3 days. Performance of tasks is held step-by-step, in teams of 5 to 7 people.

During the two years of teaching the course "Internet Entrepreneurship", we have tested the inclusion of a variety of Design Thinking tools in the Lean Startup methodology. Work on projects of technological entrepreneurship was done both in teams and individually. The team came up with the idea, tested hypotheses in customer research. The analysis of startup metrics and calculation of economic indicators of the project solution were done individually to describe business processes of startup activity and define ways of holding clients. The results were made not only in the presentation of the ideas but also in the writing of research works in which it was necessary to show the features of its creation, to give proposals for promotion.

The course "Internet Entrepreneurship" was held in the Financial University within the faculty classes (36 h, every two weeks), training practice (two weeks, from 9–00 to 13–00, four times a week). However, we are convicted, that for the success of learning of start-up skills a rich program is right what is needed, as it was shown in the case with the organisation of training practice when nothing distracts from the project, when each day begins with a warm-up of thinking, learning new techniques of design thinking, adjustments and mentoring by teachers, teamwork and research.

We have seen the primary purpose of the course is to give students an idea about the features of creating a startup, promotion, in practice, tried out all the steps from the development of innovative approaches to testing and promotion of the project solution feel like young entrepreneurs.

4 Our Experience in the Educational Process of Game Mechanics and Design Thinking

4.1 Design Thinking and Business Game "IT-Startup"

For two years already we have been actively implementing various forms of research, communication and design activities. As part of the faculty stage of the International student scientific conference, it has become a tradition for our students to participate in the hackathon, in which they study the principles of design thinking. Teams of students develop business ideas, create prototypes of products or services that solve the problems of the city, society. The competition is held in three stages: working on the idea with the help of Design Thinking and brainstorming tools, creating a prototype, and developing a presentation script. During the competition, the leading players of the teams change, practising the skills of leadership and critical thinking, as the developed idea is being brought to the discussion to third parties. At the end of the game, each team prepares visual accompaniment and presents its decision to the judges.

At the Festival of Science in 2016, students were given a task to think over the concept of environmental problems of the city with the help of IT service: from IT platforms informing about eco-actions or gathering participants of ecological patrol, eco-crowdsourcing, and social Internet projects that implement new eco-ideas. In 2017, the game was introduced for first-year students. The goal of the game was to show the feature of creating an Internet enterprise product. The emphasis was made on the feedback of judges. Students learned how to analyse the potential of the digital products market, how to present the ideas. The hackathon was organised for senior students in a more complicated version. In addition to working on the concept, students had to calculate the economic indicators of the digital market and to choose the method of monetisation of the project.

This year we have tried an unconventional format of student scientific event - Meet Up. A roundtable was organised to discuss what the critical aspects of Business development in the era of the new Digital Economy are, how the transformation of the business strategy of enterprises will affect the change in business requirements to the competencies of employees, what to expect from the society regarding universal digitisation.

However, the main event for students was the business game "IT-startup". We gave students a chance to try themselves as Project Managers, taught them to negotiate with competitors and, by passing all the risks and incidents, to achieve the position of the Great CIO. Students were very immersed in the simulation of a competitive environment, which caused agitate and even wars to capture the resources of IT projects.

We actively introduce game mechanics in the learning process. In 2017, we developed a new game based on Design thinking, so that students could get an idea of how to create innovations, evaluate their demand for employees, understand the chances of promoting a new product in digital markets. During the game "IT-startup & Design thinking", teams explored customer experience with a product, service or process, gain empathy skills, perform project work in a group, create prototypes and test hypotheses. The game gives a choice of challenges, allows the study of the subject area and ensures user experience of interaction with the product or process, recording the results of the analysis and discussion of ideas in case templates, presentation. The playing field is shown in Fig. 2, cards with a description of Design Thinking tools - in Fig. 3.

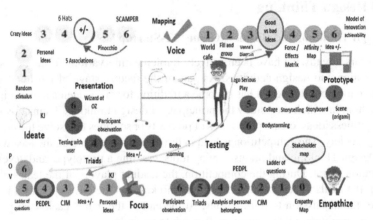

Fig. 2. Playing field in the business game "IT-startup & Design thinking" (Source: Vasilieva 2018)

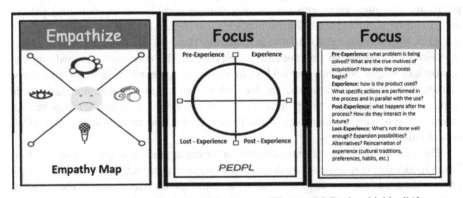

Fig. 3. Example of cards with tasks in the business game "IT-startup & Design thinking" (*fragment with PEDPL Model* (Vasilieva 2018, p. 182) (Source: Vasilieva 2018)

4.2 Business Game "Your Profession in IT": How Can We Become Professionals in the Digital World?

On the Open Day of the Financial University, we also developed and tested a business game "Your profession in IT". Applicants and their parents have a rather vague idea about what the graduates of "Business Informatics" are like, what unique competencies the students receive during the training, what makes IT such a popular economic sector in the labour market and what specific skills the students should already develop to become IT, specialists. Taking this into account, we have included the description of necessary personal qualities and competencies of 8 popular professions among graduates of IT-directions: Consultant on the implementation of information systems, presales, Product Manager, Software Developer, Engineer support group, Software Tester, Project Manager, System administrator. For each of the profession is a portrait of its average representative was created, as well as the types of behavior in conflict situations, behavioral characteristics. Schoolchildren and first-year students determined the vector of their training and the necessary competencies (knowledge and skills) of the future profession in IT in an entertaining form. A portrait of a typical representative of the profession, the type of behavior in conflict situations, behavioral characteristics was constructed. The game implements psychological methods to test subject area knowledge, identification of communication skills, logic and visualization of results, games and puzzles, depending on the track profession. Some tasks were discussed with masters in the framework of research seminars.

We give a description and examples of some tasks.

Stage 1. Choose your favorite colour.
Stage 2. Are you an extrovert or an introvert?
Task 1. Twist your fingers several times. What finger was on top? The extrovert has a left thumb on top, and the introvert has a right thumb.
Task 2. Taking a pencil or pen, on the outstretched hand align it (her) with any vertical line (door, window). Alternate closing left and right eye. Extroverts' object in hand shifts when the right eye is closed. For the introvert, it shifts when the left eye is closed.
Task 3. Twist your arms around your chest. The extrovert will have left arm on top. The arm is right for an introvert.
Stage 3. Tasks to test the skills to design: Build a house of cards, collect a cat from 2 sheets of paper, etc.

The result of the game is the set characteristic of the IT profession competency, a road map of learning and the pattern of career development (Table 1). The description of the profession reflects the elements of the Navigator developed by SAP, as a partner of our Department.

Returning to the results of teaching the course "Internet Business", we want to highlight that the primary objective is not only to see the solution of the problem of preparation of young and enterprising personnel able to expand the digital space of useful new services and innovative products, but rather to develop the qualities that allow students to solve complex non-standard situations in conditions of uncertainty. Our approbation of new forms of education in the educational process has given excellent results in final qualifying works. In their master's theses, our graduates included the results of design research and offered innovative digital development strategies for companies such as Russian Post, Sberbank. There is a remarkable experience in defending the final qualifying work this year on the basis of a team project to create a startup, as it has already been done at the Far Eastern Federal University [23].

We believe that these are important steps to the transformation of the educational process. The skills of creative thinking, teamwork and personal development, which we are developing with such new methods of training our graduates will make them competitive in the labour market, will allow them to shape their strategies for professional growth competently.

Table 1. Map of development of a specialist in the IT profession.

Specialist	To develop	To know	Career development
Project Manager	Sales skills, professional budget calculation skills, risk analysis, project management, negotiation skills, public speaking skills, preparation of reviews, articles	Scrum, Agile, PMBook, software lifecycle, system integration, IT strategy, risk management, BI, Excel	IT Director
System Administrator	Responsibility for a result, an adequate response to the conflict, multitasking	Linux, MS Windows, telecommunication solutions, it architecture, server applications, drivers	Head of Network Administration and Network Architect
Product Manager	Result Orientation, analytical thinking, manipulator, public speaking, competent speech, perception and active listening, public speaking experience, high level of stress resistance	BI, Tableau, Click, MS Excel; Direction: Business Informatics	Director of Sales and Business Development
Presales	Stress Resistance, leadership, time management, negotiations, the use of psychological techniques of influence, preparation of commercial proposals, skills resource assessment, labor input, cost, experience of public speaking, competent speech	ARIS, BPWin, business process engineering	Presales Director
Engineer Support Group	Time management, adaptability, English. language, complex negotiation skills, diligence, persuasion skills, building trust and loyalty	Scrum, Agile, PMBook, SOFTWARE lifecycle, it integration, it strategy, risk management	Support Team Leader
Consultant	Experience in complex negotiations with customers. Knowledge of different types of behavior in negotiations, understanding and experience of psychological methods of influence	ERP, CRM, BPM, system integration	Consulting Director

5 Conclusion

The trend of customer orientation and reactive and unexpected changes in customers' needs, tastes, preferences makes business change, look for new business moments, which in Gartner's terminology means a constant search for short-term opportunities used dynamically: "a business moment can come from nowhere, and yet they are becoming more and more" (Gartner Symposium/Itxpo 2013). Until recently, the human capital was perceived as the principal participant of business processes in enterprises, as an integral part of the organisational capital of the company. However, automation and the introduction of industrial technologies 4.0 replace human with programs, robots, bots, drones, etc. This does not mean that in the new era the human role in the process will be minimised. The goals, focused on the implementation of new business tasks in the conditions of constant changes, will require the ability to work in a team, to effectively use their competencies, to be focused and successful, to think outside the box and find original solutions, to actively use the accumulated individual and collective intellectual capital, which will make the use of various techniques of Design Thinking an integral part of human activity in the company.

References

1. Almeida, L.S., Prieto, L.P., Ferrando, M., Oliveira, E., Ferrándiz, C.: Torrance test of creative thinking: the question of its construct validity. Think. Skills Creativity **3**(1), 53–58 (2008). https://doi.org/10.1016/j.tsc.2008.03.003
2. Altuchova, N., Vasilieva, E., Gromova, A.: Teaching experience of design thinking in the course of "Internet-business". In: CEUR Workshop Proceedings, vol. 1761, pp. 219–225 (2016, in Russian). http://ceur-ws.org/Vol-1761/paper28.pdf
3. Altukhova, N., Vasilieva, E.: The practice of using Design Thinking techniques in the "Online Entrepreneurship" training course: from an idea to prototyping. In: Finance: Theory and Practice, vol. 21, no. 3, pp. 194–201 (2017, in Russian). https://doi.org/10.26794/2587-5671-2017-21-3-194-201
4. Bidshahri, R.: These are the most exciting industries and jobs of the future, 29 January 2018. https://singularityhub.com/2018/01/29/these-are-the-most-exciting-industries-and-jobs-of-the-future
5. Blank, S.: The Four Steps to the Epiphany: Successful Strategies for Products that Win. Wiley, Hoboken (2014)
6. Blank, S., Dorf, B.: The Startup Owner's Manual: The Step-By-Step Guide for Building a Great Company, 1st edn. K & S Ranch, Cork (2012)
7. Chermahini, S.A., Hickendorff, M., Hommel, B.: Development and validity of a Dutch version of the remote associates task: an item-response theory approach. Think. Skills Creativity **7**(3), 177–186 (2012). https://doi.org/10.1016/j.tsc.2012.02.003
8. Clark, T., Osterwalder, A., Pigneur, Y.: Business Model You: A One-Page Method for Reinventing Your Career. Wiley, Hoboken (2012)
9. De Bono, E.: Serious Creativity: Using the Power of Lateral Thinking to Create New Ideas. HarperBusiness, New York (1993)
10. De Bono, E.: Six Thinking Hats. Penguin Books, Limited, London (1999)
11. De Bono, E.: Lateral Thinking: A Textbook of Creativity. Penguin Adult, London (2010)
12. Hamza, T.S., Hassan, D.K.: Consequential creativity. Int. J. Technol. Des. Educ. **26**(4), 587–612 (2015). https://doi.org/10.1007/s10798-015-9321-4
13. Howard, T.J., Culley, S.J., Dekoninck, E.: Describing the creative design process by the integration of engineering design and cognitive psychology literature. Des. Stud. **29**(2), 160–180 (2008). https://doi.org/10.1016/j.destud.2008.01.001
14. Kelley, T., Kelley, D.: Creative Confidence: Unleashing the Creative Potential Within Us All. Currency, 1st edn. Harper Collins, London (2013)
15. Kotler, P., Kartajaya, H., Setiawan, I.: Marketing 3.0: From Products to Customers to the Human Spirit. Wiley, Hoboken (2010)
16. Liedtka, J., Ogilvie, T.: Designing for Growth: A Design Thinking Toolkit for Managers. Columbia University Press, New York (2011)

17. Michalko, M.: Cracking Creativity: The Secrets of Creative Genius. Ten Speed Press, Berkeley (1998)
18. Navigator SAP. http://sapland.ru/navigator (in Russian)
19. Nussbaum, B.: The Empathy Economy. Bloomberg, 8 March 2005. https://www.bloomberg.com/news/articles/2005-03-07/the-empathy-economy
20. Ries, E.: The Lean Start-up: How Today's Entrepreneurs Use Continuous Innovation to Create Radically Successful Businesses. Crown Business, New York (2013)
21. Silig, T.: What I wish I knew when I was 20. A Crash Course on Making Your Place in the World. HarperCollins Publishers, London (2009)
22. Simon, H.: The Sciences of the Artificial. MIT Press, Cambridge (1996)
23. Far Eastern Federal University will conduct an experiment on the protection of diplomas in the format of startups. Uchitelskaya Gazeta, 15 May 2017 (in Russian). http://www.ug.ru/news/21773
24. Vasilieva, E.: Design Thinking: a little bit about the approach and a lot about the tools of creative thinking, learning client requests and creating ideas. RU-SCIENCE (2018, in Russian)
25. Vasilieva, E.: Design Thinking as a breakthrough technology to create human-centered digital services. In: 7th International Conference on Application of Information and Communication Technology and Statistics in Economy and Education (ICAICTSEE–2017) 3–4 November, pp. 381–388 (2017). http://icaictsee.unwe.bg/past-conferences/ICAICTSEE-2017.pdf
26. Vision for the future of the digital world at the conference Gartner Symposium. ITxpo- 2013, 17 October 2013, (in Russian). http://www.crn.ru/news/detail.php?ID=84923

The Application of the Artificial Immune System for Design, Development and Using of the Hybrid System in Education

Irina Astachova[1](✉) and Ekaterina Kiseleva[2]

[1] Voronezh State University, Universitetskaya ploshchad 1, 394036 Voronezh, Russia
[2] Voronezh State Pedagogical University, Lenin Street 86, 394024 Voronezh, Russia

Abstract. The scope of the paper is dedicated to the design of theoretical and hands-on investigation of mathematical model concept for Education Progress Control System (EPCS) that might be applied for educational institutions. The versatility of the EPCS lies in its independence from any specific subject content (or related factors), allowing teachers to upload the required course directly to the educational platform, and students to choose individual courses in order to plan their educational programs of their own. To implement the designed EPCS the hybrid system design approach was chosen, because it combines the advantages of different technologies that allow solving complicated tasks. The well-known fuzzy logic design allows determining the educational content sections, but this approach causes significant difficulties for students. However, the implementation of Kohonen self-organized network (or Self-Organizing Map (SOM) is a computational method for the visualization and analysis of high-dimensional data, especially experimentally acquired information) allows classifying students involved into educational programs provided by the EPCS platform. An algorithm for optimizing the obtained target component of the system using an artificial immune system is considered.

Keywords: Mathematical model of the training and control system ·
Optimization of the content component of training · Artificial immune system

1 Introduction

In recent years, various concepts of IT-based educational platforms have spread out. According to the data available in the literature, the main differences in most cases are following: the distribution degree of control functions between the system's user and the system itself (for some cases user is allowed to choose the scenario of his/her interaction with the system, for other cases the scenario is fully or partially implement into the system and cannot be changed by the user); the amount of integrated content – theoretical courses and self-check tasks (and their combination implemented into the system); the presence or absence of education progress control function [1, 2, 7–10]. The designers of such educational systems have chosen the various combinations of parameters and the result "melting pot" has been the deliverable of the proposed educational platform. However,

V. Sukhomlin and E. Zubareva (Eds.): SITITO 2017, CCIS 1204, pp. 67–75, 2021.
https://doi.org/10.1007/978-3-030-78273-3_7

all almost all of the currently known EPCS platforms have the potential to accumulate statistical information regarding the students' educational scenarios (the courses they choose, the order that the courses were taken by them), typical mistakes that take place during students' self-checks, the overall amount of passed and failed courses, etc.

The main purpose of this work is to design the Education Progress Control System (EPCS) concept that might be applied for educational institutions and might be applied for student's education and knowledge check needs. The one of main objectives is to develop a mathematical model for such EPCS and to choose the appropriate means for its optimization. In order to develop the EPCS we have chosen the hybrid system (HS) design approach, because it combines the advantages of different technologies that allow solving complicated tasks. HS is a system combining two or more different computer technologies [3]. We have taken the parametric model of common educational process created by Monakhov [2] as a basis for the EPCS mathematical model. The parameters that holistically show the patterns of the educational process are following: goal setting parameter (the designed system of micro-goals); diagnostics parameter; educational dosing parameter for certain student's activity; the logical structure parameter of the educational project; correction parameter. The listed parameters are forming the basic design approach for the EPCS mathematical model.

The provided EPCS concept sets the purpose to split each particular educational section and its content on the micro-goals, and stores the fact of student's achievements, using the self-checks tasks embedded into the system. The self-checks is a set of mandatory training tasks that are required to be performed by a student. If a self-checks have not been performed, the correction is carried out, and then followed by the new self-checks test. The dosing of individual students activity is a set of content that is offered for students during the development of certain training section.

2   The System Model

The Fig. 1 shows the EPCS concept schema by the embedded components.

The mathematical model of the EPCS can be presented as following [11, 12]:

$$URS = \langle S, PP, T, CK, RR \rangle, \tag{1}$$

where S is the educational process; PP is the profiles factor of teachers and students; T is the educational path; CK is relates to the model of the current knowledge of certain student; RR is the profile of the educational course [5]. To store the personal information of teachers and students the profile entities are used. The educational path is represented by the information about the students' the educational path scenario within the EPCS.

In accordance to the parametric model of the educational process proposed by Monakhov [2], we have developed the following model of the educational process in the EPCS according hybrid system design approach (S)

$$S = \langle G, CT, EM, Q \rangle, \tag{2}$$

where G is the goal setting parameter, represented by the EPCS's educational micro-goals; CT is the educational courses branch, that corresponds to the logical structure of

Fig. 1. The model of hybrid learning system.

educational process; *EM* is the educational content, used for the correction and educational dosing of for the independent students; *Q* is the educational diagnostics parameter, comprising a plurality of self-check tasks. The set of educational objectives can be presented as following mathematical model:

$$G = \langle GN, GS \rangle, \tag{3}$$

where *G* is the educational branch of certain educational micro-goals; *GN* is the set of educational edges for branch's dedicated educational objectives; *GS* is the set of branch's edges, reflecting the hierarchical relationship between certain educational objectives. The learning content can be determined by using the equation below:

$$EM = \{P, E\}, \tag{4}$$

where *P* is the set of educational pages; *E* is the set of educational elements.

The self-check or knowledge diagnostics parameter *Q* might be defined as a set of self-check tasks. The set of the self-check questions (*Q*) is defined by:

$$Q = QSn\ QB, \tag{5}$$

where *QS* is the multiple sets of self-check questions; *QB* is the set of test questions sections.

To describe the content of certain educational course content we should use the following equation to determine the educational branch:

$$CT = \langle CTN, CTS \rangle, \tag{6}$$

where *CT* is the branch of the educational course content; *CTN* is the set of branch vertices, points of content; *CTS* is the set of branch edges, reflecting the relations between the involved educational content elements.

The components are models G, CT presented in the form of graphs, which can be optimized by using the appropriate well-known algorithms, for example:

CT is the branch of the educational material; CTN is the set of branches vertices, the educational content items; CTS is the set of the educational branch edges, reflecting the relations between the involved educational content elements. The content of the educational material represents as orientated graph. As the statistics weights of the edges the coefficient a_{ij} of difficulty transition from the vertexes i to j of the educational branch might be applied. Initially, these coefficients can be empirically determined by the peer review and then adjusted by using of well-known math-numerical methods. Thus, the problem of determination of the optimal educational sequence for certain educational content can be reduced to the task of optimizing of the related orientated graph.

3 Methods

The EPCS concept is divided on the components that are split on several sections (please refer to the Fig. 1 above). The main EPCS component is the algorithm that builds the educational branch (**Educational Scenario component**), and the components of this branch can be divided on micro-goals. The **Prognostication component** with the use of fuzzy logic allows determining the educational sections, which cause some difficulties for students (bad self-check statistics, long investigation periods for theoretical parts). Therefore, the fuzzy logic approach allows adjusting the micro-goals content as well. The **Educational Information component** includes theoretical and self-check materials and allows determining the dosing parameter during certain educational scenarios. The **Control Function component** directly corresponds with the diagnostics parameter of educational process.

The implementation of Kohonen self-organized network helps rank students involved into educational programs provided by the EPCS platform by three parameters: students that have not passed the self-checks and have not finished the educational scenario; students who demonstrate the knowledge level, corresponding to the current educational standards; students who demonstrate the knowledge level above the current educational standards. The **Statistics component** helps store information about the educational progress for students, who are registered in EPCS platform and these data is provided by Data Management component.

To classify students we use Kohonen self-organized network technology. The classification itself is the decomposition of objects to several sets, the number of which can be known in advance. This network consists of a single layer of neurons and learns independently (based on self-organized neuron map). In this case, an existence of a certain number of data classes is expected. The class can be prototype the vector data that is mostly typical for each class. Therefore, for each selected data vector the closest prototype can selected (and this process can be iterated across other data vectors), then the composition of all vectors (connected with the original prototype [2]) becomes a new prototype for each class.

The Kohonen self-organized network is represented as number of inputs for each neuron that is equal to the dimensional parameters of the classified object. In our case, the results of work on certain educational scenario of certain students will be classified. As it was determined above in the paper, each individual work in the educational scenario consists of four tasks – therefore, each neuron has four inputs correspondently. The number of neurons equals the number of groups that students are divided. In our case, we can divide students into four groups as following:

1. Have not passed the self-check (these students will be directed to the correction group);
2. Have shown knowledge level that corresponds to the state educational standard requirements (these students will be directed to the satisfactory group);
3. Have shown knowledge level that is above or equal the state educational standard requirements (these students can be assessed as "good");
4. Have shown the outstanding knowledge level that is above the educational standard requirements (these students can be assessed as "excellent").

However, in case of necessity the number of listed above classes can be changed by changing of the neurons number for certain neuron network map. During the initial network training, the initial values of weight matrix were set randomly so those are small values. Upon the presentation of the training sample, weight matrix is modified during self-organization process. Each column of the weight matrix represents itself as set of parameters for corresponding neuron-classifier. For each j-neuron ($j = 1, 2, \ldots, m$) the distance might be determined from the single neuron to the input vector X:

$$d_j = \sum \left(x_j - w_{ij}\right)^2. \tag{7}$$

Then the neuron with the number k, $1 \leq k \leq m$ is chosen – for this neuron the distance is minimal, (i.e., the network classifies the input vector to class number k). Therefore, at the N-step of training only the weights for neurons in the vicinity of neuron k will be modified:

$$w_{ij}^{N+1} = w_{ij}^N + \alpha_N \left(x_i - w_{ij}^N\right). \tag{8}$$

where α_N is the abstract pace of learning, expressed in number.

Initially, in the vicinity of any of neuronal neuron network can be located, but with each step further this vicinity is shrinking. Thus, at the end of the training iteration only the weights of neuron with number k are participating in the learning process. After some time period the learning pace α_N also decreases (often considered $\alpha_N = 0.9, \alpha_{N+1} = \alpha_N - 0.001$). Images of the training sample are presented sequentially, and each time there is adjustment of weights.

The Kohonen network learning algorithm consists of the steps listed below:

1. Network initialization;
2. Assignment the network coefficients $w_{ij}, i = 1, \ldots, n; j = 1, \ldots, m$ as small random values to all weight involved. Values preset: α_N – initial learning phase and D_0 – maximal distance between the weight vectors (column of matrix W);
3. Submission of the new input signal X to network;

4. Calculation of the distance from input X to all neurons of the network:

$$d_j = \sum \left(x_j - w_{ij}\right)^2, j = 1, \ldots, m. \tag{9}$$

5. Selection of neuron k, $1 \leq k \leq m$ with the minimal distance d_k from the input point that is applied to all neurons of the network.
6. Adjustment of weights of k-neuron and all neurons there are located within a distance that not exceeds D_N:

$$w_{ij}^{N+1} = w_{ij}^N + \alpha_N \left(x_i - w_{ij}^N\right). \tag{10}$$

7. Decrease of values.

Steps 2–6 might be iterated until the weights will stop shifting their values (or until the total values shift for all weights will be very small).

After the network has been trained, the classification of students' knowledge is carried out by applying the test vector to the network input and calculation of the distance from this input pint to each neuron (with further selection of the target neuron) with the smallest distance (as an indicator of the correct classification). This classification approach allows data fulfilling for the network, and can be based on the educational content of the verification work.

To increase the effectiveness of educational scenarios, diagnostics, and correction according to the objective in order to determine the educational course sections that are representing the difficulties for students the methods of fuzzy logic were used [6].

The educational prognostication is a quantitative estimation of the future condition of an object or system that is based on scientific methods. To predict the difficulties that students might face during the pass of educational scenario the methods of fuzzy logic were used that allow finding a fuzzy solution. That approach meets the requirements of the level of accuracy.

An artificial immune system is used to optimize the system of micro-targets [3]. The model of an artificial immune system is considered in [4] as a set of the following elements: the space of lymphocytes, a set of antigens, a given affinity measure that shows the degree of correspondence of each lymphocyte to antigens. The algorithm of the artificial immune system is presented in [4, 13] as follows:

1. The initial immune system is formed. The degree of adaptation lymphocytes to the antigen is calculated by the value of affinity function.
2. There is the best lymphocyte, which is an intermediate solution.
3. A mutation operator is applied to lymphocytes.
4. A selection operator is used to preserve the number of lymphocytes, it selects the lymphocytes with the highest affinity.
5. The algorithm is terminated if a specified number of completed cycles is reached or the lymphocyte affinity values don't change.

In this paper the artificial immune system was used to optimize the course tree, it is one of the components of the hybrid learning system model. The course tree defines the logical structure of the learning process. The logical structure consists of elements of the content of learning and the relations between them [14]. This relation can be unconditional, but it can be determined by the methodical position of the preparer of the training course. The following optimization scheme is presented in [5]. The logical structure of the learning content is presented as a sequence of elements of content A_1, A_2, ..., A_m. There are intra subject relations between the elements of content, A_i is used in the study of the element A_j with $i < j$. A system of relation between content elements can be specified using a graph. The following indices are used in [5] to characterize the system of constraints.

The length of the relation $A_i A_j$ is defined as follows:

$$P(A_i, A_j) = j - i. \tag{11}$$

The effectiveness of communication is called the value inverse of its length

$$E(A_i, A_j) = \frac{1}{P(A_i, A_j)}. \tag{12}$$

The average link length is determined by

$$P_{average} = \frac{1}{m} \sum P(A_i, A_j), \tag{13}$$

where $\sum P(A_i, A_j)$ is the sum of the lengths of all relations, and m is the number of relations.

The effectiveness of a logical structure is defined as a value that is the inverse of the average length and can be expressed as a percentage

$$E = \frac{100}{P_{average}}. \tag{14}$$

The algorithm for optimizing the logical structure of the content of training using an artificial immune system is as follows.

We used a graph representing relations between the elements of the content as an antigen. This is the theme "Elements of set theory" in our case.

We examined the sequence of studying the elements of the content of the topic as lymphocytes.

A measure of affinity for all lymphocytes is calculated. It is the effectiveness of the communication system, determined by the formula (14). The lymphocyte with the best affinity value is determined, it is the logical structure with the most effective system of relations in our case. It represents the current solution.

A certain part of the lymphocytes with the worst indicators is removed.

6. The mutation operator was applied to the remaining lymphocytes. We used two types of mutations.
7. The process is repeated from step 3 until a predetermined number of iterations is reached or an acceptable affinity value is reached. The result is a lymphocyte with the highest affinity from the current set.

4 Results and Discussion

The following user interface (UI) has been designed for the implementation of the EPCS platform.

The main page is common location on the UI for all users and represents itself as a connecting node between various sections of the System. The page provides two entry blocks, the first are a login into the teacher's account and the second is login as a student. The users also have the opportunity to register a new account as a student or teacher.

Once registered under the student account the user is immediately transferred to the **private student cabinet.** This page is the next binding node - being in the account, one can explore the theoretical section of the educational course material; perform practical work. If the student has been classified by the system as one who does not show the level of knowledge required by the state educational standards, he will be asked to go through the knowledge correction procedure, and then will be reassessed. Students can view all of their results with a full provision of information about the tests passed, personal data change, etc.

After registering as a teacher, the user enters the personal teacher's cabinet. The user is immediately invited to page "Students", which is designed as summary data table of all students and their tests passed.

The EPCS platform described in this article can be used during the process of distance learning for the organization and control of individual work of students, it allows conducting efficient training and student's knowledge control on any educational course (Fig. 2).

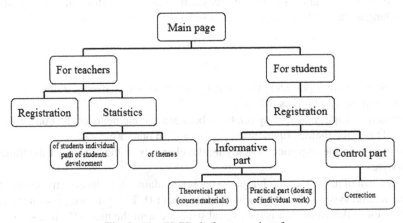

Fig. 2. The EPCS platform user interface.

5 Conclusion

The mathematical model of hybrid learning and control system, considered in the paper, provides the opportunity to optimize the learning process on various parameters using statistical information obtained in the course of system operation, which contributes to the structure of the system parameters, presented in the form of various graph.

The artificial immune system is created to optimize the system of micro-targets.

References

1. Melnikova, A.A.: Tools for modeling educational multimedia complexes: dis. … Ph.D. (Engineering), Samara (2004). (in Russian)
2. Monakhov, V.M.: Technological Foundations of the Design and Construction of the Educational Process. Peremena, Volgograd (1995). (in Russian)
3. Astachova, I.F., Firas, A.M.: Drawing Up the Schedule of Studies on the Basis of Genetic Algorithm. Proc. Voronezh State Univ. Ser.: Syst. Anal. Inf. Technol. (2), 93–99 (2013). https://www.elibrary.ru/item.asp?id=20734404. (in Russian)
4. Astakhova, I.F., Ushakov, S.A., Hitskova, Ju.V.: Model and algorithm of an artificial immune system for the recognition of single symbols. In: Advances in Computer Science. Proceedings of the 6th European Conference of Computer Science. WSEAS Press, pp. 127–131 (2015)
5. Monakhov, V.M., Vasekin, S.V., Kosino, O.A.: Design of innovative methodical system of mathematic bachelors training. Pedagogika (1), 22–31 (2015). https://www.elibrary.ru/item.asp?id=23599967. (in Russian)
6. Astachova, I.F., Shashkin, A.I., Korobkin, A.A.: Fuzzy logic design system of the prediction stability of ground mass. Proc. Voronezh State Univ. Ser.: Syst. Anal. Inf. Technol. (1), 98–106. https://www.elibrary.ru/item.asp?id=23441770. (in Russian)
7. Jurkov, N.K.: Intelligent Computer Training Systems. Publishing House of PSU, Penza (2010). (in Russian)
8. Clark, S., Baggaley, J.: Assistive software for disabled learners. Int. Rev. Res. Open Distrib. Learn. 5(3), 1–6 (2004). https://doi.org/10.19173/irrodl.v5i3.198
9. Batyrshin, I.Z., Nedosekin, A.O., et al.: Fuzzy Hybrid System. Theory and Practice. Fizmatlit, Moscow (2007). Yarushkina N.G. (ed.). (in Russian)
10. Samohvalov, E.N., Gapanuk, Yu.E.: Combining automated tutorials based on a semantic network of concepts. Eng. J.: Sci. Innov. (11), 32 (2013). https://doi.org/10.18698/2308-6033-2013-11-1068. (in Russian)
11. Fritze, P., Ip, A.: Learning engines a functional object model for developing learning resources for the WWW. In: Proceedings of the 10th World Conference on Educational Multimedia and Hypermedia & World Conference on Educational Telecommunications, ED-MEDIA/ED-TELECOM 1998, Freiburg, Germany, 20–25 June (1998). https://files.eric.ed.gov/fulltext/ED428662.pdf
12. Roberts, F.S.: Discrete Mathematical Models, with Applications to Social, Biological and Environmental Problems. Prentice-Hall, Hoboken (1976)
13. Holland, J.H.: Adaptation in Natural and Artificial Systems: An Introductory Analysis with Applications to Biology, Control and Artificial Intelligence. MIT Press, Cambridge (1992)
14. Ahuja, R.K., Magnanti, T.L., Orlin, J.B., Reddy, M.R.: Applications of network optimization. In: Handbooks in Operations Research and Management Science, vol. 7, pp. 1–83 (1995). https://doi.org/10.1016/S0927-0507(05)80118-5

The Features of Teachers' Training in the Field of Application of Information Technologies in Education

Vadim Grinshkun$^{(\boxtimes)}$ ⓘ, Irina Levchenko ⓘ, and Anastasia Pavlova ⓘ

Moscow City Teacher Training University, 2nd Selskohoziajstvenny proezd 4,
129226 Moscow, Russia

Abstract. The article observes the modern trends in teachers' training in the field of using of information technologies in education. The purpose of the article is to identify the drawbacks of the existing educational system in this field and to offer recommendations for their elimination. The authors have analyzed the experience of pedagogical high schools of Russia in teaching application of information technologies in education, in particular, the experience of Moscow City University, that was one of the first in Russia to establish Department of Application of Information Technologies in Education for conducting basics of application of information technologies in education training of future teachers. The authors identified the main drawbacks of current pedagogical training in sphere of application of information technologies in education and gave recommendations on how to make it more effective. They formulated the priority direction in training of application of information technologies in education and the main goals and objectives of training teachers in this field. The authors singled out the key elements of the content of application of information technologies in education courses for teachers, and principles characterizing the application of information technologies in education as educational discipline. Recommendations formulated in the article will be useful for educational courses creation in sphere of application of information technologies in education aimed at training of future and current teachers of schools and high schools.

Keywords: Application of information technologies in education · Teachers' training · Information and telecommunication technologies · Teaching methods · Trends in teaching · Training courses · Learning objectives

1 Introduction

1.1 A Subsection Sample

Use of means of information technologies' education, as a rule, makes real positive impact on an intensification of work of teachers, and also on learning efficiency of schoolchildren and students. At the same time any skilled teacher will affirm that against enough frequent positive effect from using of information technologies, in many cases

V. Sukhomlin and E. Zubareva (Eds.): SITITO 2017, CCIS 1204, pp. 76–83, 2021.
https://doi.org/10.1007/978-3-030-78273-3_8

the use of means of information technologies does not affect anyway on the efficiency increase of teaching process, and in certain cases such use has negative effect.

It is obvious that solution of problems of pertinent and justified using of information technologies in education should be carried out complexly and everywhere.

2 Purpose of the Research

The purpose of the article is to identify the drawbacks of the existing educational system in the field of using information technologies in education and to offer recommendations for their elimination.

3 Main Content

Training to appropriate use of means of information and telecommunication technologies should be entered into the content of teachers' training in the field of information technologies application in education. The applicable tendencies are already observed in pedagogical high schools of Russia, standard documents and programs of training and retraining of teachers. Almost all future teachers learn such disciplines as "Technical and audiovisual means (or technologies) of teachings" and "Information and communication technologies in education". To number of such disciplines it is possible to add courses which are taught in high schools: "Internet educational resources", "Methods of appraisal application and educational software usage", "Modern means of training results estimation" and some other disciplines. It is obvious that all of them, anyhow, light up the features of pedagogical activities realization in the conditions of telecommunication technologies usage. To this agenda, it is certainly necessary to add multiple courses on methods of various disciplines teaching that reflect specificity of using information technologies while teaching separate subjects in school and high school program.

Such kind of approach linked to questions of using information technologies within the limits of enumerated disciplines, has, at least, two essential drawbacks, which can be seen even in the names of these directions of students' training in pedagogical high schools.

The first drawback is separation and incoherence of the enumerated disciplines read, as a rule, by different teachers. The maintenance of these courses in many places duplicates each other. So, for example, features of development and use of electronic publications and educational resources published on the Internet, can be considered in almost all listed courses.

The second problem posed by the existing system of separation of teaching content, is that even in its name, these disciplines are focused primarily on the study of the means used in training, rather than on training teachers to work with the help of such means to increase the efficiency of education. According to the names, that are setting "tone" to teachers' training, such means, features of their device and functioning are learnt consistently, "through a comma". With this approach, it is impossible to examine all the means, which, however, is not required. Study of specific means and technologies become outdated so quickly that after the graduation of high school the teacher will have to face very different means with which they did not work.

In our opinion, the pointed directions of training and retraining teachers should be substantially and methodically combined in the uniform complex aimed at teachers' and tutors' studying of the essence and specificity of information technologies usage in education. Thus "Information technologies in education" can be used as the separate name, enough vast under the maintenance and a fundamental subject matter, and as the name and the systematizing factor of the block of the above-named subject matters already today introduced in programs of students training in pedagogical high schools.

Many specialists consider that "information technologies use in education", treated as a process, cannot represents itself as the name of an academic discipline or a unit of academic disciplines. Really, to learn the process is incorrect. But information technologies in education can be regarded as an activity – the activity of teachers aimed at providing education by the objective, authentic, actual information and means of processing. In this case information technologies in education training will represent teaching activity, that is quite correct and justified. As an example, recognized discipline, having a similar name, under which teaching activities take place, can cause a school subject "Drawing." Books with the same name each of us had more than once in their hands. Perhaps, similarly may be with the publication of textbooks and manuals titled "Information Technologies Use in Education". As another example, confirming the validity of this approach is the car driving. On the one hand, it is a process in which the car moves without a single accident on a given route, on the other hand, human activity having the appropriate knowledge, skills and abilities. It should be noted that this particular activity (not the process) is taught at the appropriate courses.

Department of Information Technologies Application in Education, established in Moscow City University, is one of the first in Russia attempted to carry out the basics of information technologies use in education training for future teachers on the basis of a number of the above-mentioned subjects. To do this, we search the purposes and principles of learning that would systematize the training of teachers, to make its content more fundamental and less dependent on the constantly changing and developing information technologies. Within this framework, the textbook "Using of Information Technologies in Education. Fundamental Basis" was created.

4   Results of the Research

Taking into account the approach to information technologies use in education as a teachers and other specialists activity the definition which is the semantic basis for training in the created course is elaborated. According to this definition information technologies use in education is understood as a field of scientifically-practical activities of the person, directed on application of technologies and means of gathering, stowage, processing and disseminating of information, providing formation of new knowledge in the sphere of education for achievement of the psychological and pedagogical purposes of training and education.

The use of information technologies in education treated as a separate discipline or a direction of teachers training (without dependence from their specialization), possesses a number of features.

First of all, it is necessary to notice that the word combination "using information technologies in education" does not contain concepts "computerization" or any other similar concepts. They are not included even into the above-mentioned definition. Thus, creation and use of the editions published in the traditional way on a paper, also is the high-grade factor of information technologies use in education. Features of constructing traditional editions, formation of their maintenance and, certainly, training with their use also is justified and it can be esteemed in such course or unit of academic disciplines. Another matter that training to the produced direction linked to use of printed editions is well enough learnt, and students are familiar with it because of other disciplines and life experience. In this connection the basic emphasis at study of information technologies usage in education should be placed on studying of resources and editions, the work that is possible through the use of computer technology.

Transferring from training of technical and technological aspects of working with computer means to training of formation, selection and appropriate use of educational electronic editions and resources should become a priority direction in training of information technologies usage in education. The modern teacher should not only have knowledge in the field of information and telecommunication technologies that is included into the content of courses on computer science studied in pedagogical universities, but also to be a specialist in application of new technologies in the professional activities.

Main objectives of teachers' training in the field of information technologies use in education should be:

- studying of positive and negative aspects of information and telecommunication technologies usage in education;
- formation of ideas about the role and place of the information technologies use in education in the information society, the species composition and areas of effective use of means of information technologies use in education, technology, processing, presentation, storage and transmission of information;
- studying of the general methods of information technologies usage, adequate to the needs of the educational process, the control and measurement of learning outcomes of the lesson, extracurricular, research, organizational and management activities of educational institutions;
- knowledge formation about requirements concerning the means of information technologies in education, the basic principles of quality assessment, teacher training strategy for the practical use of information in the field of education;
- providing additional opportunities to clarify the role and the place of information technologies in the modern world to students;
- teaching and evolving language of information technologies in education (with parallel fixation and systematic terminology).

In spite of the fact that the content of described discipline or system of training courses still is in a forming stage, already priorities now are clear, according to the basic concepts and essence of processes of information technologies usage in education. One of paramount places in the content of training in the field of information technologies usage in education is occupied with questions of pertinent, justified and an effective utilization of information and telecommunication technologies in education.

The key areas of the content of the training course that were identified are features of using information technologies in education, technical means and technologies of using information technologies in education, methods of using information technologies in educational activities, basis for the formation of educational environment and information educational space, questions of formation readiness of teachers to professional use of information technologies.

Training course of information technologies use in education (or the system of courses under this name) should include scientific basis for the creation, review and application of educational electronic editions and resources. In this area there are still many unsolved problems. These include the problem of the adequacy of such means to realities of the educational process, improving scientific, semantic and stylistic culture of content of means of information technologies, necessity of the interface, technological and information connection between separate educational editions and the resources that are used in different spheres of activity of schools and high schools.

There are several characteristic features of information technologies in education as an educational discipline and determining it unlike other similar approaches and content areas described in many recent publications. Thereupon it is enough to note such factors as:

- systematic approach - the basis of the discipline is not an enumeration of existing means and technologies of information technologies in education with their descriptions, but the needs and common characteristics of information technologies in possible types of educational activities;
- aiming to eliciting aspects of using information technologies in education, invariant to psychology-aged features of learners, specificity of educational activity of concrete educational institutions, developing of information technology and of some other factors;
- identification of variant aspects of using information technologies in education depending on various factors - psychological, methodological, technological and organizational characteristics, training and retraining of teachers taking into consideration various aspects that should be carried out using a system of specialized courses, disciplines and tutorials;
- creation of educational material, focusing teachers' attention on key issues, the search for answers which is a prerequisite for the effectiveness of information;
- systematization of terminology within teaching the language of information technologies application in education;
- orientation training, including the development of the teachers sustained motivation to participate in formation of information educational environment.

5 Conclusion

It is important to convey to future teachers that the information technologies in education achieves two strategic objectives. The first of these aims is to increase the effectiveness of all types of educational activities based on the use of information and communication technologies. The second aim is to improve the quality of training specialists with a new type of thinking, according to requirements of the informational society. Using the methods and means of information technologies the future specialists must learn to get answers to questions about what information resources are available, where they are, how to get access to them and how they can be used to improve the effectiveness of their professional activities.

Teachers should understand that use of information technology will be justified and will lead to increase the effectiveness of the training only if such kind of use will respond to the specific requirements of the educational system - if the training in full without the use of the applicable means of information technologies is impossible or it is inconvenient. It is obvious that the system of teachers' training in the sphere of information technologies of education should include acquaintance with several groups of such requirements, both in terms of the learning process itself, and in relation to other activities of teachers.

For justified and effective use of information and telecommunication technologies teachers need to know the main positive and negative aspects of information technologies usage in education, the use of electronic publications and resources. It is obvious that the knowledge of such aspects will help teachers and educators to use information technologies there where it involves the greatest advantages and minimize the possible negative aspects associated with the work of students with modern means of information technologies. Application of means of information technologies in training by the principle of "the more the better" can not lead to a real increase in the effectiveness of the functioning of the education system. Balanced and well-reasoned approach is necessary in the use of electronic publications and educational resources.

References

1. Azevich, A.I.: Educational paradigms in the era of informatization. Vestn. Moscow City Univ. Ser.: Inform. Informatiz. Educ. (2), 51–55 (2017). https://www.elibrary.ru/item.asp?id=294 08120. (in Russian)
2. Bakhtibaeva, S.A., Grinshkun, V.V., Berkimbaev, K.M., Turmambekov, T.A.: Use of information technology in teaching semiconductors physics. Indian J. Sci. Technol. 9(19), 1–6 (2016). https://doi.org/10.17485/ijst/2016/v9i19/93892
3. Bazhenova, S.A., Kartashova, L.I.: Using innovative approaches to the assessment of results of training in preparing future teachers of computer science. Vestn. Moscow City Univ. Ser.: Inform. Informatiz. Educ. (2), 38–47 (2015). https://www.elibrary.ru/item.asp?id=23714998. (in Russian)
4. Berdi, D.K., Saribaeva, A.X., Zhilisbaeva, G.N., Berkimbaev, K.M., Kornilov, V.S.: Forming information competency of future teachers in the frame of professional pedagogical activities. RUDN J. Informatiz. Educ. (1), 73–79 (2015). https://www.elibrary.ru/item.asp?id=22979053
5. Frolov, A.: Challenges and prospects of using information technologies in higher education. SHS Web Conf. 29, 02015 (2016). https://doi.org/10.1051/shsconf/20162902015
6. Grigoriev, S.G., Grinshkun, V.V., Levchenko, I.V.: Determination of the theoretical and methodological foundations of the use of electronic educational resources in education system of Moscow. Bull. Lab. Math. Nat. Sci. Educ. Informatiz. 4, 11–25 (2012). (in Russian)
7. Grigoriev, S.G., Grinshkun, V.V., Koloshein, A.P.: The technology of the use of electronic educational resources at institution of higher education. Vestn. Moscow City Univ. Ser.: Inform. Informatiz. Educ. (23), 8–13 (2012). https://www.elibrary.ru/item.asp?id=17780539. (in Russian)
8. Grigoryev, S.G., Grinshkun, V.V.: Informatization of Education. Fundamental Basics, Moscow (2008). (in Russian)

9. Grinshkun, V.V.: Development of the system of teacher training in the context of the informatization of education. In: From Informatics at School to the Technosphere of Education. Collection of Scientific Papers of International Scientific and Practical Conference, Moscow, pp. 119–125 (2016). https://www.elibrary.ru/item.asp?id=25315087. (in Russian)

10. Grinshkun, V.V.: Influence of information resources quality on formation of teachers readiness to informatization of education. Kazan Pedagog. J. (6), 28–34 (2016). https://www.elibrary.ru/item.asp?id=27719565. (in Russian)

11. Grinshkun, V.V.: Informatization and innovations within the educational and research activities of undergraduates and graduate students in a Pedagogical University. RUDN J. Informatiz. Educ. (1), 7–14 (2016). https://www.elibrary.ru/item.asp?id=25497374. (in Russian)

12. Grinshkun, V.V.: Integrative approaches to educational and innovatory activities of magistrants and postgraduate students of teachers training higher school in the conditions of informatization of education. Vestn. Moscow City Univ. Ser.: Inform. Informatiz. Educ. (1), 20–27 (2016). https://www.elibrary.ru/item.asp?id=25833754. (in Russian)

13. Grinshkun, V.V.: On important aspects of teachers training in the field of informatization of education. RUDN J. Informatiz. Educ. (4), 7–12 (2015). https://www.elibrary.ru/item.asp?id=25013310. (in Russian)

14. Grinshkun, V.V.: Preparation of future teachers in the field of informatization of education: features, problems, significance. In: Bulletin of the Laboratory of Mathematical, Natural Science Education and Informatization, pp. 121–128 (2015). https://www.elibrary.ru/item.asp?id=25287866. (in Russian)

15. Grinshkun, V.V., Krasnova, G.A.: Specific of using massive open educational electronic courses in Russian and foreign universities. RUDN J. Informatiz. Educ. 14(3), 255–266. https://www.elibrary.ru/item.asp?id=30053382. (in Russian)

16. Grinshkun, V.V., Krasnova, G.A.: New Education for New Information and Technological Revolutions. RUDN J. Informatiz. Educ. 14(2), 131–139 (2017). http://doi.org/10.22363/2312-8631-2017-14-2-131-139. (in Russian)

17. Grinshkun, V.V., Krasnova, G.A., Nukhuly, A.: Features of use of open electronic resources and mass educational courses in higher education. Vestn. Moscow City Univ. Ser.: Inform. Informatiz. Educ. (2), 8–17 (2017). https://www.elibrary.ru/item.asp?id=29408115. (in Russian)

18. Grinshkun, V.V., Shirochenko, M.E.: The organization of educational project activity of students with application of information and telecommunication technologies. RUDN J. Informatiz. Educ. 14(2), 180–187 (2017). http://doi.org/10.22363/2312-8631-2017-14-2-180-187. (in Russian)

19. Kulgildinova, T.A., Uaissova, G.I.: Realization of frame-based technologies in the context of education informatization. J. Theor. Appl. Inf. Technol. 89(1), 254–260 (2016). http://www.jatit.org/volumes/Vol89No1/26Vol89No1.pdf

20. Levchenko, I.V.: Methodical aspects of application of information technologies in educational process. Bull. Lab. Math. Nat. Sci. Educ. Informatiz. 5, 25–28 (2013). (in Russian)

21. Levchenko, I.V.: Methodical preparation of teachers using the information educational environment. In: Proceedings of the International Forum Electronic Education: From the Present to the Future, pp. 21–24 (2013). (in Russian)

22. Onalbek, Zh.K., Grinshkun, V.V., Omarov, B.S., Abuseytov, B.Z., Makhanbet, E.T., Kendzhaeva, B.B.: The main systems and types of forming of future teacher-trainers' professional competence. Life Sci. J. 10(4), 2397–2400 (2013). http://www.lifesciencesite.com/lsj/life1004/320_21859life1004_2397_2400.pdf

23. Pavlova, A.E.: Features of the organization of practical lessons on the subject "technology of development of electronic educational editions and resources". Vestn. Moscow City Univ. Ser.: Inform. Informatiz. Educ. (3), 54–58 (2016). https://www.elibrary.ru/item.asp?id=27038179. (in Russian)

24. Pavlova, A.E.: Preparation of future teachers of primary school for the use of information and communication technologies in the training process. In: Bulletin of the Laboratory of Mathematical, Natural Sciences Education and Informatization, vol. 210–213 (2013). (in Russian)

25. Pavlova, A.E.: Organization of laboratory reaserchesin the discipline "social aspects of informatization of education". Bull. Russ. Univ. Peoples' Friendsh. Ser.: Informatiz. Educ. (3), 21–25 (2016). https://www.elibrary.ru/item.asp?id=26674338. (in Russian)

26. Zaslavskaya, O.Yu.: Contents of pedagogical activity in conditions of informatization. In: Kravets, O.Ja. (ed.) Modern Informatization Problems in Simulation and Social Technologies: Proceedings of the XX-th International Open Science Conference, Yelm, WA, USA, January 2015, pp. 277–282. Science Book Publishing House, Yelm (2015)

The Combination of Technologies Supporting Interactivity and Identification of Students at the Level of Architectural Blocks of the Educational System Using Information Technology

Alexey Komarov[1]([✉]) [iD] and Victor Panchenko[2] [iD]

[1] LLC Scientific & Research Institute of Natural Gases and Gas Technologies, 5537-j Proektiruemyj Proezd vl. 15, str. 1, 142717 Razvilka, Moscow Region, Russia
[2] MIREA – Russian Technological University, Vernadsky Avenue 78, 119454 Moscow, Russia

Abstract. The article describes the basic elements of a unified landscape of educational technologies implementing ways to support interactivity and identification of students in the educational complex. Modern educational complexes using information technology (IT) should form a controlled environment with the ability to systematically collect and process information about the educational process. A permanent analysis of information about students, as well as educational materials, will allow us to identify the classes of students and educational content that are most suitable for each other in terms of time and success in learning . In the architecture of the educational system using IT, technological solutions have been identified that provide the formation of a database and a knowledge base required to solve this problem. On the basis of the specific features of the educational process implementation, it is possible to use various sets of technologies to solve certain didactic tasks, but it is the integrated application of the technologies described in the article that reveals the potential in the field of the education management quality.

Keywords: Learning management systems · Programmed education · Interactivity · Identification · Statistical analysis · SCORM · Experience API · Technology of single experiment programs · Shared content technology · Multi-screen technology of activity · Systems approach · Computer training tools

1 Introduction

The architecture of the training system using information technology - Learning Technology Systems Architecture (LTSA) - is offered to be used to formulate and consider the initial tasks of research and technological design of training systems with support for interactivity and identification of students. Figure 1 shows the architecture of the LTSA standard (third level) and problems are highlighted in descriptors, the solution of which

© Springer Nature Switzerland AG 2021
V. Sukhomlin and E. Zubareva (Eds.): SITITO 2017, CCIS 1204, pp. 84–94, 2021.
https://doi.org/10.1007/978-3-030-78273-3_9

depends on the accepted technologies for processing content materials, processing protocols and technologies for implementing single-experiment programs. The topological system of architecture models is a diagram of a directed graph (digraph) at six vertices with 15 arcs. The power of the universe of a full digraph at six vertices and thirty arcs, not counting the empty set, is 1.540.944. One of the graphs of this rather large set is accepted as the universe of the generated subsets in the LTSA architecture.

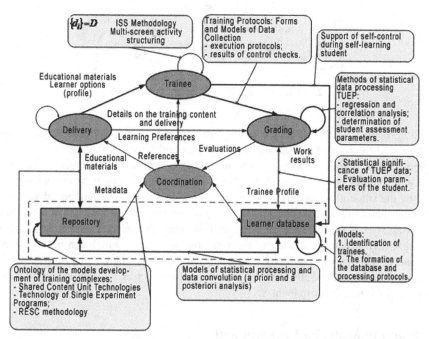

Fig. 1. Educational system architecture (3rd level) with technologies for supporting educational activities.

The LTSA architecture is, to some degree, a paradigm "label" of the universe (model), which characterizes the complexes of processes, storages and precedents of an education system built on information technologies. We represent the LTSA architecture in Fig. 2 as a pseudo-graph with six vertices in order to form a matrix description of the constituent subgraphs of the architecture.

On the diagrams of the LTSA and the graph (Fig. 1 and Fig. 2, respectively), one can distinguish a number of isolated and overlapping components of the systems corresponding to various tasks and functions, functionalities and operators implemented in the creation of educational systems. Further study of the graph allows encoding to order the groups of problems solved in the training system; it is also convenient to use the graph adjacency matrix as an image of relations.

Now let's take a closer look at the main elements of the educational complex using IT: a repository of educational materials, a block for presenting material, blocks for collecting and processing data during training, a data and knowledge system. For each element, we will use systemically linked learning support technologies [1].

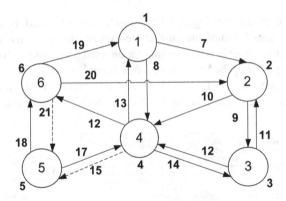

Fig. 2. LTSA pseudo-orggraph architecture diagram.

The processes of the training course preparing and its study at each stage should be supported by a set of educational technologies and have a pedagogical basis. The fragmented use of various technologies and didactic approaches adversely affects the quality of the educational process, which can be expressed in an increase in the time spent by the student on mastering the content, in a decrease in the number of successfully completed training, incorrect assessment of the students, a decrease in the image component, etc. If various technologies and didactic approaches are applied separately, this negatively affects the quality of the educational process, which can be expressed in an increase in the time spent by the student on mastering the content, in a decrease in the number of successfully completed training, incorrect assessment of the trainees, decrease in the image component, etc.

2   Training Material Development

When developing and presenting training materials (repository), a systematic approach to the description of the subject area should be applied, the basis of which is rational-empirical systems complexes (RESC) [2].

The RESC levels in the adopted notation: Y1 - sign-linguistic, Y2 - set-theoretic, Y3 - abstract algebraic, Y4 - logical-mathematical, Y5 - topological, Y6 - information, Y7 - dynamic, Y8 - heuristic, as well as operations: R (A) - operation of abstraction, R (K) - operation of concretization; subject areas are distinguished: SAK - subject area of knowledge, SAA - subject area of activity; empirical kernel systems according to Clear (E1, E2, E3): D - initial data systems, F- generation systems [3].

To organize the learner's cognitive activity (LCA) as a single-channel queuing system, it is possible to use the Technology of Shared Content Units (TREC) for a given test curriculum, that is, Technology of Unitary Experiment Programs (TUEP) [1, 4]. Shared units of content form an Information Semantic System (ISS), which is represented as a discrete space of states and transitions. The skeleton of the knowledge system forms a network of thesaurus concepts, over which a coating is constructed in the form of a module structure (fragments, portions, pages, frames).

2.1 Presentation of Training Material

The scheme of the general formulation of the educational process based on TUEP, shown in Fig. 3, to a certain extent predetermines the series of time intervals, and, consequently, the range of classes of problems for identifying the parameters of students and problems of dual clustering and pattern recognition that are available for research.

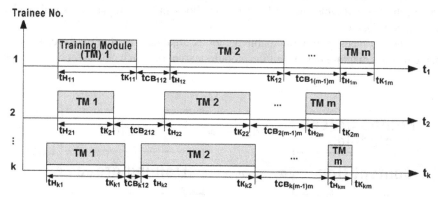

Fig. 3. Scheme of the educational process in the modular-personnel space of electronic forms of training (1,2... k - student numbers; t_H - start time of working with the module; t_k - closing time; t_{CB} - break).

As a means of organizing a program-controlled process of independent development of authors information materials of the repository (electronic libraries), the concept of "module" (TM1, TM2,...) and its components, presented in the form of viewing sequences of frames (pages), for example, TM1 (K1 ... K13) and TM2 (K1 ... K11) [4, 5]. The module frame is the basic element of the network, characterized by its volume and time spent on its study.

A frame is presented as a system that could contain uniform complex forms of presentation of semantic information: textual (- form), audio (- form: speech, sounds), visual (- form: facial expressions, gestures, plastic), graphic pictorial (- form: drawings, tables, photographs) [6].

A complex tuple, the elements of which are the accepted characters of the alphabet $\{t; S; g; C\}$ can be an analogue of the formal description of the module frame. If the formal description of the module was compared with the usual sentence of words, then we get a formal sentence, associatively separated by brackets, in which subsets of tuples are distinguished - words from a given alphabet from a variety of homogeneous forms.

For example, module frame structure M:

$$StrMk \Leftrightarrow (t; C; (S; C; t); g; t; (t; t; t)K), \tag{1}$$

Where tuples (1) defines the sequence of information in the form: (text; graphics; (speech, table, text); visualization; again text; (text; text; text) ...). Here $StrMk$ (the frame structure) defines the model of the presentation of the information flow that affects the student in real time, the contact, which in turn is defined by the cost of mastering the material by a particular student.

For each module frame according to the TUEP method, the forms of the training exercise are determined, for example, from the following series: to study (to read (action D1), to highlight key concepts, to outline (to rewrite) (D2), to type text (D3); to draw up a summary (a note for drawing up note U1): to save the headings and portion numbering as headings of the electronic note and use the data to determine the speed of typing; to note schemes and tables in an electronic notebook in the Student's Personal Folder (SPF) (note U2), etc.

For various types of programmable activities organized by the TREC technology [7], the process diagram in terms of the module-learner system it can be set out as in the Fig. 4.

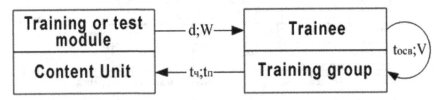

Fig. 4. Parameters and variables of the observing system of the "module - learner" type.

In the Fig. 4 we have:

$d \in D$ – the class of actions prescribed for the learner, defining the activity with elements of the module "M";

W – amounts of information presented in the elements (texts, graphs, multimedia components …);

t_u, t_n, t_{ocs} – estimates of time spent on a given activity, for reading t_u, for rewriting (possibly printing) of given fragments t_n, for pondering and comprehending of semantic information t_{ocs};

V – amount of syllabus (secondary document), $V = 0.2W$;

T – total process costs: $T = t_u + t_n + t_{ocs}$, i.e. for reading, for writing down and comprehending (mastering) of the content semantic "M".

Reading, rewriting, typing on the keyboard, taking notes in this system are elementary operations of the learner's cognitive activity. In this case an experiment is always associated with the measurement of time and analysis of the received data depending on the environment and forms of information. It can be noted that the use of TREC together with TUEP is the basis for the creation of effective tools for the analysis and management of educational activities in e-learning systems.

Features of information perception by a person, his main characteristics as an object of training should be reflected in the technologies for presenting educational material that are preferable to use. Looking ahead, we can talk about the adjustment of educational content (operations R (A)/R (K), changing the structure of modules, etc.) depending on the psychological characteristics of the personality: the preferred way of perceiving information, temperament, social and even genetic [8].

Programmed training in terms of independent LCA may relate to the regulation and systematization of the use of additional technical tools to help increase the degree of assimilation of the material. For example, an additional monitor is used in training using the Student's Multi-Screen Activity Technology (SMSAT). SMSAT was successfully applied by the authors in training to solve the transport problem, where the developed web application was used.

The expansion of the SMSAT affects the features of training using books, where cognitive activity is organized with minimal expenses for actions that are not part of the cognitive process, but often distract learners from it (switching between windows, unnecessary search for information, etc.)

Mandatory preliminary tests of students necessary for creating the optimal educational process are one of its most important stages. For example, before commissioning a gas pumping unit, preliminary tests are carried out, and the passport characteristics are adjusted in accordance with the actual condition. Why, when dealing with such a complex object as a human being, in most cases we begin the learning process without proper analysis?

Accounting for retrospective (a priori) and current (posterior) information about the student - The Technology of Preliminary and Current Tests (TPCP) should become a mandatory component of the educational process. Trainee ratings (absolute/relative) will be formed on the basis of the test results. As practice has shown, this brings a positive gaming component and elements of competition to the learning process.

2.2 Collection and Processing of Training Data

During the study, the accounting procedure and the set of the retrospective (a priori), current (a posteriori) and expert data to be registered during training and processing of observation data were determined. As part of the classes in the disciplines "General Theory of Systems", "Theory of Decision-making", relevant data were collected on various laboratory works. The following items were included in the data list: data of test books, data on attendance at classes, data on the completion of control tasks, qualimetric data of trainees for given and elementary types of activity, total time spent on laboratory work [9]. Depending on the discipline, changes in the list are possible, but the general approach remains unchanged.

Creation of an assessment system of criteria is necessary to perform an assessment of the activities of students is necessary. The identification of the object of observation as a management system implemented on the basis of the forecasting of retrospective data is formed from an intuitively obvious hypothetical relationship between the assessment of labor spent on the educational process and the assessment of the individual's preparedness for the student to perceive and understand new material based on competencies formed at the time of monitoring and developed according to the results of past experience studying the system of subjects provided for in the curriculum.

By way of example of an assessment of the student's activity, the "Rating" model of the problem used by the authors can be cited [10].

The following hypotheses are accepted for the constructive setting of the "Rating" problem at the heuristic level:

- The general hypothesis: statistical, a priori, and a posteriori data (past successes, attitude to the educational process, etc.) indirectly characterize the effectiveness of the cognitive process of individual learning.
- The particular hypothesis: a priori assessment of the student F_0 can be expressed as a function of two variables:

$$F_0 = f(\bar{y}, \bar{x}).$$

where $\bar{y}$ – student's average estimate based on a priori data (data from past experience); $\bar{x}$ – average estimate of the student's activity for the current period of the cognitive process: academic hour, lesson, month, semester, academic year.

Estimate $\bar{y}$ can be determined according to the certificate of secondary education, and later on at the initial stage according to the student's gradebook.

Estimate $\bar{x}$ – assessment depends on the attendance of classes and the activity of the student during these classes.

To determine the a priori basic assessment and the student's rating in the considered specific task "Rating", the following dependence was adopted for F_0:

$$F_0 \xleftrightarrow{def} W = \frac{1}{2}\left[\frac{1}{2}\left(\frac{\bar{y}}{5} + K_D\right) + \frac{\bar{y} \cdot K_D}{5}\right] \cdot 5, \qquad (2)$$

where $\bar{y}$ – secondary school average estimate, $\bar{y} \in [3; 5]$;

K_D – confidence coefficient; estimate of an individual's activity in the current semester of study, $K_D \approx \bar{x}$;

$\bar{x}$ – estimate of average attendance during the observation period in relative units $\bar{x} \in [0; 1]$;

W – a priori estimate of the student in points, $W \in [0; 5]$.

Constituents of the formulas (2) reflect the process of rationing and scaling of information associated with the heuristic of the following initial premises for rating scales:

$$W = [W(+) + W(\times)] \cdot \frac{5}{2}, \quad 0 \le W \le 5;$$
$$W(+) = \left(\frac{1}{5}\bar{y} + \bar{x}\right) \cdot \frac{1}{2}, \quad 0 \le W(+) \le 1;$$
$$W(\times) = \frac{\bar{y}}{5} \cdot \bar{x}, \quad 0 \le W(\times) \le 1.$$

Now:

$W(+)$ – additive component of the estimate W;

$W(\times)$ – multiplicative component of the estimate W.

Having understood the semantics adopted for the constituent of formula (2), we can proceed to its formal analysis:

$$W_b = \frac{5}{4}\left(\frac{\bar{y}}{5} + K_D\right) + \frac{\bar{y} \cdot K_D}{5} = \frac{\bar{y}}{4} + \frac{5}{4}K_D + \frac{\bar{y} \cdot K_D}{2} = 0.25\bar{y} + 1.25\bar{x} + 0.5\bar{y} \cdot \bar{x}.$$

(3)

Formula (3) is defined as a conceptual model of a student's weighted average base rating, calculated using a priori data $\bar{y}$ and observational results $\bar{x}$ (a posteriori observational data).

The model can be optimized for using the grading scale of the Unified State Exam or a 12-point grading scale in accordance with the levels of knowledge [8].

Separately, in the unit for collecting and processing information, it is worth noting the qualimetric indicators of students in the simplest types of activities, which make it possible to determine the inevitable time spent on studying educational material. The amount of information of educational material can be estimated both in characters and in bits [8].

A number of experiments to evaluate the qualimetric indicators of students in elementary types of LCA showed high variances in their final values, which indicates a significant effect of these indicators on the overall assessment of LCA. The formation of classes of students, including by their qualimetry on elementary types of activity, is obvious.

It is preferable to provide students with some tools and the results of an analysis of their activities, the inclusion of elements of control in the educational process should stimulate introspection, form the idea that control is an integral part of the training, and not closed information for the teacher. It is useful to present a number of training tasks in the form of computer simulators. Depending on the training form, the implementation of data collection of programmed training will have its own characteristics. In intramural training, it is possible to use a logging system during the execution of individual experiment programs.

When using Learning management system (LMS), it is possible to use an automated collecting data about the time spent on working with content. The basic principles for tracking time spent on working with training modules are laid down in the SCORM standard (Shareable Content Object Reference Model) and its development "Experience API" (xAPI) [11, 12]. In the course of the study, the authors used the SCORM package, based on the UEP "Processing of UEP Data" materials.

This package has been downloaded to the deployed Moodle system. A file of "clean" data was formed from the LMS database with basic data on the course of the trainees' passage of various training elements (modules) in a format ready for statistical processing.

Currently, the development of common methods for collecting data and processing them for various forms of educational systems - Data Collection and Processing Technologies (DCPT).

The software should evaluate the student's retrospective activity on the basis of the obtained a priori and posterior data in aggregate and on the basis of their convolution using the Bayes hypothesis evaluation formula. The result of the assessment may consist in recommendations for changing the form and depth of presentation of the material, means and methods of its presentation. In addition, the computerization of data processing and management tools helps to identify problem areas in the structure of the course being studied individually for each participant in the cognitive process. Technologies and the procedures for making these changes to the educational complex should be fixed in the form of Educational Complexes Adaptation Technologies (ECAT).

When using a systematic approach to the organization of training, the educational complex is formed: in terms of content - in accordance with the basics of the Rational-Empirical Complex of Systems (RECS); in terms of presentation - by using the Technology of Shared Content Units (TSCU), Technology of Unit Experiment Programs (TUEP), Technology of Multi-Screen Student Activity (TMSSA); regarding the structure of the data about the student - Technologies of Preliminary and Current Tests (TPCT); in terms of collecting and processing data on the progress of training - Data Collection and Processing Technologies (DCPT); in terms of interactivity - Technologies for the Adaptation of Educational Complexes (TAEC). The list of technologies and methods used in the author's research and noted as essential for further research during the construction of the educational complex is shown in Fig. 5.

3   Conclusion

Experience has shown, even the fragmented application of approaches and technologies belonging to the described general system of educational technologies increases the effectiveness of training. The development and adoption of common standards compliant to the achievements of didactics and modern IT, as well as their systematic application for each stage of the educational process, will lead to a transition from traditional to interactive education with constant identification of students and educational content. Education requirements will only become stricter over time, the number of areas of knowledge will grow, and, obviously, it is no longer possible to do without a cardinal improvement in approaches to learning.

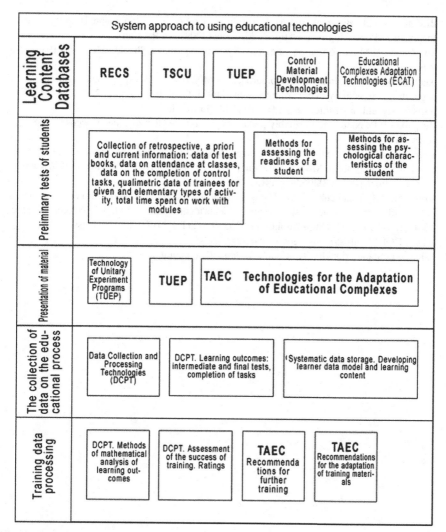

Fig. 5. The list of technologies and methods used in the construction of the educational complex.

References

1. Komarov, A.I., Panchenko, V.M.: Software complex for supporting interactive education process with opportunity of students identification. Mod. Inf. Technol. IT-Educ. **12**(3–1), 82–89 (2016). https://www.elibrary.ru/item.asp?id=27411978. (in Russian)
2. Nechaev, V.V., Panchenko, V.M., Komarov, A.I.: Interdisciplinary "system-forming" basis of educational process organization according to studies direction. Open Educ. (5), 70–77 (2012). https://www.elibrary.ru/item.asp?id=18359809. (in Russian)
3. Klir, G.J.: Architecture of Systems Problem Solving. Springer, Boston (1985). https://doi.org/10.1007/978-1-4757-1168-4
4. Norenkov, I.P., Zimin, A.M.: Information Technologies in Education. BMSTU Press, Moscow (2004). (in Russian)

5. Bashmakov, A.I., Bashmakov, I.A.: Designing of Computer Textbook and Training System. Information-Publishing House "Filin", Moscow (2003). (in Russian)
6. Solomatin, N.M.: Information Semantic System. Vysshaya Shkola, Moscow (1989). (in Russian)
7. Nechaev, V.V., Panchenko, V.M., Komarov, A.I.: Methodological aspects and technologies for supporting interactivity in e-learning systems. Int. J. Open Inf. Technol. 2(1), 17–22 (2014). https://www.elibrary.ru/item.asp?id=21019894. (in Russian)
8. Bespalko, V.P.: Nature conformably pedagogy. Narodnoe Obrazovanie, Moscow (2008). (in Russian)
9. Komarov, A.I., Panchenko, V.M., Nechaev, V.V.: Role of data and knowledge system in providing IT education. Mod. Inf. Technol. IT-Educ. (10), 116–125 (2014). https://www.elibrary.ru/item.asp?id=23020624. (in Russian)
10. Komarov, A.I., Panchenko, V.M.: Using systems approach to build education process based on technologies of interactive support and students identification. Mod. Inf. Technol. IT-Educ. 13(4), 126–133 (2017). https://doi.org/10.25559/SITITO.2017.4.406. (in Russian)
11. ADL SCORM. https://adlnet.gov/research/projects
12. E-learning Standard xAPI (Tin Can API). https://xapi.com/

How to Solve Unconventional Mathematical Problems with the Help of Electronic Visualisation

Olga Korchazhkina$^{(\boxtimes)}$ (iD)

Federal Research Centre "Computer Science and Control" of the Russian Academy of Sciences, Vavilov Str. 44-2, 119333 Moscow, Russia

Abstract. The article discusses the necessity and possibility of how to use virtual digital environments while solving unconventional mathematical problems. It also compares a few ways of solution to the Bertrand paradox problem with traditional visual methods and the MathKit virtual environment. The support of interactive modelling platforms allows students to form holistic and integrated knowledge on the subject.

Keywords: Unconventional problem · Visualization · Virtual environment · MathKit · The Bertrand paradox · Probability theory

1 Introduction

The federal document named "The Conception of the development of mathematical education in the Russian Federation" (hereinafter referred to as the Conception) was approved by the decree No. 2506-r of the Government of the Russian Federation on December 24, 2013 [2]. It claimed the priority goals of general mathematical education in transition to convergent technologies and enhancement of the prestige of engineering and technical specialties. They include formation and further development of secondary school students' abilities:

- to logical thinking, designing, communication and interaction based on broad mathematical material (from geometry to programming);
- to searching for solutions to fundamentally new mathematical problems, experiments and observations, to formation of internal (mental) representations and models for mathematical objects, to formulation and testing of hypotheses, and to overcoming intellectual obstacles;
- to real mathematics: mathematical modelling (how to build a model of the reality and interpret its results) and applying mathematics, including the use of information technologies.

At the current stage of development of the national general secondary and higher professional education, there appeared a change in the current methodological approach.

V. Sukhomlin and E. Zubareva (Eds.): SITITO 2017, CCIS 1204, pp. 95–107, 2021.
https://doi.org/10.1007/978-3-030-78273-3_10

Not only does it include purely technical means of education (*technology in education*) that is accompanied by the idea of complete management of the process of education (*technology of education*). Moreover, the modern methodological approach called *technology for education* should be provided with a full set of methods and training practices which are necessary for the development of students' thinking abilities. The approach under consideration is based on the principles of a systematic view on the conditions under which the school students' intellect is being developed. Plus, it is grounded on the formation of the qualities of mathematical thinking they need for future full-fledged professional activities and life in the information society.

One of the distinctive features marking the Russian national mathematical school is a high priority on developing skills that allows students to be independent while solving mathematical problems as creative, unconventional and non-trivial tasks. The trait mentioned above is the result of the school reform laid down by an academician A.N. Kolmogorov back in the 1960s, and that is still declared in the Conception to be one of the defining principles of the modern approach to the way mathematical education in modern Russia is organized.

To select unconventional tasks the teacher considers the requirements of the curriculum, the students' level of subject knowledge and other learning conditions. The most relevant tasks are chosen not just due to their increased complexity, but because they require students to use the research approach. Among the latter, a special role is played by problems with an ambiguous solution along with so-called mathematical paradoxes. The most famous one might, for example, be an aporia of a Greek philosopher Zeno of Elea (c. 490–430 BC) about Achilles and the tortoise.

Mathematical paradoxes have some distinctive features. On the one hand, they are quite logically derived from well-known axioms and/or theorems. Whereas, their results obviously contradict ordinary consciousness or intuitive knowledge so much that it can cast doubt on the whole range of mathematical tools used to solve them. The way out may be conducting either an experiment or a search for conceptual contradictions in the task itself or in its solution, or, sometimes, in both.

The article is to consider one of unconventional mathematical problems which originally has three logically justified but contradictory solutions – the Bertrand paradox. The solutions to the paradox problem will be analyzed from three challenging points: pedagogical technologies (methods of problem solving), information technologies (decision tools) and management technologies (high school students' cognitive learning activities at the lesson).

2 Setting Up the Task

Traditionally, the Bertrand paradox is regarded as a classical probabilistic problem which can have a single-valued solution only in case when you determine a mechanism or a method of how to select the initial random variable. The author of the problem is a French mathematician Joseph Bertrand (1822–1900), who described this probabilistic paradox in his book Calcul des probabilités ("Calculus of Probabilities") published in Paris in 1888 (according to other sources – in 1889). He presented the problem as an example of the fact that the probability when some event occurs cannot be clearly defined without choosing the initial assumptions, which give the starting point of thinking [3, pp. 130–133]. In the article, it will be shown how to organize high school students' cognitive learning activities to resolve the Bertrand paradox when the result is determined by the mechanism or method of random constructions.

The problem of such kind traditionally belongs to the field of probability theory, which, in Russia, is included in the secondary school programme on mathematics but, unfortunately, in a very limited proportion [7, p. 207]. Nevertheless, the Bertrand paradox is quite possible to be resolved by high school students with different levels of mathematical training. This forms students' mathematical culture and, in addition, meets the goals of developing their thinking abilities and achieving meta-disciplinary learning results.

Primarily, these tasks must involve students' spatial imagination. So, the use of educational creative environments and virtual laboratories, such as an electronic MathKit, provides students with an additional visual support. It facilitates the search for a solution to the problem by visualizing developing processes and moving objects. Such technological tools help to carry out intellectual processing of information, to structure and present it in the form of various interactive models. Not only does it save students' time, awaken their interest in the subject or motivate them to perform cognitive learning activities. But it also allows to emphasize significant issues while formulating and solving problems of different levels of complexity in the most rational way. It especially refers to those tasks that do not simply apply certain algorithms but require students to conduct thoughtful analysis and make reasonable decisions.

3 Comparing Traditional and Electronic Visual Methods of Solving the Bertrand Paradox

The Bertrand paradox goes as follows. Draw a unit circle of radius $r = 1$. Consider an equilateral triangle with the side l inscribed in the unit circle (Fig. 1). Suppose a chord d of the circle is chosen at random and mark its length as m. The task is to find the probability $P_{m>l}$ that a random chord is longer than the side of the triangle, that is $m > l$. The probability $P_{m>l}$ indicates how often the event $m > l$ occurs in the general chain of events of all possible m tending to infinity when the event l is fixed.

To discuss several arguments of the Bertrand paradox, it is necessary to bear in mind that the result depends on the method of constructing the set of chords. This leads to operating with either a concept of the "area", or a concept of the "linear size", or a concept of the "angular size". What the paradox emphasizes is that each argument obtained is true under particular initial assumptions. This learning situation includes the ways of how to construct a set of chords. At the same time, the most important moment in the arguments of the Bertrand paradox is a concept of the "geometric locus of mid-chords", which in all the solutions considered will differ from each other, and, obviously, cause different results.

3.1 The First Argument: The "Random Midpoint" Method

The initial assumption: construct random chords and determine the probability $P_{m>l}$ through the area ratio.

Inscribe one more circle in the equilateral triangle and call it "the inscribed circle" (in Fig. 2 it is indicated by a dashed line, and the area within it is shaded in grey). Its OR radius is obviously 1/2 (Fig. 3). Inside the unit circle, draw randomly (without any rules or bindings to certain coordinates) a few chords – d_1, d_2, d_3, d_4 and d_5, then denote their midpoints with "crosses" (Fig. 2). As you can see, chords d_1 and d_5 do not intersect the inscribed circle, while chords d_2 and d_3 do. It means that the midpoints of chords d_2 and d_3 are located inside the inscribed circle, while the midpoints of chords d_1 and d_5 – out of it. Chord d_4 is tangent to the inscribed circle: the point of tangency coincides with the chord midpoint. It is clear that the midpoint locus of all possible randomly drawn chords is the unit circle with its area $S_1 = \pi$. Whereas the inscribed circle of radius $r = 1/2$ is the locus of those chord midpoints whose chords have a length more than the side of the equilateral triangle: $m > l$. The area of the inscribed circle $S_2 = \pi/4$. So, the probability $P_{m>l}$ is determined by the ratio of the areas of the inscribed and the unit circles: $P_{m>l} = S_2/S_1 = 1/4$. It should be noted again that this is the required probability $P_{m>l}$ for randomly constructed chords that are longer than a side of the inscribed triangle. The midpoints of these chords fall within the entire (grey) area of the inscribed circle.

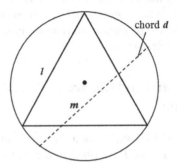

Fig. 1. The Bertrand paradox.

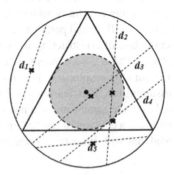

Fig. 2. The first argument of the Bertrand paradox: the "random midpoint" method ($P_{m>l} = 1/4$).

3.2   The Second Argument: The "Random Radius" Method

The initial assumption: construct random parallel chords and determine the probability $P_{m>l}$ through the linear size ratio.

Drop a perpendicular OR from the center O of the unit circle to one of the sides of the triangle and extend it to the intersection with the unit circle in point Q(Fig. 4). The length of the segment OR, as it was found out in the first argument of the Bertrand paradox is equal to half the radius of the unit circle: $OR = 1/2$. Choose a few points on the radius and construct the chords that go through these points perpendicularly to the radius. Then segment $RQ = 1 - OR = 1/2$. Segment OQ is the midpoint locus of the parallel chords which were constructed. Moreover, only those chords satisfy the condition $m > l$ whose midpoints lie on segment OR, which is half the length of segment OQ. Therefore, the probability $P_{m>l} = OR/OQ = 1/2$.

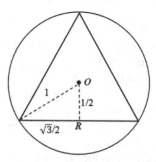

Fig. 3. The first argument of the Bertrand paradox: the "random midpoint" method – 2 ($P_{m>l} = 1/4$).

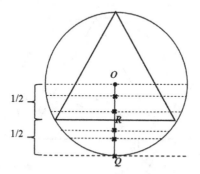

Fig. 4. The second argument of the Bertrand paradox: the "random radius" method ($P_{m>l} = 1/2$)

3.3   The Third Argument: The "Random Endpoints" Method

The initial assumption: construct random chords originating from a common point on the circumference of the unit circle and determine the probability $P_{m>l}$ through the angular size ratio.

Stiven Krants [3, p. 132] gives the third argument of the Bertrand paradox as follows. (Fig. 5). Draw the chord from vertex C of the triangle at an arbitrary angle θ to the tangent of the unit circle in the same point C. If $0° \leq \theta \leq 60°$ or $120° \leq \theta \leq 180°$, then $m \leq l$. If $60° < \theta < 120°$, then $m > l$. Therefore, the region in which the chords of length $m > l$ are enclosed is the inner angle $60°$ of an equilateral triangle. Two angles – both of $60°$ – external to the inner angle of the equilateral triangle form the region through which chords constructed from the vertex C have the length $m < l$. So, in this case the probability that a random chord is longer than a side of the inscribed triangle is: $P_{m>l} = 60°/180° = 1/3$.

The third argument can be modified into **the fourth one** and offered to students as a combination of the "random endpoints" method and the "random midpoint" method. The initial assumption: construct some chords from a common point on the circumference of the unit circle. The probability $P_{m>l}$ can be determined through the ratio of the lengths of the circular arcs that are the midpoint locus of the chords constructed.

Construct a set of chords from the vertex C of the equilateral triangle and denote each midpoint with a "cross" (Fig. 6). The midpoint locus of the chords forms one more circle (call it "the locus circle") that has the center O of the unit circle and the vertex C of the triangle on its circumference. By the way, the segment OC is the bisector of the angle C. The arc AB is enclosed inside the triangle and the inscribed circle. Those chords whose midpoints belong to the arc AB satisfy the expression $m > l$ (in Fig. 6 these are chords d_3, d_4 and d_5). So, the probability $P_{m>l}$ is determined by the ratio of the length of the arc AB to the circumference of the locus circle. Obviously, the circumference of the locus circle is equal to the circumference of the inscribed circle because they both have the radius $r = 1/2$. The length of the arc AB is $1/3$ of the circumference of the locus circle because the triangle ABC is similar to the triangle inscribed in the unit circle and is also equilateral. Therefore, $P_{m>l} = 1/3$.

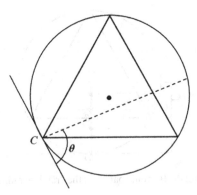

Fig. 5. The third argument of the Bertrand paradox: the "random endpoints" method ($P_{m>l} = 1/3$).

As it is clearly seen, the Bertrand paradox is a non-trivial problem in the field of probability theory and mathematical statistics. Even though the "manual" ways of solving the paradox are not very convincing, careful geometric constructions allow students to

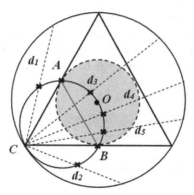

Fig. 6. The fourth argument of the Bertrand paradox: the "random endpoints" + "random midpoint" combined method ($P_{m>l} = 1/3$).

conclude that its result is significantly influenced by the methods of operating with the original probabilistic values. They can understand that the solution depends on the rules of how to construct random chords. It means that the distribution of the probability density of the original events influence the probable outcome. Nevertheless, secondary school students, who have very little experience in operating both with interdependent random events and with random variables, may take this evidence for insufficiently obvious, and the results – for paradoxical.

The way out can be found through fundamentally different methods of geometric constructions – by using electronic mathematical environments (for example, "1C Math-Kit 6.0" [4]). It gives the possibility to conduct virtual experiments by modeling and visualizing learning concepts while solving creative unconventional mathematical problems. The MathKit is that very digital tool which can be successfully used to verify the above mentioned theoretical arguments of the Bertrand paradox.

Visualization as it is, especially animated visualization, plays a key role in solving non-trivial mathematical problems. According to the information retrieval conception invented by an American psycho-cognitivist James Gibson, the perception and processing of information is an active and continuous process that is very close to how consciousness flows [1, p. 339]. Therefore, everything that the human brain perceives is not just a discrete series – a series of objects placed in Time and Space, but a continuous event that a person perceives with his/her "perceiving system": "The system is able to navigate, explore, survey, adapt, optimize, to get out of equilibrium and then come into it, whereas feelings are not able to do it "[1, p. 346]. That is, a person's perceiving system can act actively.

External objects, fallen in the external environment and perceived as an event in general, should allow the cognizant subject to be not just a contemplator, but an active researcher acting in accordance with his/her "perceiving system". Thus, the visualization of the events under investigation should stimulate students' "research behavior", which is performed through their interaction with the virtual environment.

Three screenshots of the virtual statistical laboratory interfaces working on the Bertrand paradox and the results of drawing the probability curves $P_{m>l}$ for various initial assumptions are presented in Figs. 7, 8 and 9. They depend on the way of how chords inside the unit circle can be constructed. The probability $P_{m>l}$ is counted and displayed in the pink rectangle on the right. The value $P_{m>l}$, depending on the number of trials (the number of random chords), can be seen on the graph at the bottom of the window.

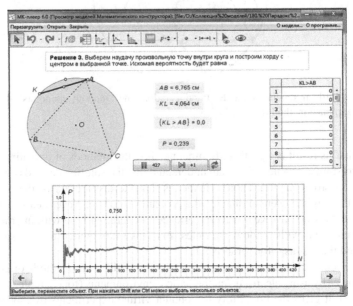

Fig. 7. Statistical confirmation of the first argument of the Bertrand paradox with the "random midpoint" method in the "1C MathKit 6.0" environment ($P_{m>l} = 1/4$).

The fourth argument of the Bertrand paradox, shown in Fig. 6, was suggested by one of the 11th-grade students while training the course on the Bertrand paradox, and has not been covered in special literature yet. That is why it cannot be found in the database of the "1C MathKit 6.0" [4], either. However, the interactive environment of the MathKit made it possible to construct the midpoint locus of the random chords and thereby prove that it really is a part of the locus circle of a unit diameter $(r = 1/2)$. It appeared to be an arc AB enclosed within an equilateral triangle and the inscribed circle. In addition, with the help of the MathKit the lengths of the arcs AB, AC and BC(Fig. 10) were calculated, which turned out to be equal to each other, and, therefore, $P_{m>l} = 1/3$. This became an experimental confirmation of the hypothesis that regardless of what method of calculating the probability $P_{m>l}$ is chosen, the result of solving the Bertrand paradox problem is influenced by the way of specifying the initial probabilistic quantities.

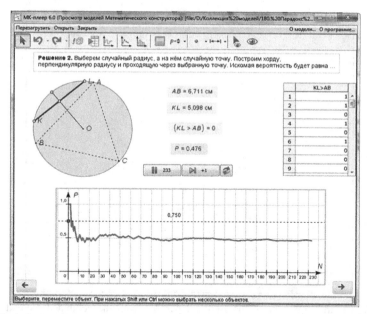

Fig. 8. Statistical confirmation of the second argument of the Bertrand paradox with the "random radius" method in the "1C MathKit 6.0" environment $(P_{m>l} = 1/2)$.

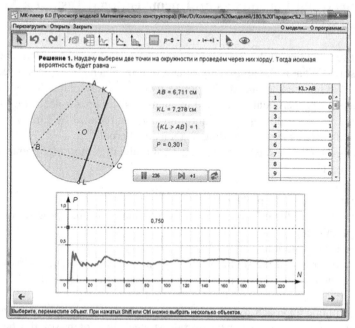

Fig. 9. Statistical confirmation of the third argument of the Bertrand paradox with the "random endpoints" method in the "1C MathKit 6.0" environment $(P_{m>l} = 1/3)$.

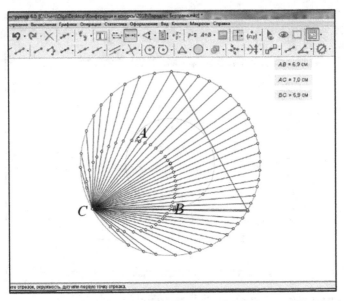

Fig. 10. The fourth argument of the Bertrand paradox with the combined method through geometrical constructions in the "1C MathKit 6.0" environment ($P_{m>l} = 1/3$).

4   The Bertrand Paradox as an Unconventional Task at a Math Lesson

All the above solutions to the Bertrand paradox problem have shown that the answer to the question "What is the probability of an event in which $m > l$, if an event m has taken place?" is not predetermined. The polysemy of the results of the Bertrand paradox demonstrates the "experimental nature of mathematics" [3, pp. 43–45], which does not yield to the traditional principle of algorithmization introduced by Euclid – that is a strictly formalized manner of recording mathematical proof.

Formally, the plan of solving a mathematical problem is most often represented as follows [8, p. 91]:

1. a clear statement of the problem;
2. a clear analysis of the initial data: what axioms and/or theorems can we use?
3. thorough thinking;
4. searching for a solution;
5. accurate recording of the solution found: its presentation with the help of conventional mathematical symbols in the form of a clear logical algorithm.

An algorithmic approach to the solution to the Bertrand paradox problem can be applied only at certain stages, when the overall "strategic line" of the solution has already been determined. But it cannot be obtained without a clear idea of what happens with multiple constructions done in various ways.

Probability theory and, in particular, measure theory, admits a variety of understanding what a random event on which another random event depends is: "the probability of an event is determined by the assumption that certain predetermined conditions are satisfied" [9, p. 185]. It means that different distributions of the probability density of the fact that the initial event takes place lead to different probability distributions of the occurrence of the resulting event.

In addition, the Bertrand paradox is a classic example of a *modified task* that involves variable approaches to the solution when students try to solve the problem in different ways, to consider it from different sides, using various aspects in the initial problem. This approach allows one to trigger associative links that have a straight or even a remote relationship to the original task. In all cases it still contributes towards calling to memory either similar tasks, or similar methods of performing activities. These activities tend to keep students' interest in the problem, remove their fatigue of prolonged looking for solutions, help them to concentrate on essential details of the task.

George Pólya, an American mathematician, originally Hungarian, who dedicated his research to the processes of solving mathematical problems, pointed out that in order to preserve the students' motivation "we must put a new question related to the problem. This new view reveals untested possibilities of creating links with the previously acquired knowledge and gives hope for establishing new useful links. The new question holds our interest because it alters the problem revealing its new sides" [6, pp. 55–56]. Those conceptual questions can be as follows:

– What will happen if we reformulate the problem this or that way?
– What will happen if we need to find another value?
– How will the way of our thinking and actions change if we exclude some points of the problem or add some new data?

Such options of variation suggested by George Pólya include decomposition and compilation of new combinations, introduction of auxiliary elements, generalization, specialization and using analogy.

Searching for the solution to the Bertrand paradox problem with the use of visual models can be carried out at least within three lesson models, which depend on the level of students' mathematical knowledge and training.

Lesson model one (for students with a high level of mathematical training). *The goal of students' cognitive learning activity is to master how to solve probabilistic problems independently.* Figure 1 sets the problem. By brainstorming the students suggest a variety of options what value the probability $P_{m>l}$ can have. These versions are actually hypotheses. The teacher selects some of the most plausible hypotheses and invites students to justify each of them. To do this the students are divided into groups and choose their own solutions to confirm or disprove their hypothesis, using algorithmic methods for solving geometric problems (Figs. 2, 3, 4 and 5). Then the results are being discussed and compared. At the final stage of the lesson, statistical experiments from the "1C MathKit 6.0" database are demonstrated (Figs. 7, 8 and 9). Watching them the students can compare their own outcomes with the results of each virtual experiment.

Lesson model two (for students with an average level of mathematical training). *The goal of students' cognitive learning activity is to justify the influence of initial* *assumptions on the results of solving probabilistic problems.* Figure 1 sets the problem. The teacher and the students discuss possible ways of constructing a set of chords. The students are divided into groups, choose one of the methods of the initial assumptions (how to construct the chords) and try to find a solution to the problem (Figs. 2, 3, 4 and 5). In the end, all solutions are being discussed, and as a check, the teacher demonstrates virtual experiments from the "1C MathKit 6.0" database (Figs. 7, 8 and 9).

Lesson model three (for poorly motivated students or for students with a low level of mathematical training). *The goal of students' cognitive learning activity is to justify the ambiguity that the solution to probabilistic problems can have.* Figure 1 sets the problem. The teacher demonstrates how to construct a set of chords and possible solutions (Figs. 2, 3, 4 and 5). The students discuss the solutions performing frontal or group work and choose "the most believable" ones from their point of view. Then the teacher demonstrates virtual experiments from the "1C MathKit 6.0" database (Figs. 7, 8 and 9), thereby showing that solutions to probabilistic problems can lead to ambiguous results depended on the initial assumptions.

5   Conclusion

The experience in solving the Bertrand paradox demonstrates its great possibility for high school students to develop their mental abilities, regardless of their subject knowledge or corresponding goals of cognitive learning activities. Firstly, students comprehend the importance of hypotheses while solving creative and non-trivial tasks. Secondly, they realize how important the initial assumptions in probabilistic problems, which determine not only the choice of the method, but also the result of the solution, are. And finally, students learn to find and resolve contradictions arising during their cognitive learning activities. One more point deals with the tools of electronic visualization in solving probabilistic problems. Some functions of the tools represent a field where virtual statistical experiments can be carried out. Because of that, an integrated picture of the matter can be created in the students' minds. The fact really allows to confirm or challenge the hypothesis and theoretical thinking got with traditional methods and due to this, to become an additional effective source of holistic knowledge.

References

1. Gibson, J.J.: The Ecological Approach to Visual Perception. Psychology Press, Hove (1986)
2. The Concept of Development of Mathematical Education in the Russian Federation. http://bda-expert.ru/doc/2013-12-24-koncepciya-math-obrazovanie-rf.zip. (in Russian)
3. Krantz, S.G.: The Proof is in the Pudding: The Changing Nature of Mathematical Proof. Springer, New York (2011). https://doi.org/10.1007/978-0-387-48744-1
4. Mathematical Designer. E-Version 6.0. 1S, Moscow (2017). http://obr.1c.ru/educational. (in Russian)
5. Penrouz, R., Gardner, M.: The Emperor's New Mind: Concerning Computers, Minds and the Laws of Physics, 1 edn. Oxford University Press, Oxford (2002)
6. Polya, G.: How to Solve It: A New Aspect of Mathematical Method. Princeton University Press, Princeton (1945)

7. Savinov, E.S.: Approximate Main Educational Program of Educational Institution. Basic school, Prosveshcheniye Publ. , Moscow (2011). (in Russian)
8. Sverdlik, A.G.: How emotions affect abstract thinking and why mathematics is incredibly accurate: how the cerebral cortex works, why its possibilities are limited and how emotions, complementing the work of the cortex, allow a person to make scientific discoveries. In: Abramovich, F., Schrader, S. (eds.) Scientific. LENAND Publ., Moscow (2016). (in Russian)
9. Halmos, P.R.: Measure Theory. Springer, New York (1950). https://doi.org/10.1007/978-1-4684-9440-2

Development of the Creativity of Students at the Study of Filled Sets of Julia with Mathematical Methods and Information Technologies

Valeriy Sekovanov$^{(\boxtimes)}$ ⓘ, Vladimir Ivkov ⓘ, and Alexey Piguzov ⓘ

Kostroma State University, Dzerzhinskij Street 17, 156005 Kostroma, Russia
piguzov@ksu.edu.ru

Abstract. In the article, the formation of the creative qualities of students is analyzed using the example of the Mandelbrot set and the Julia sets. The connection between the points of the Mandelbrot set and the Julia sets for the degree of complex argument 2 is considered. A program that demonstrates this link is developed. An algorithm for constructing the Mandelbrot set of an arbitrary natural degree is given.

Keywords: Creativity · Flexibility of thinking · The Julia set, the Mandelbrot set · Information technology · Fractal · Iteration · Algorithms for constructing Julia sets · Creative quality

1 Introduction

In this article, we focus our attention on the most important creative qualities of students – the flexibility of thinking and the ability to establish unexpected relationships between objects and phenomena on the example of studying the filled sets of Julia.

Questions related to the creativity, fractals and sets of Julia were studied in monographs, scientific papers and teaching aids [see 1–14].

In domestic psychology the term "flexibility of thinking" was introduced into practice by Menchinskaya N.A. [1]. She described several cases of inhibition of the process of actualization of solution methods which are very familiar to the subject "under the pressure of stronger and more obsessive tendencies... coming from the side of the latter in time experience." Bogoyavlensky D.N. and Menchinskaya N.A. identified three main indicators of flexibility of thinking:

1. the reasonable variation of modes of action;
2. the ease of restructuring of knowledge and skills and their systems in accordance with changed conditions and
3. easy switching from one mode of action to another.

V. Sukhomlin and E. Zubareva (Eds.): SITITO 2017, CCIS 1204, pp. 108–116, 2021.
https://doi.org/10.1007/978-3-030-78273-3_11

As it is noted in the psychological and pedagogical literature, the flexibility (mobility) of cognitive processes is related to the changing aspects of the examination of objects, phenomena, their properties and relationships, the ability to change the intended way of solving the problem if it does not satisfy those conditions that are identified in the process of solving and can not be taken into account from the very beginning. This flexibility is evident in the active reconstruction of the initial data, understanding and use of their relativity. In this paper this situation is illustrated by the use of various algorithms for constructing the filled sets of Julia and the analysis of the connection of the Julia sets with the Mandelbrot set.

2 Problem Statement

Let's consider the Julia sets and the sets for polynomials $f(z) = z^p + c, p \geq 2$ which definitions are analogous to the definitions of sets for quadratic functions. The Julia set for the polynomial of the complex variable $f(z) = z^p + c, p \geq 2$, denoted by $J(f_c)$, is defined as $J(f_c) = \partial\{z : f^{(n)}(z) \to \infty, \ n \to \infty\}$, where ∂ is the boundary of the region of attraction of infinity, and $f^{(n)}(z) = f\left(f^{(n-1)}(z)\right), n = 2, 3, \ldots$.

As in [2] we mean the set of points z of the complex plane whose orbits are caught by the filled sets of Julia for the polynomial of the complex variable $f(z) = zp + c$, $p \geq 2$ (and denoted by $\overline{J(f_c)}$). Note that the real Julia set is the boundary of the filled set of Julia. The orbit of every point of the Julia set is quite complicated even for the case $p = 2$ see [2]. In a simplified version we will understand the fact that the orbit is caught, as its attraction by some cycle, which includes periodic points of the function $f(z) = z^p + c$.

For $c = 0$, the filled set of Julia is the circle of unit radius with center at the origin, and the Julia set is the circumference, the boundary of this circle. Let's justify this statement. Let $f_0(z) = z^p, p \geq 2$. Then $z_n = f_0^{(n)}(z) = z^{p^n}, \ n = 1, 2, \ldots$. If $|z| < 1$, then $\lim_{n \to \infty} z_n = 0$, and for $|z| > 1 \ \lim_{n \to \infty} z_n = \infty$. If $\lim_{n \to \infty} z_n = \infty, |z| = 1$, then $|z_n| = 1$.

Thus, a circle of unit radius with center at the origin is the filled set of Julia. Note that for $c \neq 0$ the Julia set will have a fractal structure.

The following Theorem 1 which generalizes the following theorem 8.1.1, proved in [2] for quadratic polynomials of a complex variable, is true.

Theorem 1. Suppose that $f(z) = z^p + c$, where $|c| < 2$, and $p \geq 2, p \in ¥$. Let $z \in £$ and $z_n = f_c^{(n)}(z)$ for $n = 1, 2, 3, \ldots$. If there is an n_0 such that $\left|z_{n_0}\right| \geq 2$, then $\lim_{n \to \infty} z_n = \infty$.

That is, the orbit $z_n = \left\{f_c^{(n)}(z)\right\}_{n=1}^{\infty}$ tends to infinity and z z does not belong to the Julia set $\overline{J(f_c)}$. (For a proof, see [10]).

Theorem 1 gives the basis for constructing the filled set of Julia.

Figure 1a and Fig. 1b shows the algorithm for initializing and selecting the image scale. With this part of the program, a step for analyzing the points of the complex plane simulated by the computer monitor is selected.

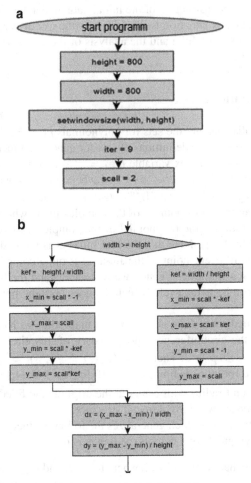

Fig. 1. a. Initializing process and choosing a scale. b. Initializing process and choosing a scale.

Figure 2 shows the algorithm for constructing the filled set of Julia.

Let's give examples of constructing the Julia sets for second, third, fourth, tenth, fifteenth and thirtieth polynomials for $c = 0.25$ (Fig. 3).

Using the algorithm shown in Fig. 2, the orbit of the point is calculated, analyzed, and the starting point is displayed depending on the value of the module of the corresponding iteration of the function.

Let's show, with the help of Theorem 1, that with increasing n, the filled set of Julia tends to a circle of radius 1 with center at the origin. Indeed, in this case $c = 0.25 < 2$.

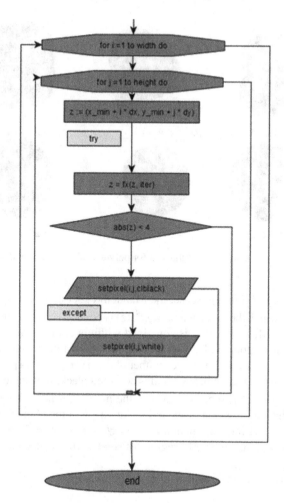

Fig. 2. Construction of the filled set of Julia for a polynomial of the complex plane.

Let $z \in \pounds$ and $|z| < 1$. There exist $p \in ¥$ and $n_0 \in ¥$ such that $z_n = f_c^{(n)}(z)$ of the function $f(z) = z^p + 0.25$ is greater than 2 modulo.

According to Theorem 1 $z_n = f_c^{(n)}(z) \to \infty$, then point $z \in \pounds$ does not belong to the filled set of Julia. The Julia sets in Fig. 3, obtained with the help of computer experiments, confirm our conclusion.

The Mandelbrot set allows to determine the form of the Julia set. This unexpected connection is not obvious and requires confirmation with the help of mathematical methods and illustrations with the help of computer experiments.

By the Mandelbrot set of the function $f_c(z) = z^p + c$ we mean the set of points from the complex plane for which the orbit of zero is bounded.

To carry out the computer experiment of constructing Julia sets and to analyze the connection of Julia sets with the Mandelbrot set, we will proceed from the following

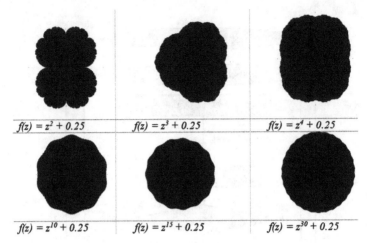

Fig. 3. Construction of the Julia sets for polynomials of different degrees.

considerations. In the geometric sense, the Mandelbrot set is the set of points c in the complex plane for which the sequence $z_n = f_c^{(n)}(z)$ is bounded and does not go to infinity.

Besides, all the Mandelbrot set is contained within a circle of radius 2. Therefore, we assume that if for a point with a sequence of iterations of the function $f(z) = z^2 + c$ with initial value $z = 0$ after some large number of them ($M \geq 100$ [4]) $|f_c(z)| < 2$, then the point belongs to the Mandelbrot set and is coloured black. If at some stage the value of sequence $z_n = f_c^{(n)}(z)$ is greater than two, the point does not belong to the set and remains white. Thus, we obtain a black and white image of the Mandelbrot set (Fig. 4).

The Mandelbrot set for the function $f_c(z) = z^p + c$ for $p = 2$ consists of a large (main part) and an infinite number of regions of smaller size, called buds (Fig. 4 on the left).

Let's note the most important properties of the Mandelbrot set at $p = 2$:

1. the Mandelbrot set serves as an indicator for the filled sets of Julia when the function $f_c(z) = z^p + c$ is iterated;
2. the Mandelbrot set is connected;
3. the Mandelbrot set is symmetric with respect to the real axis;
4. the Mandelbrot set is not symmetric with respect to the imaginary axis.

An algorithm that establishes a connection between the Mandelbrot set and the filled sets of Julia of the function $f_c(z) = z^p + c$ is given in [10].

In our program, we can construct the Julia set for point c by selecting this point in the plane of the Mandelbrot set (by clicking the left mouse button). To construct the Julia set, we use the algorithm from [4, p. 171]. For a chosen point c, we iterate the function $f_c(z) = z^2 + c$ for each point of the square $[-2; 2] \times [-2; 2]$.

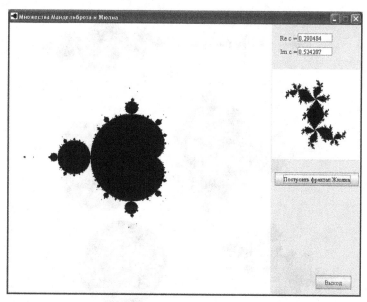

Fig. 4. Construction of the Mandelbrot set and the Julia set with the help of the author's program.

1. Select the size of the output area on the screen $a \times b$ (in pixels) and the coordinates of the area shift. In our case, $a = b = 200$, $a_0 = 600$, $b_0 = 300$. The minimum and maximum values of the real and imaginary parts of the complex argument $a \times b$ xmin = ymin = -2, xmax = ymax = 2.
   Then the calculated shift steps of the argument values are:
   $dx = (xmax - xmin)/(a - 1)$
   $dy = (ymax - ymin)/(b - 1)$.
2. For all points of the output area nx and ny, we calculate the values of the argument (within the cycle from 0 to 200):
   $x = xmin + nx * dx$
   $y = ymin + ny * dy$.
   We perform the iterative calculation process $f_c(z) = z^2 + c$;
   $xk = x * x - y * y + Re\_c$
   $yk = 2 * x * y + Im\_c$
   $k ++$.
3. Calculate the radius of the orbit of the current point r = xk * xk + yk * yk and if it is less than some value (100, according to [4]) or the number of iterations exceeds 200, we finish the iterative process.
4. If at the end of the process $r < 100$, output the black point and go to the next point.

Performing an analysis of the connection between the Mandelbrot set and the filled set of Julia, we come the following conclusion. When moving over the black body of the Mandelbrot set, the Julia set will deform (Fig. 5). When a point leaves the Mandelbrot set, the corresponding Julia set "explodes", turning into "dust" (Fig. 6).

To consolidate the training material on the sets of Julia and Mandelbrot, we offer the following tasks:

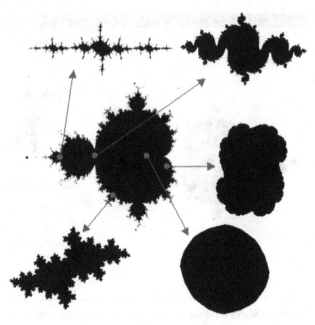

Fig. 5. The correspondence of the interior points of the Mandelbrot set to the Julia set.

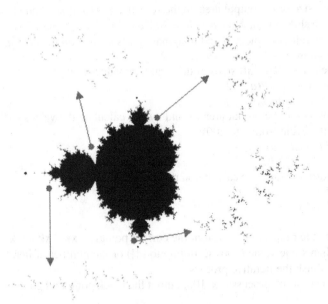

Fig. 6. The correspondence of exterior points of the Mandelbrot set to the Julia set.

1. Show that the Mandelbrot set for the function $f_c(z) = z^2 + c$ is symmetric with respect to the real axis and is asymmetric with respect to the imaginary axis.

2. Show that the Mandelbrot set for the function $f_c(z) = z^3 + c$ is symmetric with respect to the real and imaginary axes.
3. Show that the Mandelbrot set for the function $f_c(z) = z^4 + c$ is symmetric with respect to the real axis and is asymmetric with respect to the imaginary axis.
4. Show that the Mandelbrot set for the function $f_c(z) = z^5 + c$ is symmetric with respect to the real and imaginary axes.
5. On the basis of items 1 to 4, it is proposed to give a hypothesis about the symmetry properties of the Mandelbrot set and to justify it.

In addition, as self-learning tasks, it is proposed to carry out the proposed algorithm for constructing Julia sets in various development environments or even using mathematical packages.

3 Conclusion

In conclusion, we note that the developed method of studying the filled sets of Julia of complex polynomials enables students to learn the integration of mathematical methods with information technologies, which positively affects their motivation for studying mathematics and computer science, develops creativity and research competences.

Acknowledgements. The study was carried out at the expense of a grant from the Russian Science Foundation (project No. 16-18-10304).

References

1. Bogoyavlensky, D.N, Menchinskaya, N.A.: Psychology of Knowledge Digestion at School. APS RSFSR Publ. (1959). (in Russian)
2. Crownover, R.M.: Introduction to Fractals and Chaos, 1st edn. Jones & Bartlett Publishers Inc., London (1995)
3. Sekovanov, V.S.: The contribution of academician A. N. Kolmogorov in the formation of fractal geometry and dynamical systems theory. In: Proceedings of the Teaching Fractal Geometry and Computer Science in High School and School in the Light of the Ideas of Academician A.N. Kolmogorov. KGU, Kostroma, pp. 146–150 (2016). https://elibrary.ru/item.asp?id=28817645. (in Russian)
4. Peitgen, H.-O., Richter, P.H.: The Beauty of Fractals: Images of Complex Dynamical Systems. Springer, Heidelberg (1986). https://doi.org/10.1007/978-3-642-61717-1
5. Sekovanov, V.S.: How to teach fractal geometry at Nekrasov Kostroma State University. Vestn. Kostroma State Univ. **19**(5), 153–154 (2013). https://elibrary.ru/item.asp?id=20935968. (in Russian)
6. Sekovanov, V.S.: On Julia Seto of some rational functions. Vestn. Kostroma State Univ. **18**(2), 23–28 (2012). https://elibrary.ru/item.asp?id=18942762. (in Russian)
7. Sekovanov, V.S.: Training Fractal Geometry as a Means of Forming the Creativity of Students of Physical and Mathematical Specialties of Universities: dis. ... Dr. Sci. (Pedagogy), Moscow (2007). (in Russian)
8. Sekovanov, V.S.: What Is Fractal Geometry? Synergetics: From the Past to the Future, Ser. 75, No. 114, LENAND, Moscow (2016). (in Russian)

9. Sekovanov, V.S.: Elements of the Theory of Discrete Dynamical Systems. Lan', St. Petersburg (2017). (in Russian)
10. Sekovanov, V.S.: Elements of the Theory of Fractal Sets. LIBROKOM, Moscow (2013). (in Russian)
11. Sekovanov, V.S., Ivkov, V.A.: Multistage mathematics and information task "strange attractors". Vestn. Kostroma State Univ. **19**(5), 155–157 (2013). https://elibrary.ru/item.asp?id=20935969. (in Russian)
12. Sekovanov, V.S., Ivkov, V.A.: Development of the special course "The Julia Set and Mandelbrot Sets". Mod. Inf. Technol. IT-Educ. (7), 587–592 (2011). https://elibrary.ru/item.asp?id=23020796. (in Russian)
13. Sekovanov, V.S., Ivkov, V.A., Piguzov, A.A., Fateev, A.S.: Execution of mathematics and information multistep task "building a fractal set with L-systems and information technologies" as a means of creativity of students. Mod. Inf. Technol. IT-Educ. **12**(3–1), 118-125 (2016). https://elibrary.ru/item.asp?id=27411983. (in Russian)
14. Sekovanov, V.S., Mironkin, D.P.: Study of Baker's map as means of creativity formation in students and pupils with distance learning using. Vestn. Kostroma State Univ. **19**(1), 190–195 (2013). https://elibrary.ru/item.asp?id=19058410. (in Russian)

Research and Development in the Field
of New IT and Their Applications

Development of the Research Stand for Remote Interaction with Speech Database in the Cloud Storage

Irina Bazhenova[✉] [ID]

Lomonosov Moscow State University, Leninskie gory, 1, GSP-1, 119991 Moscow, Russia

Abstract. Cloud data storage provides a convenient framework for organizing remote work with speech databases. The article discusses the problem of constructing a research stand based on the use of cloud services for a obtaining of the estimation evaluation characteristics for integrated speech database.

The use of this stand will allow to determine the basic technological solutions to mechanisms for implementing remote access to the accumulated and systematized data in the speech database.

The use of cloud services as a new paradigm for the organization of infrastructure and the creation of distributed applications allow to develop a package of cloud web-services for unified multi-platform remote access to speech data-base in the cloud storage.

Keywords: Cloud computing · Cloud storage · Speech database

1 Introduction

Development and creation of a research stand for remote interaction with speech databases in the cloud infrastructure allowed to develop basic technological solutions for mechanisms for implementing remote access to accumulated data and to formulate an optimal conceptual model for annotating stored speech databases [1].

In order to develop basic technological solutions for the mechanisms for implementing remote operational access to the accumulated and systematized data in the speech databases, the criteria for selecting a cloud data warehouse with the most optimal characteristics for the allocation and use of the integrated speech database were initially formed. These criteria included:

- scalability of the database used in the cloud storage;
- ability to store large amounts of data, which characterizes speech databases, which are based on files of sounding speech;
- ease of management and processing of data in the cloud storage, the ability to use the language of work with data;
- providing security mechanisms for stored data;
- using of integrated data storage in the cloud and server storage;

© Springer Nature Switzerland AG 2021
V. Sukhomlin and E. Zubareva (Eds.): SITITO 2017, CCIS 1204, pp. 119–126, 2021.
https://doi.org/10.1007/978-3-030-78273-3_12

- the ability to connect the cloud infrastructure to a local data center;
- providing convenient programming interfaces for interacting with information from a speech database located in the cloud storage;
- the ability to unify the mechanisms of access to data located both in the cloud storage and in the traditional server database;
- availability of convenient tools for administering the cloud data warehouse.

A particularly important criterion is the ability to expand the basic tools that provide access to the cloud database and the functionality of such a database. On the other hand, the development of an integrated speech database requires the ability to connect the cloud infrastructure to a local data center.

The most advanced cloud data stores were analyzed based on these criteria. Considered such cloud-based data storage services as Amazon SimpleDB, Amazon Simple Storage, Amazon Relational Database Service, Google Cloud SQL, Oracle Database as a Service, Azure & SQLAzure.

Amazon Relational Database Service (RDS) implements service of databases which functions independently, representing the separate VPS servers optimized for work with databases. Amazon RDS supports work with several popular databases of various manufacturers, such as: MySQL community edition; Oracle Database Standard Edition One; Oracle Database Standard Edition; Oracle Database Enterprise Edition.

Amazon RDS provides very flexible means of configuring access to database servers using security groups, access control at the level of individual IP addresses and subnets.

Google App Engine (GAE) is an infrastructure that provides an API for storage services and data downloads. This API for App Engine allows you to deploy applications written in several supported programming languages, such as Python, Java, PHP. The disadvantage is that Google App Engine does not provide deploying applications on virtual machines, as in Amazon EC2.

Data can be stored in a non-relational store in Cloud Datastore, in Cloud Storage, or in Google Cloud SQL.

Google Cloud SQL is an instance of a MySQL database in the Google cloud.

This cloud database has the functionality of a regular MySQL database that has already been installed and requires no additional software installation to use it.

The Google Cloud SQL cloud is a web service that supports the creation and use of a relational database together with App Engine applications.

To interact with Google Cloud SQL, you can use the MySQL client, external applications that provide access to the database through MySQL database drivers, and App Engine applications in Java, Python, PHP. A Google Cloud SQL instance can use up to 16 GB of RAM and up to 500 GB of database space. This is the main restriction, which excludes the use of this cloud storage for large-scale speech databases. However, for small object-oriented speech databases, the 500 GB size may be sufficient.

Using Google Cloud SQL when developing a distributed integrated system has one more significant drawback for working with a cloud database. This is the lack of the ability to create custom stored functions, which are usually carried over to most of the implementation of the business logic of the project.

The Windows Azure platform offers a variety of storage services that allow you to place data in a reliable, scalable data warehouse in the cloud, and supports two types of data warehousing [1]:

- Windows Azure Storage for storing tables, large objects and queues;
- SQLAzure, which is a full-featured database.
- the use of SQL Azure as the basis for developing a speech database provides the following significant advantages [3]:
- easy installation and deployment;
- absence of expenses for maintenance of infrastructure. Instead, only operational expenses are provided for use;
- instead of a server license or processors, as for MS SQL Server, you can use more flexible payment options for actual consumption of resources;
- wide availability, both from any point of the network, and through a wide range of supported technologies;
- high resiliency provided by triple data replication
- management and recovery inside the cloud;
- flexible scalability;
- support of the relational data model
- interaction similar to MS SQL Server, using T-SQL.

One of the advantages of Azure cloud architecture for building a research stand on its base can be considered the availability of free subscription for research activities and unconditional free subscription for students.

2 Development of a Research Stand for Working with Speech Databases

The use of Windows Azure and SQL Azure was chosen based on the cloud comparison criteria defined above. This cloud storage is most convenient both from the point of view of development, and from the point of view of controllability and scaling, to create a distributed system for remote work with an integrated linguistic database. An important factor in the choice of this cloud storage was the ability to build a distributed storage system for the speech database, which provides the ability to use data stored not only in the cloud, but also in the local data center.

The scheme of the developed research stand using the cloud infrastructure of Windows Azure and SQL Azure is shown in Fig. 1.

The architecture of the developed software consists of the following components [4]:

- web sites that implement a graphical user interface for working with a speech database;
- cloud services;
- MS SQLServer database [4];
- SQL Azure databases [2], located in the cloud infrastructure in various data centers;
- the storage of BLOB objects in Windows Azure;

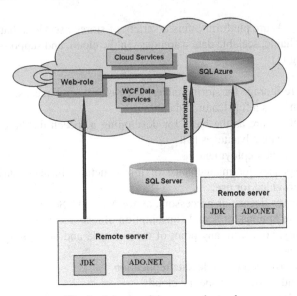

Fig. 1. Scheme of the research stand.

- extra-cloud applications for Windows Azure Storage and SQL Azure on java and c#;
- web-applications for access to SQL Azure; WCF data services;
- data access applications from SQL Azure using LINQ;
- services for working with LOB-data;
- services for creating relational data from hierarchical speech databases, where a large amount of linguistic information is traditionally accumulated;
- services for creating and managing an integrated speech database.
- the services of obtaining relational data from hierarchical speech databases allow:
- create a hierarchical data model for linguistic information from speech databases;
- add linguistic information for speech databases in the form of hierarchical structures, using both predefined structures and the ability to specify an arbitrary hierarchical structure based on the use of a subset of the xml representation standard of the document;
- convert the hierarchically organized speech databases to relational databases.

The initial task of creating a software package for working with an integrated speech database was to determine the presentation of data from an integrated speech database to build a model for the functioning and use of the cloud integrated speech database and to develop tools that solve the task of maintaining an integrated speech database in a cloud data warehouse.

To create annotated speech databases, it is necessary to supplement linguistic information in verbal-speech databases with phonograms of sounding speech with annotated data. Adding annotated speech files to the linguistic database has significantly improved the performance of performing search queries for data from cloud and remote data warehouses.

To create annotated speech databases, the tools were added to the research stand [5], allowing you to create and edit annotations for sounding speech files (see Fig. 2).

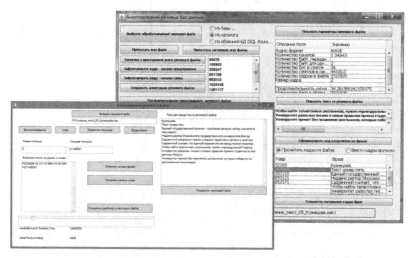

Fig. 2. Annotation program for the sounding speech file.

The developed integrable verbal-speech database contains information in the for-mat of audio files. To perform search queries for linguistic information, an annotated data describing the sound files stored in the database is included in the created verbal-speech database. The availability of annotated data makes it possible to implement effective mechanisms for searching fragments of sounding speech in verbal-speech databases.

Figure 3 shows an algorithm for processing linguistic information in an integrated speech database.

Creating an integrated speech database as a collection of cloud data storage with local and remote storage allows you to vary the completeness of data placed in the cloud storage. Database services are ranked by the completeness of the functionality and the level of availability of information from the integrated speech database. Services deployed in the cloud infrastructure are limited by the interaction with the cloud storage of the speech database. While services hosted on a remote server have full access to both the cloud data store and to the speech database hosted on the remote server. This approach allows, along with the use of cloud architecture for the formation of speech databases, to limit the spectrum of data carried to the cloud.

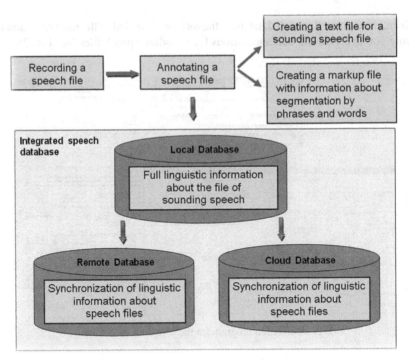

Fig.3. Algorithm for processing and managing speech files in a database.

3   Use of the Research Stand

On the basis of the developed research stand, a set of experiments on the use of cloud services was conducted to obtain temporal evaluation characteristics of work with the integrated speech database. Tests were carried out with two different cloud data stores to determine the dependence of the speed of query execution for fragments of sounding speech from the data acquisition mechanism on the generated research stand (Table 1).

Table 1. Dependence of speed of execution of requests from the mechanism of obtaining data.

The size of the speech file in bytes	Access via a SELECT query (sec)		Access with data processing in a stored procedure (sec)	
	SQL Azure in Western Europe	SQL Azure in the central part of the USA	SQL Azure in Western Europe	SQL Azure in the central part of the USA
4 291 744	1,592	5,11	7,296	3,04
9 101 546	5,031	20,839	9.128	22,24
12 370 420	8,014	31,76	18,12	24,9
16 038 822	7,62	39,87	20,15	27,92

A set of tests was performed, the result of which is shown in the graph (see Fig. 4). The purpose of these tests was to determine the dependence of the read speed of one byte of the speech file on the file size and the mutual placement of the web service and the cloud data store.

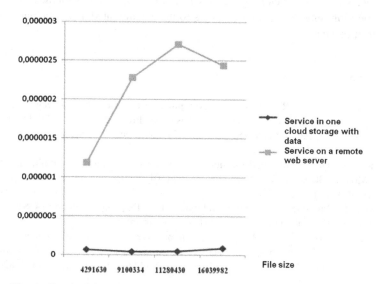

Fig. 4. Graph of the dependence of the read time of one byte on the file size.

As you can see from the graph above, for large sizes of speech files, the relative read speed of a unit of data decreases for services located on remote Web servers.

The developed software, which uses SQL Azure as the basis for storing the speech database, allows testing the following access mechanisms:

- access to SQL Azure from the code of stored procedures and functions;
- access to SQL Azure from code running on the Windows Azure infrastructure. Remote applications interact with cloud services via standard Internet protocols (HTTP/HTTPS, SOAP, REST), and cloud services provide access to SQL Azure;
- access to SQL Azure from the code located on the client side;
- access to SQL Azure from both code running on the Windows Azure infrastructure and from code running on the remote server infrastructure. The client-side code can also access SQL Azure directly or through cloud services.

4   Conclusion

Further, after the conceptual data model of the created integrated speech database is formed and a presentation sample of the test data is created, the task is to distribute the data between the cloud infrastructure and the remote server in order to vary the completeness of the available data. The developed research stand will allow testing the mechanisms of interaction between the cloud infrastructure and a local data center located in a remote infrastructure.

The software developed on the basis of the proposed research stand allows the aggregation of automatically saved statistical data. The analysis of the accumulated statistical data of which will allow developing the basic technological solutions for the mechanisms for implementing remote operational access to the accumulated and systematized data in the speech databases.

References

1. Bazhenova, I., Potapova, R., Potapov, V.: Development of the research cloud technology stand-alone system (regarding integrated speech databases). In: Proceedings of the 17th International Conference Speech and Computer (SPECOM 2015), vol. 2, pp. 1–7. University of Patras Press, Patras (2015)
2. Bazhenova, I.: The use of cloud technology in distance learning programming languages. Vestnik Moscow State Linguist. Univ. (13), 45–52 (2014). https://elibrary.ru/item.asp?id=216 81015. (in Russian)
3. Bazhenova, I.: Database Application Development for Cloud Data Warehouses. SQL Azure. LAP LAMBERT Academic Publishing (2013). (in Russian)
4. Bazhenova, I.., Potapova, R., Potapov, V.: Comparative analysis of different mechanisms of work with the integrated speech database in the cloud data storage. Vestnik Moscow State Linguist. Univ. Hum. (15), 19–27 (2016). https://elibrary.ru/item.asp?id=39248266. (in Russian)
5. Potapova, R., et al.: Speech Communication in Information Space. LENAND, Moscow (2017).(in Russian)

Modelling Heterogenous Robot Squads in Unstable Situations

Valentina Baranyuk⬥, Daria Minyaylo⬥, and Olga Smirnova⁽⊠⁾⬥

MIREA – Russian Technological University, Vernadsky Avenue 78, 119454 Moscow, Russia

Abstract. The report considers the issues of information interaction at destabilizing the state of the mixed robotic grouping. The equilibrium state is achieved by applying the principles of maintaining the quasi-stability state of the system and exchanging of pertinent data flows between objects. Within the framework of this, the spheres of their application, schemes of possible information interaction are examined using the example of unmanned aerial vehicles. In addition, an approach is described for planning the actions of a group of unmanned aerial vehicles under the conditions of "balancing on the brink" and the basic principle of pertinence. Pertinent information flows correspond to the specific information needs of each object in the mixed robotic group, what does not require additional resources for processing the received information. Moreover, the results of modeling the behavior of mixed robotic groups in the conditions of "balancing on the brink" with the exchange of the information, streams by the example of a group of unmanned aerial vehicles are presented. The simulation was performed using the developed special software and described using the IDEF0 functional modeling methodology. The developed functional model shows all the requirements, limitations, information and other resources involved in the process of achieving the goal by a group of unmanned aerial vehicles.

Keywords: Mixed robotic groups · Multi-agent systems · UAV · Stabilization of the system · Pertinent data flows · Balancing on the brink · Decentralized management · Functional model

1 Introduction

The civil unmanned aircraft takes a special place in the modern world. Due to the modern achievements in the field of communications, aerial photography and industrial control systems, the spectrum of tasks which are solved with the help of the unmanned aerial vehicles has expanded significantly: monitoring of the territory in case of emergency, ground mapping, people's search, etc. In comparison to the manned aircrafts the major advantage of the unmanned aerial vehicle is the relatively low cost of production and the ability not to risk the pilot's life.

2 Purpose of the Unmanned Aerial Vehicles

The unmanned aerial vehicles (UAVs) vary greatly in their size and technical specifications. The UAVs of aircraft and helicopter type are the most prevailing in the civilian

© Springer Nature Switzerland AG 2021
V. Sukhomlin and E. Zubareva (Eds.): SITITO 2017, CCIS 1204, pp. 127–134, 2021.
https://doi.org/10.1007/978-3-030-78273-3_13

purposes today. Out of them, we can distinguish small and ultra-small type of the UAV. By small and ultra-small we mean the UAV with characteristics presented in Table 1.

Table 1. T-class characteristics of the UAVs.

Type of the UAV	Weight, kg	Flight height, km	Flight time, hours
Small	Up to 50	Up to 3–5	3–8
Ultra-small	Up to 50	Up to 1	About 2

In comparison with larger UAVs the class of small and ultra-small unmanned vehicles has a number of advantages. This class has a relatively low cost price. The advantages also include their lightness, small size, maneuverability, ease of control. They do not require any specialized ground infrastructure, special personnel and can be controlled and serviced by the staff of the regular organizations. Among the disadvantages we can identify the fact that such configuration does not allow to equip them with large capacity batteries, which limits the duration of an autonomous flight [1].

The market of production and use of the unmanned vehicles is constantly evolving. Today, they are most in demand in the field of ground monitoring for cartography, in the interests of protection and needs of the emergency services. A complete list of the applications of civil vehicles of this type is shown in Fig. 1 [2].

The prospects for the use of self-controlled UAVs are constantly expanding. Along with such tasks as increasing the duration of the flight, the payload on board and reducing the cost of production, one of the key topical positions is the task of organizing a group flight of the UAVs. The implementation of the UAV group control significantly increases the efficiency of achieving the specified goal. It is advisable to use the multi-agent approach to create such distributed intelligent [3]. The main advantage of this approach is that it allows to implement a dynamic redistribution of tasks between the agents, as well as a dynamic change in the behavior of the group.

The interaction of the UAVs in a group represents itself the control of the actions of the unmanned vehicles and control of their implementation, ensuring flight safety, assessing the relative position of the group and its objects. The acquisition and transmission of information is the provision of communication between the objects of the control system, for example, between the UAV group and the ground complex [4]. The control of the group generally includes determining the location of the group and the system's elements, accounting for the number of the system's objects. In most cases, the UAV is controlled by an on-board navigation and control system, which includes [5]:

- navigation system;
- a system of sensors and signals that provides UAV traffic parameters;
- various types of antennas and sensors for task performance;
- autopilot module (hereinafter – AP).

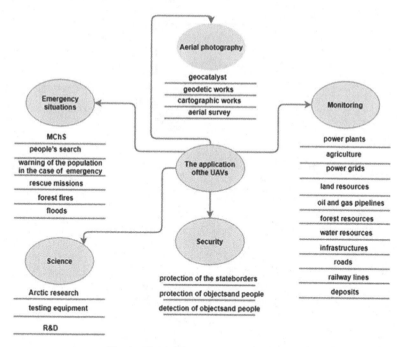

Fig. 1. Fields of application of the UAV.

The transmission of information flows is possible not only between a single UAV with a station (Fig. 2a), but also between a group of unmanned vehicles and a ground station (Fig. 2c), and within the group itself (Fig. 2b).

3 Modeling of the Task Execution by a Robotic Grouping in the Conditions of "Balancing on the Edge"

Nowadays, one of the developers' key tasks in this field is to design strategies for group decentralized autonomous control of the UAVs taking into account their information interaction [7]. A particular and most interesting case is the design of the strategy of group decentralized autonomous control of the UAVs in conditions of "balancing on the edge" due to the exchange of the pertinent information flows.

The approach to planning the actions of group of the unmanned aerial vehicles in conditions of "balancing on the edge" implies the preservation of the state of quasi-stability of the system when its state deviates to the stability boundaries by making a decision by the distributed intellect in a critical situation (behavior in situations requiring leadership determination in the group, self-sacrifice and etc.) [8].

An important issue in the process of functioning of mixed robotic groups is the exchange of information between the objects (agents) of the system. The transmitted information is the main element in a collective control strategy in mixed robotic groups. Within the framework of information interaction for solving the assigned tasks, the

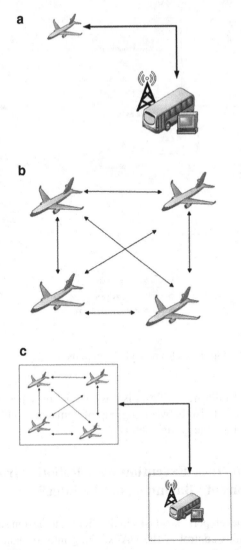

Fig. 2. a. The information flows between a single UAV with a station. b. The information flows between a group of unmanned vehicles. c. The information flows between a group of unmanned vehicles and a ground station.

objects of mixed robotic groups should exchange only the pertinent information flows. – Information flows, characterized by the degree of proximity of the expected and obtained results. Pertinent information flows correspond to the specific information needs of each object in the mixed robotic group, which does not require additional resources for processing the received information [7].

Consider the approach to planning the actions of mixed robotic groups in the conditions of "balancing on the edge" on the example of the UAV group, whose main tasks

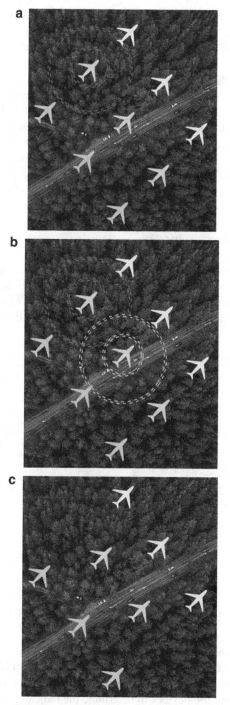

Fig. 3. a. Transmission of the pertinent information flows. b. Transmission of the pertinent information flows. c. Transmission of the pertinent information flows. (Color figure online)

are ground monitoring, including in hard-to-reach areas, in carrying out search activities to coordinate the actions of land groups in an emergency situation.

Each UAV has its own zone of visibility, action radius and spectrum of tasks. We will assume that the UAV group consists of 3 functional groups, each of which includes 3 agents that move to the target point, without exceeding the boundaries of the radio communication between each other. Nine agents are doing the ground monitoring, while one of the agents signals a deviation of the system to the stability boundary. When the percentage of deviation becomes critical for the system, the agent transmits the pertinent information to the nearest agent in its functional group (Fig. 3a). The agent who received the information takes over the tasks of the retired agent and informs the others about it (Fig. 3b). The remaining group implements the rebuilding (Fig. 3c).

Circular dashed lines in Fig. 3a, 3b and 3c show the transfer of the information flows:

- red – signal about destabilization;
- yellow – signal about receiving tasks.

For a more detailed description of the process which is under our consideration, the most interesting is the methodology of functional modeling IDEF0, the main purpose of which is the modeling of the process, by creating its graphical representation. Figure 4 shows the context diagram of the process "Implementation of the assigned task by the UAV group".

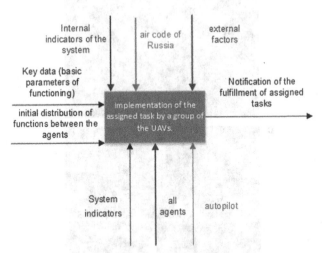

Fig. 4. Context diagram of the process "Implementation of the assigned task by the UAV group".

The main aim for the UAV group is to fulfill the assigned task. The input data are the basic parameters of functioning and the initial distribution of functions between the agents. The output data is the notification of the implementation of the assigned tasks. As the mechanisms used the devices to determine the indicators of the system, agents and AP. As a controlling influence used the internal indicators of the system, external factors and the air code of the Russian Federation.

A more detailed description of block A0 is presented on the child diagram – the first level of decomposition (Fig. 5).

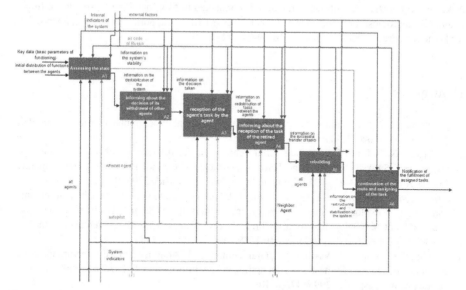

Fig. 5. The first level of decomposition of the process "Implementation of the assigned task by the UAV group".

The first level decomposition scheme details the interaction of the UAV group in the conditions of "balancing on the edge", including the agent's assessment of his internal state, informing the other agents about the decision of his retirement, the agent receiving the task of the retiring agent, informing about the reception of the task of the retired agent, general rebuilding, continuation of the route and the assigning of task. The constructed model makes it possible in a visual form to obtain information on the functioning of a group of the unmanned vehicles in conditions of "balancing on the edge" while using the pertinent information flows.

4 Conclusion

Application of the proposed solutions to preserve the state of quasi-stability of the system due to the exchange of the pertinent information flows during the control of the UAV group makes it possible to bring the internal state of the system back to a state of equilibrium under conditions of "balancing on the edge" due to the efficient, autonomous and rapid compensation of the changes that have appeared. The developed functional model shows all the requirements, limitations, information and other resources that involved in the process of achieving the goal by the UAV group.

Due to this interaction, the probability of achieving the specified goal, even in emergency situations and with the failure of several members of the group, increases significantly, and under favorable conditions of the whole route, the group is able to perform a wide spectrum of tasks in a shorter time, which is a key factor in search of the events and a number of other tasks.

Acknowledgments. The following research is conducted in Moscow State University of Information Technologies, Radiotechnics and Electronics (MIREA) supported by Russian Foundation for Basic Research under the Grant № 16-29-04326.

References

1. Zinchenko, O.N.: Unmanned Aerial Vehicles: the use aerial photographs in order to map. Part 1. Racurs, Moscow (2011). (in Russian)
2. Voropaev, N.P.: Use of unmanned aerial vehicles in the interests of EMERCOM of Russia. Vestnik Sankt-Peterburgskogo Universiteta Gosudarstvennoi Protivopozharnoi Sluzhby MCHS Rossii (4), 13–17 (2014). https://elibrary.ru/item.asp?id=22967082. (in Russian)
3. Kothari, M., Postlethwaite, I., Gu, D.: Multi-UAV path planning in obstacle rich environments using Rapidly-exploring Random Trees. In: Proceedings of the 48th IEEE Conference on Decision and Control (CDC) Held Jointly with 2009 28th Chinese Control Conference, Shanghai, pp. 3069–3074 (2009). http://doi.org/10.1109/CDC.2009.5400108
4. Amelin, K.S., Antal, E.I., Vasiliev, V.I., Granichinav, N.O.: Adaptive control autonomous group of unmanned aircraft. Stohasticheskaja optimizacija v informatike. **5**, 157–166 (2009). https://elibrary.ru/item.asp?id=12994147. (in Russian)
5. Bento, M.F.: Unmanned aerial vehicles: an overview. Inside GNSS. **3**(1), 54–61 (2008). https://www.insidegnss.com/auto/janfeb08-wp.pdf
6. Allan, R.J.: Survey of agent based modelling and simulation tools. Technical report: DL-TR-2010-007, Version 1.1, Science and Technology Facilities Council (STFC) Daresbury Laboratory, Daresbury, Warrington, WA4 4AD (2010)
7. Sigov, A.S., Nechaev, V.V., Baranyuk, V.V., Smirnova, O.S.: Approaches to group control and information–driven interaction in heterogeneous robot squads. In: CEUR Workshop Proceedings: Selected Papers of the First International Scientific Conference Convergent Cognitive Information Technologies, 25–26 November 2016, vol. 1763, pp. 146-151 (2016). http://ceur-ws.org/Vol-1763/paper18.pdf. (in Russian)
8. Baranyuk, V.V., Miniyailo, D.V., Smirnova, O.S.: Planning brinksmanship behavioral patterns for heterogeneous robot squads. Int. J. Open Inf. Technol. **4**(12), 16–20 (2016). https://www.elibrary.ru/item.asp?id=27543355. (in Russian)

Automatic Text Processing for Historical Research

Anna Glazkova$^{(\boxtimes)}$ ⓘ, Valery Kruzhinov ⓘ, and Zinaida Sokova ⓘ

University of Tyumen, Volodarskogo Str. 6, 625003 Tyumen, Russia
{a.v.glazkova,v.m.kruzhinov,z.n.sokova}@utmn.ru

Abstract. This article is devoted to the main possibilities of using natural language text processing technologies for historical research. The authors present a taxonomy of biographical facts and use text mining technologies (extraction of information from texts) to obtain biographical information from texts in Russian in accordance with the proposed types of biographical facts. The conducting of biographical research implies the need to view and study large amounts of textual information. The considerable part of the sources is currently presented in electronic form, which allows researchers to apply modern methods of extracting information to them. The article presents an overview of the main areas of application of technologies for automatic processing natural language texts in the humanities and describes the approach to the creation and implementation of the instrument for the extraction and systematization of biographical facts. This instrument will be useful to both historians and other users interested in biographical research.

Keywords: Digital humanities · Natural language processing · Text mining · Information extraction · Historical methodology

1 Introduction

It is a common knowledge that historian has to work with a huge amount of information. This information can be represented in different forms (manuscripts, archive documents, etc.) and associated with different aspects of human life (social, political, economic, private and others).

At the moment the significant part of the world's text sources and documents are available in digital form. Many historical texts are also digitized. Paper documents translation into electronic form is motivated by the aim of preserving cultural heritage and making it more accessible to scientists and other people interested in history. Text processing methods serve to accelerate the processing of digital information. Therefore, the use of natural language processing tools can improve the quality of historical research, reduce the amount of information that a researcher needs to view and increase the effectiveness of his work [1, 2].

The arrival of word processors, electronic mail, online libraries and the Internet made computers the part of the daily life of most humanities scholars [3]. In connection with

© Springer Nature Switzerland AG 2021
V. Sukhomlin and E. Zubareva (Eds.): SITITO 2017, CCIS 1204, pp. 135–146, 2021.
https://doi.org/10.1007/978-3-030-78273-3_14

the volume of existing information, it is often difficult to extract facts from the texts, especially if they are not found explicitly in the texts. In this regard, there is a need to develop methods and tools for efficient processing of information stored in electronic sources.

In the article the authors propose an approach to developing a system for extracting biographical facts from the text, describe the available results and discuss the prospects.

2   Text Mining

2.1   The Concept of Text Mining

There is no canonical definition of *text mining*. Usually researchers use a definition based on the definition of data mining: text mining is a set of methods for detecting previously unknown, non-trivial, practically useful and accessible interpretations of knowledge. Text mining is the analysis of data contained in natural language text [4, 5].

The key groups of text mining tasks are text classification and categorization, information retrieval, processing of changes in text collections and development of means for presenting information to the user.

2.2   Text Classification and Categorization

The document classification consists in assigning documents (texts) from the collection to one or several groups (classes) of similar texts (for example, by author, theme or style). Text classification can occur with the participation of a person and without it. In the second case it is called text *categorization* [2, 4].

Text classification system should refer the texts to some predefined classes (convenient for it). In terms of machine learning, it is necessary to do this with training samples (supervised learning), for which the user must provide the text classification system with a set of classes, as well as samples of documents belonging to these classes.

The second case of classification is called document categorization or clustering. In this case, the computer system itself must determine the set of clusters by which texts can be distributed. In machine learning, the corresponding task is called unsupervised learning. In this case, the user must tell the computer system the number of clusters to which he would like to split the processed collection (it is implied that the algorithm of the program already has a procedure for selecting characteristics).

2.3   Information Retrieval (IR)

Information retrieval is a process of searching unstructured documentary information that satisfies information needs.

IR helps to identify a set of documents all those that are devoted to the subject and satisfy a predetermined search condition (query) or contain the necessary information-relevant data.

The process of information retrieval includes a sequence of operations aimed at collecting, processing and providing information. In general, it consists of six stages [5, 6]:

1. clarification of an information need;
2. formulating an information request;
3. definition of a set of possible holders of information arrays (sources);
4. search for information from identified information arrays;
5. acquaintance with the received information;
6. estimation of search results.

Depending on the specifics of the information retrieval researchers consider address, semantic, document, factual types of IR (Table 1) [7, 8].

Table 1. Information retrieval types.

Type of IR	Necessary conditions
Address IR	1. The document has an exact address; 2. Ensuring a strict order of the location of documents in a storage device or in the system store
Semantic IR	1. Translation of the document content and information requests from natural language into an information retrieval language and compiling search results; 2. Creation of a search description in which an additional search condition is specified
Document IR	Document tagging
Factual IR	Availability of means of fact extraction

Address information retrieval is a process of searching documents for purely formal characteristics specified in the request. Addresses of documents can be addresses of web servers and web pages and elements of bibliographic records, and addresses of documents storage in the repository.

Semantic information retrieval is an information retrieval for searching documents for their content. The fundamental difference between address and semantic types of information retrieval is that in case of address information retrieval the document is viewed as an object from the point of view of form, and in semantic information retrieval it is considered as a carrier of some content. Due semantic search a set of documents is used without specifying addresses. This is the fundamental difference between catalogs and libraries. A library is a collection of bibliographic records without addresses.

Document information retrieval is a process of searching for information corresponding to the user's request in the repository of the primary documents information retrieval system or in the secondary documents database. There are two types of documentary search:

1. library search, aimed at primary documents detection;
2. bibliographic search, aimed at detection information about documents presented in the form of bibliographic records.

Factual information retrieval is an extraction of the facts that correspond to the information request.

Facts include information extracted from documents, both primary and secondary, and obtained directly from sources of their origin. There are two types of factual search:

documentary and factual, aimed at the search in the documents for fragments of text containing facts;

fact creation, suggesting the creation of new factual descriptions in the search process by logically processing the found factual information.

There has been a few recent works related to information extraction. Among others, some works are devoted to digital humanities [9–12]. Thus, Adamovich and Volkov [12] presented the system for biographical facts extraction from historical texts using a tree-like representation of facts. In the paper [13] the authors tackle the relation classification task using a convolutional neural network that performs classification by ranking (CR-CNN). Meerkamp and Zhou [14] presented an architecture for information extraction from text that augments an existing parser with a character-level neural network. Homma et al. [15] developed a hierarchical neural network proposed for sentence classification to extract product information from product documents. The network classifies each sentence in a document into attribute and condition classes on the basis of word sequences and sentence sequences in the document. T. Gogar et al. [16] proposed a method for spatial text encoding, which allows us to encode visual and textual content of a web page into a single neural net.

3   Text Mining Applications for Historical Science

3.1   The Stages of Historical Data Processing

All historical data go through several stages from its origin to presentation. The life cycle of historical data consists of six steps (Fig. 1).

The first step of the life cycle is *creation*. The main aspect of this step consists of the physical creation of digital data. Examples of activities in this phase would be the data entry plan, digitization of documents, or considering the appropriate database software.

The next step is *enrichment*. The main goal of this stage is to enrich the data created in the previous step with metadata, describing the historical information in more detail. This phase also comprises the linkage of individual data that belongs together in the historical reality, because these data belong to the same person, place or event.

Editing includes the actual encoding of textual information and extends to annotating original data with background information, bibliographical references and links to related passages.

In the stage of *retrieval* proceed information is retrieved, that is, selected, looked up, and used.

Information *analyzing* means quite different things in historical research. It varies from qualitative comparison and assessment of query results, to advanced statistical analysis of datasets.

Fig. 1. The life cycle of historical data.

Historical information is to be communicated in different circumstances through multiple forms of *presentation*. It may take very different shapes, varying from electronic text editions, online databases, virtual exhibitions to small-scale visualizations.

3.2 Biographical Data in Historical Research

Due to the fact that the world's text resources are constantly increasing, the urgency of tasks related to reducing the amount of time spent viewing electronic text sources is also growing. Such tasks include classification and clustering of documents, automatic annotation and abstracting, fact extraction from natural language texts. Thus, conducting biographical research involves working with facts relating to human life. These facts can relate to various aspects of life – social, political, cultural or personal. The search for diverse biographical information is carried out using various resources. In particular, such resources are the Internet, electronic libraries and other digital text sources.

Information retrieval for electronic resources is associated with a number of difficulties. So, the researcher can not always clearly formulate a search query. In addition, a number of biographical facts are in the text in an implicit form. These features force the user to view large amounts of textual information in search of relevant facts for research. In addition, the texts containing biographical facts have a different structure. They are divided into strictly documentary (autobiographies, scientific biographies, summaries) and non-strictly documentary texts (memoirs, essays, chronicles). Fact extraction for texts that have a clear structure (personnel records, summaries) is easily amenable to automation. However, processing texts that do not have a regulated structure requires additional analysis of syntactic and semantic links between words and sentences of the text. Thus, an important fundamental scientific problem is the development of methods and algorithms for extracting biographical facts from texts in natural language, including the identification of relationships between entities and the systematization of the facts obtained.

In connection with the need to solve the described problem, the task of automatically extracting biographical facts from the natural language text is really actual. As part of our research, we use the concept of a *person's information portrait*. An information portrait means the name of a person (a named entity that identifies an individual) and many related facts. In the most general form, a fact is a relation on a set of words. To solve practical problems, it is necessary to specify the types of relations that will be used to extract the facts. Specification of the concept of "fact", that is, the identification of such relationships in the text that must be extracted during the construction of an information portrait, is one of the tasks of this study.

4 An Approach to Biographical Facts Extraction

4.1 The Stages of Biographical Facts Extraction

The purpose of our further study is to automate the construction of person's information portraits based on texts in natural language. In other words, the research is aimed at solving the problem of extracting biographical facts from texts written in natural language.

We consider three stages of constructing information portraits (Fig. 2).

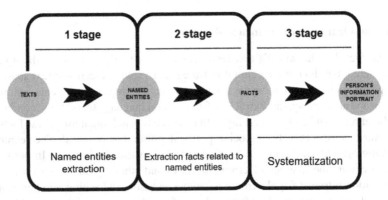

Fig. 2. The stages of information portraits construction.

The first stage is the extraction of named entities that serve as person's identifiers. A named entity is a word or phrase that denotes a proper name. In this study, named entities are words or combinations of words that denote people. These are personalities, the facts about which will be extracted in the future. At this stage, we use automatic tools to find the names of people in the text. This search can be organized using both a dictionary of names and external attributes of named entities (capital letters, specific suffixes of surnames, etc.)

The next step is to extract from the text the facts relating to the received named entities. The fact is a kind of relation in a set of words. To develop methods for extracting facts and their practical implementation, it is first of all necessary to concretize the set of relations that will be used in the framework of this study. In other words, it is necessary to select those types of relations on a set of words that will be considered facts and extracted in the course of text analysis.

In our work we consider the following types of facts based on the work [17]: nonbiographical facts and biographical facts that are divided into personal (place of birth, nationality, etc.) and professional facts (education, occupation, etc.). The complete taxonomy of facts is presented in Fig. 3.

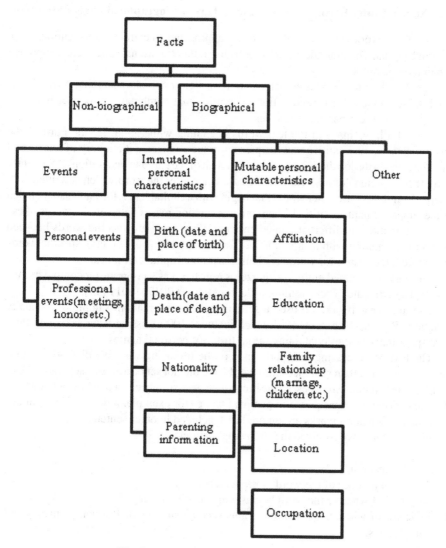

Fig. 3. The taxonomy of biographical facts.

Based on the constructed information portraits we plan to develop an ontological knowledge database for storing biographical information. Thus, the information obtained at the stages of extraction of named entities and facts will become available for further use in other tasks and applications and will be useful for both historians and other people interested in biographical research. The peculiarity of this project is its principled focus on the needs of historians and biographers. We plan that the technology being developed will help researchers reduce the amount of information needed to view information and not skip the facts that are found implicitly in the text.

4.2 Named Entity Recognition as a First Stage of Biographical Facts Extraction

As part of our work, we used and tested two approaches to extract named entities from texts in Russian. The first rule-based approach is rather traditional. The second approach is based on neural networks.

The flowchart for rule-based named entity recognition is shown in Fig. 4. We developed the instrument for named entity recognition that combines approaches based on dictionaries and rule-based approaches.

First of all, we mark in the text words beginning with capital letters. Further, the text indicates named entities that are present in the connected dictionary of names and surnames and in the job dictionary (like "President of the Russian Federation", "Secretary of State for Foreign Affairs" etc.). In the case when after the word which is written with a capital letter there are other words that begin with a capital letter, they are also included in the supposed named entity. If there are punctuation marks between the words, these words are marked as different named entities. When there are specific words between the words beginning with a capital letter (for example, "de" or "de la"), specific words are ignored, the search for words beginning with the capital continues.

Currently, the named entity recognizer is registered as a program for computers. We received a certificate of registration of the program № 2017616011 [19].

To train our network, we used a set comprising of a random sample of manually annotated Persons-1000 texts [20] which includes 1000 Russian news texts and their corresponding xml-files containing initial forms of personal names.

The text preprocessing was performed in the following way. We divided the texts into sentences and then sentences into words. We did not set ourselves a separate task of dividing the text into sentences, so the breakdown was simply carried out by punctuation. If punctuation marks are part of a personal name (for example, a dot after the initial), then such punctuation marks are ignored and included in other sentences.

For each word we received the following features:

1. Word embeddings.
2. The serial number of the word in the sentence.
3. Indicator of whether the word begins with a capital letter.
4. Indicator of whether the word contains specific suffixes of Russian surnames and patronymics.

The used recurrent neural model has two hidden layers with sigmoid activation. Each hidden layer contains 200 neurons. For optimization we have chosen the Adam optimizer and exponentially decaying learning rate.

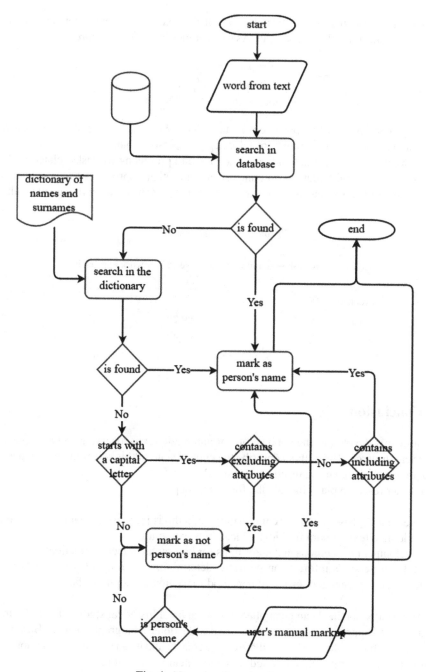

Fig. 4. Named entity extraction.

The Table 2 contains quality indicators of rule-based and neural network named entity recognition for the test sample. As a target metric, we use F-score:

$$Precision = \frac{TP}{TP+FP},$$
$$Recall = \frac{TP}{TP+FN},$$
$$\text{F-score} = 2 \cdot \frac{Precision \cdot Recall}{Precision - Recall},$$

TP – the number of true positive personal names, *FP* – the number of false positive personal names, *FN* – the number of false negative personal names.

As we see, the neural network approach is quite promising for tasks related to the processing of natural language. In comparison with other approaches to named entity recognition for the Russian language, the proposed approaches show rather good results.

Table 2. The final results.

Metric	Rule-based approach, %	Neural network approach, %
Precision	96.6	93.4
Recall	90.79	89.29
F-score	93.6	91.3

5　Conclusion

The article is devoted to the applications of automatic text processing technologies in historical research. The authors describe the current state of this scientific direction and also present their scientific results in this field.

Further research plans include the following steps:

1. selecting the best method or combination of methods for personal names extraction;
2. building a text corpora for biographical facts extraction;
3. development of methods and algorithms for biographical facts extraction;
4. building person's information portraits: determining the roles of participants in a fact; development and testing of a method for removing duplicate facts.

The results obtained can be applied in biographical historical studies. In the future, the developed approaches can be tested on real collections of biographical texts. Based on these texts, a biographical facts database can be created and it can be used by biographers, historians and other people interested in biographical information.

Acknowledgements. The authors wish to thank all those who participated in the field exercise and helped to make it a successful endeavor.

The reported study was funded by RFBR according to the research project 18-37-00272.

References

1. Hockey, S.: Electronic Texts in the Humanities: Principles and Practice. Oxford University Press, Oxford (2000). https://doi.org/10.1093/acprof:oso/9780198711940.001.0001
2. Manning, C., Raghavan, P., Schütze, H.: Introduction to Information Retrieval. Cambridge University Press, Cambridge (2008)
3. Merono-Penuela, A., et al.: Semantic technologies for historical research: a survey. Semant. Web. **6**(6), 539–564 (2015). https://doi.org/10.3233/SW-140158
4. Landje, D.V., Snarskij, A.A., Bezsudnov, I.V.: Internet: Navigation in Complex Networks: Models and Algorithms. Librokom (URSS), Moscow (2009).(in Russian)
5. Piotrowski, M.: Natural language processing for historical texts. Syn. Lect. Hum. Lang. Technol. **5**(2), 1–157 (2012). https://doi.org/10.2200/S00436ED1V01Y201207HLT017
6. Basegroup Labs: Data Analysis Technologies. http://basegroup.ru. (in Russian)
7. Text Mining (Big Data, Unstructured Data). http://www.statsoft.com. (in Russian)
8. Boolean retrieval. In: Manning, C., Raghavan, P., Schütze, H. (eds.) Introduction to Information Retrieval, pp. 1–18. Cambridge University Press, Cambridge (2008). https://nlp.stanford.edu/IR-book/pdf/01bool.pdf
9. Schweizer, T.J., Alassi, S., Mattmüller, M., Rosenthaler, L., Harbrecht, H.: Integrating historical scientific texts into the Bernoulli-Euler online platform. In: Digital Humanities. Montreal, Canada (2017). https://dh2017.adho.org/abstracts/147/147.pdf
10. Grimmer, J., Stewart, B.M.: Text as data: the promise and pitfalls of automatic content analysis methods for political texts. Polit. Anal. **21**(3), 267–297 (2013). https://doi.org/10.1093/pan/mps028
11. Zwaan, J., Smink, W., Sool, A., Westerhof, G., Veldkamp, B., Wiegersma, S.: Flexible NLP pipelines for digital humanities research. In: Proceedings of the 4th Digital Humanities Benelux Conference 2017, Montreal, Canada (2017). https://dh2017.adho.org/abstracts/215/215.pdf
12. Adamovich, I.M., Volkov, O.I.: The system of facts extraction from historical texts. Syst. Means Inform. **25**(3), 235–250 (2015). https://doi.org/10.14357/08696527150315. (in Russian)
13. Santos, C., Xiang, B., Zhou, B.: Classifying relations by ranking with convolutional neural networks. In: Proceedings of the 53rd Annual Meeting of the Association for Computational Linguistics and the 7th International Joint Conference on Natural Language Processing, Beijing, China, vol. 1, pp. 626–634 (2015). https://doi.org/10.3115/v1/P15-1061
14. Meerkamp, P., Zhou, Z.: Information Extraction with Character-Level Neural Networks and Free Noisy Supervision. Cornell University Library. https://arxiv.org/pdf/1612.04118.pdf
15. Homma, Y., Sadamitsu, K., Nishida, K., Higashinaka, R., Asano, H., Matsuo, Y.: A hierarchical neural network for information extraction of product attribute and condition sentences. In: Proceedings of the Open Knowledge Base and Question Answering (OKBQA), Osaka, Japan, pp. 21–29 (2016). https://www.aclweb.org/anthology/W16-4403
16. Gogar, T., Hubacek, O., Sedivy, J.: Deep neural networks for web page information extraction. In: Proceedings of AIAI 2016: Artificial Intelligence Applications and Innovations, Thessaloniki, Greece, pp. 154–163 (2016).
17. Gogar, T., Hubacek, O., Sedivy, J.: Deep neural networks for web page information extraction. In: Iliadis, L., Maglogiannis, I. (eds.) AIAI 2016. IAICT, vol. 475, pp. 154–163. Springer, Cham (2016). https://doi.org/10.1007/978-3-319-44944-9_14
18. Glazkova, A., Kruzhinov, V., Sokova, Z. Automatic compilation of Person's information portraits as an instrument of historical research. In: CEUR Workshop Proceedings: Supplementary Proceedings of the 6th International Conference on Analysis of Images, Social Networks and Texts (AIST-SUP 2017), Moscow, Russia, 27–29 July 2017, vol. 1975, pp. 56–62 (2017)

19. Glazkova, A.V.: Named-entity biographic recognizer (NERbiografija). Patent RF, no. 2017616011 (2017). (in Russian)
20. "Persons-1000" Collection. http://ai-center.botik.ru/Airec/index.php/ru/collections/28-persons-1000. (in Russian)

Hadoop/Hive Data Query Performance Comparison Between Data Warehouses Designed by Data Vault and Snowflake Methodologies

Yuri Grigoriev$^{(\boxtimes)}$ ⓘ, Evgeny Ermakov ⓘ, and Oleg Ermakov ⓘ

The Bauman Moscow State University, 2ed. Baumanskaya Str. 5-1, 105005 Moscow, Russia
grigoriev@bmstu.ru

Abstract. The article discusses the difference between Data Vault and Snowflake methodologies in Hadoop infrastructure. The history of Data Vault methodology development from the original version to the modern is showed. The main components of Data Vault are described: hubs, communications, satellites. A comparison of the Data Vault approach with the classic star and snowflake approaches is performed. TPC-H test schema is designed using the Data Vault methodology: business entities are identified and converted to hubs, their rela-tionships are allocated to satellites. Result storage size and query execution time comparison between Data Vault and Snowflake is performed.

Keywords: Data vault · Snowflake · Data warehouse · Hive · Hadoop · SQL

1 Introduction

In the 80–90s of the last century, in response to the rapid growth of accumulated data and the need to handle them, OLAP [1], multidimensional cubes and data warehouse (DWH) technologies were created [2], which is now an important part of the IT infrastructure of any enterprise. Data growth has not slowed down, and the modern IT industry is working with large data (Big Data) [3], which poses new challenges for DWH engineers all around the world. The answer to this challenge is the creation of new approaches both in the storage and processing of information, and new methodologies for designing DWH.

One of the key technologies for processing big data is the Hadoop technologies stack. Based on the MapReduce paradigm, Hadoop has become the basis for a whole ecosystem of services and applications: Spark, Kafka, Oozie, etc. One of the such application is Hive, a system that combines a classic relational approach to working with data and processing with MapReduce tasks.

V. Sukhomlin and E. Zubareva (Eds.): SITITO 2017, CCIS 1204, pp. 147–156, 2021.
https://doi.org/10.1007/978-3-030-78273-3_15

The answer to the complexity associated with scalability, presentation flexibility and data granularity is the new approaches to DWH design, different from the Snowflake scheme. The Data Vault (DV) approach introduces new entity types: Hub, Link, Satellite, Bridge, PIT - and tightly regulates the composition of entity data fields. This approach allows to quickly respond to changing the data structure with minimal consequences for the DWH structure, while the complexity of performing requests to DWH is significantly increased.

With all the diversity of approaches and technologies, the DWH architector faces the problem of choosing the best approach in each specific case, while the problem of compatibility between approaches and technologies remains open and relevant. This article explores the question of how the use of the DWH design methodology in the Hive/Hadoop stack complicates the design process and affects the query performance.

2   Modern Approaches to the DWH Design

2.1   Approaches Development History

Normalization as an approach was originally created in the early 1960s by Edgar F. Codd and Christopher J. Date for online transaction processing systems (OLTP). In the early 1980s, this approach was adapted to the increasing demands of data warehouses, which resulted in the creation of the Snowflake scheme, which was introduced in the second half of the 1980s in data modeling (Fig. 1).

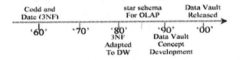

Fig. 1. Approaches development history.

Low performance and low flexibility with changes in the data structure of both the third normal form (3NF) and Snowflake schemes began to manifest themselves in the 90s during the ever-increasing amounts of data. The Data Vault model was designed to overcome these shortcomings, preserving the strengths of the 3NF architecture and the Snowflake architecture [4]. The main advantage of this approach is the ability to quickly respond to changes in the needs of business units without making significant changes to the DWH scheme. In 2012, the development of the methodology DataVault 2.0, which adds optimizations for BigData and NoSQL technologies, was announced.

2.2   The Classic Snowflake Approach

Classical DWHs are built on the basis of a multidimensional data model, which involves the use of two basic entities: individual dimensions (time, geography, customer, account) and facts (sales volume, income, quantity of goods) analyzed by the selected dimensions. A multidimensional data model can be physically implemented both in multidimensional

DBMS and in relational ones. In the relational DBMS, it is performed according to the "star" or "snowflake" scheme (Fig. 2a, b). These schemes involve the allocation of fact tables and dimension tables: each fact table contains detailed data and foreign keys on the measurement tables. The theory of constructing a multidimensional data model and its implementation in the relational structure is widely covered both in the foreign [5, 6] and in the domestic literature [7].

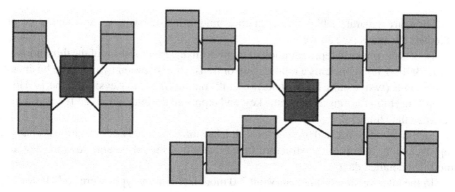

Fig. 2. Star (left) and snowflake (right) scheme.

2.3 Data Vault Approach

The DataVault model v.1.0 uses 3 kinds of tables: Hub, Link and Satellite. In the later version of the DataVault 2.0 model, two more types were added: bridge and point-of-view (PIT) [8] (Fig. 3).

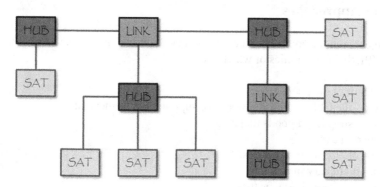

Fig. 3. Data Vault scheme.

You have to use the following standard entity attributes using Data Vault concept:

- The surrogate key, an optional component, perhaps a smart key or a serial number;
- The Load Date Time Stamp, which records when the key was first loaded into the vault;
- Source of data (Record Source) - registration of the source system, used to reverse track the data.

Hubs are separate tables that contain a unique list of business keys and a set of standard attributes (see above).

Link is the physical representation of many-to-many relationships of the third normal form (3NF). Link represents a relationship or transaction between two or more business components (two or more business keys). Link contains the Hub Keys: from the 1st Hub to the N-th Hub - forming a composite key, and represent the interactions and connections between the Hubs.

Satellites are contextual (descriptive) Hub key information. The description is changing over time, therefore the structure of the Satellites should be able to store new or modified detailed data.

In the later version of the DataVault 2.0 model, two more types were added: bridge and point-of-view [8].

A point-of-view is a modified satellite that contains the hub key and timestamps of all other satellites associated with the hub. In fact, the point-of-view is a prepared skeleton for join in order to get attributes at any time, which significantly reduces the execution time of the request.

A bridge is an extension of a link entity that allows you to bind more than one entity, which also increases the execution time of queries by decreasing the join operation.

3   DWH Design for the TPC-H Test Using the Snowflake and Data Vault Approaches

As a subject area for comparing the approaches described above, the TPC-H test was selected [9], the main entities of which are:

- Part - a unit of the goods sold;
- Partsupp - the table of links between the supplier and the details;
- Supplier - supplier of goods (details)
- Customer – buyer
- Nation – dictionary of countries;
- Region - dictionary of regions;
- Orders - goods purchases facts table;
- Lineitem - order contents.

To emulate the data flow from external systems, the following rules for loading in-formation into the data warehouse were taken:

- The data comes from two external systems: the order accounting system and the supplier management system;
- From the order accounting system, the data is loaded into the store every day in the Lineitem and Order entities;
- From the vendor management system, the data is downloaded once a week in Part, PartSupp, Supplier, Customer entities, and the information in them is not changed much (no more than 10% of the records are updated);
- Nation and Region entities are for reference, so they are updated on demand.

To generate a database in hive under the Star scheme, a script from Hortonworks was used [10]. The ER-scheme is shown in Fig. 4 at the same time, for the Part, Part-Supp, Supplier, Customer measurements, which are changed once a week, the 2nd type of slowly changing dimension is used [11].

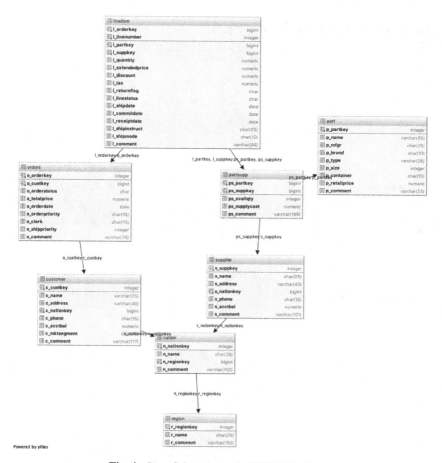

Fig. 4. Snowflake scheme for TPC-H database.

In order to rebuild the database schema for the requirements of the Data Vault methodology, the following transformations were performed:

1. Business entities were selected and converted into Hubs: hub_customer, hub_nation, hub_orders, hub_region, hub_supplier;
2. Relationships are established between business entities in accordance with the TPC-H scheme. Each existing relationship is transformed to the implementation scheme of M-M: link_customer_nation, link_customer_order, link_lineitem, link_nation_region, link_part_supp, link_supplier_nation;
3. All the data on business entities and their connections are allocated to satellites and separated by context. So, for example, the general information about the part is stored in sat_part_info, where the name, producer, brand and type are described, and all information about the container is stored in sat_part_container, where the package size and the container identifier are saved.

The conversion results are shown in Fig. 5.

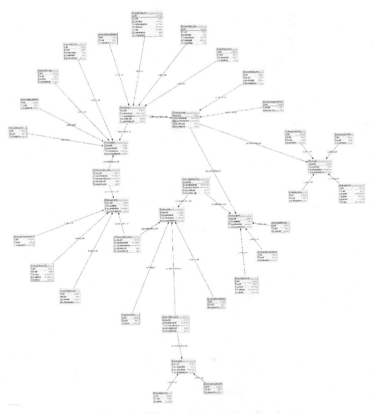

Fig. 5. Data Vault scheme for TPC-H database.

4   Comparing the Query Characteristics of Data Vault and Snowflake DB in Hive

As a test stand, 8 machines Hadoop cluster, deployed in a virtual environment, was used. Features of the nodes: 4Gb RAM, 200Gb hard drive. HDFS services were deployed at seven nodes, and one node was used as cluster monitor. Cloudera was used as a Hadoop distribution.

For the experiments, a TPC-H database with a coefficient $sf = 5$ was generated. After that, weekly data downloads from external systems were simulated for 4 weeks. The result of the emulation was also saved in a database with a schema based on the Data Vault. The tables were saved in HDFS in the column format *orc*.

4.1   Storage Size Comparison

Tables 1 and 2 show the size of the tables and the number of rows in each of them for the Snowflake and Data Vault methodologies, respectively.

Table 1. Table size (Showflake).

Table name	Number of rows	Table size
customer	3 000 000	0.16
lineitem	29 999 795	0.81
nation	100	0
region	20	0
orders	7 500 000	0.18
part	4 000 000	0.1
partsupp	16 000 000	0.58
supplier	200 000	0.01

The total size of Snowflake was 1.84 Gb, Data Vault - 1.85 Gb.

It can be seen from the tables that for data tables and unchanged measurements, the size in Data Vault is slightly increased by adding additional fields. At the same time, slowly changing measurements weigh significantly more in Snowflake than in the Data Vault, since they stores changes in records. For Snowflake, this is due to the choice of the 2nd type of slowly changing dimensions but using other types would result in either loss of information or a change in the scheme (departure from Snow-flake).

Table 2. Table size (Data Vault).

Table name	Number of rows	Table size
Hub_customer	750 000	0
Hub_nation	25	0
Hub_orders	7 500 000	0
Hub_parts	1 000 000	0
Hub_region	5	0
Hub_supplier	50 000	0
Link_customer_nation	1 125 000	0.03
Link_customer_order	11 250 000	0
Link_lineitem	44 999 694	0.15
Link_nation_region	39	0
Link_part_supp	6 000 000	0.01
Link_supplier_nation	75 000	0
Sat_customer_acct	1 125 000	0.01
Sat_customer_comment	1 125 000	0.02
Sat_customer_info	1 125 000	0.03
Sat_lineitem_comment	44 999 713	0.45
Sat_lineitem_info	44 999 713	0.38
Sat_lineitem_line	44 999 713	0.12
Sat_lineitem_ship	44 999 713	0.22
Sat_nation_comment	39	0
Sat_nation_info	39	0
Sat_orders_comment	11 250 000	0.14
Sat_orders_info	11 250 000	0.02
Sat_orders_price	11 250 000	0.03
Sat_orders_ship	11 250 000	0.02
Sat_part_comment	1 500 000	0
Sat_part_container	1 500 000	0
Sat_part_info	1 500 000	0.01
Sat_part_price	1 500 000	0
Sat_partsupp_comment	6 000 000	0.18
Sat_partsupp_info	6 000 000	0.03
Sat_region_info	9	0
Sat_region_comment	9	0
Sat_supplier_acct	75 000	0
Sat_supplier_comment	75 000	0

4.2 Query Execution Time Comparison

To compare the query execution time, a series of experiments was performed, the results of which are given in Table 3.

Table 3. Query execution time comparison.

Query name	Snowflake avg(s)/std(s)	Data Vault avg(s)/std (s)
Reading table *Part*	0.70/0.17	0.52/0.12
Reading table *partsupp*	23.33/1.21	92.24/2.23
Reading table *lineitem*	79.92/1.98	210.92/6.92
Q17	163.42/3.28	477.12/16.24
Q1	77.39/2.13	179.80/3.34

The results visualization is shown in Fig. 6.

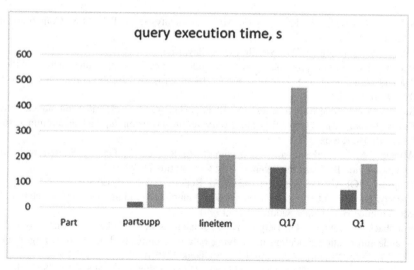

Fig. 6. Query execution time by different architectures.

It can be seen that Data Vault strongly loses snowflake in all kinds of complex queries. This can be explained by the fact that hive uses the MapReduce approach to implement the query, in which it is extremely computationally difficult to implement multiple tables join.

5 Conclusion

Comparison of Data Vault and Snowflake approaches to data warehouse design, historical preconditions for the new methodologies creation, main differences and key features of each approach are considered. The TPC-H data warehouse was designed using the Data Vault methodology.

For the experiments, a TPC-H database with a coefficient $sf = 5$ was generated. After that weekly data downloads from external systems were simulated for 4 weeks. The results of the emulation were stored in a database with the Data Vault based schema. The tables were saved in HDFS in the column format orc.

On the basis of full-scale experiments, it was shown that the size of fact tables and immutable dimensions in the Data Vault is slightly increased by adding additional fields.

When performing queries Data Vault strongly loses snowflake in all kinds of complex queries. This can be explained by the fact that hive uses the MapReduce approach to implement the query, in which it is extremely computationally difficult to implement join multiple tables.

In the future, it is planned to compare the approaches of Anchor modeling with Data Vault and Snowflake and suggest methods for optimizing the execution time of hive requests for modern methodologies.

References

1. Salley, C.T., Codd, E.F.: Providing OLAP to user-analysts: an IT mandate. Computerworld **27**(30) (1998)
2. Inmon, W.: Building the Data Warehouse. Willey, New York (1992)
3. Ivanov, P.D., Vampilova, V.Zh.: Big data technologies and their application in modern industrial enterprise. Eng. J. Sci. Innov. (8), 3 (2014). https://www.elibrary.ru/item.asp?id=225 09394. (in Russian)
4. Sidorov, A.A.: Modern approaches to architecture data warehouses. Data vault model. Ration. Enterp. Manag. (3), 44–45 (2010). http://www.remmag.ru/admin/upload_data/remmag/10-3/Lanit.pdf. (in Russian)
5. Almeida, M.S., Ishikawa, M., Reinschmidt, J., Roeber, T.: Getting Started with Data Warehouse and Business Intelligence. IBM Corporation (1999)
6. Pendse, N.: OLAP Architectures: The OLAP Report, 18 January 1998
7. Sperley, E.: The Enterprise Data Warehouse: Planning, Building, and Implementation, 1st edn. Prentice Hall, Upper Saddle River (1999)
8. Rönnbäck, L., Regardt, O., Bergholtz, M., Johannesson, P., Wohed, P.: Anchor modeling – agile information modeling in evolving data environments. Data Knowl. Eng. **69**(12), 1229–1253 (2010). https://doi.org/10.1016/j.datak.2010.10.002
9. Transaction Processing Performance Council: TPC BenchmarkTM H Standard Specification Revision 2.17.2 (2017). http://www.tpc.org/tpc_documents_current_versions/pdf/tpc-h_v2.17.2.pdf
10. Graziano, K.: The Business Data Vault. Vertabelo Database Modeler, 3 November 2015. https://www.vertabelo.com/blog/data-vault-series-the-business-data-vault/
11. Hive benchmark. https://datacadamia.com/db/hive/benchmark#documentationreference

Heuristic Algorithm and Results of Computational Experiments of Solution of Graph Placement Problem

Boris Melnikov[1] (ID), Vladislav Dudnikov[2] (ID), and Svetlana Pivneva[2]([✉]) (ID)

[1] Russian State Social University, Wilhelm Pieck Str. 4, build. 1, 129226 Moscow, Russia
[2] Togliatti State University, Belorusskaja Str. 14, 445020 Togliatti, Russia

Abstract. Most of the problems on graphs are hard problems. Therefore, it is obvious that an exhaustive approach to solving problems will rarely succeed. Approaches considered by other authors are related to evolutionary modeling, genetic algorithms and other stochastic algorithms, and they have some success. However, some shortcomings are seen in these approaches. The authors propose an approach that is heuristic, but not stochastic. The paper presents a generalized mathematical model of the problem that enables considering the problem of placement in n-dimensional space as a problem of searching for permutations of n elements. This eliminates such shortcomings of algorithms for placing graphs, such as the possibility of control over the process of operation of the algorithm and the strong dependence of the search capabilities on the time complexity of the algorithm. The presented heuristic algorithm Hebene was built based on the corresponding mathematical description. Computational experiments were undertaken for all pairwise nonisomorphic connected graphs up to order 9 inclusive. The algorithm found the optimal solution in more than 50% of cases, the algorithm also yielded acceptable solutions in other situations.

Keywords: Heuristic algorithm · Graph placement problem · Computational experiments

1 Formal Setting of the Graph Placement Problem

It is common knowledge that a large number of graph-based problems are intractable [1]. This is primarily due to the fact that, in order to solve them, an exponentially large number of variants often need to be searched through, which normally renders complete enumeration impossible.

Thus, if we look at the general graph of the traveling salesman problem with 25 vertices based on the setting from [1], at the rate of search of 35 million variants per second, checking all the solutions will take as much time as has passed since the Big Bang (about 13.7 billion years). However, problems that arise in real applications, may have not 25, but many thousands of vertices. Therefore, it is obvious that a brute-force approach to solving problems would scarcely be successful.

V. Sukhomlin and E. Zubareva (Eds.): SITITO 2017, CCIS 1204, pp. 157–166, 2021.
https://doi.org/10.1007/978-3-030-78273-3_16

The graph placement problem was earlier addressed by other authors, e.g. in [2–4]. Evolutionary modeling algorithms and other stochastic algorithms (genetic algorithms, evolutionary algorithms, simulation normalization algorithm [5], etc.) were used in those papers with a some success. However, such approach has certain disadvantages:

- Inability to control the process of the algorithm (due to its stochastic nature);
- It is difficult to describe a class of problems for which this set of parameters (e.g., for a genetic algorithm) yields solutions close to optimum;
- Strong dependence of search abilities on the algorithm time complexity (parameters for the genetic algorithm can be set so that the optimum will still be found, but the running time will be close to the time of the complete enumeration algorithm).

In view of the foregoing imperfections, the authors suggest an approach that is heuristic, rather than stochastic (which eradicates the above disadvantages).

This section contemplates problem setting and suggests new terms to describe the general graph placement problem. The term "graph placement model" introduced by us is used throughout the paper. Content-wise graph placement model consists of the following components:

- a graph;
- a set of positions where the graph vertices are to be placed;
- a function that formally converts a natural number (position number) to a position from a set of positions;
- an estimating function.

Also, the model is used to describe the placement problem classes (e.g. the class of the problem of graph placement in the plane).

The proposed description of the placement problem generalizes the settings earlier proposed in [2, 3, 6].

Definition 1. *Graph placement model.*

We will call the quadruple a graph placement model $M = \langle G, M_\eta, H, f \rangle$, here

- $G = \langle V, E \rangle$ is a graph (V is a set of vertices, E is a set of edges);
- M_η is a set of multidimensional space placements (i.e., a set with elements $x_\eta = \langle m_1, m_2, ..., m_n \rangle$, where $m_i \in \mathbb{N}^\eta$, $n = |V|$);
- $H : X \to M_\eta$ (here X is a set of all placements $x = \langle x_1, x_2, ..., x_n \rangle$, with the property that $(\forall x_i, x_j \in V)(x_i \neq x_j)$);
- $f : M_\eta \to \mathbb{R}^+$

We will also introduce some terms that will be encountered in the paper, which are based on [7]:

- the model signature is a triple $\langle M_\eta, H, f \rangle$;
- model variant is defined by a subset of all possible entries. A variant of the model is a model with its specified signature;

- a special case of the problem is given based on the model variant with a specific graph definition.

The following problems can be examples of the model variant:

- the problem of placing graph vertices on a plane "in a coordinate grid";
- graph visualization problem described in the same way: the points of the coordinate plane are numbered, and the number of edge crossings in the graph is selected as an estimating function;
- the problem of placing elements of integrated circuits - in the simplest case, this problem, as per [8], matches the graph visualization problem.

We will discuss in more detail the example of graph visualization problem model. A triple like this can be the signature for such model $\langle M_2, I, g \rangle$:

- M_2 is a set of two-dimensional space positions;
- I is a function that converts the placement $x \in X$ in the placement $x_2 \in M_2$;
- $g(x_2)$ is a function that computes the number of edge crossings in the given placement.

Figure 1 represents a special case of graph visualization problem. A dotted line marks the grid of placement, in the grid corners the position numbers and their coordinates are marked. Thus, if $x = \langle 5, 4, 3, 2, 1 \rangle$, then $I(x) = \langle (0; 0), (1; 0), (0; 1), (1; 1), (0; 2) \rangle$, and $g(I(x)) = 1$.

The model $\langle G, M_1, H, f \rangle$ will be called the model of graph placement in a ruler, and $\langle G, M_2, H, f \rangle$ the model of graph placement in a grid (on a plane).

1.1 The Problem of Graph Placement Minimization

The problem is to minimize the function of the model f. If we consider the previous variant of the model for graph visualization problem, the problem is to minimize the number of edge crossings, that is, to find such a placement $x^* = \langle 1, 2, ..., n \rangle$ that $g(I(x^*)) \rightarrow \min_{x \in X} g(I(x^*))$.

The problem can be described in a more formal way as follows.

Thus, a special case of the placement problem is given. A placement should be found $x^* = \langle x_1^*, x_2^*, ..., x_n^* \rangle$ such that

$$(\forall x \in X)(f(H(x^*)) \leq f(H(x)),$$

where X is a set of all permutations $\langle 1, 2, ..., n \rangle$.

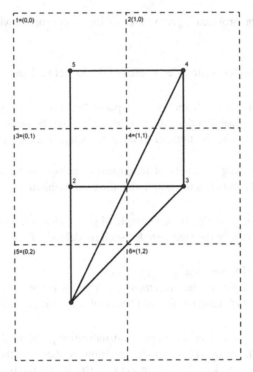

Fig. 1. Example of a special case of graph visualization problem.

The paper goes on to contemplate variants of the model with

$$f(x) = \sum_{i=1}^{n-1} \sum_{j=i+1}^{n} a(x_i, x_j) d(x_i, x_j), \tag{1}$$

where $a(x_i, x_j)$ – element of adjacency matrix of graph, $d(x_i, x_j)$ is a function that determines the distance in any metric space between a pair of placement positions x.

2 Heuristic Algorithm of Pseudooptimal Graph Placement

We will describe pseudooptimal graph placement algorithm named *Hebene* (abbreviated HEuristics of BEst NEighbor) using flowcharts. Figure 2 shows a flowchart of *HebeneIter* procedure. *HebeneIter* procedure is a single iteration of the *Hebene* algorithm.

Figure 3 presents *Hebene* algorithm flowchart that uses *HebeneIter* procedure.

The algorithm shown in flowcharts is divided into two procedures. First procedure exchanges all pairs of vertices, and if the value of the target function improves, it returns true value, otherwise it returns false. Second procedure executes first procedure until it returns false.

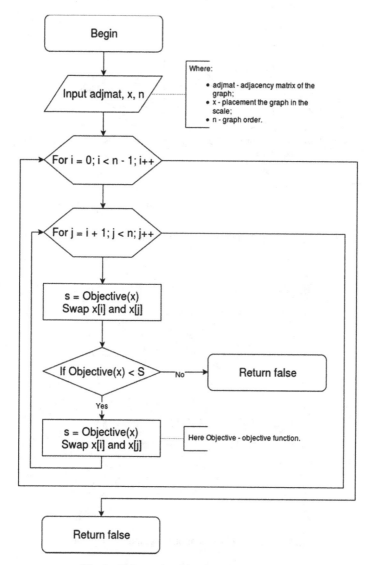

Fig. 2. *Hebene* algorithm iteration flowchart.

3   Computational Experiment

First of all, we will give a clear example of the work of *Hebene* algorithm aimed at graph placement in the plane. Figures 4 and 5 represent the same graph, however, the graph in Fig. 4 is selected as the one with a random placement, while the placement for the Fig. 5 graph is found by *Hebene* algorithm. The purpose of the algorithm was minimizing the number of intersections between the edges.

Now we will present the results of our computational experiments in more detail. To conduct computational experiments, the authors considered all pairwise nonisomorphic

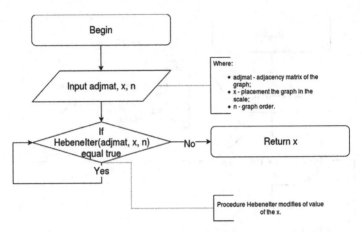

Fig. 3. *Hebene* algorithm flowchart.

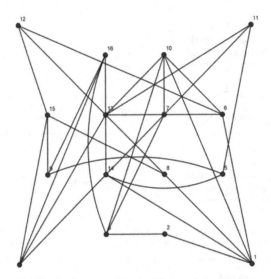

Fig. 4. Random placement of the graph in the plane.

connected graphs of orders 3 to 9. The number of connected pairwise nonisomorphic graphs for the calculated orders is listed in Table 1. Line p indicates the order of the graphs, and line C_p – the number of pairwise nonisomorphic connected graphs.

For each graph minima of the problem of graph placement minimization were then calculated using the complete enumeration algorithm. This provided data to compare the capabilities of the proposed heuristic algorithm.

Figures 6, 7 and 8 show comparison graphs of optimal solutions found (using complete enumeration method), and solutions found using *Hebene* algorithm for orders 7, 8 and 9, respectively.

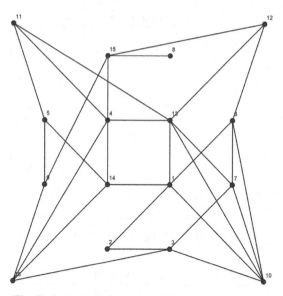

Fig. 5. Optimized placement of the graph in the plane.

Table 1. Number of pairwise non-isomorphic graphs.

p	3	4	5	6	7	8	9
C_p	2	6	21	112	853	11117	261080

It is noteworthy that complete enumeration did not find optimal solutions for all order 9 graphs. Out of 261080 graphs, optimal solutions were found for 18961 graphs. Consequently, Fig. 5 shows a comparison graph only for optimal solutions found.

We can see from the comparison graphs that they are similar, specifically in the property that the relative number of optimal solutions found by *Hebene* algorithm is more than 50% for the orders under consideration (3 to 9). Also, as can be seen from the graphs below, the difference between the optimal solutions and the solutions found by *Hebene* algorithm increases as the number of graphs decreases.

This review of the experiment results demonstrates distribution of solutions found by *Hebene* algorithm as compared to optimal solutions. However, let us also consider the quantitative estimate for all graphs combined. We will take as an estimate the ratio of the total number of values of the estimating function for all optimal solutions to the number of values of the estimating function for the solutions found by *Hebene* algorithm. Specifically:

$$O^h(G) = \frac{\sum\limits_{g \in G} f(x^*)}{\sum\limits_{g \in G} f(x^h)},$$

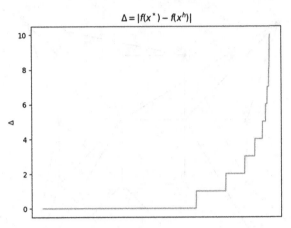

Fig. 6. Comparison graph for graphs of order 7.

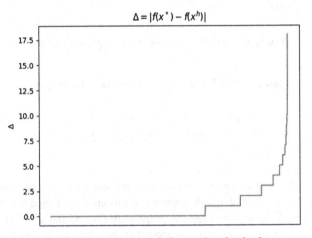

Fig.7. Comparison graph for graphs of order 8.

where G is a set of all pairwise nonisomorphic graphs, x^*, same as before, is optimal solution for this graph, x^h is the solution found using *Hebene* algorithm. The results of such criterion for the graphs under consideration are summarized in Table 2.

This criterion shows how optimal solutions are for all graphs. In other words, if the value of the criterion is equal to 1, the algorithm will always find the optimal solutions. For clarity, we will show the criterion value for the same graphs, but for randomly selected solutions, i.e.:

$$O^r(G) = \frac{\sum\limits_{g \in G} f(x^*)}{\sum\limits_{g \in G} f(x^r)},$$

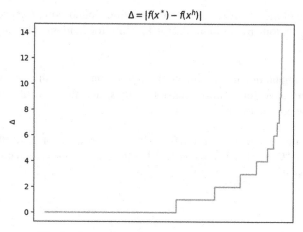

Fig. 8. Comparison graph for graphs of order 9.

Table 2. Criterion results $O^h(G)$ for the graphs under consideration.

p	7	8	9
$O^h(G)$	0.9641	0.9729	0.9612

where x^r is the randomly selected solution for graph g [9]. Table 3 summarizes the results of the assessment $O^r(G)$ for same graphs as above.

Table 3. Results of $O^r(G)$ criterion for reviewed graphs.

p	7	8	9
$O^r(G)$	0.5496	0.5340	0.4456

4   Conclusion

Therefore, computational experiments for the suggested algorithm were carried out for all pairwise non-isomorphic graphs up to order 9 inclusive (as mentioned earlier due to computational complexity, not all graphs of order 9 were considered). During the computational experiments it was established that:

- the distribution of objective function values for solutions found using *Hebene* algorithm is sufficiently close to the distribution of objective function values for solutions found using complete enumeration, and the number of optimal solutions found using *Hebene* exceeds 50%;

- the total value of the objective function for solutions found using *Hebene* differs from the optimal solutions by no more than 4%, while for random solutions the average value is 50%;

Based on computational experiments it can be concluded, that the algorithm has proved to be effective for small dimension graphs, and therefore it requires further research for higher dimension graphs.

Acknowledgements. The work was carried out within the framework of the RFBR grant project No. 17-46-630560 "Conceptual innovation model of the socio-ecological and economic system of the Samara region".

References

1. Garey, M.R., Johnson, D.S.: Computers and Intractability: A Guide to the Theory of NP-Completeness. W.H. Freeman & Co., New York (1979)
2. Emelyanov, V.V., Kureichik, V.M., Kureichik, V.V.: Theory and Practice of Evolutionary Modeling. Fizmatlit Publ., Moscow (1982).(in Russian)
3. Balyuk, V.V.: Genetic algorithms for solving the problem of placing VLSI elements. Izvestiya SFedU. Eng. Sci. (8), 65–71 (2006). https://www.elibrary.ru/item.asp?id=12792652. (in Russian)
4. Kostina, M.A., Melnikova, E.A.: Artificial intelligence algorithms in the problem of graph visualization. Sci. Vector Togliatti State Univ. (3), 32–35 (2014). https://www.elibrary.ru/item.asp?id=22888640. (in Russian)
5. Melnikov, B.F., Eyrih, S.N.: On the approach to combining truncated branch-and-bound method and simulated annealing. Proc. Voronezh State Univ. Ser. Syst. Anal. Inf. Technol. (1), 35–38 (2010). https://www.elibrary.ru/item.asp?id=15199645. (in Russian)
6. Dudnikov, V.A.: Genetic algorithm for solving the optimization problem of locations graph vertices in the line. Heurist. Alg. Distrib. Comput. **2**(2), 60–68 (2015). https://www.elibrary.ru/item.asp?id=29383559. (in Russian)
7. Hromkovich, J.: Deterministic approaches to algorithmics for hard computing problems. Part I: the main definitions. Heurist. Alg. Distrib. Comput. **1**(2), 30–42 (2014). https://www.elibrary.ru/item.asp?id=22030663. (in Russian)
8. Lisyak, M.V.: Hybrid algorithm for multicriteria placement of VLSI elements. Izvestiya SFedU. Eng. Sci. (7), 77–84 (2012). https://www.elibrary.ru/item.asp?id=17864078. (in Russian)
9. Melnikov, B.F., Sayfullina, E.F.: Applying multiheuristic approach o randomly generating graphs with a given degree sequence. Univ. Proc. Volga Region Phys. Math. Sci. (3), 70–83 (2013). https://www.elibrary.ru/item.asp?id=21315166. (in Russian)

Building of Virtual Multidocuments Mapping to Real Sources of Data in Situation-Oriented Databases

Valery Mironov⬤, Artem Gusarenko$^{(\boxtimes)}$ ⬤, and Nafisa Yusupova⬤

Ufa State Aviation Technical University, Karl Marx Str. 12, 450008 Ufa, Russia
{mironov,gusarenko}@ugatu.su, yussupova@ugatu.ac.ru

Abstract. Within the framework of the Polyglot Persistence approach, a situationally-oriented database is considered - an information processor within a web application that processes XML/JSON documents based on the HSM hierarchical situational model. A flexibility task in HSM of mapping virtual documents for real data from various physical storages is discussed. In order to embed new data warehouses, it is suggested to follow the principle of invariance, the model does not change when embedding a new mapping. An approach mapping embedding is proposed, which provides for each new type of storage the development of three modules: manipulation, loading and saving, implemented as callback functions. To embed three modules working with the repository, a common plug-in technology is used. The approach is illustrated by the example of mapping to the table of the relational database SQLite. The advantages of the approach and practical implementation on the PHP platform are discussed and demonstrated on SQLite database.

Keywords: Situation-oriented database · Web application · Dynamic model · Finite state model · NoSQL · HSM · XML · DOM

1 Introduction

Recently, in the field of data processing technologies, the Polyglot Persistence approach is widely discussed - the sharing of data from heterogeneous storages within a single application [1]. This approach develops in close interaction with the NoSQL movement (Not only SQL - the use of nonrelational databases along with relational ones) [2]. In contrast to the relational approach (based on the SQL language), when all the application functions are carried out based on a relational database, and the database management system (DBMS) focused on a wide range of storage features and data retrieval for solving "any problems", NoSQL approach focuses on an effective solution within a single DBMS for relatively narrow classes of tasks, usually connected with web processing of so-called "big data" (Big Data). The Polyglot Persistence approach involves the use combination flexible different types of data warehouses managed by different databases within a single application. In this case, access to individual repositories is controlled by the corresponding "native" DBMS, and a front-end server is created for coordination and

V. Sukhomlin and E. Zubareva (Eds.): SITITO 2017, CCIS 1204, pp. 167–179, 2021.
https://doi.org/10.1007/978-3-030-78273-3_17

integration [2]. The development of the front-end server requires programming in Web-based procedural languages using application programming interfaces (APIs) provided by the respective storages.

This article discusses the use of context-oriented databases (front-line database) as a front-end server. SODB based on MDA (Model-Driven Approach - an approach to the management of Web-based applications highly abstract models and notations [1–7]), implementing virtual repository of documents in hierarchical XML and/or the JSON, shown on many disparate real-world data, with access in the context of the current situation [17–20].

The architectural features of the SODB in terms of Polyglot Persistence are explained in Fig. 1.

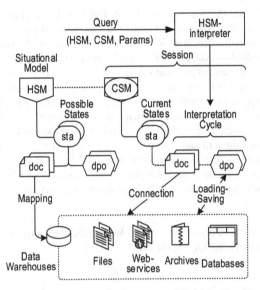

Fig. 1. DBMS architecture in the aspect of Polyglot Persistence.

The developer constructs in a declarative form and places the HSM-Hierarchical Situation Model in the form of a hierarchy of submodels that define possible states and transitions of the serviced business process. In HSM-states, virtual documents (*doc* - Virtual Multi-Document) are defined, which determine the mapping to real data of various kinds: local files, remote web services, archives, databases, etc. In addition, the states declare data processing objects (*dpo* - Data Processing Object) that reference virtual documents. Each situational model stored in the SODB is processed by the HSM interpreter on external requests. An external query generates an HSM interpretation cycle, and the interconnected sequence of cycles forms an interpretation session. On each cycle for the HSM being processed, the interpreter builds the Current State Model (CSM) model, monitoring the state transitions of the submodels - on the first session cycle - relative to the initial states, on the subsequent cycle - relative to the current states of the previous cycle. In addition, on each cycle for the current states, in accordance with the definitions of *doc* and *dpo*, virtual document mapping objects and data processing objects are created. Data processing objects process documents from real repositories. Thus, the SODB enables the developer to set conditions and rules for accessing data in situationally-oriented form and takes on routine operations of interaction with real data. This simplifies the programming of applications that support business processes with the situational nature of development.

2   The Task of Embedding New Mappings

In the early versions of SODB, data was processed in the form of XML documents from local files, access to which was carried out directly. The mapping task occurred when you had to process documents stored in zip archives, in databases, and provided by remote web services also. An intermediate layer of virtual documents was introduced, which maps the internal documents of the SODB to external data located in various repositories. Virtual documents are specified by means of doc-elements, which are placed in the HSM-model as the child elements of states (Fig. 2).

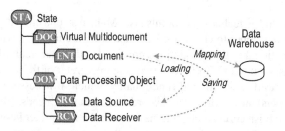

Fig. 2. Specification of virtual multidocument in model.

Each doc-element defines a so-called virtual multidocument, which can contain multiple mappings to a single repository. A virtual multidocument is characterized by its external type – *type*, which corresponds to the data store type, as well as the virtual type – *vtype* corresponding to the type of the internal SODB document. Currently built-in mappings support virtual types of XML and JSON, as well as external types:

- XML and JSON are documents stored in local files or retrieved for reading by the GET method from remote web services over the HTTP protocol;
- ZIP - documents, packed in zip-archives;
- MySQLi - documents from the relational database MySQL, stored either entirely in the table cell ("concentrated" method), or ("distributed" method).

The virtual document processing declarations are separated from the handling declarations of virtual documents and are specified in the HSM-model using data processing objects. The problem of diversity, which it is almost impossible to cover entirely. First, there is a wide variety of different data storages, both traditional relational and NoSQL-storages, which are rapidly developing at the present time. For example, the

PHP platform has built-in modules for interacting with more than two dozen databases, not counting the solutions that are offered by independent developers. Embedding all of them will require a lot of labor. Secondly, it is a variety of mapping functions. Many options, functions and modes. For example, the module for interacting with the MySQL database in PHP includes many methods and properties. The implementation of them in full implies greater labor intensity. While a particular application requires only a small subset. If modern databases are blamed for complexity, then the integrator of the set of databases, realizing all their capabilities, will be super complicated.

It is often necessary to implement only some functions of working with the repository, rather than managing it in its entirety. For example, extracting and saving documents, and the creation of a database, tables, views is implemented by the database administrator. In these conditions, flexibility is necessary.

In fact, this approach has long been known - add-ins can also be used in the interpreter and in the model. The question is how to implement this in this case, in relation to the SODB.

3   The Idea of Embedding Mappings

The idea is to use plug-in technology for this task. Make it so that embedding a new mapping requires the developer to create well-defined software modules with standardized interfaces and functionality that are simply connected to the interpreter of the situational models. Then this would not affect the core of the interpreter of the situational models, but will allow to build in the limited functionality, which, if necessary, can be further extended by independent developers in accordance with their needs. This requires you to develop and establish certain conventions for both the interpreter kernel and plug-ins - what modules should be used, how to connect them to the interpreter, how to call the modules, how to exchange information with modules (interaction interfaces), and so on.

The composition of the mapping embedding modules and their interaction with the interpreter core is explained in figure submodel presented in the center (Fig. 3, b) sub:Proc reflects the basic moments of setting virtual documents and processing the relevant real data.

The sta:Main state of the submodel serves the normal operation situation, and sta:Errors - the error situation. In the sta:Main state, a multi-document doc:MD1 is defined with a mapping to a real data storage of some type T1, containing two virtual documents: ent:D1 and ent:D2. In addition, in this state, the DOM – dom:P1, specifying the processing of virtual documents, is defined. Loading a document into a DOM-object can be specified either by using the explicit source element src:S1 with the doc-attribute, or by using the implicit one in the form of the loadDoc attribute in the dom-element itself. Similarly, unloading (saving) a document from a DOM-object can be specified either using an explicit receiver element rcv:R1 with the doc-attribute, or with an implicit - in the form of thesaveDoc attribute in the dom-element itself. Attributes doc, loadDoc, and saveDoc refer to the virtual documents D1 and D2 of the multidocument MD1.

During the processing of the situational model, the HSM-interpreter creates in the operative memory global arrays, available when processing various HSM-elements

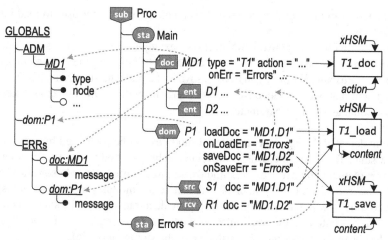

Fig. 3. Modules for embedding the mapping and their interaction with the interpreter core: a - global arrays; b - HSM model; c - mapping embedding modules.

(Fig. 3, a). So, when processing a doc-element in an array of VAD (Associated Data Memory), a sub-array with the key-the local name of the multidocument (in this case MD1) is entered. In this sub-array, the element type (key type) is placed, a reference to the corresponding node in the situational model (node key), as well as specific objects providing this type of mapping (for example, identifiers and connection parameters serving the communication channel with the database in which it is stored documentation). When processing a dom-element, the interpreter creates a global DOM-object with a key-the name of the dom-element (in this case dom: P1), in which the virtual document is processed. Similarly, when processing an arr-element, oriented to JSON-documents, the interpreter creates a global associative array with a key - the name of the arr-element (not shown in the figure). If errors are detected during the processing of doc/dom/arr -elements, the interpreter creates the appropriate sub-arrays in the global ERRs error array, where it records error information.

Thus, the specificity of a particular type mapping of a virtual document to real data is manifested in three separate stages of the interpretation of the situational model. This makes it advisable to introduce three independent modules that take into account the features of the embedded mapping (Fig. 3, c):

1. The module for manipulating the multidocument (in our example T1_doc). This module is invoked by the interpreter when processing the doc-element so that it creates specific objects of interaction with the storage of this type and/or performs certain actions with data in the repository. As inputs to the module, the xHSM reference is transmitted to the current HSM-element of the situational model and the value of the action attribute that defines the required actions;

2. The module for loading the document (in our example - T1_load). It starts when the dom-element is processed with the loadDoc attribute and the src-element with the doc-attribute and must return as content result a virtual XML document

extracted from the real data storage. This result the interpreter uses to load into the DOM-object;

3. The module for saving the document (in our example - T1_save). It starts when the dom-element is processed with the saveDoc attribute and the rcv-element with the doc-attribute. From it, you need to save in the real data storage an XML content document that was unloaded by the interpreter from the DOM-object and passed to the module as an input parameter.

Errors detected during the execution of modules can be processed by transitioning to a new state. To do this, the onErr attribute can be specified in the doc-element, and in the dom-element, the onLoadErr and onSaveErr attributes, whose values are the name of the transition state. If an error is detected, the modules must return a result of true, according to which the interpreter will provide a transition to the state specified in the onErr attribute (for the manipulation module), in the onLoadErr attribute (for the loader) or in the onSaveErr attribute (for the storage module).

In the research prototype of the HSM-interpreter on the PHP platform, mapping embedding modules are implemented as call-back functions. The interpreter "on the fly" generates the name of the function, based on the type of mapping and the functionality of the module, and calls it to execute.

The operation of the HSM-interpreter when processing VAD with mapping to various formats of real data is based on the use of built-in PHP modules for interaction with external data: files, databases, archives, web services, etc. For internal data processing, interaction through global associative arrays. In accordance with this approach, when processing a situational model for each virtual document specified in a state that is current on this interpretation cycle, the interpreter creates an eponymous global array in the operative memory in which the parameters and objects necessary for accessing real documents are placed. With further processing of sources and data receivers referencing a virtual document, the interpreter accesses the corresponding global array, thereby obtaining the information necessary to access the real documents. Errors detected during the processing of virtual documents are also reflected in the global array - an array of errors, the presence of which allows you to program the response to errors - change the current state, notify the user of an error, and so on.

4   Embedding the Mapping with the SQLite Example

This work illustrates the proposed approach by the example of mapping virtual documents on the SQLite database - a simple relational database that does not requires a stand-alone server, but implemented in the form of module libraries. This will store XML/JSON documents in the cells of the database tables of this type. We will be guided by the advanced version supported in PHP by the SQLite3 module [3] and we will use the appropriate type when specifying virtual documents. Let us need simple ways of saving the document entirely in the table cell and, accordingly, extracting the document from it (the "concentrated" approach). In accordance with the above, for embedding you need to create three callback functions: SQLite3_doc, SQLite3_load and SQLite3_save. These functions have been programmed and connected as plugins.

`SQLite3_doc function`. This function is executed by the HSM-interpreter when processing a doc-element with the attribute `type = "SQLite3"` and acts based on the value analysis of the action attribute. For our simple case, it provides three options for action:

- `action = "connect::databaseData#flags"` - connects to the specified database. A new instance of the SQLite3 class object is created from the PHP library, which for later use is placed in the VAD global array element corresponding to the doc-element being processed. When the SQLite3 object is created, the database is automatically created if it is not available at the specified address, and opens (with the specified flags, if any) for access through the object;
- `action = "disconnect"` - the connection to the database is terminated using the close method of the SQLite3 object, and the object itself is deleted from the VAD array;
- `action = "exec::requests"` - SQL queries are sent to the database using the exec method of the SQLite3 object. At a time, a series of queries on the SQL dialect used in SQLite3 can be passed.
- If the syntax of the action attribute is violated, as well as when errors occur in the operation of the SQLite3 object, the internal `ErrTrigger` function of HSM-interpreter error handling is invoked, to which the corresponding message is sent as a parameter.

`SQLite3_load function`. This function is executed by the HSM-interpreter at the initial processing of the dpo-element with the attribute `srcDoc`, which refers to a doc-element of the SQLite3 type. It returns a document extracted from the table cell of the SQLite3 database, to load it into the processing object.

The value of the `srcDoc` attribute in the global VAD array is used to find the description of the desired doc-element. A corresponding entry element is searched for and its cell attribute is parsed:

$$cell = "table.column [string]",$$

where the `table` is the name of the table (the default is the docs table); `column` - column name in the table (default column is `doc`); string is the row ID of the `rowid` table (default is 1). Based on these parameters, a SQL query is generated

`SELECT column FROM table WHERE rowid = string`,

which is sent to the database using the `querySingle` method of the SQLite3 object. The result of this query, which is a retrieved document, is returned by this function as a result string.

If the syntax of the cell attribute is violated or when errors occur in the functioning of the SQLite3 object, the internal `ErrTrigger` function of the error processing is called in which the appropriate message is sent as a parameter.

`SQLite3_save function`. This function is executed by the HSM-interpreter at the final processing of the dpo-element with the attribute `srcSave`, which refers to a doc-element of the SQLite3 type. It gets a textual representation of the document extracted from the processing object to store it in the table cell of the SQLite3 database.

By the value of the `srcDoc` attribute in the global VAD array, a description of the desired doc-element is searched, and a corresponding entry element is searched for and is parsed in the same way as is done by the `SQLite3_load function`. Based on the parameters of the cell attribute, an SQL query is generated

```
INSERT OR REPLACE INTO table (rowid, column)
(string, 'Content'),
```

where `Content` is a string with the content of the document received by the function as an input parameter. The query is sent to the database using the exec method of the SQLite3 object to be stored in the corresponding cell.

As in the previous function, if the syntax of the cell attribute is violated or when errors occur in the functioning of the SQLite3 object, the internal `ErrTrigger` function of error processing is called, to which the corresponding message is sent as a parameter.

5   Example of a Model with a Mapping to SQLite

As an example of using the mapping capabilities on SQLite, consider a situation model that provides a document from a remote web service and stores it in a cell in a SQLite table, and then retrieved and displayed to the user. First, consider this task for an XML document (Fig. 4), and then for a JSON document (Fig. 5).

In Fig. 4, a model of some XML-services of the Central Bank of Russia http://www.cbr.ru/scripts/ (a guide to currency codes, lists of quotations of currency, dynamics of quotations of the US dollar and precious metals for the current year). Details the structure of the XML document used in the example - the list of the latest currency quotes generated on the XML_daily.asp web page. The root XML element `ValCurs` contains two `attributes`: `Date` - the date of quotations, and `name` - the name of the document. It includes a number of child `Currency` XML elements corresponding to certain currency types, with the `ID attribute` - the currency identifier - and the child XML `elements`: `NumCode` and `CharCode` - numeric and symbolic currency codes; `Nominal` and `Name` - denomination and name of the currency; `Value` - the price for the nominal.

HSM model sta:SQLite-Processing, shown in Fig. 4, b, specifies:

- a virtual multidocument `doc:CentroBank` with the document `ent:Last` - the list of the latest quotes;
- The virtual multidocument `doc:xmlDoc` with the `ent:cell` document that is located in the cell of the first row of the doc-column of the docs table is mapped to the DB/sqlitedocs database. The first instance of `doc:xmlDoc` uses the action attribute to create a database (if it is not available) and connect to it. The second instance of `doc:xmlDoc` sends two SQL statements to the database to delete the docs table (if it exists) and to create a new instance of this table (thereby ensuring the self-sufficiency of this example in terms of independence from its previous execution; whether it is required);

- `sub:proc` subcode, whose states `sta:proc` and `sta:errProc` provide processing of the XML document of current currency quotes in normal conditions and when errors occur.

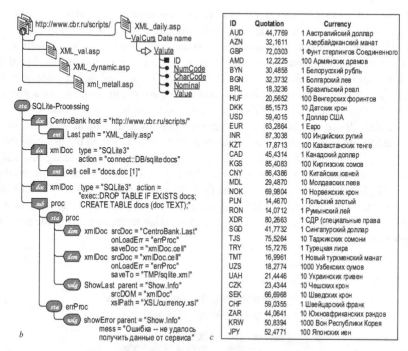

Fig. 4. An example of using a mapping on SQLite for XML documents: a) - a model of XML-services of the Central Bank of Russia; b) - HSM model of obtaining XML-document through a service with saving in SQLite; c) - the result of processing the document for display to the user.

In the `sta:proc` state, the first instance of `dom:xmlDoc` creates a DOM-object and loads into it the XML virtual document Last (the list of quotations) specified in `doc:CentroBank`. The `onLoadErr` attribute specifies the transition state in case of an error when loading the DOM-object. The `saveDoc` attribute instructs to save the contents of the DOM-object as a cell document of the `xmlDoc` virtual multidocument, i.e., in the cell of the SQLite database table.

The second instance of the element `dom:xmlDoc` demonstrates retrieving a document previously stored in the SQLite database in the DOM-object. The `saveTo` attribute instructs to save the contents of the DOM-object in the TMP/sqlite.xml file for test control.

Widget-element `wdg:showLast` demonstrates the processing of the XML document loaded in the DOM-object. It creates an image for the user by XSL-transformation of the contents of the DOM-object an XML document loaded into the DOM-object specified by the `srcDOM` attribute is transformed into HTML-code according to the stylesheet specified by the `xslPath` attribute. The result of the transformation (Fig. 4,

c) represents the table, each line of which corresponds to the currency, the value of the CharCode is displayed in the "Code" column, the "Value" column is shown in the "Quotation" column, and the Nominal and Name clings are in the "Currency" column. The generated HTML-code is embedded in the parent widget specified by the parent attribute.

In the sta:errProc state, an error message is generated using the wdg:showError widget; the message text is specified by the mess attribute.

In Fig. 5 shows an HSM-model, similar to the model on Fig. 4, b and designed to solve the same problem, but based on JSON documents. Here, the processing of the XML document received from the web service is specified using the arr-element that generates the data processing object as an associative array. This initiates the automatic conversion of the document to JSON format and loading it into an associative array.

The JSON document, like the previous example XML document, is stored in the cell of the SQLite table, and then extracted from there for display in the user's browser. The wdg:showLast widget in this example demonstrates the processing of a JSON document loaded into an associative array. The image for the user here is formed by Smarty-template the JSON-document from the associative array specified by the attribute srcArr, is transformed into HTML-code according to the tpl-template specified by the tplPath attribute. The result of the transformation is the same as in the previous example (see Fig. 4, c).

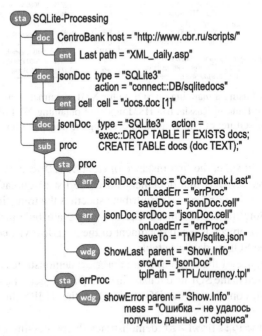

Fig. 5. An example of mapping using on SQLite for JSON documents.

The examples examined are programmed, debugged and tested on the HSM-interpreter prototype. This confirms the operability of the proposed approach. For the convenience of the readers, the HSM-code of the situational models, the contents of the files used in the examples, are presented on the site of the project of situationally oriented databases http://hsm.ugatu.su/codesamples/ (for access in the left menu "Categories" select the item "Virtual documents "and the sub-item" SQLite", then select the item corresponding to the model).

6   Issues of Effectiveness

Compared with previous SODB. The ability to embed new maps not only by authors, but also by other developers in accordance with their needs. This simplifies the adaptation to the needs of the developer - in the amount of functionality that is required in this case.

Note that, although the software processing of documents in the examples is different (in the first case, the XML document is used as a tree in the DOM-object, in the second - the JSON-document representation in the form of an associative array), the situational models differ insignificantly. This indicates a high level of abstraction of the HSM-language in general.

Compared with manual programming. The effect of using the proposed approach is to reduce the complexity of programming a web application built based on SODB, in comparison with traditional "manual" programming in server scripting languages such as PHP. This is achieved through a higher level of abstraction of the HSM-model, when the many routine operations necessary to implement the functions specified in the declarative form in the definitions of virtual multidocuments are assigned to the HSM-model interpreter. These operations include establishing a connection to a real data storages, converting real data to an XML format, loading, processing, and uploading data. The calculations carried out by the authors show that this reduces the amount of program code (in comparison with manual PHP programming) to the part necessary for processing virtual XML documents up to 15 times, which gives a 5-fold reduction in the total volume of the HSM-model code (for the examples considered).

7   Conclusion

Thus, the concept of virtual documents mapped to real data warehouses allows the use of situational-oriented databases as a front-end server in web applications implementing the Polyglot Persistence approach. Practical implementation in the conditions of a wide variety of storages requires a mechanism for embedding mappings. The proposed technology for mappings embedding is based on the development for each new type of storage of three modules with standardized names and interfaces that are called by the interpreter. The manipulation module provides connection to the storage and transmission of specific requests to it; the loader extracts the virtual document from the store to be loaded into the data processing object; the save module writes a virtual document retrieved from the data processing object to the storage. The proposed approach is illustrated by the example of embedding a mapping on a relational database SQLite for data processing objects in XML and JSON formats. A high level abstraction of the declarative situational model in comparison with procedural programming languages, that the smaller the amount of program code. Uniformity of models of processing documents from various physical storages. As a result, simplification and convenience of programming web applications.

References

1. Delgado, A., Marotta, A., González, L.: Towards the construction of quality-aware Web Warehouses with BPMN 2.0 business processes. In: 2014 IEEE Eighth International Conference on Research Challenges in Information Science (RCIS), Marrakech, pp. 1–6 (2014). https://doi.org/10.1109/RCIS.2014.6861041
2. Delgado, A., Marotta, A.: Automating the process of building flexible Web Warehouses with BPM systems. In: 2015 Latin American Computing Conference (CLEI), Arequipa, pp. 1–11 (2015). https://doi.org/10.1109/CLEI.2015.7360005
3. Bogacheva, A.N., Zilov, A.A., Soloviev, A.V., Tishchenko, V.A., Shchelkacheva, I.V.: Experience in the use of map services to display geographic data from the database Nika. Proc. Inst. Syst. Anal. Russ. Acad. Sci. **66**(3), 45–54 (2016). https://www.elibrary.ru/item.asp?id=27165918. (in Russian)
4. Keyno, P., Siluyanov, A.: Design and implementation of a declarative web-interface modeling language interpreter on a high-performance distributed systems. J. Appl. Inform. **10**(1), 55–70 (2015). https://www.elibrary.ru/item.asp?id=23030387. (in Russian)
5. Pinheiro, P.V.P., Endo, A.T., Simao, A.: Model-based testing of RESTful web services using UML protocol state machines. In: Brazilian Workshop on Systematic and Automated Software Testing (2013)
6. Agustin, J.L.H., del Barco, P.C.: A model-driven approach to develop high performance web applications. J. Syst. Softw. **86**(12), 3013–3023 (2013). https://doi.org/10.1016/j.jss.2013.07.028
7. Daniel, F., Matera, M.: Model-driven software development. In: Daniel, F., Matera, M. (eds.) Mashups. DSA, pp. 71–93. Springer, Heidelberg (2014). https://doi.org/10.1007/978-3-642-55049-2_4

Methods, Algorithms and Software for the UML Class Diagram Refactoring

Olga Deryugina⑩ and Evgeny Nikulchev(✉) ⑩

MIREA – Russian Technological University, Vernadsky Ave. 78, 119454 Moscow, Russia

Abstract. This article considers the problem of UML class diagram refactoring. It gives a brief overview of the approaches to the UML class diagram describing, transformation and refactoring. Article also proposes a software tool for the UML class diagram refactoring called UML Refactoring. This software tool provides import of diagrams in XMI format, OO-metrics calculation. UML Refactoring tool searches for the transformations, which decrease a fitness function value. Article presents an algorithm of a prototype CLANG plugin, which receives C++ source code at the input and returns UML class diagram in XMI format.

Keywords: UML refactoring · UML diagram refactoring · UML diagram transformation · Class diagrams · UML diagrams · UML · MDA

1 Introduction

With the growth of a UML class diagram size increases time needed for designer to analyze and edit it: searching for the diagram elements becomes more complicated as well as making changes or standard metrics calculating.

So for the UML class diagrams of a big size it becomes important to use software tools, which provide automated analysis, editing and equivalent transformations application.

To be able to analyze (calculate metrics, search for elements, to which design pattern should be applied, etc.) and transform UML class diagrams the abstract data structure should be used. The abstract data structure can be based on various types of formal methods. Formal methods of UML class diagram description are proposed in the Table 1.

Main approaches to the UML class diagram transformation are described in the Table 2.

Refactoring is the restructuring of the system, which keeps it's functionality invariant. Usually refactoring is conducted on the source code level and is aimed at improving such characteristics as understandability, modifiability and maintainability.

The most significant works on the refactoring are the following: [12–15]. These works describe object-oriented design patterns, refactoring recipes, object oriented design principles, etc.

However, some of the refactoring methods, which were introduced for the source code level, can be conducted on the UML class diagram level. Model refactoring has

V. Sukhomlin and E. Zubareva (Eds.): SITITO 2017, CCIS 1204, pp. 179–191, 2021.
https://doi.org/10.1007/978-3-030-78273-3_18

Table 1. Formal methods of the UML class diagram description.

Method	Advantages	Disadvantages
Graphical [1]	Visualization	Complexity of the computer processing
Based on the specialized modeling languages [2–6]	Standardization. Automatic validation	For the XMI format: search complexity is O(n)
Based on the algebra of logic [7–9]	High level of formalization	Complexity of the computer processing
Based on the graph theory [10, 11]	High level of formalization. Well-developed methods of computer processing	It is not obvious how to describe UML class diagram packages

Table 2. Main approaches to the UML class diagram transformation.

Approach	Advantages	Disadvantages
Determined	Computational effectiveness	Low modifiability
Specialized model transformation languages	Standardization. High modifiability	Transformation description can be rather complicated
Graph transformations	Well-developed mathematical methods	None

several advantages. First, model transformations applied on the design stage can reduce software development cost. Second, model transformation are less error-prone than code refactoring.

UML class diagram refactoring approaches are described in the Table 3.

1.1 Search Based Approach to the UML Class Diagram Refactoring

Algorithm takes at the input UML class diagram d, a fitness function n, a set of transformations T and a permissible accuracy level ε.

Algorithm gives at the output UML class diagram d' whose fitness value is locally or globally optimal.

Search based approach is connected with the Search Base Software Engineering (SBSE) methods [16]. SBSE methods solve software engineering problems using heuristic algorithms (GA, simulated annealing, swarm intelligence, etc.

Some researchers conduct UML class diagram refactoring using SBSE methods [17–26], including design pattern application, design of the software system hierarchy, class structure design, specification based software design.

The disadvantage of the search based approach is that the result of the heuristic algorithm can have optimal fitness value but be not satisfiable for the user.

Search based UML class diagram tools include the following: Darwin [19], Dearthoir [24], CODe-Imp [25], Bunch tool [26], etc.

Table 3. Main approaches to the UML class diagram refactoring

Approach	Description	Advantages	Disadvantages
Search based [17–26]	Algorithm takes at the input fitness function, UML class diagram, a set of transformations and permissible accuracy level. Heuristic algorithm searches for a diagram, which has the optimal fitness value	1. Algorithm finds at least a local extremum of the fitness function 2. Well-developed evolutional methods, including: genetic algorithm, simulated annealing, swarm intelligence algorithms, etc.	The result of the heuristic search can be not satisfiable for the user
Advisory system [27]	Algorithm takes at the input fitness function, UML class diagram, a set of transformations. Algorithm proposes to the user a list of transformations, which improve fitness function value	The final decision is given to the user, who has more information about the system	Extremum for the fitness function is very likely no to be found

1.2   Advisory system approach to the UML class diagram refactoring

Algorithm takes at the input UML class diagram d, a fitness function n, a set of transformations T and a permissible accuracy level ε.

Algorithm gives at the output UML class diagram d' with the improved fitness value. The user makes the final decision which transformations are necessary to be applied.

The disadvantage of the advisory system approach is that the result fitness value is not likely to be optimal.

In terms of the advisory system approach the problem of the UML class diagram refactoring can be formulated as follows:

Assume that there is a UML class diagram d, a set of semantically equivalent transformations T, and a fitness function $f(d)$.

Then it is required to find such a set of pairs $\{t, E\}$, that:

$$d' = t(d, E), \quad \Delta f(d') < 0,$$

where E is a subset of the diagram elements (classes, interfaces, relations), d' is a diagram, attained as a result of the initial diagram d transformation.

To be able to develop advisory systems of the UML class diagram refactoring the following tasks need to be solved:

1. Develop formal method of the UML class diagram description and an abstract data structure to store, analyze and transform UML class diagram.
2. Formulate quality criteria for the UML class diagrams, which can be formulated as the fitness function.
3. Develop algorithms of analysis and transformation of UML class diagrams.

2   UML Refactoring Tool Providing Analysis, Transformation and Refactoring of UML Class Diagrams

UML Refactoring project is devoted to the advisory approach of the UML class diagram refactoring. The official site of the project is www.uml-refactoring.ru.

Main functional blocks of the software tool are shown in Fig. 1.

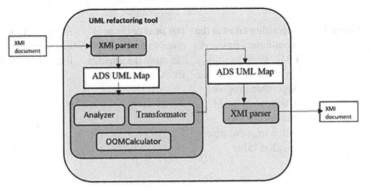

Fig. 1. Main functional blocks of the UML Refactoring tool.

UML Refactoring tool supports XMI format [2], which was developed as a data interchange standard for various modelling tools.

User can export UML class diagram to the XMI format and import it in the UML refactoring tool. After that analysis process starts: user selects a fitness function, object-oriented metrics are calculated (Avg. CBO, Avg. DIT, Avg. NOC, Avg. DAC, Avg. NLM, Avg. NOM, DAC2, DSC), Analyzer searches for the elements of the diagram to which it is reasonable to apply transformation (Interface Insertion, Façade, Strategy).

UML class diagrams are stored in the UML Refactoring tool in the UML Map abstract data structure. This data structure provide UML model storage, analysis and transformation. It is based on hash maps of UML model elements. The reduced UML class diagram of the UML Map abstract data structure is shown in Fig. 2.

The DSC (Diagram Structural Complexity) metric was proposed in [27] as the possible quality criterion for the refactoring. The DSC metric can be formulated as follows:

$$DSC(d) = k_1 \cdot |C| + k_2 \cdot |I| + k_3 \cdot |R| + k_4 \cdot \sum_{i=0}^{n} |A_i| + k_5 \cdot \sum_{i=0}^{n} |M_i| + k_6 \cdot \sum_{j=0}^{m} M_j,$$

(1)

where $DSC(d)$ is the structural complexity of the diagram d;

C is the number of classes of the diagram d;
I is the number of interfaces of the diagram d;
R is the number of relations of the diagram, d;
A_i is the number of attributes of the class $c_i \in C$, $i \in 0 \ldots n$;
M_i is the number of methods of the class $c_i \in C$, $i \in 0 \ldots n$, except methods, which belong to interfaces i_l, $l \in 0 \ldots k$, realized by the class c_i of interfaces, where k is the number of interfaces, realized by the class c_i;
M_j' is the number of methods of the interfaces $i_j \in I$, $j \in 0 \ldots m$.

Structural complexity quality criterion is important as long as complexity affects software modifiability, maintainability and understandability.

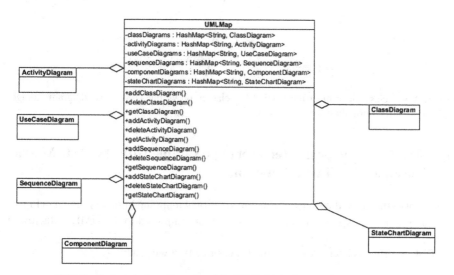

Fig. 2. Reduced class diagram of the UML Map abstract data structure.

The detailed UML class diagram of the classes, providing analysis and transformation of UML class diagrams is shown in Fig. 3.

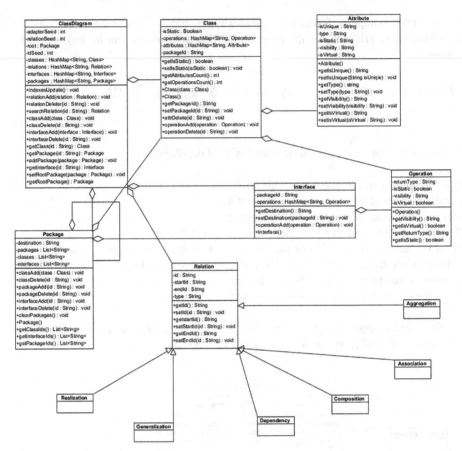

Fig. 3. UML class diagram of the UML Map classes providing UML class diagram storage, analysis and transformation.

3   UML Class Diagram Refactoring Example with the DSC Metric Chosen as the Fitness Function

Fragment of the UML diagram of the agent-relational mapping library is shown in Fig. 4. This diagram was exported to the XMI format and imported to the UML Refactoring tool.

DSC metric has been chosen as the fitness function with the

$$k_1 = 0.01, \; k_2 = 0.01, \; k_3 = 1.00, \; k_4 = 0.01, \; k_5 = 0.01, \; k_6 = 0.01.$$

The result of the analysis is shown in Fig. 5.
Metrics, which has been calculated for the diagram, are shown in Table 4.

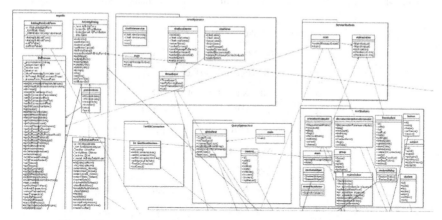

Fig. 4. Fragment of the UML class diagram of the *ArPlatform* library.

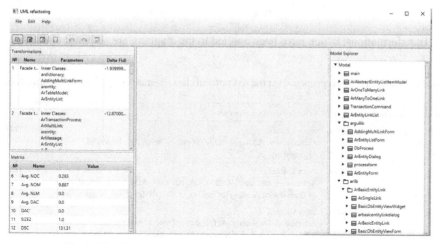

Fig. 5. Result of the diagram analysis using UML Refactoring tool.

Transformations proposed for the diagram are shown in Table 5.

Table 4. Metrics calculated for the ArPlatform class diagram using UML Refactoring tool.

Number	Metric	Value
1	Number of classes	106
2	Number of interfaces	0
3	Number of relations	118
4	Avg. DIT	0.434
5	Avg. CBO	1.66
6	Avg. NOC	0.283
7	Avg. NOM	9.877
8	Avg. NLM	0.0
9	Avg. DAC	0.0
10	DAC'	0.0
11	SIZE2	1.0
12	DSC	131.31

Transformations, which have been applied to the diagram, are shown in Table 6.

Table 5. Transformations proposed for the ArPlatform class diagram using UML refactoring tool.

Number	Transformation	Subset of diagram elements	$\Delta f(d)$
1	Façade transformation	Inner Classes: ArDictionary; AddingMultiLinkForm; ArEntity; ArTableModel; ArEntityList	−1.93999
2	Façade transformation	Inner Classes: ArTransactionProcess; ArMultilink; ArEntity; ArMessage; ArEntityList; ArTransaction; ArManyToOneLink; ArOneToManyLink; MappingConfig	−12.8700
3	Façade transformation	Inner Classes: ArEntity; ArDictionary; ArTransactionProcess; AddingMultiLinkForm; ArEntityDialog; ArEntityForm; DbConnectionParametersModel; ArTableModel; ArEntityList; ArTransaction; TransactionCommand; ArNotifier	−9.87
4	Façade transformation	Inner Classes: ArMessage; ArTransactionProcess; ArTransaction; arEntityParameters; ArLocation	−2.9399

(*continued*)

Table 5. (*continued*)

Number	Transformation	Subset of diagram elements	$\Delta f(d)$
5	Façade transformation	Inner Classes: ArEntityForm; ArEntity; ArEntityDialog; ArTableModel;	−0.9499
6	Façade transformation	Inner Classes: ArTableModel; ArDictionary; AddingMultiLinkForm; ArEntity; ArEntityForm; ArEntityList	−2.9300
7	Façade transformation	Inner Classes: ArEntityList; ArDictionary; ArAbstractEntityList; ArTransactionProcess; AddingMultiLinkForm; ArEntity; ArEntityDialog; DbConnectionParametersModel; ArTableModel; ArEntityListItem; TransactionCommand; ArNotifier;	−6.8700
8	Façade transformation	Inner Classes: ArTransaction; ArTransactionProcess; ArEntity; ArMessage; ArEntityParameters; ChatLocalCenter; ArLocation;	−4.9200
9	Façade transformation	Inner Classes: ArEntityParameters; ArTransactionProcess; MainWindow; ArMessage; DbProcess; ArTransaction; ArLocation; ArNotifier	−6.9099
10	Façade transformation	Inner Classes: ChatLocalCenter; ArTransaction; ArLocation	−0.9600
11	Façade transformation	Inner Classes: TransactionCommand; ArEntity; ArEntityList; ArNotifier	−1.9499
12	Façade transformation	Inner Classes: ArLocation; ArTransactionProcess; ArMessage; ArTransaction; DbConnection; ArEntityParameters; ChatLocalCenter; ArNotifier	−5.9099
13	Façade transformation	Inner Classes: ArNotifier; ArNultiLink; ArTransactionProcess; ArEntity; MainWindow; DbProcess; ArEntityList; ArManyToOneLink; rOneToManyLink; DbConnection; MappingConfig; ArentityParameters; ransactonCommand; ArLocation;	−10.8500

Table 6. Transformations proposed for the ArPlatform class diagram using UML refactoring tool.

Number	Transformation	Subset of diagram elements	$\Delta f(d)$
1	Façade transformation	Inner Classes: ArTransactionProcess; ArMultilink; ArEntity; ArMessage; ArEntityList; ArTransaction; ArManyToOneLink; ArOneToManyLink; MappingConfig	−12.8700
2	Façade transformation	Inner Classes: MainWindow; DbProcess; FacadeClass225	−20.9500
		Total:	−33.8200

As the result of the refactoring fitness function value decreased to 97.49.

To be able to automatically build UML class diagram of the *ArPlatform* library a prototype CLANG [28] plugin CPPToXMI has been developed. This plugin takes C++ source code at the input and returns UML class diagram in the XMI format at the output.

Algorithm of the CPPToXMI plugin can be described as follows:

```
//class diagram to be created
ClassDiagram diagram = new ClasasDiagram()
std::list<list<string>> agregations = new
std::list<list<string>>()
for each CXXRecordDecl RD
  if RD->isClass()
    bool class_is_abstract = get_is_abstract(RD)
    attributes_temp = get_attributes(RD)
    methods_temp = get_methods(RD)
  //create aggregation pairs
    for each attribute in attributes_temp
      list<string> agregation_pair = new list<sting>()
      agregation_pair.push_back(attribute_class_name)
      agregation_pair.push_back(class_temp.get_is())
      agregations.push_back(agregation_pair)
    if (!class_is_abstract & attributes_temp.size>0)
      //get class name, generate id
      class_temp.set_name(get_class_name(RD))
      class_temp.set_id(generate_ID())
      class_temp.set_is_abstract(class_is_abstract)
      class_temp.add_methods(methods_temp)
      class_temp.add_attributes(attributes_temp)
      diagram.add_class(class_temp)
      if (RD->getNumBases()>0)
        //add generalization relations to diagram
        for each base in RD->getNumBases()
          Generalization relation = new Generalization()
          relation.set_start_id(class_temp.get_id())
          relation.set_end_id(get_parent_id())
          diagram.add_relation(relation)
      //add dependency relations
      for each method in methods_temp
        if method.hasBody()
          Stmt body =  method.getBody()
          for each child in body
            if child is MemberExpr
              Dependency relation = new Dependency()
              relation.set_start_id(class_temp.get_id())
              relation.set_end_id(get_id(child))
  else
```

```
//add interface
Interface interface_temp = new Interface()
interface_temp.set_name(get_name(RD))
interface_temp.set_id(generate_id())
interface_temp.add_methods(get_methods(RD))
  diagram.add_interface(interface_temp)
//create aggregation relations
for each aggregation_pair in aggregations
  class_name = agregation_pair.front()
  string end_id = agregation_pair.back()
  if (diagram.has_class(class_name))
    Aggregation relation = new Aggregation()
    relation.set_id(generate_id())
    relation.set_start_id(diagram.get_id(class_name))
    relation.set_end_id(end_id)
    diagram.add_relation(relation)
save_diagram(diagram.to_xmi(), path)
Method diagram.to_xmi() can be described as follows:
//add XMI prefix
string str = prefix
for each interface in interfaces
  str+= interface.to_xmi()
for each class in classes
  str+=class.to_xmi()
  for each relation in relations
    if (relation.get_start_id() == class.get_id())
      str+=relation.to_xmi()
//add XMI suffix
str+=suffix
return str
```

4   Conclusion

This paper describes methods and algorithms which are used in the UML Refactoring tool to analyze, transform and refactor UML class diagrams. The proposed tool provides metric calculation (Avg. CBO, Avg. DIT, Avg. NOC, Avg. DAC, Avg. NLM, Avg. NOM, DAC2, DSC) and transformation application (Interface Insertion, Façade and Strategy).

An example of the UML class diagram refactoring has been proposed with the DSC metric chosen as the fitness function.

Acknowledgements. The work results were used within framework of the state task of the Russian Ministry of Education and Science, project No. 8.2321.2017 "Development and adaptation of control systems for compensation of dynamic deflecting effects on mobile objects in a state of dynamic equilibrium".

References

1. Booch, G., Rumbaugh, J., Jacobson, I.: The Unified Modeling Language User Guide. Addison-Wesley Professional, Boston (2005)
2. XML Metadata Interchange (XMI) Specification. Version 2.4.2. https://www.omg.org/spec/XMI/2.4.2/About-XMI
3. Evans, A., France, R., Lano, K., Rumpe, B.: The UML as a formal modeling notation. In: Bézivin, J., Muller, P.-A. (eds.) UML 1998. LNCS, vol. 1618, pp. 336–348. Springer, Heidelberg (1999). https://doi.org/10.1007/978-3-540-48480-6_26
4. XQuery 3.0: An XML Query Language. http://www.w3.org/TR/xquery-30
5. XSL Transformations (XSLT). http://www.w3.org/TR/xslt
6. Meta Object Facility™ (MOF™) 2.0 Query/View/Transformation™ (QVT™). http://www.omg.org/spec/QVT/index.htm
7. Efrizoni, L., Informatika, T., Wan-Kadir, W.M.N., Mohamad, R.: Formalization of UML class diagram using description logics. In: 2010 International Symposium on Information Technology, Kuala Lumpur, vol. 3, pp. 1168–1173 (2010). https://doi.org/10.1109/ITSIM.2010.5561621
8. Schmitt, P.H.: UML and It's Meaning (2003). https://formal.iti.kit.edu/beckert/teaching/Spezifikation-SS04/skriptum-schmitt.pdf
9. Beckert, B., Keller, U., Schmitt, P.H.: Translating the object constraint language into first-order predicate logic. In: Proceedings, VERIFY, Workshop at Federated Logic Conferences (FLoC), pp. 113–123 (2001)
10. Kerkouche, E., Chaoui, A.A., Bourennane, E.B., Labbani, O.: A UML and colored petri nets integrated modeling and analysis approach using graph transformation. J. Obj. Technol. 9(4), 25–43 (2010). https://doi.org/10.5381/jot.2010.9.4.a2
11. Rahmoune, Y., Chaoui, A., Kerkouche, E.: A framework for modeling and analysis UML activity diagram using graph transformation. Procedia Comput. Sci. 56, 612–617 (2015). https://doi.org/10.1016/j.procs.2015.07.261
12. Kerievsky, J.: Refactoring to Patterns. Addison-Wesley Professional, Boston (2004)
13. Fowler, M.: Refactoring: Improving the Design of Existing Code. Addison-Wesley, Boston (2000)
14. Martin, R., Martin, M.: Agile Principles, Patterns, and Practices in C#. Pearson Education, Boston (2007)
15. Gamma, E., Helm, R., Johnson, R., Vlissides, J.: Design patterns: abstraction and reuse of object-oriented design. In: Nierstrasz, O.M. (ed.) ECOOP 1993. LNCS, vol. 707, pp. 406–431. Springer, Heidelberg (1993). https://doi.org/10.1007/3-540-47910-4_21
16. Harman, M., Mansouri, S.A., Zhang, Y.: Search-based software engineering: trends, techniques and applications. ACM Comput. Surv. 45(1), 11 (2012). https://doi.org/10.1145/2379776.2379787
17. Amoui, M., Mirarab, S., Ansari, S., Lucas, C.: A genetic algorithm approach to design evolution using design pattern transformation. Int. J. Inf. Technol. Intell. Comput. 1(2), 235–244 (2006)
18. Bowman, M., Briand, L.C., Labiche, Y.: Solving the class responsibility assignment problem in object-oriented analysis with multi-objective genetic algorithms. IEEE Trans. Softw. Eng. 36(6), 817–837 (2010). https://doi.org/10.1109/TSE.2010.70
19. Hadaytullah, Vathsavayi, S., Räihä, O., Koskimies, K.: Tool support for software architecture design with genetic algorithms. In: 2010 Fifth International Conference on Software Engineering Advances, Nice, pp. 359–366 (2010). https://doi.org/10.1109/ICSEA.2010.61
20. Lutz, R.: Evolving good hierarchical decompositions of complex systems. J. Syst. Arch. 47(7), 613–634 (2001). https://doi.org/10.1016/S1383-7621(01)00019-4

21. Simons, C.L., Parmee, I.C.: Single and multi-objective genetic operators in object-oriented conceptual software design. In: Proceedings of the 8th Annual Conference on Genetic and Evolutionary Computation (GECCO 2006), pp. 1957–1958. Association for Computing Machinery, New York (2006). https://doi.org/10.1145/1143997.1144324

22. Deryugina, O.: Improving the structural quality of UML class diagrams with the genetic algorithm. ITM Web Conf. **6**, 03003 (2016). https://doi.org/10.1051/itmconf/20160603003

23. O'Keeffe, M., Cinnéide, M.O.: Towards automated design improvement through combinatorial optimisation. In: Workshop on Directions in Software Engineering and Environments (WoDiSEE 2004), 26th International Conference on Software Engineering, Edinburgh, UK, pp. 75–82 (2004). https://doi.org/10.1049/ic:20040214

24. O'Keeffe, M., Cinnéide, M.O.: Search-based refactoring for software maintenance. J. Syst. Softw. **81**(4), 502–516 (2008). https://doi.org/10.1016/j.jss.2007.06.003

25. Mancoridis, S., Mitchell, B.S., Rorres, C., Chen, Y., Gansner, E.R.: Using automatic clustering to produce high-level system organizations of source code. In: Proceedings. 6th International Workshop on Program Comprehension. IWPC 1998 (Cat. No. 98TB100242), Ischia, Italy, pp. 45–52 (1998). https://doi.org/10.1109/WPC.1998.693283

26. Deryugina, O.A., Nikulchev, E.V.: Software tool for automated UML class diagram refactoring using given quality criteria. Cybern. Program. **1**, 107–118 (2017). https://doi.org/10.7256/2306-4196.2017.1.21934

27. Clang: a C language family frontend for LLVM. http://clang.llvm.org

28. Ryadchikov, I., et al.: Development of robotic mobile platform with the universal chassis system. IOP Conf. Ser. Mater. Sci. Eng. **312**(1), 012021 (2018). https://doi.org/10.1088/1757-899X/312/1/012021

Modeling of Complex Systems over Bayesian Belief Network

Viktoriya Taran[1]([⊠]) [iD] and Tatyana Gubina[2] [iD]

[1] V.I. Vernadsky Crimean Federal University, 295007 Simferopol, Russia
victoriya_yalta@ukr.net
[2] Bunin Yelets State University, Kommunarov Str. 28, 399770 Yelets, Russia

Abstract. The article analyzes the factors that have an impact on the activation of complex natural processes and their catastrophic consequences. Solar activity, precipitation and seismic activity have chosen as the most significant factors, a sharp increase in which leads to activation of natural processes such as landslides, mudflows, natural and forest fires, snow avalanches, hurricanes, tornados, squalls, volcanic eruptions, etc. Intermediate and resulting indicators have chosen to describe and evaluate the course of the processes under consideration: Natural Hazards, Time Frame and Cash. The construction of the Bayesian Belief Network for modeling of complex natural processes on the Northern Mountainous Coast of Black Sea, its structure and training by filling in probability tables are considered. Experts fill conditional probabilities for dependent or intermediate vertices. The values of unconditional probabilities have filled according to observation data for top-level vertices. The managing or controlling factor is determined as Funds Invested and its importance has discussed. Simulation of various scenarios of the course of natural processes has carried out, for which the probability of occurrence of certain states of the resulting outcome indicators is calculated.

Keywords: Modeling · Forecasting · Complex systems · Catastrophic consequences of complex natural processes · Landslide processes · Bayesian Belief Network

1 Introduction

The Northern Coast of the Black Sea, with its unique climate conditions, historical, natural and economic resources, is the region most often affected by natural disasters and exogenous processes. In addition, this narrow strip of the coast has more than 50% of all peninsula roads, and the urbanization density is more than double that of the average for the Northern Mountainous Coast of Black Sea [1]. Thus, complex natural processes pose a significant threat; they destroy not only roads, but also buildings and all kinds of structures, and cause great damage to their operation [2]. Despite the development of modeling and forecasting methods, the prediction of the natural processes activation, which can entail catastrophic destructive consequences, detrimental to economic activity, is one of the main problems of the modern scientific world. The identification of all factors, the determination of the degree of their influence on the course and activation of

V. Sukhomlin and E. Zubareva (Eds.): SITITO 2017, CCIS 1204, pp. 192–202, 2021.
https://doi.org/10.1007/978-3-030-78273-3_19

catastrophic processes and the forecasting of possible consequences remain an ongoing challenge and an actual task, and, moreover, the work is made more complex by the risk that there are some unforeseen situations in the system, which is also a complex task of analyzing the random dynamic processes [3].

There is a narrow focus of research on the forecasting of complex natural processes in the Northern Mountainous Coast of Black Sea, observation, monitoring, cartographic studies and expert evaluation of a specialist. The weak link in this area is the limited use of modern information technologies and intellectual decision-making systems, the lack of a systematic approach [4, 5].

This Article seeks to analyze the factors having a direct impact on the activation of complex natural processes, the modeling of these processes with the help of the Bayesian Belief Network, and building a forecast model.

2   Identification of Factors Affecting the Activation of Catastrophic Natural Processes

Complex natural processes taking place on the Northern Mountainous Coast of Black Sea and in other regions are of a complex random nature. They depend on many factors, have considerable uncertainty, and therefore are very difficult to forecast [5].

Let us highlight the complex natural processes leading to catastrophic consequences:

- hydrometeorological hazards;
- flooding;
- low water;
- landslips;
- processing of shores of seas and reservoirs;
- natural fires;
- mud flows;
- snow avalanches;
- earthquakes;
- tsunami;
- hurricanes, tornadoes, squalls;
- volcanic eruptions;
- extreme air temperatures [6].

It was been revealed that the occurrence of any catastrophic natural phenomena, as well as landslide processes, directly depends on the solar activity and its 11-year cycle. Thus, we name the solar activity as the first and the main factor [1, 5].

In addition to the solar activity, rainfalls of two opposite types have a great influence:

- summer showers, as a result of which the land is not soaked, and large streams of water rushing from the mountains carry the top layer of the soil to the sea, washing away its organic component and eroding ravines;

- winter drizzling rain, which moisten the soil abundantly, deeply soaking it and filling the underground karst cavities – in that way natural water reservoirs for the summer appear; they create soil strains, resulting in land movements - spring land-slides, downfalls and mud flows.

Another factor to be consider is seismic activity. The Northern Mountains of Black Sea are relatively young mountains, and they react to earthquakes. But we will only consider earthquakes with epicenters, located not more than 200 km from the Coast and with a magnitude not exceeding 8,5 K, i.e. the level of released energy in the epicenter corresponds to 8.5 K.

As a factor of the so-called regulation of natural processes or management, consider the following factor: investing in fortification and protective structures. All these factors are attributing to the primary or most significantly affecting the activation of catastrophic natural processes, a drastic change of which leads to a change in the course of these processes and their activation.

There are a large number of observation stations for monitoring the natural conditions on the Black Sea's northern mountain coast, such as: meteorological stations, a seismic station, observatories and research institutes. Meteorological stations are equipped with modern instruments for collecting weather data. The seismic station is equipped with accurate and sensitive sensors, which have no analogues on the North Coast of the Black Sea. The hydrogeological research department examines landslide processes from the geological point of view, monitors and keeps records of these processes since 1945. Observatories conduct observations of solar activity, have a large set of monitoring data since 1900. The branch of the Institute of Marine Geology and Geophysics is engaged in studying and monitoring the states of the earth's surface, sea currents and changes in the relief of the seabed.

Therefore, we chose such factors as precipitation, solar activity, seismic activity for modeling and forecasting complex natural processes. Many scientists use these factors to build their models and make calculations for the forecast.

All these indicators are processing independently of each other, although the single center for the study of natural phenomena of the Northern Mountainous Coast of Black Sea could solve the problems of forecasting and predicting natural processes that entail catastrophic consequences. In this case it is not possible to apply classical regression analysis or autoregressive models, which are used most often in the field, since the error of such calculations is too great, in addition, the forecast interval is often too large or whether, on the contrary, too small for timely decision-making and implementation of the decision.

3   Building a Bayesian Belief Networks

The logical-probabilistic approach, in which the propositional formulas (given over a certain alphabet) are the model of the statement, is of particular interest from the point of view of modeling the reasoning process of the expert. This is traditional for formal logic and the degree of confidence in the truth (or stochastic uncertainty of the truth) of these propositional formulas and the bond strength between them are characterizing by probability estimates: both scalar (point) and interval [7]. Due to their high transparency, the ability to combine empirical data with expert knowledge and their apparent relevance to uncertainty, Bayesian Belief Networks can make a significant contribution to the study and modeling of complex systems of a different nature [11].

A Bayesian Belief Network (BBN) is represented by a pair (G, P), where $G = \langle X, E \rangle$ is a directed acyclic graph on a finite set X (its vertices are the listed factors and the expected intermediate and result indicators) connected by a set of oriented edges E, set of conditional probability distributions. Thus, Bayesian Networks are a convenient tool for describing complex processes and events with uncertainties. To describe the Bayesian Network, it is necessary to determine the structure of the graph and the parameters of each node. This information can be obtaining directly from data or from expert estimates [8]. A graph has written as a set of conditions for independence, as each variable is independent of its parents G. The second component of the pair is a set of parameters that defines the network. From a mathematical point of view, BBN is a model for representing probabilistic dependencies, as well as the absence of these dependencies. At the same time, the link $A \rightarrow B$ is the cause, when the event A is the cause of the occurrence of B, affects the value accepted by V. BBN is called the cause (causal), when all links are causal [9].

To make decisions using a Bayesian Belief Network in conditions of uncertainty, the basis is the calculation of the probabilities of the transition strategies from one to the other state of the system. Evaluation of indeterminate forms in the BBN has performed by calculating the probabilities of the states of vertices based on available information about the value of other vertices of the network, thanks to these messages, the system proceeds to the next state [10].

A model based on the Bayesian belief network allows you to combine both statistical data and expert assumptions about the nature of behavior and the relationships between elements [11, 12]. Bayesian networks are one of the representations of knowledge bases with uncertainty [13].

Under uncertainty, the basis for decision-making with the help of the Bayesian belief network is the calculation of the probabilities of transition strategies from one to the other state of the system [14, 15].

We construct the graph of the Bayesian Belief Network in the form of a "tree", where the top-level contains the vertex-factors with unconditional probabilities, which are determined at the beginning of the simulation from experiments or observation results. These are the factors listed above: Solar activity, Seismic activity and Precipitation and Invested funds. We will work with the *Netica* program, which is a shareware product. At the second level, we place one vertex: "Natural risks", i.e. we can expect the activation of natural processes and the risk of causing catastrophic destruction. The next level will also consist of only one vertex: "Time Terms" - the forecast of the time interval, during which the catastrophic consequences of the course of natural processes will manifest (or not manifest).

The last fourth level is the result of modeling "Total Cash", i.e. the final amount of funds that will be required to eliminate catastrophic consequences, including the funds invested in reinforcement measures.

Each of the listed vertices, except for "Investment" and "Time Terms", will have three types of values: Few, Medium and Catastrophic. "Investment" will contain such values: "In Full", "Medium", "Few". For the vertex "Time Terms", we define the following possible values: "Two days", "Week", "Month", "Do Not". The Bayesian network, taking into account all the above, is shown in Fig. 1.

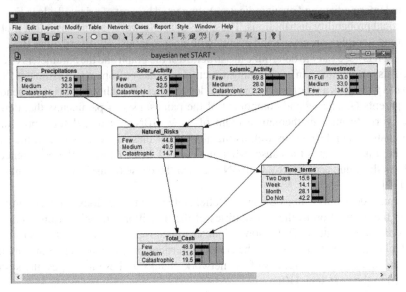

Fig. 1. Bayesian Belief Network for complex natural processes modeling.

The Bayesian network training is done by filling in conditional probability tables for the vertices of the middle and lower levels and unconditional probabilities for the vertex-factors that lie at the upper level (from the results of observations). Tables are filled using expert evaluations, exhibited by experts (Fig. 2). At the same time, if the vertex has three variants of values, then the training table will include $3n + 1$ conditional probabilities, for which the condition should be fulfilled: the sum in the line is 100 (100%). For example, the probability table for the "Natural Risks" vertex has $3n$ lines, i.e. $3^4 = 81$ lines, and each line has three probability values, the total number of probability values is 243. The main distinguishing feature of the proposed model is the distribution of all values for each graph node into three groups, and for the vertex "Temporary risks" – there are even by four, while the classical Bayesian networks operate with only two values of the variables: 0 and 1. By increasing the number of values that can take by graph nodes (the vertex) the size of the tables of conditional probabilities increases dramatically. This concerns the vertices of the second, third and fourth levels. We will perform simulations with the help of the shareware pro-gram Netica.

Precipitation	Solar_Activity	Seismic_Activity	Invested_Funds	Small	Average	Catastrophic
Small	Small	Small	In Full	95	4	1
Small	Small	Small	Average	90	8	2
Small	Small	Small	Small	80	18	2
Small	Small	Average	In Full	85	12	3
Small	Small	Average	Average	75	20	5
Small	Small	Average	Small	65	28	7
Small	Small	Catastrophic	In Full	82	16	2
Small	Small	Catastrophic	Average	72	25	3
Small	Small	Catastrophic	Small	62	30	8
Small	Average	Small	In Full	83	15	2
Small	Average	Small	Average	73	22	5
Small	Average	Small	Small	63	30	7
Small	Average	Average	In Full	74	22	4
Small	Average	Average	Average	70	23	7
Small	Average	Average	Small	66	24	10
Small	Average	Catastrophic	In Full	72	22	6
Small	Average	Catastrophic	Average	70	24	6
Small	Average	Catastrophic	Small	68	24	8
Small	Catastrophic	Small	In Full	70	23	7
Small	Catastrophic	Small	Average	67	25	8
Small	Catastrophic	Small	Small	64	27	9
Small	Catastrophic	Average	In Full	67	28	5
Small	Catastrophic	Average	Average	63	30	7
Small	Catastrophic	Average	Small	60	31	9
Small	Catastrophic	Catastrophic	In Full	65	30	5

Fig. 2. Filling in the conditional probabilities tables of the Bayesian Belief Network.

After filling all the tables of conditional and unconditional probabilities, we get this result. The probabilities for the vertices are distributed as follows:

- "Natural risks": "Few" - 44.8%, "Medium" - 40.5%, "Catastrophic" - 14.7%;
- "Time Terms": "Two Days" - 16.6%, "Do Not" - 42.2%;
- "Total cash": "Not much" - 48.9%, "Medium" - 31.6%, "Catastrophic" - 19.5%.

This indicates that with generalized input data, sharp catastrophic destruction from natural processes is not expected. The investment is at an average level, no special costs are required to eliminate the consequences of complex natural processes.

4 Simulation of Complex Natural Processes Using the Bayesian Belief Network

To construct an operational forecast, after filling in all tables of conditional probabilities, you must enter new input values. We set the initial conditions for the upper level for operational (short-term) modeling.

Let, for example, there have been strong (catastrophic) atmospheric precipitation against the background of sharply increased solar activity, while the seismic activity is medium, and the investments have been at a low level. The result of the forecast shows that the activation will take place at a catastrophic level "Natural Risk" (65%), with the probability of small and averages disruptions of 10% and 25%, respectively, and it should be expected within the next two days (52.1%), the greatest probability of destruction requiring additional large scale investments (56.0%), as shown in Fig. 3.

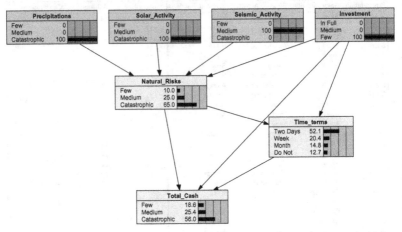

Fig. 3. The Bayesian Belief Network for predicting the course of complex natural processes and their consequences.

Let's consider three scenarios:

– funds are invested in small (insufficient) volume (Few);
– funds are invested in average volume, but, maybe, at the wrong time (Medium);
– funds are fully invested (In Full).

Let's consider the probabilities of the three remaining nodes of the Bayesian network: "Natural Risks", "Time Terms" and "Total Cash". The obtained results are tabulating in the constructed Table 1, which reflects the changes in the control factor and its influence on the vertices of the lower levels. We leave the previously selected values for the first level vertices. Let's construct the forecast for the received model, we will change only values of the controlling factor.

Thus, we can see from the table that with a small investment of funds, the level of "Natural Risks" is threateningly increasing to 65%, i.e. the probability of catastrophic destructions caused by natural processes increases to 65%. At the same time, natural processes with catastrophic consequences are expecting to occur within two days with a probability of 52.1%, within one week – 20.4%, which indicates the necessity of mandatory preventive measures, and possibly the need to prepare and mobilize forces for future elimination of such consequences. The total amount of cash will be required at the same time in a catastrophic amount with a probability of 56.0%, and only slightly more than 20% the probability of an average cost level.

With medium-sized investments, (i.e. funds are providing, but maybe not always on time and not always in full), the reviewed indicators are less threatening. The probability of catastrophic consequences is reducing to 54%, the waiting period for the manifestation

Table 1. The results of the forecast when the managing factor "Investment" changes.

Investment		Few (100%)	Medium 100%	In_Full (100%)
Natural risk, %	Few	2	14	20
	Medium	25	32	38
	Catastrophic	65	54	42
Time frame, %	2 days	52.1	32.1	16.6
	Week	20.4	22.1	17.2
	Month	14.8	20.8	27.6
	Do Not	12.7	25.0	38.6
Cash, %	Few	18.6	30.3	42.3
	Medium	25.4	34.2	36.5
	Catastrophic	56.0	35.5	21.2

of these processes is up to 32.1% and 22.1%, and the catastrophic total costs are reducing to 35.5% (Fig. 4).

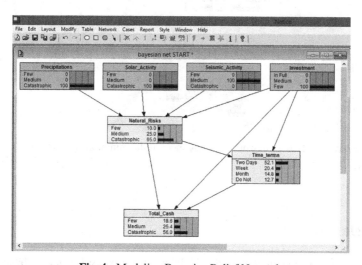

Fig. 4. Modeling Bayesian Belief Network

These values of the considered graph vertices depend not only on the controlling factor "Invested funds", but also on the current state of nature, which is describing by rest of the vertices of the first level.

The table shows that atmospheric precipitation and solar activity necessarily lead to activation of complex natural processes, but the level of destruction and cata-strophic consequences can will been significantly reduced if the strengthening measures have been taken place in advance, i.e. funds investment, strengthening the most dangerous sections of roads, communications, retaining walls, structures, etc.

If we set a goal: to find out what possible characteristics we get, if we want to minimize total costs, then the Bayesian networks allow us to recalculate the probability of the graph state even for top-level vertices, i.e. in the opposite direction. Figure 5 shows the result of the simulation. Yes, indeed, preliminary investments must be made in a much larger volume, but at the same time, the natural risks of activating natural processes that have catastrophic consequences are reduced up to 22.5%, and the occurrence time of catastrophic consequences is delayed by a month (28.6%), or such natural disasters won't even occur (43.0%).

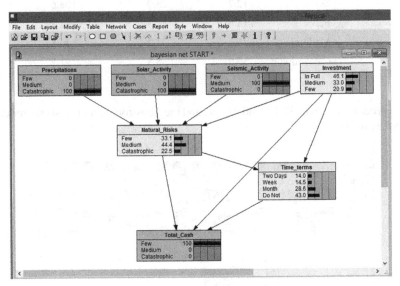

Fig. 5. The Bayesian Belief Network for assessment of the minimization of the total amount of money.

5   Conclusion

Thus, the factors were been identified, which have the greatest impact on the activation of natural processes with disastrous consequences. The Bayesian Belief Network was been built to model complex natural processes on the Northern Mountainous Black Sea Coast. A graph was been drawn up for the Bayesian Belief Network, and the network was trained by filling in tables of unconditional and conditional probabilities. The states of the vertices of the Bayesian Belief Network was been defined and the corresponding calculations were made for them. The controlling factor was been chosen as "Investments". The calculation of the management strategy was been carried out using the indicator: "Investments to strengthen hazardous zones" (pre-invested funds).

The Bayesian network makes it possible to update the decision-making strategies in accordance with the selected criteria after obtaining new observations for the hydrometeorological, seismic, solar and complex natural processes of the Northern Mountainous Black Sea Coast. The model obtained helps to optimize the costs of preventing the catastrophic consequences of complex natural processes or their elimination. The resulting Bayesian network can easily will been expanded with the help of new vertices taking into account new information on the state of the flow of the process under investigation [4].

Therefore, the Bayesian Belief Network can been used to model complex processes and systems under uncertainty. Thus, such a model is becoming increasingly popular. Bayesian networks would also be useful for modeling and forecasting processes of various origins, including complex natural processes, since the model allows us to take into account the structural and statistical uncertainties of the processes under study.

However, it is necessary to take into account some deviations, including the low flexibility of frequently used software packages, the difficulty of obtaining expert knowledge, and the impossibility of simulating feedback loops [16].

Bayesian Belief Network was been proposed for the first time for use in scientific developments in the field of natural disasters of the Northern Mountainous Black Sea Coast. This model is adequate and offers the decision maker the results of calculations for developing and making managerial decisions. It is been planned to continue research and development of methods for assessing the adequacy of the constructed models of the Bayesian Belief Network in the future [4].

References

1. Krucik, M.D.: Protection of Mountain Roads from Landslides. Kolomija (2003). (in Ukrainian)
2. Selin, Yu.N.: System analysis of ecologically dangerous processes of different nature. Syst. Res. Inf. Technol. (2), 22–32 (2007). http://journal.iasa.kpi.ua/article/view/127652. (in Ukrainian)
3. Taran, V.N.: Practical introduction of the developed methods of prognostication of landslide processes of the South Bank of Crimea. Bull. Natl. Tech. Univ. "KhPI". Ser. "Inf. Model." (21), 162–172 (2010). https://www.elibrary.ru/item.asp?id=19057693. (in Russian)
4. Taran, V.N.: Modeling of natural catastrophic processes of the Southern coast of Crimea with the help of the Bayes network. Auditorium (3), 47–54 (2016). https://www.elibrary.ru/item.asp?id=27184309. (in Russian)
5. Taran, V.N.: Clusterization of data for forecasting for landslide processes of the Southern coast of Crimea. Inf. Process. Syst. (6), 276–280 (2010). http://www.hups.mil.gov.ua/periodic-app/article/7863/eng. (in Ukrainian)
6. Puchkov, V.A., Akimov, V.A., Sokolov, Yu.I.: Disasters and Sustainable Development in the Context of Globalization. EMERCOM of Russia, Moscow (2013). https://www.elibrary.ru/item.asp?id=20823662. (in Russian)
7. Romanov, A.V., Levenets, D.G., Zolotin, A.A., Tulupyev, A.L.: Incremental synthesis of the tertiary structure of algebraic Bayesian networks. In: 2016 XIX IEEE International Conference on Soft Computing and Measurements (SCM), St. Petersburg, pp. 28–30 (2016). https://doi.org/10.1109/SCM.2016.7519673

8. Khlopotov, M.V.: Bayesian network in student model engineering for competence level evaluation. Naukovenie (5), 36 (2014). https://www.elibrary.ru/item.asp?id=23039405. (in Russian)
9. Bidjuk, P.I., Terent'ev, A.N.: Construction and methods of learning Bayesian networks. Taurida J. Comput. Sci. Theory Math. (2), 139–154 (2004). http://tvim.info/files/2004-2-139.pdf. (in Russian)
10. Terentyev, A.N., Bidyuk, P.I.: Method for probabilistic inference from training data in Bayesian networks. Cybern. Syst. Anal. **43**(3), 93–99 (2007). http://www.kibernetika.org/annotations/2007/7referats3.pdf. (in Ukrainian)
11. Kharitonov, N.A., Tulupyev, A.L., Zolotin, A.A.: Software implementation of reconciliation algorithms in algebraic Bayesian networks. In: 2017 XX IEEE International Conference on Soft Computing and Measurements (SCM), St. Petersburg, pp. 8–10 (2017). https://doi.org/10.1109/SCM.2017.7970479
12. Goryainov, S.V., Kuznetsov, A.Y., Tushkanov, E.V., Kuznetsova, O.V., Romanova, E.B.: Analysis of Bayes mathematical systems of pattern recognition for identifying the objects on hyperspectral photographs. In: 2017 XX IEEE International Conference on Soft Computing and Measurements (SCM), St. Petersburg, pp. 40–42 (2017). https://doi.org/10.1109/SCM.2017.7970489
13. Zolotin, A.A., Tulupyev, A.L.: Matrix-vector algorithms of global posteriori inference in algebraic Bayesian networks. In: 2017 XX IEEE International Conference on Soft Computing and Measurements (SCM), St. Petersburg, pp. 22–24 (2017). https://doi.org/10.1109/SCM.2017.7970483
14. Taran, V.N.: The analysis of Bayesian networks for modeling of complicated natural processes. In: Proceedings of the of the 1st All-Russian Scientific and Practical Internet Conference "Remote Educational Technologies", IT ARIAL, Simferopol, pp. 192–196 (2016). https://www.elibrary.ru/item.asp?id=27306766. (in Russian)
15. Taran, V.N.: Bayesian networks for modeling complex systems. In: 2017 IEEE II International Conference on Control in Technical Systems (CTS), St. Petersburg, pp. 240–243 (2017). https://doi.org/10.1109/CTSYS.2017.8109535
16. Landuyt, D., Broekx, S., D'hondt, R., Engelen, G., Aertsen, J., Goethals, P.L.M.: A review of Bayesian belief networks in ecosystem service modelling. Environ. Model. Softw. **46**, 1–11 (2013). https://doi.org/10.1016/j.envsoft.2013.03.011

The Development of an Intelligent Simulator System for Psychophysiological Diagnostics of Trainees on the Basis of Virtual Reality

Dmitry Chernykh[1] (iD), Rimma Gorokhova[2](✉) (iD), and Petr Nikitin[2] (iD)

[1] Volga State University of Technology, Lenin Sq. 3, 424000 Yoshkar-Ola,
the Republic of Mari El, Russia
[2] Financial University under the Government of the Russian Federation, 49 Leningradsky
Prospekt, 125993 Moscow, Russia
{RIGorokhova,PVNikitin}@fa.ru

Abstract. The paper discusses possible application of high technology including virtual reality (VR) in diagnostics of individual typological features of the person. The authors have revealed application features of virtual reality in diagnostics of psychophysiological professionally important qualities that determine potential or actual abilities to a certain effective professional activity. They have classified psychophysiological features as well as application features of virtual reality in diagnostics of the former. The main methods of medicine, diagnostic medicine, virtual reality technology aimed at diagnostics, identification of respondents' state, professional orientation are determined on the base of an integral methodological approach.

The analysis of various intellectual simulators aimed at psychophysiological diagnostics of students on the basis of virtual reality is performed. The possibilities of their application for the determination of psychophysiological, professionally significant personality traits are considered on the basis of intellectual simulators developed by the authors. The conditions for using virtual reality in the process of training, vocational training and retraining, methodical and didactic features of the use of simulators have been revealed.

Keywords: Intelligent training system · Virtual reality · Psychophysiological features · Diagnostics

1 Introduction

1.1 Types of Human Psychophysiological Characteristics

Nowadays information technology is vigorously developing and penetrating into all sectors of human activities - from everyday life to industrial and defense enterprises.

Engineering psychology is no exception. It studies psychological patterns of the working activity of a person in management and control systems, and a person's information interaction with technical devices of the mentioned systems. The systems of

V. Sukhomlin and E. Zubareva (Eds.): SITITO 2017, CCIS 1204, pp. 203–214, 2021.
https://doi.org/10.1007/978-3-030-78273-3_20

so-called virtual reality, where a person has an opportunity to find themselves in an absolutely different environment that does not greatly differ from the real one by cognitive dimensions, are currently becoming more prevalent.

The concept of virtual reality is treated differently in the scientific community. Some authors [1] refer virtual reality to a computer-generated environment that creates an illusion of the user's presence in the world offered by a software system. However, the majority [2, 3] define virtual reality as a technology of human-computer interaction which ensures immersion of the user into a 3D interactive information environment. In this paper we use the second definition. Application of high technology including virtual reality is an effective means both for training and for diagnostics of individual typological features of the person.

Psychophysiological dimensions are found to be of the greatest interest among human individual typological features. In terms of engineering psychology it deals with psychophysiological professionally important qualities that refer to human individual features determining potential or actual abilities to a certain effective professional activity. The mentioned qualities are formed by genetic, medical, biological, social and psychological factors. Requirements to psychological and psychophysiological professionally important qualities are raising along with increasing extremeness of operational environment. Optimal staff recruitment and a degree of work efficiency are in line with correlation between the personal dimensions determined by a diagnostic process and demands of the occupation.

A maturity level of professional activity and capabilities to improve psychophysiological characteristics are conditioned by the type of higher nervous activity. I.P. Pavlov's classification is believed to be the most authoritative typology of higher nervous activity. The key parameters of this classification are intensity of processes of excitation and inhibition, their balance and flexibility. The correlation of these processes gives four temperament types: sanguine, choleric, phlegmatic, and melancholic. The diagnostics of professionally important qualities should take into account the mentioned types which are to be defined beforehand by using special methods (Eysenck Personality Questionnaire, N.N.Obozov Personality Questionnaire). The outcomes of these tests can eventually help to make final diagnostic conclusion more complete [4]. The main psychophysiological characteristics relating to professional activity of a person are believed to be adaptive tracking, measuring by eye, neuroticism, extroversion, responsiveness, etc. [5, 6]. At the same time a set of key qualities is determined by a specific professional activity. Identification of professionally important qualities is necessary as it allows us to construct a specialist competency model, to reveal professional activity peculiarities important for understanding the specific character of such professional training. It sets out the relevance of this work.

1.2 Diagnostics of Psychophysiological Characteristics

Nowadays we have a number of computer-based methods for evaluation of professionally important qualities. A system of measures, which helps identify people who are most suitable for training and further professional activity in a certain occupation due to their personal traits, plays a special part in evaluation of professional aptitude. Diagnostics of psychophysiological characteristics is aimed at defining people whose abilities and individual psychophysiological capacities meet requirements set out by the specificity of training and professional activity in a certain occupation.

The information of psychophysiological features of any given profession is generalized in a professiogram that outlines peculiarities of this professional activity. First of all, it is necessary to present what operations and main working actions and functions are to be performed in case of mastering a chosen profession. These data are initially included both in the principal educational program of speciality training and in the work programs in each subject. The professiogram should include knowledge and skills required for certain operations, typical psychophysiological states such as emotional tension, fatigue, monotony of actions, physical and intellectual job complexity, algorithms of actions to be performed by a person. Then, significance of different psychological attributes and personal qualities for effective performance of this activity should be estimated. For this purpose, in accordance with the given description of professional operations it is necessary to define personal attributes that ensure performance of each such operation and determine the degree of importance of different psychic functions for attaining a final effect of a working process, the charging time of a psychic function throughout a working process. The outcome of such an analysis is definition of the most significant parameters that characterize the human ability to professional activity.

Construction of a professiogram helps define professional aptitude as it is based not only on evaluation of psychic processes, but also on evaluation of a number of professional working operations. It is necessary to perform diagnostics in order to define professional aptitude of the people who are currently choosing a profession as well as the people who already have some professional skills or are taking a course of rehabilitation and returning into profession. Psychology and diagnostic medicine pay a special attention to reliability and differentiation requirements to the used methods. Application of virtual reality for diagnostics should also take into consideration receiving statistically stable outcomes in several examinations of subjects, and at the same time a certain method should be used for investigation of a definite psychic function of a person. There are different tests such as nervous system tests, temperament tests; interest, inclination, activity priority tests; memory, thinking, attention, perception tests, tests for giftedness. However, in order to define the professional aptitude of a person it is more effective to use a set of tests specially selected for revealing a development level of those psychological qualities and capabilities that are demanded for a certain profession. The test outcomes make it possible to give recommendations for further professional activity in a chosen occupation, for successful training and professional improvement, to identify possible adaptation to profession, occurrence of emergency situations and exposures.

Psychophysiological diagnostics of professional orientation with the use of different types of tests implies examination and evaluation of some psychological parameters of attention, memory, motor coordination, etc. important for successful training and professional activity in a chosen occupation as well as an analysis of completed professional operations. One of the prevailing methods for evaluation of personal psychological characteristics is Sixteen Personality Factor Questionnaire, 16PF, developed by Raymond Cattell. Cattel's method is commonly used in psychodiagnostic practice both abroad and in Russia. This Questionnaire is universal and practical, reveals comprehensive information of a personality. Professional Self Identity Questionnaire on the basis of J. Holland's theory of career choice is also widely used. The Questionnaire is based on the belief that any successful career directly depends on how much one's personality corresponds to the type, spirit and demands of the profession. Statistics proves that all successful people achieve their highest and fullest development only in the professional environment that conforms to their personality type. The people of integrity and consistency are those who have managed to realize their core values [7].

The comparison of professional diagnostic methods shows 60% effectiveness of such an evaluation method as professional aptitude tests. Thus, Bennett Mechanical Comprehension Test is used to reveal abilities to engineering professions.

Among psychodiagnostic methods applied within a social psychological approach of evaluation instrument methods are becoming more prevalent. They are used for investigations of attention capacity, short-term and permanent memory, reaction rate, reaction accuracy, etc. Diagnostic means with virtual reality interfaces play a special part in application of instrument methods.

2 Features of Virtual Reality for Diagnostics of Psychophysiological Characteristics

2.1 The Effectiveness of Diagnosis Using Virtual Reality

Virtual reality is characterized by a number of peculiarities that facilitate more effective diagnostics. Yu.P. Zinchenko et al. consider a possibility of complete control over an observer's attention and system customizability to be the main advantage of virtual reality technology [8].

In addition to it, such factors as a possibility of motivation, control and interaction, practicability, interactivity, spatial orientation, and multisensory activity are also described in the literature as advantages of virtual reality systems [8]. It is noted that the virtual reality interface is an effective teaching tool for people with limited health capacities. V.V. Selivanov believes that application of virtual reality in teaching can help implement a principle of visualization more effectively and establish better relations with real situations [2].

Beside a big number of outlined advantages there are some restrictions connected with financial, technical and conceptual difficulties [8]. It is also reasonable to assume [1] that the effect of presence in the virtual reality depends on the individuality and can be observed not in every instance. Moreover, it is shown by experiments [1] that an output device (a screen or 3D glasses) does not affect time of test completion, and on the contrary, it makes a great impact on correctness of task performance - a screen image causes a less number of errors.

In diagnostics of human psychophysiological characteristics the study of interaction between visual perception and motor activity is of the greatest interest as in modern technical systems an operator plays a key role [5] and should have highly developed visual and motor skills, especially in cases of hazardous situation risks.

Virtual reality technology makes it possible to study different ways of interaction between the person's perception of the events going on around and their actions. The non-existing (virtual) reality, which surrounds a person and into which a person gets immersed, integrates with their real actions and movements in the "non-existing" space.

Virtual reality technologies suppose an effect of presence in the virtual reality and communicate the effect of immersion into the virtual environment to test persons in different ways depending on the equipment [2, 9]:

- a virtual reality program is displayed on the PC monitor and special glasses are used, in this case the degree of immersion is the least, only individual sessions are possible;
- a program uses a big inclined screen, the image is projected to the back side of the screen, special glasses and a remote control device are necessary;
- a virtual room with projections on three walls and the floor, semitransparent 3D glasses combining VR image with real image, additional accessories such as a sensor glove for tactile perception or a joystick for control of one's movements in the virtual reality. The room can be used individually or by student or test groups.

Thus, application of virtual reality implies instrument methods and at the same time promotes a search for new methods aimed at recording human reactions. VR interface diagnostic devices play a special part, they help identify reactions characterizing human professional features and capabilities.

In this connection, evaluation of conformity of the individual possibilities to certain professional activities taking into account individual peculiarities of sensor, cognitive and motor reactions becomes more relevant.

2.2 Intellectual System of Professional Rehabilitation on Virtual Reality Technology

At the present time the Volga State University of Technology is developing an intelligent training system for career guidance and professional rehabilitation. The system comprises methods of psychology, diagnostic medicine and virtual reality technology and is aimed at diagnostics, career guidance, inclusive teaching and learning and professional rehabilitation within an integral methodological approach.

The intelligent training system performs a complex investigation of human psychophysiological characteristics and cognitive mechanisms and focuses on identifying the professional potential of test persons and their professional orientation, on their professional training and further training.

The intelligent training system implemented as a complex smart expert system on the base of uniquely designed methods of studying human psychophysiological state with the use of fuzzy logic and a fuzzy set device will make it possible to construct an individual psychophysiological portrait of a test person and develop an individual program of professional training which can be implemented with the use of the developed system.

In addition to it, it is supposed to make a comprehensive evaluation of human professional efficiency on the base of learning outcomes using this intelligent training system. The evaluation outcomes help make scientifically valid recommendations for professional rehabilitation with the use of information technology and virtual reality systems.

Application of methods combining traditional techniques of experimental psychology and modern VR technologies becomes more relevant. Virtual reality used for examination of cognitive functions such as memory span, perception and attention makes it possible to estimate their parameters in the conditions of noise pollution of the space or a short-term stimulation.

In order to observe manifestation of psychophysiological features in the conditions of solution of complex cognitive tasks it is necessary to immerse test persons in the virtual environment demanding motor activity and space orientation. This can be a base for the development of tests aimed at revealing professional capabilities and professional aptitude to a number of occupations such as operators, drivers, pilots, sportsmen, engineers [5, 10], etc.

The development of such methods has become real due to the innovative technology of virtual reality which gives not only more realistic 3D incentives, but provides a test person with greater mobility in task solution. The proposed method uses the following techniques for organization of incentives and test person's actions.

All activities of the test person are followed by recording an electroencephalogram, a galvanic skin reaction, an electrocardiogram, etc. It is supposed that in some possible situations the cognitive processes (perception, memory, thinking) can prevail over one's own motor activity as well as in other situations the subject's activity is added with one's own motor activity actualized as goal motor actions while the degree of interaction between the cognitive processes and motor activity can be adjusted by "misalignment" of the visual and motor components. As a result, interaction of the cognitive processes and actions can cause a significant change in efficiency of task solution. The proposed method makes it possible to conduct multifactorial psychological and psychophysiological experiments for research into:

1. interaction between the cognitive processes (perception, memory, thinking) and behavior (actions);
2. influence of degrees and forms of motor-cognitive cooperation on the subject's successful practical activities;
3. particularities of brain and autonomic nervous system activities in the context of an actual goal behavior.

Some author's methods of measuring psycho-physiological features of a person, with the use of additional reality should be considered [4].

3   Methods for Measuring Psycho-Physiological Characteristics of a Person

3.1   Method for Determining the Time of Perception of Visual Information [11]

A method for determining the latent period of a person's visual perception is known. In this method, a test object with equal background illumination is formed and affects the apple of the eye with a flash from the light source, with subsequent fixation of changes in the diameter of the apple of the eye under the influence of a flash of light.

As a test object, the apple of the eye of a test person is used, and the light source is positioned from the eye at a distance less than the focal length, after which a light pulse is formed with an amplitude equal to the background preset duration Ti, the trailing edge of which coincides with the moment when the test person began to contract his apple of the eye, and the latent period of visual perception of the pupillary reaction of a person is determined by the value of Ti.

The disadvantage of the method is the need to use special equipment to fix the moment of the contraction of the apple of the eye of a test person, the dependence of the diameter of the apple of the eye on background illumination.

There are some studies of the time parameters of stimulus identification and decision making about the reaction that constitute the "middle term" of the reflex. To measure the temporal parameters of the sensory phase of the reflex, a reverse masking technique is used, which makes it possible to determine the time of perception necessary to transfer information to the central nervous system and its identification.

The time of perception is the period from the moment of the start of the exposure of the test short stimulus to the activation of the masking stimulus, when the latter can no longer interfere with the recognition of the test stimulus. During the research, the test persons are presented with one of 3 to 4 letters on the electroluminescent screen and after a certain period of time includes a masking stimulus - a single flash with a duration of 100 mcs. The masking stimulus is switched on after 20 ms after the end of the exposure of the letter. Then a pause between test and masking stimuli with each sample is increased by 10 ms, until the subject does not recognize the letter. The time of perception of letter stimuli is measured.

The disadvantage of the method is the low accuracy in determining the time of perception of visual stimuli and the dependence of the time of perception of the letter information on the parameters of the stimuli, as it is known that in the recognition of stimulus features such as the location of the stimulus contour, its orientation and size, the timing specifications of the identification are different. The low accuracy of determining the time of perception of visual stimuli is due to the value of the sampling of the change in the pause duration between the letter stimulus and the masking stimulus which is equal to 10 ms.

The closest method to the technical essence of the proposed method is a method for determining the time of perception of visual information by presenting to the test person a sequence of two light impulses of a predetermined duration, for example, equal to 50 ms separated by a pause equal to, for example, 150 mcs repeating after a constant time interval of about 1,5 s, the duration of the pause between the light impulses is reduced until the test person determines the moment of subjective fusion of two light impulses into one, and in the first stage of the measurement the duration of a pause between two light impulses with a predetermined constant speed of about 20 ms/s is reduced until the test person determines an estimated subjective fusion of two light impulses into one; in the second measurement step, the pause time between two light impulses with a predetermined constant speed of about 5 ms/s is increased, until the subject determines the moment of subjective feeling of separation of two light impulses; in the third stage of measurements the duration of a pause between two light impulses with a predetermined constant speed of about 2 ms/s is reduced, until the test person determines the moment of subjective fusion of two light impulses into one, characterized by the fact that the time of human perception of the visual information is taken as equal to the sum of the duration of the light impulse and the duration of the pause between two light impulses at the moment of subjective fusion of two light impulses into one, determined at the third stage of measurements.

The disadvantage of the method is:

- low accuracy in determining the time of perception of visual information, as it is determined by continuous change of the duration of a pause between two light impulses, and the human eye is more sensitive to the perception of a discretely varying duration;
- the limited conditions for determining the time of perception of visual information;
- binding to stationary equipment.

There are helmet-mounted systems of target designation and indication (HSTDI) - obligatory for modern combat planest and helicopters. The HSTDI projects the image on a transparent screen, which is in front of the pilot's eyes and fixed on his helmet. As the screen is transparent, the pilot can simultaneously observe both the external situation and the information displayed: basic flight parameters, tactical and navigational information.

Devices for displaying augmented reality are more perspective for the research work. Among such devices, lightweight glasses of the augmented reality of EpsonMoverio BT-200 or GoogleProjectGlass and miniature contact lenses of the augmented reality of Innovega (iOptik system) are known. The innovative iOptik system can work in conjunction with specialized glasses. Its user is focused simultaneously on several objects of different remoteness, and the perception of one object does not interfere with the perception of the other.

However, these technical means are not intended to determine the time of perception of visual information.

The technical result achieved by the claimed invention is to increase the accuracy of determining the time of perception of visual information, to provide the possibility of expanding the conditions for determining the time of perception of visual information, for example, when performing motor or other exercise test, in the course of any activity, in stationary conditions or ground, water or flight movements of a test person.

The technical result is achieved by presenting to a test person a sequence of two light impulses of duration of 50 ms, separated by a pause equal to 150 ms, repeated through a constant technical lapse of 1,5 s during a motional or load test or during any activity, under stationary conditions or ground, water or flight movements. In the first stage of measurements, the duration of a pause between two light impulses is reduced until the test person determines the moment of the fusion of two light impulses into one, in the second stage of measurements the duration of a pause between two light impulses is increased until the test person determines the moment of sensation of the separation of two light impulses, the time of human perception of visual information is taken equal to the sum of the duration of the light impulse and the duration of the pause between two light impulses at the time of sensation of the separation of two light impulses determined at the second stage of the measurements, **the new is that** the light impulses are presented with the help of portable devices that form augmented reality, in the first stage, the duration of the pause between two light impulses is reduced with each subsequent presentation discretely with a given constant step 0,5 ms. In the second stage, the duration of the pause between two light impulses is increased for each subsequent presentation discretely with a given constant step of 0.1 ms, the duration of the pause between two light pulses at the moment of sensation of the separation of two light pulses is fixed, further, during the execution of the motional or load test or in the process of any activity the test person is presented with light impulses with the last fixed duration of the pause periodically with a given period, if the testee feels the fusion of two light pulses into one, the duration of a pause between two light impulses is increased with each subsequent presentation discretely with a given constant step of 0.1 ms until the subject determines the moment of sensation of the separation of two light impulses, the duration of a pause between two light impulses at the moment of sensation of separation of two light impulses is fixed, if the test person feels two light impulses separate, the duration of a pause between two light pulses is reduced with each subsequent presentation discretely with a predetermined constant step of 0.1 ms until the test person determines the moment of fusion of two light impulses into one, the duration of a pause between two light impulses at the moment of the fusion of two light pulses into one is fixed.

The proposed method for determining the time of perception of visual information is as follows.

A device (helmet, glasses or lenses) which forms augmented reality and which is a part of the research software and hardware complex is fixed on a test person. The researcher from the program library of the complex chooses and sets the test person the mode of the motional or load test, or the test person is engaged in some activity.

Then, a sequence of two light pulses of 50 ms duration, separated by a pause equal to 150 ms, repeating through a constant time interval of 1.5 s, is applied to the device that forms the augmented reality.

In the first stage of measurements, the duration of a pause between two light impulses is reduced with each subsequent presentation discretely at a predetermined constant step of 0.5 ms until the test person determines the moment of the fusion of two light pulses into one.

In the second stage of measurements, the duration of a pause between two light pulses is increased for each subsequent presentation discretely at a predetermined constant step of 0.1 ms, until the subject determines the moment of sensation of separation of two light impulses. The duration of a pause between two light impulses at the moment of sensation of the separation of two light impulses is fixed.

The time of human perception of visual information is taken equal to the sum of the duration of the light impulse and the duration of the pause between two light impulses at the moment of sensation of the separation of two light impulses determined at the second stage of measurements.

Then periodically with a specified period, the test person is presented with light impulses with the last fixed duration of the pause. If the test person feels the fusion of two light pulses into one, the duration of a pause between two light impulses is increased with each subsequent presentation discretely with a given constant step of 0.1 ms until the person determines the moment of sensation of separation of two light impulses.

The duration of a pause between two light impulses at the moment of sensation of the separation of two light pulses is fixed.

If the subject feels two light pulses separate, the duration of a pause between two light impulses is decreased at each subsequent presentation discretely with a given constant step of 0.1 ms, until the subject determines the moment of the fusion of two light pulses into one. The duration of a pause between two light pulses at the moment of the fusion of two light pulses into one is fixed.

The fixation of the duration of a pause is made according to the relative actions or signals of the person, which are fixed by the software-hardware complex or by the researcher. When the test person is moved from the researcher at a considerable distance, communication and information exchange is carried out via the radio channel.

The proposed method for determining the time of perception of visual information allows:

– to increase the accuracy of determining the time of perception of visual information;
– to expand the conditions for determining the time of perception of visual information due to the possibility of carrying out tests in natural or artificial conditions, including tests when moving on land, in water or in air;
– to determine the time of perception of visual information with simultaneous presentation to the test person the symbolic characters or other additional information necessary for the test to be carried out near or far from the researcher in online mode;
– to control the functional state of the test person, in particular the development of fatigue during the motional or load test or in the course of any activity according to the dynamics of the time of perception of visual information.

Famous technical solutions and means can be used in the implementation of this method. Well-known or original software may be used for computer processing of information.

The described method for determining the time of perception of visual information differs from those well-known for new properties, which cause a positive effect. The method allows determining the time of perception of visual information in conditions under which it was impossible to perform earlier.

In addition to the above described method, the authors developed the following methods based on the technology of additional reality:

• *a method for determining the excitation time of a human visual analyzer*, which allows [12]:

– to expand the conditions for determining the time of excitation of the human visual analyzer due to the possibility of carrying out tests under natural or artificial conditions, including tests when moving on land, in water or in air;
– to determine the time of excitation of the visual analyzer of the person with simultaneous presentation of the symbolic characters or other additional information necessary for the test to be performed near or far from the researcher in the online mode;

- to control during the performance of the motional or load test or in the course of any activity the functional state of the subject, in particular the development of fatigue according to the dynamics of excitation of the visual analyzer.

The described method for determining the time of excitation of the human visual analyzer differs from those well-known because of the new properties that cause a positive effect.

- *a method for determining the time of inertia of the human visual system*, which allows [13]:

  - to expand the conditions for determining the time of inertia of the human visual system due to the possibility of carrying out tests under natural or artificial conditions, including tests under stationary conditions or when traveling on land, in water or in air;
  - to determine the time of inertia of the human visual system with simultaneous presentation of the symbolic characters or other additional information necessary for the test to be carried out near or far from the researcher in online mode;
  - to control during the performance of the motional or load test, or in the course of any activity the functional state of the subject, in particular the development of fatigue according to the dynamics of the time of inertia of the visual system.

4 Conclusion

Application of modern computer technologies makes possible objective psychophysiological diagnostics revealing test persons' psychic characteristics relating to their professional orientation. Virtual reality becomes a new effective research method of experimental psychology. Virtual reality technology gives unique opportunities for attaining new objectives of innovative higher education.

Acknowledgement. The research work is done by the support of RF Ministry of Education and Science grant No. 25.1095.2017/ПЧ and Russian Foundation for Basic Research grant No. 16-08-00386.

References

1. Averbukh, N.V., Shcherbinin, A.A.: The presence phenomenon and its influence upon intellectual task performance within virtual reality settings. Psychol. J. High. Sch. Econ. **8**(4), 102–119 (2011). https://www.elibrary.ru/item.asp?id=20147373. (in Russian)
2. Selivanov, V.V., Selivanova, L.N.: Virtual reality as teaching method and aid. Educ. Technol. Soc. **17**(3), 378–391 (2014). https://www.elibrary.ru/item.asp?id=21979557. (in Russian)
3. Chernysheva, A.V., Boychenko, T.A., Reznichenko, G.A.: Virtual reality in science and technology. Hum. Bull. BMSTU (8), 7 (2015). https://www.elibrary.ru/item.asp?id=24147147. (in Russian)

4. Gorokhova, R., Nikitin, P., Chernykh, D., Petrenko, O.: Application features of virtual reality in diagnostics of human psychophysiological characteristics. In: The European Proceedings of Social and Behavioural Sciences - RPTSS 2017, vol. XXXV, Article no: 48, pp. 411–419 (2018). https://doi.org/10.15405/epsbs.2018.02.48

5. Tatjanenko, S.A.: Professionally important qualities of contemporary engineers. In: Proceedings of the VII International Research Conference "Topical Issues of Pedagogy and Psychology", JeNSKE, Novosibirsk, Part II, pp. 147–151 (2011). https://sibac.info/archive/pedagog/01.08.2011-II.pdf. (in Russian)

6. Petukhov, I., Steshina, L., Kurasov, P., Tanryverdiev, I.: Decision support system for assessment of vocational aptitude of man-machine systems operators. In: 2016 IEEE 8th International Conference on Intelligent Systems (IS), Sofia, pp. 672–679 (2016). http://doi.org/ https://doi.org/10.1109/IS.2016.7737383

7. Samojlik, N.A.: The questionnaire "diagnostics of the personality's professional and value orientations": a technology of its development and psychometric characteristics. Russ. J. Educ. Psychol. (7), 141–166 (2016). https://www.elibrary.ru/item.asp?id=27115250. (in Russian)

8. Zinchenko, Yu.P., Menshikova, G.Ya., Bayakovskii, Yu.M., Chernorizov, A.M., Voiskunsky, A.E.: Virtual reality technology in the context of world and national psychology: methodological aspects, achievements and prospects. Natl. Psychol. J. 1(3), 54–62 (2010). https://www.elibrary.ru/item.asp?id=16533395. (in Russian)

9. Bakhareva, V.A., Zakharova, U.S., Serbin, V.A., Feshchenko A.V.: The technology of virtual and augmented reality in the educational environment of university. Open Distance Educ. 4(60), 12–20 (2015). https://doi.org/10.17223/16095944/60/2. (in Russian)

10. Boguslavets, M., Bavula, A., Karpenko, V.: Preparation of marine engineers based on use virtual learning environments. Tidings Baltic State Fish. Fleet Acad. Psychol. Pedagogical Sci. 2(36), 162–165 (2016). https://www.elibrary.ru/item.asp?id=26225531. (in Russian)

11. Afonshin, V.E., Rozhentsov, V.V., Nikitin, P.V.: Method for determining the excitation time of the human visual analyzer. Patent RF, no. 2626597 C1 (2017). (in Russian)

12. Afonshin, V.E., Rozhentsov, V.V., Nikitin, P.V.: Method for determining the time of inertia of the human visual system. Patent RF, no. 2626686 C1 (2017). (in Russian)

13. Afonshin, V.E., Rozhentsov, V.V., Nikitin, P.V.: Method for determining the time of perception of visual information. Patent RF, no. 2626687 C1 (2017). (in Russian)

Scientific Software in Education and Science

Comparative Analysis of New Semi-empirical Methods of Modeling the Sag of the Thread

Marina Berminova⒟, Aliya Galyautdinova⒟, Alexandra Kobicheva⒟, Valery Tereshin⒟, Dmitry Tarkhov$^{(\boxtimes)}$ ⒟, and Alexander Vasilyev⒟

Peter the Great St. Petersburg Polytechnic University, Polytechnicheskaya Str. 29, 195251 Saint-Petersburg, Russia

Abstract. We propose a new approach to the construction of multilayer neural network models of real objects. It is based on the method of constructing approximate multilayer solutions of ordinary differential equations (ODEs), which was successfully used by the authors earlier. The essence of this method is to modify known numerical methods for solving ODEs and applying them to a variable-length interval. Classical methods produce a table of numbers as a result; our methods provide approximate solutions in the form of functions. This approach allows refining the model when new information is received. In accordance with the proposed concept of constructing models of complex objects or processes, this method is used by the authors to construct a neural network model of a freely sagging real thread. Measurements were made using experiments with a real hemp rope. Originally, a rough rope model was constructed in the form of an ODE system. It turned out that the selection of unknown parameters of this model does not allow satisfying the experimental data with acceptable accuracy. Then, using the author's method, three approximate functional solutions were constructed and analyzed. The selection of the same parameters allowed us to obtain the approximations, corresponding to experimental data with accuracy close to the measurement error. Our approach illustrates a new paradigm of mathematical modeling. From our point of view, it is natural to regard conditions, such as boundary value problems, experimental data, as raw materials for constructing a mathematical model, the accuracy and the complexity of which must correspond to the initial data.

Keywords: Ordinary differential equation (ODE) · Boundary value problem · Approximate solution · Multilayered solution · Mathematical model · Semi-empirical model · Neural network · Experimental data · Model refinement

1 Introduction

When modeling real objects, it is often impossible (or very difficult) to describe the physical processes occurring in them accurately. In this regard, we have to be content with differential equations and additional conditions (initial, boundary, and some other relations) that reflect the behavior of the simulated object insufficiently accurately. As a result, an exact solution of differential equations (which are mathematical models of

© Springer Nature Switzerland AG 2021
V. Sukhomlin and E. Zubareva (Eds.): SITITO 2017, CCIS 1204, pp. 217–228, 2021.
https://doi.org/10.1007/978-3-030-78273-3_21

the above-mentioned physical processes) does not allow us to construct an adequate (acceptable) mathematical model of the object under study. Also, each real object has features that cannot always be taken into account from general considerations. In these conditions, it is reasonable to refine the model of the object, based on the observations of it.

Refinement of physical models and corresponding differential equations is a difficult task. It is not always possible to obtain a sufficiently accurate model, modifying only the coefficients of the equation without changing its structure.

We used neural network modeling methods to solve such problems [1–11, 19–25]. The essence of this approach is that an approximate solution is sought in the form of a neural network function of the selected type, the parameters (weights) of which are selected by methods of nonlinear optimization of the functional that characterizes the quality of the solution. (Note that a similar approach can also be used to calculate the geometric transformation that connects point clouds in three-dimensional space, by minimizing the functional that characterizes the quality requirements to the solution.) This method has some similarities with the finite element method (FEM), without requiring the solution of the somewhat artificial problem of fragmentation (triangulation) of the domain. The local nature of the functions that are characteristic of the finite element method makes it difficult to solve the problem of constructing a solution from heterogeneous data – differential equations and additional conditions. The neural network solution is more resistant to errors in the data, but the process of building it is very time-consuming. Recently, neural network models of this kind are commonly called physics-informed neural networks (PINN) [12–15].

We propose a different approach [1, 2, 4, 6–11, 20], consisting of two stages. At the first stage, an approximate solution (or set of solutions) of the differential equations considered is constructed as a function for which the parameters of the problem are input variables. At the second stage, this function is refined by observations, and the refinement process can continue when new data are received.

Our approach differs from the approach [16–18] in that we replace with the semi-empirical (for example, neural network) model not part of a system that is difficult to model by differential equations, but the whole system, including differential equations. Our approach is preferable in the situation when the accuracy of the object description by differential equations is low.

The advantage of this approach is the significantly less computational complexity of building a model and selecting its parameters compared to the above-mentioned neural network approach. The compactness of the built models makes it convenient to use them in embedded systems. Another significant advantage of this approach is the fact that the constructed model automatically includes the parameters of the problem.

In this article, this approach is illustrated by the problem of calculating the sagging line of the hemp rope, which is difficult to solve by standard methods.

2   A Semi-empirical Model of the Sagging Thread

First, we construct a simple model for a thread based on the boundary value problem. Let us consider a freely hanging inextensible thread of length l, fixed at its ends at the same level.

We will introduce all the notations necessary for the calculations: here L is the distance between the supports, s – the length of the section of the curve, θ – the angle of inclination of the tangent (it is counted from the direction of the horizontal axis x counterclockwise), $\mathbf{A}$ and $\mathbf{B}$ – the vectors of the reaction forces of the supports, $\mathbf{q}$ – the distributed load caused by the weight of the thread. Let us take into account that $B = mg/2$, $q = mg/l$, where m – the weight of the thread, and g – the magnitude of the acceleration of gravity. We also denote E – Young's modulus of thread material, J – the moment of inertia of the cross-section.

To take into account the flexural rigidity, we use the equation

$$EJ\frac{d^2\theta}{ds^2} = (B - qs)\cos\theta + A\sin\theta, \tag{1}$$

with boundary conditions: $\theta(0) = 0$, $\theta(l) = 0$.

According to the given above formulas and notations, Eq. (1) reduces to the form

$$\frac{d^2\theta}{ds^2} = \frac{mg}{EJ}\left(0.5 - \frac{s}{l}\right)\cos\theta + \frac{A}{EJ}\sin\theta.$$

We make the change of variable $t = 2s/l - 1$. In this case, Eq. (1) takes the form

$$\frac{d^2\theta}{dt^2} = -a\,t\cos\theta + b\sin\theta. \tag{2}$$

Constants – the parameters a and b – are unknown and are to be determined from experimental data.

Equation (2) is supplemented by boundary conditions $\theta(0) = \theta(1) = 0$.

To find the sagging line of the thread in parametric form, we can use the system of Eqs. (3):

$$\begin{cases} \frac{dx}{ds} = \cos\theta, \\ \frac{dy}{ds} = \sin\theta. \end{cases} \tag{3}$$

The behavior investigation of the solutions of this equation showed that the desired form of the thread cannot be obtained. Previously, we solved this kind of problem by neural network approach [19, 21–25] which leads to a time-consuming process due to the training and selection of network weights which are parameters, artificially introduced into the problem.

To speed up the computation and artificial exclusion from the decision parameters, we use options of a multilayered approach to constructing an approximate solution of ordinary differential equations [1, 2, 4, 6–11, 20]. We transform the ODE (2) to the ODE system.

$$\begin{cases} \dfrac{d\theta}{dt} = z, \\ \dfrac{dz}{dt} = -a\,t\cos\theta + b\sin\theta. \end{cases}$$

To solve this problem, several explicit methods of solution were applied. Below is a description of three of them. We denote by $f(t, \theta) = -at\,\cos(\theta) + b\,\sin(\theta)$.

The First Method. The first step is done by Euler's method

$$\theta_1 = \theta_0 + hc = hc, \quad z_1 = z(0) + hf(0,0) = c.$$

Here is $c = z(0)$.

The second step is done according to the refined Euler method [26]

$$\theta_2 = \theta_0 + 2hz_1 = 2hc, \quad z_2 = c + 2hf(t_1, \theta_1) = c + 2hf(h, hc),$$

We choose $h = t/4$, whence $z_2(t) = c + \frac{t}{2}f\left(\frac{t}{4}, \frac{t}{4}c\right)$. Next, we make the step of the refined Euler method

$$\theta_3(t) = \theta_0 + 4hz_2(t) = tc + \frac{t^2}{2}f\left(\frac{t}{4}, \frac{t}{4}c\right) = tc + \frac{t^2}{2}b\sin\left(\frac{t}{4}c\right) - \frac{t^3}{8}a\cos\left(\frac{t}{4}c\right).$$

The Second Method. The first step is done by Euler's method $\theta_1 = \theta_0 + hz_0 = hz_0$. The second step is done by the Störmer method [26].

$$\theta_2 = 2\theta_1 - \theta_0 + h^2 f(h, \theta_1) = 2hc + h^2 f(h, hc).$$

In this case $h = t/2$, whence

$$\theta_2 = tc + \frac{t^2}{4}f\left(\frac{t}{2}, \frac{tc}{2}\right) = tc + \frac{t^2}{4}\left(b\sin\frac{tc}{2} - at\cos\frac{tc}{2}\right).$$

The Third Method. . We start on the right. The boundary conditions have the form $z(1) = c, \theta(1) = 0$. The first step is done by the corrected Euler method [26]

$$\theta_1 = \theta_0 + hc + \frac{f(1,0)}{2}h^2 = hc - \frac{a}{2}h^2.$$

The second step is done by the Störmer method

$$\theta_2 = 2\theta_1 - \theta_0 + h^2 f(1 - h, \theta_1) = 2hc - ah^2 + h^2 f\left(1 - h, hc - \frac{a}{2}h^2\right).$$

In this case $h = t/2$, whence

$$\theta_2 = (1 - t)c - a\frac{(1-t)^2}{4} + \frac{(1-t)^2}{4}f\left(\frac{1+t}{2}, \frac{(1-t)c}{2} - a\frac{(1-t)^2}{8}\right)$$

$$= (1 - t)c - a\frac{(1-t)^2}{4} + \frac{(1-t)^2}{4}$$

$$\times \left(b\sin\left(\frac{(1-t)c}{2} - a\frac{(1-t)^2}{8}\right) - a\frac{(1+t)}{2}\cos\left(\frac{(1-t)c}{2} - a\frac{(1-t)^2}{8}\right)\right)$$

Equations for the coordinates of the line are obtained by integrating (3) using the Simpson method

$$x(s, \mathbf{a}) = \frac{s}{6m}\left(1 + \cos\theta(s, \mathbf{a}) + 4\sum_{i=1}^{m}\cos\theta\left(\frac{s}{2m}(2i - 1), \mathbf{a}\right) + 2\sum_{i=1}^{m-1}\cos\theta\left(\frac{s}{m}i, \mathbf{a}\right)\right);$$

$$y(s, \mathbf{a}) = \frac{s}{6m}\left(\sin\theta(s, \mathbf{a}) + 4\sum_{i=1}^{m}\sin\theta\left(\frac{s}{2m}(2i-1), \mathbf{a}\right) + 2\sum_{i=1}^{m-1}sin\theta\left(\frac{s}{m}i, \mathbf{a}\right)\right). \quad (4)$$

Here is $\mathbf{a}$ – a vector with coordinates a, b and c. Identification of a, b and c carried out by minimization of the error functional

$$J = \sum_{i=1}^{M}(x(s_i, \mathbf{a}) - x_i)^2 + \sum_{i=1}^{M}(y(s_i, \mathbf{a}) - y_i)^2, \quad (5)$$

which includes observational data $\{x_i, y_i\}_{i=1}^{M}$. To do this, we use the approximate solution (4), constructed by one of the three methods indicated.

3 Results of Calculation

Identifying the parameters a, b and c, we get the following graphs (Figs. 1, 2, 3, 4, 5, 6, 7, 8, 9 and Table 1):

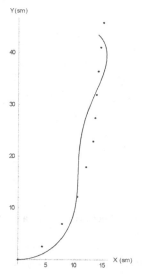

Fig. 1. The right half of the graph are lines $\{x(s, \mathbf{a}), y(s, \mathbf{a})\}$, obtained by the first method.

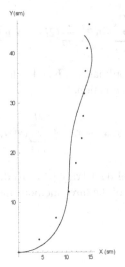

Fig. 2. The right half of the graph are lines $\{x(s, \mathbf{a}), y(s, \mathbf{a})\}$, obtained by the second method.

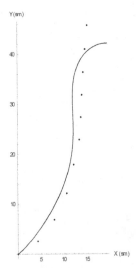

Fig. 3. The right half of the graph are lines $\{x(s, \mathbf{a}), y(s, \mathbf{a})\}$, obtained by the third way and the experimental points for $L = 0.3\,m$.

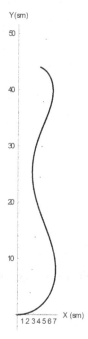

Fig. 4. The right half of the graph are lines $\{x(s, \mathbf{a}), y(s, \mathbf{a})\}$, obtained by the first method.

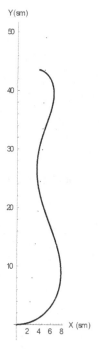

Fig. 5. The right half of the graph are lines $\{x(s, \mathbf{a}), y(s, \mathbf{a})\}$, obtained by the second method.

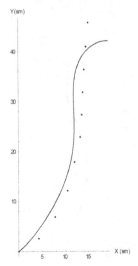

Fig. 6. The right half of the graph are lines $\{x(s, \mathbf{a}), y(s, \mathbf{a})\}$, obtained by the third way and the experimental points for $L = 0.1\, m$.

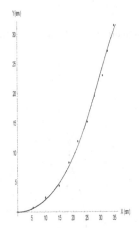

Fig. 7. The right half of the graph are lines $\{x(s, \mathbf{a}), y(s, \mathbf{a})\}$, obtained by the first method.

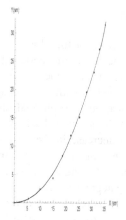

Fig. 8. The right half of the graph are lines $\{x(s, \mathbf{a}), y(s, \mathbf{a})\}$, obtained by the second method.

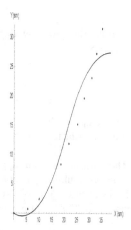

Fig. 9. The right half of the graph are lines $\{x(s, \mathbf{a}), y(s, \mathbf{a})\}$, obtained by the third way and the experimental points for $L = 0.7\,m$.

Table 1. Dependence of the root-mean-square error σ on the length L.

L, cm	Root-mean-square error σ		
	First way	Second way	Third way
10	3.83321	14.7184	2.06525
20	2.56196	2.60111	2.09851
30	2.78654	2.73364	2.30488
40	1.78029	1.71293	2.01957
50	1.08483	1.0084	1.70125
60	0.395341	0.305341	1.59632
70	0.677857	0.569207	2.31278
80	0.597448	0.59966	1.88719
90	0.426384	0.426259	1.54927

4   Results and Discussion

The mathematical model construction of the object or process is connected, usually with the approximate solution of the differential equations with coefficients inaccurately given of miscellaneous data, which may also include experimental data. In a fairly good situation (when the equations, together with the boundary and other conditions, are chosen successfully, i.e. they correspond to the real object with sufficient accuracy), the refinement of the solution of the problem leads both to a decrease in the error in satisfying the equation, and to a decrease in the error in satisfying the measurement data. However, if the choice of the equations for the model is not the right one, it is possible to improve the model by selecting the most appropriate one from a series of models that correspond to varying degrees to the original differential model. We offer to choose them from a variety of models built using our proposed approach and selection of adjustable parameters to meet the experimental data. This improvement was observed in our model problem. The effectiveness of the proposed approach was also confirmed in the study.

Acknowledgments. This work has been supported by the grants of the Russian Science Foundation (RSF) – project № 21-11-00095.

References

1. Tarkhov, D.A., Vasilyev, A.N.: Semi-empirical Neural Network Modeling and Digital Twins Development. Academic Press, Elsevier, Amsterdam (2019). https://doi.org/10.1016/C2017-0-02027-X
2. Tarkhov, D.A., Vasilyev, A.N.: The construction of the approximate solution of the chemical reactor problem using the feedforward multilayer neural network. In: Kryzhanovsky, B., Dunin-Barkowski, W., Redko, V., Tiumentsev, Y. (eds.) NEUROINFORMATICS 2019. SCI, vol. 856, pp. 351–358. Springer, Cham (2020). https://doi.org/10.1007/978-3-030-30425-6_41
3. Afanaseva, M.N., Vasilyev, A.N., Kuznetsov, E.B., Tarkhov, D.A.: The best parametrization for solving the boundary value problem for the system of differential-algebraic equations with delay. J. Phys. Conf. Ser. **1459**(1), 012003 (2020). https://doi.org/10.1088/1742-6596/1459/1/012003
4. Vasilyev, A., Kuznetsov, E., Leonov, S., Tarkhov, D.: Comparison of neural network and multilayered approach to the problem of identification of the creep and fracture model of structural elements based on experimental data. In: Sukhomlin, V., Zubareva, E. (eds.) SITITO 2018. CCIS, vol. 1201, pp. 319–334. Springer, Cham (2020). https://doi.org/10.1007/978-3-030-46895-8_25
5. Galyautdinova, A.R., Sedova, J.S., Tarkhov, D.A., Varshavchik, E.A., Vasilyev, A.N.: Comparative test of evolutionary algorithms to build an approximate neural network solution of the model boundary value problem. In: Kryzhanovsky, B., Dunin-Barkowski, W., Redko, V., Tiumentsev, Y. (eds.) NEUROINFORMATICS 2018. SCI, vol. 799, pp. 67–76. Springer, Cham (2019). https://doi.org/10.1007/978-3-030-01328-8_5
6. Lazovskaya, T., Tarkhov, D.: Multilayer neural network models based on grid methods. In: IOP Conference Series: Materials Science and Engineering, 11th International Conference on "Mesh Methods for Boundary-Value Problems and Applications", 20–25 October 2016, Kazan, Russia, vol. 158, p. 012061 (2016). https://doi.org/10.1088/1757-899X/158/1/012061

7. Bolgov, I., Kaverzneva, T., Kolesova, S., Lazovskaya, T., Stolyarov, O., Tarkhov, D.: Neural network model of rupture conditions for elastic material sample based on measurements at static loading under different strain rates. J. Phys. Conf. Ser. **772** (2016). In: Joint IMEKO TC1-TC7-TC13 Symposium: Metrology Across the Sciences: Wishful Thinking? 3–5 August 2016, Berkeley, USA, p. 012032 (2016). https://doi.org/10.1088/1742-6596/772/1/012032

8. Filkin, V., et al.: Neural network modeling of conditions of destruction of wood plank based on measurements. J. Phys. Conf. Ser. **772** (2016). In: Joint IMEKO TC1-TC7-TC13 Symposium: Metrology Across the Sciences: Wishful Thinking? 3–5 August 2016, Berkeley, USA, p. 012041 (2016). https://doi.org/10.1088/1742-6596/772/1/012041

9. Vasilyev, A., et al.: Multilayer neural network models based on experimental data for processes of sample deformation and destruction. In: CEUR Workshop Proceedings, Selected Papers of the First International Scientific Conference Convergent Cognitive Information Technologies (Convergent 2016), Moscow, Russia, 25–26 November 2016, vol. 1763, pp. 6–14 (2016). http://ceur-ws.org/Vol-1763/paper01.pdf. (in Russian)

10. Tarkhov, D., Shershneva, E.: Approximate analytical solutions of mathieu's equations based on classical numerical methods. In: CEUR Workshop Proceedings, Selected Papers of the XI International Scientific-Practical Conference Modern Information Technologies and IT-Education (SITITO 2016), Moscow, Russia, 25–26 November 2016, vol. 1761, pp. 356–362 (2016). http://ceur-ws.org/Vol-1761/paper46.pdf. (in Russian)

11. Vasilyev, A., Tarkhov, D., Shemyakina, T.: Approximate analytical solutions of ordinary differential equations. In: CEUR Workshop Proceedings, Selected Papers of the XI International Scientific-Practical Conference Modern Information Technologies and IT-Education (SITITO 2016), Moscow, Russia, 25–26 November 2016, vol. 1761, pp. 393–400 (2016). http://ceur-ws.org/Vol-1761/paper50.pdf. (in Russian)

12. Raissi, M., Perdikaris, P., Karniadakis, G.E.: Physics-informed neural networks: a deep learning framework for solving forward and inverse problems involving nonlinear partial differential equations. J. Comput. Phys. **378**, 686–707 (2019). https://doi.org/10.1016/j.jcp.2018.10.045

13. Raissi, M.: Deep hidden physics models: deep learning of nonlinear partial differential equations. J. Mach. Learn. Res. **19**, 1–24 (2018). https://www.jmlr.org/papers/volume19/18-046/18-046.pdf

14. Raissi, M., Perdikaris, P., Karniadakis, G.E.: Physics informed deep learning (part I): data-driven solutions of nonlinear partial differential equations. arXiv:1711.10561v1 [cs.AI] (2017)

15. Raissi, M., Perdikaris, P., Karniadakis, G.E.: Physics informed deep learning (part II): data-driven discovery of nonlinear partial differential equations. arXiv:1711.10566v1 [cs.AI] (2017)

16. Prostov, Y., Tiumentsev, Y.: A hysteresis micro ensemble as a basic element of an adaptive neural net. Opt. Memory Neural Netw. **24**(2), 116–122 (2015). https://doi.org/10.3103/S1060992X15020113

17. Egorchev, M.V., Tiumentsev, Yu.V.: Learning of semi-empirical neural network model of aircraft three-axis rotational motion. Opt. Memory Neural Netw. (Inf. Opt.) **24**(3), 210–217 (2015). https://doi.org/10.3103/S1060992X15030042

18. Kozlov, D.S., Tiumentsev, Yu.V.: Neural network based semi-empirical models for dynamical systems described by differential-algebraic equations. Opt. Memory Neural Netw. (Inf. Opt.) **24**(4), 279–287 (2015). https://doi.org/10.3103/S1060992X15040049

19. Vasilyev, A.N., Tarkhov, D.A.: Mathematical models of complex systems on the basis of artificial neural networks. Nonlinear Phenom. Compl. Syst. **17**(3), 327–335 (2014). http://www.j-npcs.org/online/vol2014/v17no3p327.pdf

20. Budkina, E.M., Kuznetsov, E.B., Lazovskaya, T.V., Shemyakina, T.A., Tarkhov, D.A., Vasilyev, A.N.: Neural network approach to intricate problems solving for ordinary differential equations. Opt. Memory Neural Netw. **26**(2), 96–109 (2017). https://doi.org/10.3103/S10609 92X17020011

21. Budkina, E.M., Kuznetsov, E.B., Lazovskaya, T.V., Leonov, S.S., Tarkhov, D.A., Vasilyev, A.N.: Neural network technique in boundary value problems for ordinary differential equations. In: Cheng, L., Liu, Q., Ronzhin, A. (eds.) ISNN 2016. LNCS, vol. 9719, pp. 277–283. Springer, Cham (2016). https://doi.org/10.1007/978-3-319-40663-3_32

22. Gorbachenko, V.I., Lazovskaya, T.V., Tarkhov, D.A., Vasilyev, A.N., Zhukov, M.V.: Neural network technique in some inverse problems of mathematical physics. In: Cheng, L., Liu, Q., Ronzhin, A. (eds.) ISNN 2016. LNCS, vol. 9719, pp. 310–316. Springer, Cham (2016). https://doi.org/10.1007/978-3-319-40663-3_36

23. Shemyakina, T.A., Tarkhov, D.A., Vasilyev, A.N.: Neural network technique for processes modeling in porous catalyst and chemical reactor. In: Cheng, L., Liu, Q., Ronzhin, A. (eds.) ISNN 2016. LNCS, vol. 9719, pp. 547–554. Springer, Cham (2016). https://doi.org/10.1007/978-3-319-40663-3_63

24. Kaverzneva, T., Lazovskaya, T., Tarkhov, D., Vasilyev, A.: Neural network modeling of air pollution in tunnels according to indirect measurements. J. Phys. Conf. Ser. **772** (2016). In: Joint IMEKO TC1-TC7-TC13 Symposium: Metrology Across the Sciences: Wishful Thinking? 3–5 August 2016, Berkeley, USA, p. 012035 (2016). https://doi.org/10.1088/1742-6596/772/1/012035

25. Lazovskaya, T.V., Tarkhov, D.A., Vasilyev, A.N.: Parametric neural network modeling in engineering. Recent Patents Eng. **11**(1), 10–15 (2017). https://doi.org/10.2174/187221211 1666161207155157

26. Hairer, E., Nørsett, S.P., Wanner, G.: Solving Ordinary Differential Equations I:Nonstiff Problem. Springer, Heidelberg (1987). https://doi.org/10.1007/978-3-662-12607-3

Neural Network Installation of the Functional Dependence of Mechanical Behavior in the Expansion of Elastic Material from Temperature

Ekaterina Filchuk[1] , Juriy Kasparov[1] , Tatyana Kaverzneva[1] , Juliya Sedova[1] ,
Oleg Stolyarov[1] , Dmitriy Tarkhov[1] , Evgeniy Varshavchik[1] ,
and Ildar Zulkarnay[2,3](✉)

[1] Peter the Great St. Petersburg Polytechnic University, Polytechnicheskaya Str. 29,
195251 Saint-Petersburg, Russia
[2] Bashkir State University, Zaki Validi Str. 32, 450076 Ufa, Republic of Bashkortostan, Russia
[3] Ufa Federal Research Center of the Russian Academy of Sciences, October Av. 71,
450054 Ufa, Republic of Bashkortostan, Russia

Abstract. The influence of temperature on mechanical characteristics during stretching of elastic material is investigated, functional dependence is created by means of neural networks. Perceptrons with a varying number of neurons were used. High-strength heat-resistant complex filaments were the samples in experiments. The tests were carried out at 5 different temperature levels. On the basis of the obtained data, the functional dependence of each of the parameters on the temperature of the material was revealed. For polyester thread, methods for processing data from an accelerated experiment are given, which make it possible to significantly shorten the time of its carrying out. The methods considered are universal and can be applied to other elastic materials.

Keywords: Neural networks · Elastic material · Stretching · Neural network model

1 Introduction

The aim of this paper is to establish the dependence of the elastic material's elongation on temperature and, as a consequence, to construct a strain prediction as a function of the tension and temperature in sufficiently wide ranges.

In work [1] processes of deformation of elastic materials and prediction by neural networks of the moment of sample rupture at specific values of temperatures were described. Similar studies were carried out in [2], but at different deformation rates. In our work, in addition, the dependence of the stretching of the sample at any temperatures in a given range is investigated and a functional description of the behavior of the material at an arbitrary temperature on the basis of deformation at certain specific values is constructed.

© Springer Nature Switzerland AG 2021
V. Sukhomlin and E. Zubareva (Eds.): SITITO 2017, CCIS 1204, pp. 229–237, 2021.
https://doi.org/10.1007/978-3-030-78273-3_22

2   Investigation of Aramid Thread

The experiments were carried out at five different temperatures: 100, 150, 200, 250 and 300 °C on an Instron universal measuring unit, equipped with a thermal chamber. Samples were fixed in the clamps of the test installation at a certain temperature and stretched at a constant speed of movement of the upper clamp of 100 mm/min. The result was obtained in the form of a stretching curve representing the relationship between elongation and stress arising inside the test sample. After fixing the samples in the clamps installed in the heat chamber, they were heated to a predetermined temperature level, held for 10 min and subjected to stretching prior to rupture. The obtained diagrams of expansion are shown in Fig. 1. From the diagrams obtained, it can be seen that with the change in the test temperature, the behavior of the specimens under tension and, as a consequence, their mechanical characteristics under tension, changes.

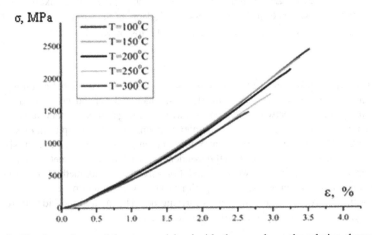

Fig. 1. The dependence of the stress arising inside the sample on the relative elongation.

The elastic properties of various materials are difficult to predict, due to their complex mechanical behavior. To solve such problems, neural networks are used because of their adaptability and resistance to errors in the data.

The neural network was used in the work in 3 stages. At the first stage, a perceptron with two neurons was used to approximate the measurement results, in order to obtain a function representing the dynamics of the stretching for a particular temperature.

Using the species function $\sigma(\varepsilon) = c_1 \tanh(a_1(\varepsilon - xc_1)) + c_2 \tanh(a_2(\varepsilon - xc_2))$, it was possible to approximate the dependence of the tension on the relative elongation quite accurately. Here ε is the relative elongation, and $\sigma(\varepsilon)$ is the tension corresponding to it. The coefficients $a_{1,2}$, $c_{1,2}$ and $xc_{1,2}$ were sought from the condition of minimum mean square error. Similar methods were used by us earlier in [1–3].

In the process of approximation, we obtained a plot of dependence between the tension and the relative elongation. Below is an example of a graph for approximating experimental data by a neural network model (Fig. 2) and deviating the model from the data (Fig. 3).

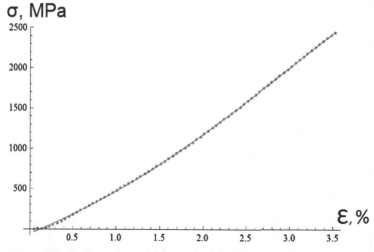

Fig. 2. Dependence of the tension on elongation at 100 °C.

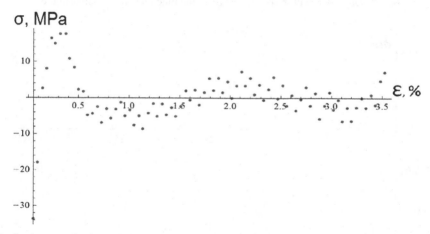

Fig. 3. An error in the neural network approximation of the experimental dependence of the tension on the relative elongation at 100 °C.

At the second stage of using the neural network, having obtained coefficients of the function $\sigma\,(\varepsilon)$ for each of the temperatures, we used a new network with 1 neuron to determine the dependence of each of the coefficients on the material temperature. For this problem we used dependencies of the form $c_3 - c_4 \tanh(a_3(T - xc_3))$. Here T is the temperature of the material. Dependence coefficients were still sought from the condition of the minimum of the error functional (Figs. 4 and 5).

At the third stage of the application of neural networks we used a perceptron with one neuron to approximate the dependence of the rupture tension σ_b on temperature. Its graph is presented at Fig. 6.

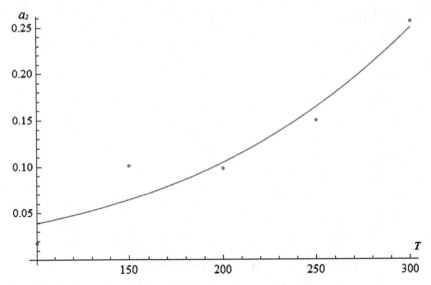

Fig. 4. Dependence of the coefficient a_2 of the function $\sigma(\varepsilon)$ on temperature.

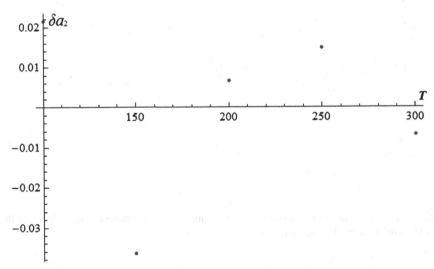

Fig. 5. An error in the neural network approximation of the coefficient a_2 of the function $\sigma(\varepsilon)$ as a function of temperature.

As a result, we have obtained a function that allows us to find the critical temperature at which the rupture tension on the sample becomes zero, that is, the temperature at which the sample melts. In laboratory studies for a given load, the thread loses its elastic properties at a similar temperature, hence finding a function by neural networks gives a fairly accurate prediction (Fig. 7).

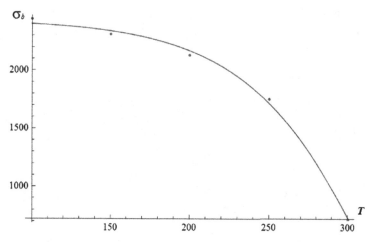

Fig. 6. Functional dependence of the points of rupture on temperature.

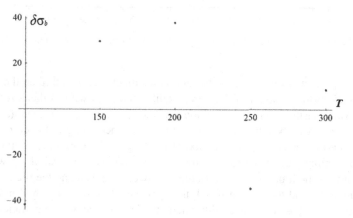

Fig. 7. An error in the neural network approximation of the functional dependence of the coordinates of the points of rupture on temperature.

3 Investigation of Polyester Thread

Consider the behavior of another elastic material - polyester thread. Having carried out similar tests on the tension of the sample at various temperatures, we obtain a graph of the dependence of the tension in the sample on the time of its stretching. The jumps in the graph represent an increase in temperature in the experimental setup (Fig. 8).

The main problem of this experiment is its duration. Due to the fact that the functional dependence on each individual section approaches the linear one, there is a desire to predict this linear asymptotics with respect to the initial segment of each section of the curve. Finding the approximation of the initial deformation in each section at a certain temperature, we find the strain prediction for the rest of this section. If the discrepancy

σ, MPa

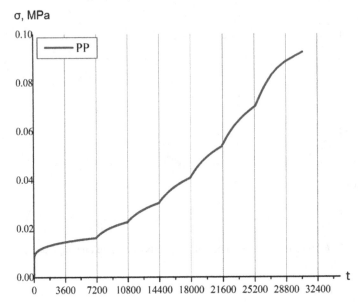

Fig. 8. Dependence of the tension in the material on time at different temperatures.

between the predicted function and the laboratory function is small, then the obtained function predicts the behavior of the sample quite accurately with further stretching.

Approximating the parts of the function is a function $\sigma(t) = (c + d\,t)\tanh(a\,t)$, which most accurately describes the stretching of the sample according to the computational emulations carried out. Using the method of least squares, we find the coefficients for the growing initial part of the sample for each section. The interval along which the approximation is built up, until the difference between the data and the prediction on a small segment behind the one on which the approximation was built will not become small enough. Next, we investigate the functional dependence of the coefficients of the functions found for different temperatures in the experimental setup and derive their functional dependence.

The resulting functional dependences are a theoretical prediction of the behavior of the sample at all temperatures (Fig. 9, 10 and 11). For the coefficients, we plot the temperature dependence of the form $b\tanh(\alpha(T - Tc))$. For an example, we give an approximation of the coefficient d representing the dependence of this coefficient on temperature.

Using the given functions of the dependence of the coefficients on the temperature for the material stretching function and knowing the behavior of the sample at a temperature of 48°, we predict the stretching of the material at 55° and compare the obtained dependence with the experimental one (Fig. 11).

As we see, knowing the law of stretching the material at several temperature values of the sample under study, we can accurately predict the behavior of the material at a higher temperature.

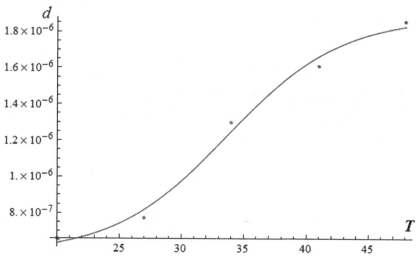

Fig. 9. Dependence of the coefficient d on temperature.

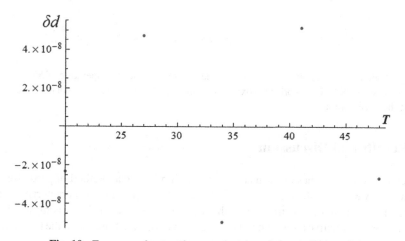

Fig. 10. Error neural network approximation of the coefficient d.

This method of predicting the behavior of a sample has a very important area of applicability. Often it is necessary to predict the deformation of materials arising during a long time. But in the laboratory, we can force the deformation of the material by increasing the temperature in the experimental setup.

And, finding the equivalent of stretching the heated sample for a time, if the test was conducted at room temperature, we can predict the stretching of the material for any time interval at a constant temperature.

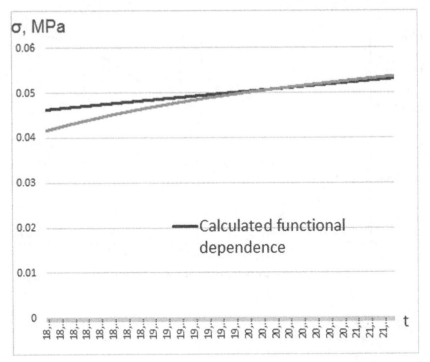

Fig. 11. Calculated functional dependence of the tension on time at temperature of 55°, obtained in the course of neural network approximation, and the experimental dependence established during the observation.

4   Results and Discussion

The conducted researches allow us to build a certain universal method of predicting the behavior of various elastic materials with changing their mechanical characteristics. This method is based on the construction of the dependence of the tension arising within the sample from the relative elongation of the elastic material as a function of the temperature in the form of a suitable neural network approximation.

Since for each individual test material there is a dynamics of the change in elastic characteristics, the task arises to accumulate a unique data bank based on materials where the prediction of their behavior is particularly important from the point of view of ensuring safety during their long-term operation. The operation of any technical objects, including buildings, structures, devices (for example, ropes, slings, safety ropes) and their individual elements is associated with a certain risk of their destruction or break-up, which can still be prevented, sometimes with data on the change in the mechanical characteristics of the materials from which they are made. Technical means used to rescue people in extreme situations, must be continuously improved with the advent of new materials that increase the possibility of rescue, for example, in high-temperature conditions or when a falling person needs to be taken from a building height to a canopy.

Building standards set certain service life of objects, but the statistics of various accidents shows how difficult it is to calculate them. In modern conditions it became necessary to take into account the influence of temperature climatic changes on the duration of safe operation of various materials and their wear and tear. In our studies, the temperature "loading" of the samples allows us to perform a kind of "aging" of materials with the construction of a model for predicting the deformation of the filament material during its stretching.

Acknowledgements. This paper is based on research carried out with the financial support of the grant of the Russian Scientific Foundation (project № 18-19-00474).

References

1. Bolgov, I., Kaverzneva, T., Kolesova, S., Lazovskaya, T., Stolyarov, O., Tarkhov, D.: Neural network model of rupture conditions for elastic material sample based on measurements at static loading under different strain rates. In: Journal of Physics: Conference Series, 2016 Joint IMEKO TC1-TC7-TC13 Symposium: Metrology across the Sciences: Wishful Thinking?, Berkeley, USA, 3–5 August 2016, vol. 772, p. 012032 (2016). https://doi.org/10.1088/1742-6596/772/1/012032
2. Vasilyev, A., et al.: Multilayer neural network models based on experimental data for processes of sample deformation and destruction. In: CEUR Workshop Proceedings, Selected Papers of the First International Scientific Conference Convergent Cognitive Information Technologies (Convergent 2016), Moscow, Russia, 25–26 November 2016, vol. 1763, pp. 6–14 (2016). http://ceur-ws.org/Vol-1763/paper01.pdf. (in Russian)
3. Filkin, V., et al.: Neural network modeling of conditions of destruction of wood plank based on measurements. In: Journal of Physics: Conference Series, 2016 Joint IMEKO TC1-TC7-TC13 Symposium: Metrology across the Sciences: Wishful Thinking?, Berkeley, USA, 3–5 August 2016, vol. 772, p. 012041 (2016). https://doi.org/10.1088/1742-6596/772/1/012041
4. Aranda-Iglesias, D., Vadillo, G., Rodríguez-Martínez, J.A., Volokh, K.Y.: Modeling deformation and failure of elastomers at high strain rates. Mech. Mater. **104**, 85–92 (2017). https://doi.org/10.1016/j.mechmat.2016.10.004
5. Zéhil, G.-P., Gavin, H.P.: Unified constitutive modeling of rubber-like materials under diverse loading conditions. Int. J. Eng. Sci. **62**, 90–105 (2013). https://doi.org/10.1016/j.ijengsci.2012.09.002
6. Kaverzneva, T.T., Smirnova, O.V.: Wear-out effect of construction equipment and hand tools on workers' labor conditions. Saf. Technosphere **2**(3), 14–18 (2013). https://doi.org/10.127 37/446. (in Russian)
7. Efremov, S.V., Kaverzneva, T.T., Tarkhov, D.A.: Neural Network Modeling in Labor Protection. Publishing House of SPbSPU, Saint-Petersburg (2014). (in Russian)

Comparison of Multilayer Methods of Solutions to the Spectral Cauchy Problem for the Wave Equation

Alexander Vasilyev[1] , Dmitry Tarkhov[1] , and Tatiana Lazovskaya[2]([⊠])

[1] Peter the Great St.Petersburg Polytechnic University, Polytechnicheskaya Str. 29, 195251 Saint-Petersburg, Russia
[2] Khabarovsk Federal Research Center of the Far Eastern Branch of the Russian Academy of Sciences, Dzerzhinskogo Str. 54, 680000 Khabarovsk, Russia

Abstract. This article continues the authors' research on the methods of constructing approximate multilayer solutions of differential equations as functions. These methods are based on the use of classical formulas for the approximate solution of differential equations for a variable interval. They have been used successfully by the authors in solving problems for ordinary differential equations. The solution to the initial-boundary value problems for partial differential equations encounters certain difficulties. We test the proposed methods of overcoming these difficulties in the first place on simple problems with known analytical solution. Here we consider the problem for the simplest wave equation with one space variable in the case of special initial conditions (Gaussian) and zero boundary conditions at infinity. We compare different methods by computational experiments: the Euler method, the corrected Euler method, the Störmer method and its modifications. The results of applying these methods are compared with the known analytical solution.

Keywords: Computational methods · Wave equation · Initial-boundary value problem · Finite difference method · Multilayer approximate solution

1 Introduction

In articles [1–5] the authors presented for the first time methods of constructing approximate solutions of differential equations in the form of functions based on classical finite-difference schemes. Since then, work on the study of such multilayer solutions and their properties for different types of equations has been continued [2–5]. The analysis of the dependence of the accuracy of the constructed solution on the selected basic schemes and the selected number of layers is carried out.

In this paper, we consider the solution of the one-dimensional wave equation as a representative of the linear hyperbolic partial differential equation. The equation is solved on the entire spatial axis with the initial condition for the solution in the form of a Gaussian (with zero initial condition for the derivative of the solution) with the possibility of extending to an arbitrary function.

© Springer Nature Switzerland AG 2021
V. Sukhomlin and E. Zubareva (Eds.): SITITO 2017, CCIS 1204, pp. 238–250, 2021.
https://doi.org/10.1007/978-3-030-78273-3_23

2 Statement of the Problem and Description of Methods

We consider the one-dimensional wave equation

$$\frac{\partial^2 y}{\partial t^2} = \frac{\partial^2 y}{\partial x^2} \tag{1}$$

with special initial conditions

$$y(0, x) = f(x), \quad \frac{\partial y}{\partial t}(0, x) = 0, \tag{1a}$$

where $t \in R^+$ – time, $x \in R$ – space variable.

Note that the initial conditions of the form $y(0, x) = 0$, $\frac{\partial y}{\partial t}(0, x) = f(x)$ can be considered similarly.

The method of the articles [1, 2, 5] consists in the application of the selected difference scheme for the interval with a variable right end. Equation (1) was considered as an equation with respect to the variable t in the operator form

$$\frac{\partial^2 y}{\partial t^2} = A(y), \tag{2}$$

where $A(y) = \frac{\partial^2 y}{\partial x^2}$.

We would like to implement the methods that are a modification of the formulas for the numerical solution of equations and systems of first-order equations, so we rewrite the problem (1) as a system

$$\begin{cases} \dfrac{\partial y}{\partial t} = z, \\[2mm] \dfrac{\partial z}{\partial t} = A(y), \end{cases} \tag{3}$$

where the auxiliary function $z(t, x)$ satisfies all necessary conditions.

It is known [6] that linear combinations of shifts and strains of standard functions of neural network bases (sigmoids, Gaussians, and others) can approximate arbitrary functions from a wide class. Therefore, in this paper, we consider the initial boundary value problem for Eq. (1) with the condition of the form

$$y(0, x) = y_0(x) = \exp(-x^2), \quad x \in R. \tag{4}$$

Function (4) is the simplest radial basis function (RBF). In general, the initial condition of a sufficiently general form can be approximated by the expression

$$y(0, x) = f(x) \cong \sum_{i=1}^{n} \omega_i \exp\left(-a_i^2(x - b_i)^2\right). \tag{4a}$$

Let us construct an approximate solution of the problem (1) $u(t, x)$ for the initial condition (4). Then, for the initial condition of the form (4a), the general view of the solution of the problem (1) will look like

$$U(t, x) \cong \sum_{i=1}^{n} \omega_i u(t, a_i(x - b_i)).$$

To solve problems (2)–(4) we have considered several basic methods [7, 8]. We considered both the methods used to solve first-order differential equations – variations of the Euler method, and the Störmer method for solving second-order problems of a special kind.

Throughout the number N means the number of layers of the final multi-layer approximation $y_N(t, x)$, which, including, the size of the step $h(t) = t/N$ depends on.

1. The Euler method, which for formulation (3)–(4) has the form:

$$\begin{cases} z_{k+1}(t, x) = z_k(t, x) + h(t) \cdot \frac{\partial^2 y_k(t,x)}{\partial x^2}, \\ y_{k+1}(t, x) = y_k(t, x) + h(t) \cdot z_k(t, x), \end{cases} \tag{5}$$

where $k = 0, ..., N-1$. Note that to the condition (4) is added by relation $z_0(t, x) = 0$.

2. Refined Euler's method for the problem (3)–(4):

$$\begin{cases} z_{k+1}(t, x) = z_{k-1}(t, x) + 2h(t) \cdot \frac{\partial^2 y_k(t,x)}{\partial x^2}, \\ y_{k+1}(t, x) = y_{k-1}(t, x) + 2h(t) \cdot z_k(t, x), \end{cases} \tag{6}$$

where $k = 1, ..., N - 1$. Here, in addition to the condition (4), there are relations

$$y_1(t, x) = y_0(t, x), \quad z_0(t, x) = 0, \quad z_1(t, x) = h(t) \exp(-x^2).$$

3. Corrected Euler's method for the problem (3)–(4):

$$\begin{cases} z_{k+1}(t, x) = z_k(t, x) + h(t) \cdot \frac{\partial^2 y_k(t,x)}{\partial x^2} + \frac{1}{2}h^2(t) \cdot \frac{\partial^2 z_k(t,x)}{\partial x^2}, \\ y_{k+1}(t, x) = y_k(t, x) + h(t) \cdot z_k(t, x) + \frac{1}{2}h^2(t) \cdot \frac{\partial^2 y_k(t,x)}{\partial x^2}, \end{cases} \tag{7}$$

where $k = 0, ..., N - 1$. The initial conditions coincide with the conditions for the classical Euler method.

4. The Störmer method for the problem in the formulation (2), (4):

$$y_{k+1}(t, x) = 2y_k(t, x) - y_{k-1}(t, x) + h^2(t) \cdot \frac{\partial^2 y_k(t, x)}{\partial x^2}, \tag{8}$$

where $k = 1, ..., N - 1$. Initial conditions $y_1(t, x) = y_0(t, x)$.

5. The Störmer method with the first step according to the corrected Euler method:

$$y_{k+1}(t, x) = 2y_k(t, x) - y_{k-1}(t, x) + h^2(t) \cdot \frac{\partial^2 y_k(t, x)}{\partial x^2}, \tag{9}$$

where $k = 1, ..., N - 1$. The initial condition for the first step

$$y_1(t, x) = \exp(-x^2)(1 + (2x^2 - 1)h(t)).$$

3 Modifications Based on the Störmer Method

The calculations of the spatial variable derivatives in the iterative schemes (5)–(9) are too cumbersome and take a significant time of the whole computational process. It seemed to us to be natural replacing the second derivative with its difference approximation. As a starting point, we used the Störmer method for the problem in the formulation (2), (4).

Both the selection of the step $h(t)$ in the Störmer method and the step of the derivative approximation gives possibilities for different modifications of the formula (8). In this paper, we have considered the following options.

1. The step of approximation of the derivative H does not depend on the step $h(t)$ of the Störmer method itself. The solution has an additional parameter H. The iterative formula has the form.

$$y_{k+1}(t,x,H) = 2y_k(t,x,H) - y_{k-1}(t,x,H) + h^2(t) \cdot \frac{y_k(t,x+H,H) + y_k(t,x-H,H) - 2y_k(t,x,H)}{H^2},$$

where $k = 1, ..., N - 1$. As before, we consider $h(t) = t/N$, where N – the number of layers.
2. The step of approximation of derivative $H = \sqrt{h(t)}$.
3. The step of approximation of derivative $H = h(t)$.

4 Results of Computing

Approximation of the solution of problem (1) provided (4) was calculated according to the formulas (5)–(9) for various numbers of layers N. For different values of the time variable, from $t = 0$ to $t = 3$ (we consider the equation in dimensionless form), the maximum approximation error was calculated – the maximum error module in 1000 equidistant points with respect to the analytical solution $y * (t, x)$ of the problem (1):

$$e_{max}(t) = \max\{|y * (t,x) - y(t,x)|; \quad x = i \cdot 15/1000, \ i = 1, ..., 1000\}.$$

Table 1. The maximum error e_{max} at the point $t = 0.1$.

	$N = 5$	$N = 10$	$N = 20$	$N = 50$
Euler method	0.0055	0.0045	0.0018	0.00155
Refined Euler method	0.0004	0.038	0.0015	0.00245
lCorrected Euler method	0.0000066	0.0000018	0.00000045	0.000000073
Störmer method	0.0019	0.00096	0.00049	0.00019
Corrected Euler + Störmer method	0.00156	0.00091	0.00042	0.00108

Table 2. The maximum error e_{max} at the point $t = 1$.

	N = 5	N = 10	N = 20	N = 50
Euler method	0.21	0.205	0.0065	0.0081
Refined Euler method	0.033	0.221	0.0064	0.0165
Corrected Euler method	0.0164	0.00345	0.00084	0.000136
Störmer method	0.067	0.036	0.0182	0.0076
Corrected Euler + Störmer method	0.053	0.0343	0.0152	0.0382

Table 3. The maximum error e_{max} at the point $t = 3$.

	N = 5	N = 10	N = 20	N = 50
Euler method	1.65	1.68	0.6	0.29
Refined Euler method	17.1	8.55	0.17	0.535
Corrected Euler method	3.43	0.162	0.023	0.0035
Störmer method	6.2	0.056	0.028	0.0123
Corrected Euler + Störmer method	1.48	0.045	0.024	0.063

As we can see from the Tables, in the case when it is necessary to approximate the solution in the very near future ($t = 0.1$), it is possible to apply the usual Euler method by selecting a sufficient number of layers. The best result, in this case, is given by the corrected Euler method (Tables 1, 2 and 3).

We illustrate some of the results with graphs.

We consider the case $N = 20$ (Fig. 1).

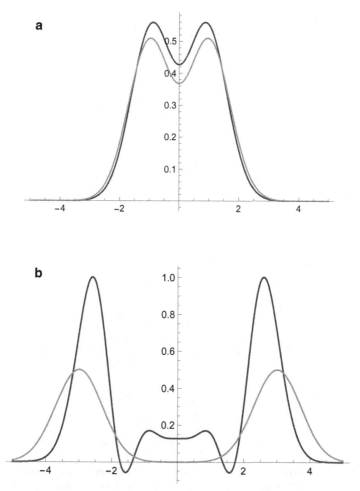

Fig. 1. (a) Graphs of exact solution (brown line) and approximate solution, constructed by the Euler method (blue line) when $t = 1$. (b) Graphs of exact solution (brown line) and approximate solution, constructed by the Euler method (blue line) when $t = 3$. (Color figure online)

The Euler method works only on the initial time interval when $t > 1$ the behavior of the approximate solution constructed using this method is very different from the exact solution (Fig. 2).

The results of the refined Euler method are substantially better. The outcome is all the more important in connection with the fact that the formulas of this method are the simplest because the movement is carried out through a step.

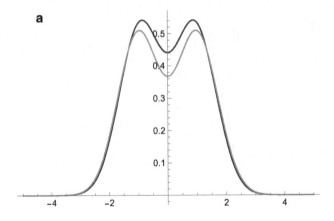

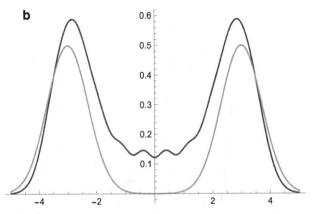

Fig. 2. (a) Graphs of exact solution (brown line) and approximate solution, constructed by the refined Euler method (blue line) when $t = 1$. (b) Graphs of exact solution (brown line) and approximate solution, constructed by the refined Euler method (blue line) when $t = 3$. (Color figure online)

We give error graphs for subsequent methods, as the approximate solution and exact solution curves are visually indistinguishable (Fig. 3).

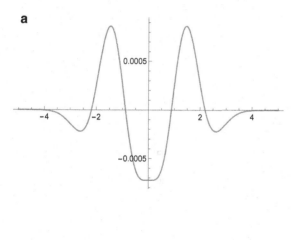

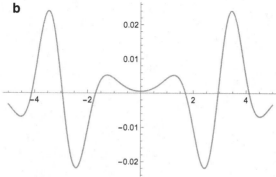

Fig. 3. (a) Graphs of the difference between the exact solution and the approximate solution, constructed by the corrected Euler method when $t = 1$. (b) Graphs of the difference between the exact solution and the approximate solution, constructed by the corrected Euler method when $t = 3$.

The corrected Euler method is the most accurate of all considered. Its labor intensity is also the greatest, but the increase in labor intensity, in this case, is justified, especially at small values of time t (Fig. 4).

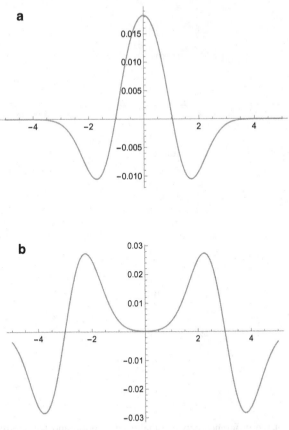

Fig. 4. (a) Graphs of the difference between the exact solution and the approximate solution, constructed by the Störmer method when $t = 1$. (b) Graphs of the difference between the exact solution and the approximate solution, constructed by the Störmer method when $t = 3$.

The results of the application of the Störmer method are significantly better than that of the refined Euler method, with similar labor intensity, which makes it possible to recommend it for such problems.

Figure 5 shows that the application of such a hybrid method leads to a noticeable increase in accuracy compared to the conventional Störmer method, especially when $t = 3$. At the same time, the labor intensity of calculations (and the complexity of the corresponding analytical formulas) is practically unchanged.

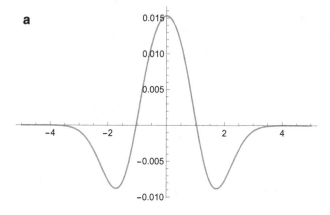

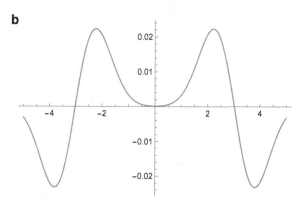

Fig. 5. (a) Graphs of the difference between the exact solution and the approximate solution, built by the Störmer method with the first step according to the corrected Euler method when $t = 1$. (b) Graphs of the difference between the exact solution and the approximate solution, built by the Störmer method with the first step according to the corrected Euler method when $t = 3$.

If to make the above modification to the Störmer method – to replace the second derivative with respect to x by the corresponding divided difference, the results practically do not change if the second or third step adjustment is applied (Figs. 6 and 7).

Note that by this modification we obtain a continuous analog of the difference scheme usual for this problem.

a

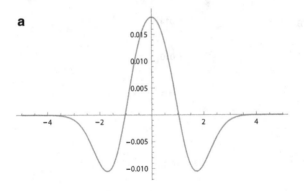

b

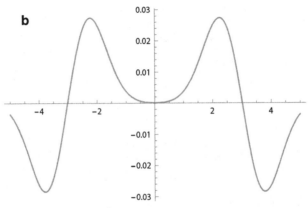

Fig. 6. (a) Graphs of the difference between the exact solution and the approximate solution, built by the Störmer method with the replacement of the second derivative concerning x by the corresponding divided difference with $H = \sqrt{h(t)}$ when $t = 1$. (b) Graphs of the difference between the exact solution and the approximate solution, built by the Störmer method with the replacement of the second derivative concerning x by the corresponding divided difference with $H = \sqrt{h(t)}$ when $t = 3$.

a

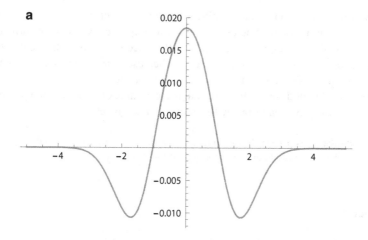

b

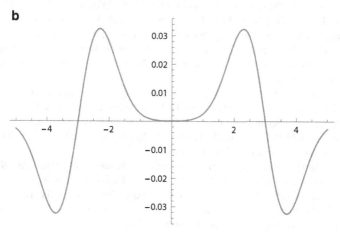

Fig. 7. (a) Graphs of the difference between the exact solution and the approximate solution, built by the Störmer method with the replacement of the second derivative with respect to x by the corresponding divided difference with $H = h(t)$ when $t = 1$. (b) Graphs of the difference between the exact solution and the approximate solution, built by the Störmer method with the replacement of the second derivative with respect to x by the corresponding divided difference with $H = h(t)$ when $t = 3$.

5 Conclusion

This article demonstrates that the methods [1, 2] can be successfully used to construct approximate solutions of not only ordinary differential equations [2–4], but also partial differential equations (see also [5]). The main difference offered methods from the classical methods for these problems is to find an approximate solution in the form of a single function, rather than a table of numbers (as in the case of using the grid method) or a piecewise continuous or piecewise smooth approximation (as in the case of the finite element method). Such representation is more convenient for further use - research of dependence on parameters, specification according to experiment data, etc. Such representation is more convenient for further use – research of dependence on parameters, specification according to experiment data, etc.

The proposed methods naturally extend to more complex problems – nonlinear, with the replacement of some conditions with experimental data, etc.

Acknowledgments. This paper is based on research carried out with the financial support of the grant of the Russian Scientific Foundation (project №18–19-00474).

References

1. Lazovskaya, T., Tarkhov, D.: Multilayer neural network models based on grid methods. In: IOP Conference Series: Materials Science and Engineering, 11th International Conference on "Mesh methods for boundary-value problems and applications", Kazan, Russia, 20–25 October 2016, vol. 158, p. 012061 (2016). https://doi.org/10.1088/1757-899X/158/1/012061
2. Vasilyev, A., Tarkhov, D., Shemyakina, T.: Approximate analytical solutions of ordinary differential equations. In: CEUR Workshop Proceedings, vol. 1761, Selected Papers of the XI International Scientific-Practical Conference Modern Information Technologies and IT-Education (SITITO 2016), Moscow, Russia, November 25–26 2016, pp. 393–400 (2016). http://ceur-ws.org/Vol-1761/paper50.pdf. (in Russian)
3. Vasilyev, A., et al.: Multilayer neural network models based on experimental data for processes of sample deformation and destruction. In: CEUR Workshop Proceedings, Selected Papers of the First International Scientific Conference Convergent Cognitive Information Technologies (Convergent 2016), Moscow, Russia, November 25–26 2016, vol. 1763, pp. 6–14 (2016). http://ceur-ws.org/Vol-1763/paper01.pdf. (in Russian)
4. Tarkhov, D., Shershneva, E.: Approximate analytical solutions of Mathieu's equations based on classical numerical methods. In: CEUR Workshop Proceedings, Selected Papers of the XI International Scientific-Practical Conference Modern Information Technologies and IT-Education (SITITO 2016), Moscow, Russia, 25–26 November 2016, vol. 1761, pp. 356–362 (2016). http://ceur-ws.org/Vol-1761/paper46.pdf. (in Russian)
5. Lazovskaya, T., Tarkhov, D., Vasilyev, A.: Multi-layer solution of heat equation. In: Kryzhanovsky, B., Dunin-Barkowski, W., Redko, V. (eds.) NEUROINFORMATICS 2017. SCI, vol. 736, pp. 17–22. Springer, Cham (2018). https://doi.org/10.1007/978-3-319-66604-4_3
6. Haykin, S.: Neural Networks: A Comprehensive Foundation. Prentice Hall, New York (1999)
7. Verzhbitsky, V.M.: Basics of Numerical Methods. Vysshaja shkola, Moscow (2002).(in Russian)
8. Hairer, E., Nørsett, S.P., Wanner, G.: Solving Ordinary Differential Equations I: Nonstiff Problem. Springer, Heidelberg (1987). https://doi.org/10.1007/978-3-662-12607-3

Network Analysis Software Within the Framework of Political Science in Russia

Ilia Bykov[1]([✉]) [iD], Denis Martyanov[1] [iD], and Natalia Ryabchenko[2] [iD]

[1] Saint-Petersburg State University, 13B Universitetskaya Emb.,
199034 Saint-Petersburg, Russia
i.bykov@spbu.ru
[2] Kuban State University, Stavropolskaya Str. 149, Krasnodar 350040, Russia

Abstract. This article is devoted to the analysis of the peculiarities of empirical research in Russia consistent with the methodology of network analysis. The article gives deals with software items and analytical cases, which show the application of the network analysis for both fully developed social networks and communities, as well as for identification and analysis of the network structures within the conventional channel of authority. The field of network research in Russia is circumscribed by the online space due to the availability and diversity of ways to identify, extract and record network data, which impedes transposition of online research findings into the whole social space. Besides, the authors of the article put a particular emphasis on the underworked area of mathematic methods used for network analysis, which is essential for a detailed interpretation of findings of the applied network research. The article also touches upon the issue of the forms of network analysis: principal form of network analysis in Russia is a structural network analysis, which allows an ultimate upgrade to network research.

Keywords: Network analysis · Political science · Research software · IT-education

1 Introduction

Several years ago Vladimir Gel'man, a political scientist from Russia with international reputation, published an article about unfortunate state of political science in Russia mentioning among other institutional and political factors a general theoretical, non-empirical approach in political studies. He emphasized an opinion that "Many Russian political scientists can endlessly discuss all sorts of grand theories and dance around big names ranging from Foucault to Huntington, but have never bothered themselves with things like Boolean analysis or regression models (and some of them have never even heard terms such as "R-square")" [1, p. 30]. The gap between theoretical and empirical political studies in Russia exists for sure, however, it is highly interesting to find out how the network approach as a primarily empirical technique is treated by political scientists in Russia.

In this article we are going to discuss the state of application of network analysis in Russian political science which is supposed to be empirically oriented and rely heavily

© Springer Nature Switzerland AG 2021
V. Sukhomlin and E. Zubareva (Eds.): SITITO 2017, CCIS 1204, pp. 251–260, 2021.
https://doi.org/10.1007/978-3-030-78273-3_24

on special scientific software. However, our study shows that network analysis approach while widely discussed and welcomed has a small outcome in Russia if we take into consideration results of empirical or comparative studies. List of publications with the results of empirical studies of politics in Russian is very short. Based on the personal research practice we argue that there is a huge gap in political studies between well-known SPSS-program, which is applied to the certain degree as a tool of empirical research in Russia, and special scientific software for network analysis. The article seeks to help political scientists who would like to use network analysis in their studies.

2 Method

Methodologically, the article relies chiefly on secondary sources, including translations of Russian sources and sources written in English by Russian political scientists, while drawing on our interactions with a variety of political scientists affiliated with academic and research institutions in Russia. Throughout the article we consider network analysis as method of investigating social structures through the use of networks and graph theory. The work was performed as a research initiative to invite attention to the software applications in the political studies. Since the subject has not been really investigated in scientific literature, the study has to have an exploratory design, aiming to draw a general picture. The article begins by tracing the opportunities and limitations of applied network analysis in political science in general, and what special software is available for political scientists in Russia. Next, we discuss the spread of network analysis in the Russian political science. Here, we describe usually used pieces of software and research techniques. After that, we study the practice of network analysis application by the Krasnodar school of political science. Krasnodar krai is a southern region of Russia, which rather recently started to be known abroad since the Winter Olympic Games in Sochi. In terms of scientific achievements this region has not been recognized yet. However, there is a well-known (at least in Russia) group of political scientist there which promotes network analysis application.

3 Network Analysis in Political Science: Opportunities and Limitations

Network analysis is an interdisciplinary research a program that seeks to describe and predict the structure of connections between objects. Unlike the usual approaches in social sciences, the network analysis proceeds from the assumption that the attributes of the actor are secondary, in contrast to the relationships in which the actor is composed. Thus, the network analysis is based on the perception of the structure as a cluster of connections of different actors. It is usually based on empirical data, uses mathematical models and gives visual representation of the bond structure. Research with network analysis tends to define network using big data analysis.

Since 1970, when the first specialized program of this kind was published, about a hundred programs were created. They differ among themselves quite significantly in various parameters: functionality, working environment, user in interface convenience, etc. It is believed that the first the program for the automatic construction of sociograms was created in 1970, and it was called SOCK. With its help, the first generated sociogram of intellectual circles in the United States was constructed. As the initial data, the texts of scientific and journalistic periodicals were used.

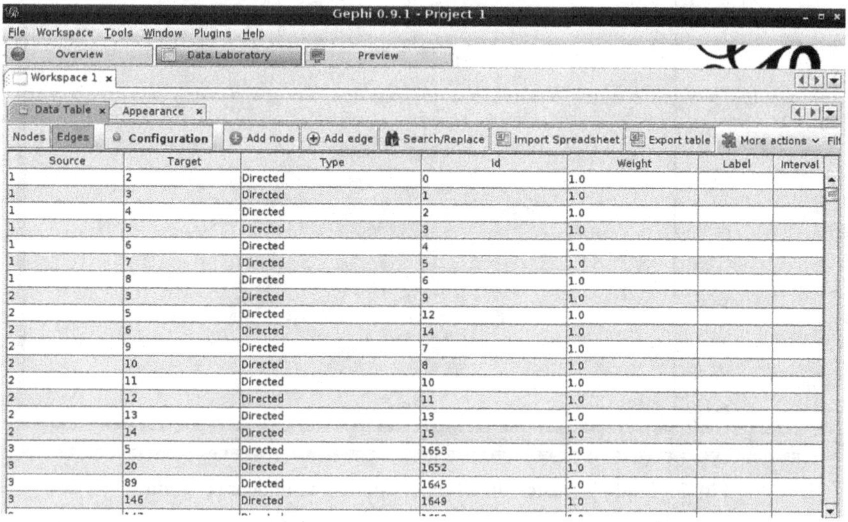

Fig. 1. Working with the data in Gephi. Source: Gephi program.

There is a wide variety of special programs for social networking analysis today. It is believed that there are about one hundred of special softwares for network analysis [2–4]. Among most known we would like to mention such programs as Gephi, CFinder, Cytoscape, NetMiner, Pajek, SocNetV, StOCNET, etc. They all use graphic interfaces, run in Windows, contain network data, are able to produce visualized output, and compute network statistics. Typical working interface includes sheet with network data (see Fig. 1). The most useful tool for political analysis deals with visualization of clusters or group of vertices which structures the networks.

The limits to use special software for network analysis usually starts with translation problem. Not all programs for network analysis are translated from English. More over, the quality of the existing translations is very disputable (Fig. 2).

The second problem includes relevance or specification of the given software for tasks of the study in hand. Sometimes, it is necessarily to write a new program in *Python* or other programming language in order to be able to collect and sort out the data from the Internet. Thus, to use network analysis the political scientist has to have knowledge and skills in statistics, linguistics, and data science.

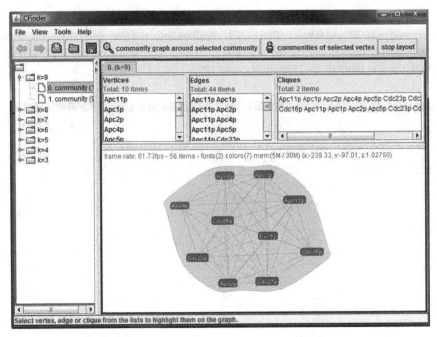

Fig. 2. Finding clusters in CFinder. Source: CFindeer program.

4 State and Scope of Current Political Studies with Network Approach in Russia

According the Russian Scientific Citation Index, there are about four thousand political scientists in Russia. However, it was not easy to find out results of empirical studies with network analysis. Especially, if we are talking about statistically significant results. The most interesting studies were made in the field of political social networking and mainly about *Vkontakte* users. *Vkontakte* is a social network service, highly popular in Russia. The paper by A. Gruzd and K. Tsyganova about Pro- and Anti-Maidan groups during the 2013/2014 Ukrainian Crises is one of the good examples of that approach [5]. The paper has not only good research design and visualization, but also pretends on statistical significance, which is rather unusual for political science in Russia. Another plus for the article includes thorough description of data collection and evaluation with Package *R* and its social network libraries "Statnet" and "Igraph" were used to manage, analyze, and visualize network data.

The similar research premises were used in the paper by Sergei Suslov about on-line political sphere of St. Petersburg [6]. He found that on-line political communication is divided on two political segments or clusters: liberal oriented and nationalist oriented (see Fig. 3). He argued that communists and socialists are almost invisible. It is very interesting, but due to the fact that all data were collected from *VK* and *Facebook* was not included in the study we have to take these results into consideration.

There is another interesting study of social structure of political protest in St. Petersburg around the St. Isaacs's Cathedral in 2017 [7]. The authors map and analyze the case of protest against the transfer of the St. Isaacs's Cathedral in St. Petersburg, Russia, to the Russian Orthodox Church using network analysis. The study reveals seven social groups participated in the protest. The big plus of the study includes the analysis of the dynamic of the protest movement, which is rather rear in this sort of studies. Unfortunately, we have not found discussion of statistical significance in this article.

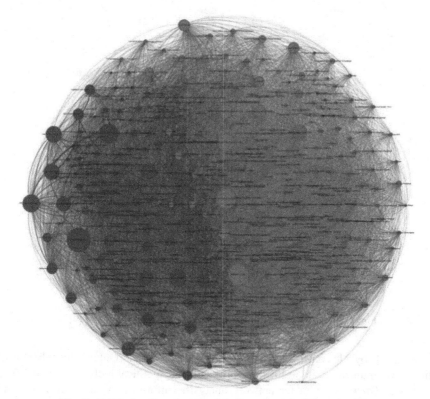

Fig. 3. Political online clusters of St. Petersburg in *VKontakte* [6].

Political elite studies are not often use network approach. However, there is a paper by E. Frideya and V. Smirnov about elite transformation in Lithuania after the USSR's collapse [8]. The study does not suggest a visualization and has no statistical significance because the data are very limited. We think that it is possible to study political elites with network analysis, though it is hardly possible to have significant results with small sample.

International relations as an interdisciplinary field of studies has been studied with network approach abroad. In Russia, we found one study which visualizes international conflicts after the Second World War [9]. The results of the study are presented in Fig. 4. It is very unexpected, but the United States is not in the center of the figure though Iraq is. We are not arguing with the results, but pointing out that they are not intuitive. It looks like the United States can not be smaller player than the Soviet Union. Also, we have not found discussion of statistical significance in this article.

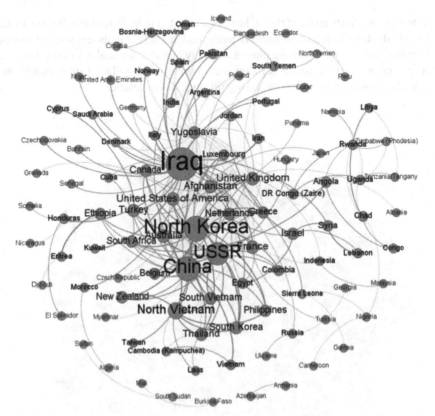

Fig. 4. Mapping international conflicts after second world war [9].

The article by Alexander Sherstobitov addresses very important problem about how political communication in on-line networks influence political mobilization [10]. The author uses *Pajek* as a tool for network analysis. Unfortunately, we have not found discussion of statistical significance in this article, which leaves the question unanswered. However, the problem of influence is central for network analysis because public opinion is formed by different factors. We believe that network analysis has to be used as an additional tool in political studies.

5   Practice of Network Analysis in Political Science: A Case of the Krasnodar School

Network analysis is common for the research and identification of social networks and communities which are based on popular social platforms, such as Facebook and VKontakte (the examples of the research of which are given above). Nevertheless, network analysis can be applied for identification and research with different social platforms. Therewith, "horizontal structures" imply the systems of connections within one or adjacent levels of the hierarchical structure, which complete and extend the system's structural and functional capacity (or having a detrimental impact on it). Overall, horizontal connections are crucial in order to enhance sustainability and flexibility of any system. Provided they are properly structured, the system acquires holographic features, when subsystems continue to perform as a system, even if substantial damages have been inflicted. Network analysis allows treating horizontal structures as networks.

One of the results of the study "Network resources of developing local policy in the context of new political reality", conducted by Krasnodar political scientists under N.A. Ryabchenko's leadership, a notion of a local network policy was conceptualized [11, 12]. "Local network policy" is treated as an activity focused on shaping political significance of regional and municipal geographical entities by means of tools and techniques of online sphere. Theoretical model of local network policy was defined. It included the following structural elements:

- local authorities;
- local online communities;
- local mass media online tools;
- local online media (municipal online journalism);
- small-size and mid-size business.

To analyze the degree of involvement of local authorities into the process of shaping local network policy local authority websites have been analyzed. Therewith, regarding the issue of local authority sites as a means of network local policy we can define two areas of concern. The first area implies low participation of users in terms of the website use (attendance, posts, comments, links etc.), and their participation in assessing website's performance. The second area deals with low performance of the websites: regardless of legislative standards, technical capacity of websites fail to comply with the content presented, which results in low network participation. These fields overlap and cause cross-expansion or contraction, due to an elevated level of users demand on social action within the online space, and vice versa. Obviously, these changes are being suspended.

However, the practice of social websites use shows that local authorities try to adjust to the users needs and perform to improve social services. According to the data presented by "Infometr" company, the most popular social platform among the bodies of authority is *Twitter*. This platform is also a leader as for the amount of posts and users. These data indicate a common trend of Russian segment of the online space. Regardless of occasional attempts to ban the use of social platforms by civil officials, social networks, which are based on these platforms, boost the dissemination of any topical item of information exponentially. Furthermore, they allow to monitor the general public feedback to a particular performance of the local authority. Undoubtedly, the use of social platforms poses a number of topical questions, but the modern online social networks feature the most consistent area, capable of carrying out a social action. As for the local authorities, their presence and performance in the social platforms must not be aimed at image-making, rather, it should operate according to the function of the body of local authority, which means enhancing interaction of the authorities and general public.

There are some difficulties when it comes to the use of social platforms. Firstly, it is common for the local authorities, represented in the social platforms, to repeat a news feed, in which case they neglect technical capacity of the social platforms used.

Secondly, the fact that there are fake accounts and bots (users, who do not actually exist but still have an account) to represent a local authority. To solve these problems, it is essential to introduce the restrictions for social platforms use by the bodies of authority, including the local authorities.

Having considered all these things above, the researchers encountered the questions, whether the system of local authority official websites is consistent with the network structure and what peculiarities of the connections within such a network are? To answer the questions a software program "Network Analysis of the public policy actors" has been developed. It collected the data on content traffic among local authority official websites, as well as among the municipality websites, the Governor and the Administration of Krasnodar krai, and presented the process as a social graph. As a result, a directed flow social network "Network analysis of public policy actors Krasnodar krai" (Fig. 5) has been developed. The given network comprises of 79 vertices with 124 directed interconnections. A directed flow social network represents a network with a clearly defined direction of connections between its vertices.

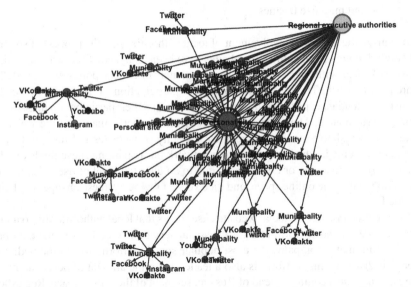

Fig. 5. Network analysis of public policy actors in Krasnodar krai. Source: Processed and composed by the authors.

Figure 5 shows a network, which has been formed by the municipality websites, represented by a vertex "unicipality"; personal sites of the Heads of municipalities (Governor of Krasnodar krai website included) a vertex "Personal site"; official presence of the municipalities in the social platforms (Krasnodar krai Administration included) vertices "*VKontakte*", "*Facebook*", "*YouTube*", "*Twitter*", "*Instagram*"; Krasnodar krai Administration website a vertex "*Regional executive authorities*". The conducted analysis shows sheer absence of connections between the "unicipality" vertex, whose interaction is only possible through a network mediator (a function performed by the "*Regional executive authorities"* and *"Personal site"* vertices). Provided we exclude the above mentioned vertices from the communicative interaction, the social graph will become just a collection of separate sites (Fig. 6).

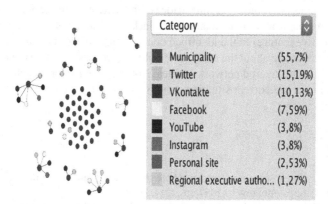

Fig. 6. Network analysis of public policy actors in Krasnodar krai (principal vertices excluded). Source: Processed and composed by the authors.

Thus, the "Regional executive authorities" and "Personal site" are the principal vertices in the given social network and function as hubs. Indeed, the research does not include the end users (Krasnodar krai population) of the information flow, which is being produced by the authorities, and the analysis would definitely show that the same users are subscribed to different municipality social accounts and visit different authority websites. However, end users do not function as a channel of information exchange between the municipality sites. Figure 6 shows, that local authorities, similarly to the average in Russia, prefer *Twitter* as a social platform for personal accounts, though interaction, which presumably exists between the municipal presence on different social platforms, has not been identified even within one social platform. This example shows the prospects of application of network analysis not specifically for fully-formed/shaped social networks and communities, but also for assessment of the degree of interaction within a network on a horizontal level of different socio-political systems.

6 Conclusion

The development of online space as a files/area of political practices operation, which function not only within the global communication channel, but also within the space, which produces new actors of public policy, requires new approaches to conducting applied studies, with network analysis in particular. Multiple network data, accumulated during the use of social platforms by online users, require classification, detailed analysis and interpretation in terms of their impact on social reality. Network analysis application in Russia is hindered by the following factors: absence of independent network analysis software; thus, the research field lacks hybrid research teams, which would be able to define the network analysis objectives within the frameworks of the humanities field and design particular software programs for the applied online networks analysis to be conducted; interpretation of network findings analysis fail to be conducted, unless proper applied mathematical tools and instruments, capable of developing new sociological interpretative methods of data network analysis, have been created. Besides, the majority of critical comments is as converges into an idea of the deficiency of the network research, as it is based on structural network analysis and lacks a cultural constituent, and does not attribute qualitative features to the identified connections within a network. A particular mention should be made about the analysis of political processes, which are to be treated as dynamic and multi-layered network entities. Not only such an approach would assist the interpretation of the current situation, but also make the development of prognostic models feasible.

References

1. Gelman, V.: Political science in Russia: scholarship without research? Eur. Polit. Sci. **14**(1), 28–36 (2015). https://doi.org/10.1057/eps.2014.33
2. Carrington, P.J., Scott, J., Wasserman, S. (eds.): Models and Methods in Social Network Analysis. Cambridge University Press, Cambridge (2005)
3. Bykov, I.A.: Empirical studies of politics with network analysis methods. Politicheskij analiz. (11), 49–59 (2011). https://www.elibrary.ru/item.asp?id=19118583. (in Russian)
4. Nooy, W., Mrvar, A., Batagelj, V.: Exploratory Social Network Analysis with Pajek: Revised and Expanded, 2nd edn. Cambridge University Press, Cambridge (2011)
5. Gruzd, A., Tsyganova, K.: Information wars and online activism during the 2013–2014 crisis in Ukraine: examining the social structures of Pro- and Anti-MaidanGroups. Policy Internet **7**(2), 121–158 (2015). https://doi.org/10.1002/poi3.91
6. Suslov, S.I.: Saint-Petersburg's political online communities clusters in "Vkontakte". Vestnik Saint Petersburg Univ. Ser. 12. Psychol. Sociol. Educ. (4), 69–87 (2016). https://doi.org/10.21638/11701/spbu12.2016.405. (in Russian)
7. Nosikov, A.A., Turygin, F.V., Myskin, E.B., Pelin, A.A.: Protesting against the Isaak Cathedral's return to the Russian orthodox Cherch: network analysis of conflict dynamics. In: Bulletin of Center of Ethnoreligious Studies, no. 1, pp. 65–82 (2017). https://www.elibrary.ru/item.asp?id=29337419. (in Russian)
8. Fidria, E.S., Smirnov, V.A.: Transformations of the networks of political elites of Lithuanian Republic during the post-soviet period (1992–2012). Polit. Expert. Politex. **8**(3), 76–97 (2012). https://www.elibrary.ru/item.asp?id=20800336. (in Russian)
9. Aleskerov, F., Kurapova, M., Meshcheryakova, N., Mironyuk, M., Shvydun, S.: A network approach to analysis of international conflicts. Politicheskaja nauka = Polit. Sci. (4), 111–137 (2016). https://www.elibrary.ru/item.asp?id=27685865. (in Russian)
10. Sherstobitov, A.S.: "Network publicness" as a new factor of political mobilization in contemporary Russia: network analysis. Vestnik Saint Petersburg Univ. Ser. 6. Int. Relat. (3), 99–105 (2013). https://www.elibrary.ru/item.asp?id=20268233. (in Russian)
11. Ryabchenko, N.A., Miroshnichenko, I.V., Gnedash, A.A., Morozova, E.V.: Crowdsourcing systems on Facebook platform: experiment in implementation of mathematical methods in social research. J. Theor. Appl. Inf. Technol. **85**(2), 136–145 (2016). http://www.jatit.org/volumes/Vol85No2/3Vol85No2.pdf
12. Ryabchenko, N.A., Gnedash, A.A.: Structure, types of users and the practices of online-social networks as a field of political practices. Int. Rev. Manag. Mark. **5**(1S), 115–120 (2015). https://www.econjournals.com/index.php/irmm/article/view/1628

The Estimation of the Individual Travelling Salesman Problem Complexity Extreme Values

Galina Zhukova[1] and Mikhail Ulyanov[2,3]($\boxtimes$)

[1] National Research University Higher School of Economics, Myasnitskaya Str. 20,
101000 Moscow, Russia
gzhukova@hse.ru
[2] V.A. Trapeznikov Institute of Control Sciences of Russian Academy of Sciences,
Profsoyuznaya Str. 65, 117997 Moscow, Russia
[3] Lomonosov Moscow State University, Leninskie gory 1, 119991 Moscow, Russia

Abstract. This article is about the probability distribution of the maximum of the logarithm of the complexity of an individual travelling salesman problem. The complexity is defined as a number of nodes of the decision tree, which was created by the branch and bound algorithm. We applied our earlier results that the distribution of the logarithm of the complexity of travelling salesman problem can be approximated by the normal distribution. In combination with the representation of the distribution of maximum of normally distributed random variables, we obtain the approximation for the distribution of the maximum of the complexity in cases of infinitely large samples. The accuracy of the approximation was visualized on the graph. In order to simplify the approximation for comparatively small samples, we used the normal distribution with the parameters equal to the expectation and standard deviation of approximation for infinitely large samples. This allowed us to obtain representations for the normal distribution, which approximates the distribution of the maximum of the natural logarithm of the complexity in series of m travelling salesman problem of size n. The quality of the representations was analysed by the experiment. On the graph, we showed the quantiles of the theoretical distribution of the maximum of the logarithm of the complexity and the sample's quantiles in the case of samples of 500 and 1000 travelling salesman problem.

Keywords: Travelling salesman problem · TSP · Branch and bound method · B&B · Complexity · Sample maximum · Largest observation

1 Introduction

The travelling salesman problem (TSP) is a problem of finding a Hamiltonian circle of minimal sum of arc weight in a complete weighted graph without self-loops. This graph is represented by its adjacency matrix, which is called a cost matrix. A Hamiltonian circle of minimal sum of arc weight is an optimal solution of the travelling salesman problem. In cases of a directed graphs, the travelling salesman problem is called asymmetric.

© Springer Nature Switzerland AG 2021
V. Sukhomlin and E. Zubareva (Eds.): SITITO 2017, CCIS 1204, pp. 261–270, 2021.
https://doi.org/10.1007/978-3-030-78273-3_25

Travelling salesman problem belongs to the class of NP-hard problems, while asymmetric travelling salesman problem, which we study further in this paper, is the most algorithmically difficult amongst different kinds of travelling salesman problems. A wide range of heuristic algorithms does not guarantee that an optimal solution will be found, while in cases of the asymmetric travelling salesman problems even an ε-polynomial algorithm does not exist. In a range of practical problems which leads to the asymmetric travelling salesman problem, it is desirable to obtain an exactly optimal solution. This paper is devoted to the study of one characteristic of exact algorithm which implements the classical Branch and Bound method.

We mostly study the characteristic of an individual travelling salesman problem such as complexity which we define as a number of nodes of a decision tree generated by implementing the Branch and Bound algorithm (according to [1]). The value of the complexity of an individual travelling salesman problem was calculated experimentally by the direct counting of nodes created by processing the program which implements the Branch and Bound algorithm. Our and our colleagues' previous results in this topic [2–7] are connected with the consideration of probability distribution and some numerical characteristics of complexity of an individual asymmetrical travelling salesman problem which are solved by the Branch and Bound algorithm. We ascertained that a probability distribution of the natural logarithm of the complexity of an individual travelling salesman problem is close to a normal distribution [4], moreover, we can use the normal distribution as the approximation of the distribution of maximum of the complexity of the individual travelling salesman problem.

It is ascertained that the distribution of the natural logarithm of complexity is close to the normal distribution [4], and the dependence of the parameters of the normal distribution on the problem dimension we can consider as approximately linear [2, 3]. This means that the complexity distribution itself (when problem dimension is fixed) is close to the lognormal distribution, consequentially, "worse" (in terms of complexity) problems are comparatively rare, but their complexity, unfortunately, by orders of magnitude are higher than the average values.

In this aspect, obviously, it is interesting to study the distribution of the maximum values of complexity both in subsets of a sample for a fixed dimension, and for the behaviour of the parameters of this distribution when the dimension of the travelling salesman problem is varied. This study of the distribution of the maximum values of complexity is the purpose of this article.

The basis of this study was the fact that the distribution of the natural logarithm of complexity is close to the normal distribution, so we can use the results about the probability distribution of the maximum of normally distributed random variable $X = N(\mu, \sigma)$ [8]. In order to simplify the approximation for comparatively small samples, we also used the normal distribution $N(\mu*, \sigma*)$ with the parameters $\mu*$ and $\sigma*$ equal to the expectation and standard deviation of approximation for infinitely large samples.

Further in the article the dependence of parameters $\mu*$ and $\sigma*$ on the dimension of the travelling salesman problem is analysed. The quality of the approximation is estimated by comparing the quantiles of the normal distribution (which have the calculated approximate values $\mu*$ and $\sigma*$ of the parameters) with sample quantiles of maximum values of the complexity in the series of 500 and 1000 travelling salesman problems.

It has also been experimentally established that the maximum values obtained from samples of volume 500 and 1000 mostly fall within the interval $[\mu * -3\sigma*, \mu * +4\sigma*]$.

2 Theoretical Basis of the Analysis

Let us give the formula [8] for the maximum value $X_{\max}$ observed in the sample of the volume m from the normal distribution $N(\mu, \sigma)$

$$X_{\max} = \mu + \sigma \sqrt{2\ln m} - \sigma \frac{\ln\ln m + \ln 4\pi}{2\sqrt{2\ln m}} + \frac{\sigma}{\sqrt{2\ln m}} v, \tag{1}$$

where v is a random variable with probability density

$$j_1(t) = e^{-t-e^{-t}}, \tag{2}$$

under condition of infinitely large sample volume m. Let us write (1) in the form

$$X_{\max} = \mu + \sigma \frac{4\ln m - \ln\ln m - \ln 4\pi + 2v}{2\sqrt{2\ln m}}. \tag{3}$$

For a linear function $X_{\max} = kv + b$ of a random variable v, we have

$$q_p^{\max} \approx B + K * q_p^v, \tag{4}$$

where $B = \mu + \sigma \frac{4\ln m - \ln\ln m - \ln 4\pi}{2\sqrt{2\ln m}}$, $K = \sigma \frac{v}{\sqrt{2\ln m}}$, q_p^v, are random variable v quantiles of level p.

We use the results obtained earlier [1, 3] that the distribution of the natural logarithm of complexity can be considered to be approximately normal with parameters that depend on the dimension of the problem as follows [1]:

$$\sigma \approx an + b, \quad \mu \approx dn + f, \tag{5}$$

where $a = 0.018$, $b = 0.392$, $d = 0.176$ и $f = 1.644$ are experimentally obtained values of the parameters. This fact allows us to establish the dependence of parameters B and K on travelling salesman problem dimension n by substitution (5) into (4):

$$B = dn + f + (an + b) \frac{4\ln m - \ln\ln m - \ln 4\pi}{2\sqrt{2\ln m}}, \quad K = (an + b) \frac{v}{\sqrt{2\ln m}}. \tag{6}$$

We also used standard normal distribution as an approximation of the distribution of the maximum of the natural logarithm of complexity as follows. For a linear function $Y = kX + b$ of a random variable X, we have

$$EY = kEX + b, \quad DY = k^2 DX, \tag{7}$$

Hence, according to formulas (3) and (7) we obtain

$$EX_{\max} = \mu + \sigma \frac{4\ln m - \ln\ln m - \ln 4\pi + 2Ev}{2\sqrt{2\ln m}}, \quad DX_{\max} = \sigma^2 \frac{Dv}{2\ln m}. \tag{8}$$

Hence, for parameters $\mu*$ and $\sigma*$ of the normal distribution which we use to approximate the distribution of the maximum of the natural logarithm of complexity we have

$$\mu* = \mu + \sigma \frac{4 \ln m - \ln \ln m - 0.01}{2\sqrt{2 \ln m}}, \quad \sigma* = \sigma \frac{0.9}{\sqrt{\ln m}}. \tag{9}$$

We took into account that the random variable v with probability density (2) has $Ev \approx 0.577$, and $Dv \approx 1.645$. Table 1 contains the values of the expressions $\frac{4\ln m - \ln \ln m - 0.01}{2\sqrt{2\ln m}}$ and $\frac{0.9}{\sqrt{\ln m}}$ for samples of volume from 500 to 100000.

Table 1. Coefficients by σ in formulas (6) for samples of volume from 500 to 10000.

Sample volume m	$\frac{4\ln m - \ln\ln m - 0.01}{2\sqrt{2\ln m}}$	$\frac{0.9}{\sqrt{\ln m}}$
100 000	4.4	0.07
10 000	3.9	0.09
1 000	3.3	0.12
500	3.1	0.13

With increasing sample size, the expectation of the maximum value observed in the sample increases (for a fixed dimension of the travelling salesman problem), but the standard deviation, on the contrary, decreases.

Substituting (5) into (9), we finally obtain:

$$\mu* = 1.76n + 1.644 + \frac{4\ln m - \ln \ln m - 0.01}{2\sqrt{2\ln m}}(0.018n + 0.392),$$
$$\sigma* = \frac{0.016n + 0.353}{\sqrt{\ln m}}. \tag{10}$$

The quantiles $q_p^{\max}$ of level p of the maximum of the natural logarithm of complexity of the travelling salesman problem of dimension n in the sample of volume m can be represented (similarly to [1]) in the form

$$q_p^{\max} \approx \mu* + \sigma* * q_p^{N(0,1)}, \tag{11}$$

here $q_p^{N(0,1)}$ are quantiles of level p of the standard normal distribution, and the values of $\mu*$ и $\sigma*$ are calculated by (10).

3 Computational Experiment

The computational experiment consisted of solving individual asymmetric travelling salesman problems using the classical branch and bound method with cost matrices of dimension from 25 to 50. As the elements of the cost matrix we used normally distributed pseudo-random numbers with parameters $\mu = 10^4$ and $\sigma = 100$ rounded up to integers. When carrying out the computational experiment, 10^5 cost matrices A_i, $i = 1, 10^5$ of each dimension from 25 to 50 were generated.

For each cost matrix we obtained the complexity $C(A_i)$, which is the number of generated nodes of the search tree. The obtained sample of complexities for a fixed dimension will be called a series. Thus, we obtained 26 experimental series of volumes 10^5 each.

To study the distribution of the logarithm of the maximum of the complexity, these series were divided into disjointed subsets s_i, $i = 0, 1, 2, ..., (10^5/m - 1)$, of the volume $m = 500, 1000, 10000$ as follows:

$$s_i = \{x_{mi}, x_{mi+1}, ..., x_{mi+m-1}\}, \tag{12}$$

where $x_r = \ln(C(A_r))$. In each subset s_i the maximum element $x_i^{\max}$ was found, and then from these maxima we created the samples of the logarithm of the maximum.

Further, we assume that we observe a random variable $X_m^{\max}$ which is equal to the maximum value in the sample of the volume m obtained by observing a normally distributed random variable with parameters μ and σ. From the samples $\{ x_i^{\max} \}|_{i=0}^{m-1}$, we compute the sample quantiles q_t, $t = 5, 25, 75, 95$, and also the median of the random variable $X_m^{\max}$. Then, using the formulas (4), we find the theoretical quantiles q_t, $t = 5, 25, 75, 95$, and the median of the normally distributed random variable, and represent the results obtained on the graph (see Fig. 1). We also presented on the graph (see Fig. 2) the theoretical quantiles q_t, $t = 5, 25, 75, 95$, and the median of the normally distributed random variable, which we calculated using the formulas (11).

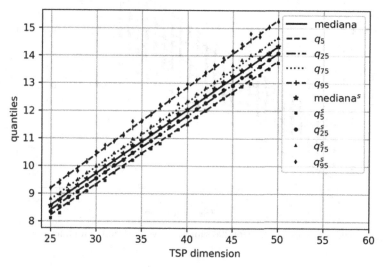

Fig. 1. Theoretical and sample quantiles (200 samples of volume 500).

By observing a normally distributed random variable with parameters μ and σ, as a rule, we obtain a sample that is mainly concentrated in the interval $[\mu - 3\sigma; \mu + 3\sigma]$ (probability of falling into this interval is 99.7%).

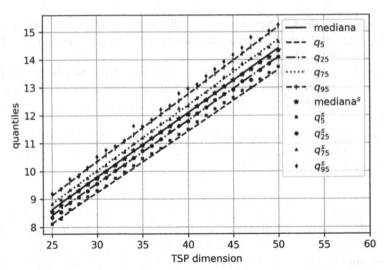

Fig. 2. Theoretical and sample quantiles (200 samples of volume 500), approximation by normal law.

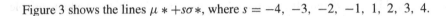

Figure 3 shows the lines $\mu * + s\sigma *$, where $s = -4, -3, -2, -1, 1, 2, 3, 4$.

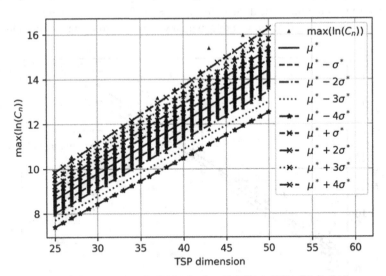

Fig. 3. Samples of max $\ln C_m$ (for 200 samples of volume 500) with lines $\mu * + s\sigma *$.

Thus, for the rough estimation of the maximum number of nodes of the search tree that are to be generated when solving the travelling salesman problem by the branch and bound method without pre-computation of the initial record tour, formulas (4)–(6), (10)–(11) can be used. These results can also be used to predict the maximum running time of the software implementation of the branch and bound method with a problem dimension greater than 50 (in conjunction with the results of [9]).

4 Forecast

The results obtained are used to estimate the maximum of the value of the natural logarithm of the complexity of the individual travelling salesman problem observed in the sample volume for cost matrix dimension from 60 to 200. The results of the calculations are given in Tables 2, 3, 4, 5, 6 and 7.

Table 2. The average of the maximum of the natural logarithm of complexity.

Sample volume m	TSP dimension n						
	60	70	80	90	100	150	200
500	16.7	19.0	21.3	23.7	26.0	37.5	49.1
1 000	17.0	19.4	21.7	24.1	26.4	38.2	49.9
10 000	17.9	20.4	22.8	25.3	27.7	40.0	52.3

Table 3. Values $\mu * + 4\sigma *$ for the maximum of the natural logarithm of complexity.

Sample volume m	TSP dimension n						
	60	70	80	90	100	150	200
500	18.9	21.4	24.0	26.6	29.2	42.0	54.9
1 000	19.0	21.6	24.2	26.8	29.4	42.4	55.4
10 000	19.7	22.3	25.0	27.7	30.3	43.7	57.1

Table 4. Values $\mu * - 3\sigma *$ for the maximum of the natural logarithm of complexity.

Sample volume m	TSP dimension n						
	60	70	80	90	100	150	200
500	15.1	17.2	19.3	21.5	23.6	34.2	44.7
1 000	15.5	17.7	19.8	22.0	24.1	35.0	45.8
10 000	16.6	18.9	21.2	23.5	25.8	37.2	48.7

Table 5. The sample quantile of the level 5% of the maximum of the natural logarithm of complexity.

Sample volume m	TSP dimension n						
	60	70	80	90	100	150	200
500	15.8	18.0	20.2	22.5	24.7	35.7	46.7
1 000	16.2	18.4	20.7	22.9	25.2	36.4	47.6
10 000	17.2	19.5	21.9	24.3	26.6	38.5	50.3

Table 6. The sample quantile of the level 95% of the maximum of t he natural logarithm of complexity.

Sample volume m	TSP dimension n						
	60	70	80	90	100	150	200
500	17.6	20.0	22.4	24.9	27.3	39.4	51.5
1 000	17.8	20.3	22.8	25.2	27.7	39.9	52.2
10 000	18.6	21.2	23.7	26.3	28.8	41.5	54.3

Table 7. The median of the complexity of travelling salesman problem (up to order).

Sample volume m	TSP dimension n						
	60	70	80	90	100	150	200
500	10^7	10^8	10^9	10^{10}	10^{11}	10^{16}	10^{21}
1 000	10^7	10^8	10^9	10^{10}	10^{11}	10^{17}	10^{22}
10 000	10^8	10^9	10^{10}	10^{11}	10^{12}	10^{17}	10^{23}

5   Conclusion

Thus, in the article we studied the dependence of the maximum of the natural logarithm of the complexity of the individual travelling salesman problem observed in the sample (for a fixed dimension of the problem) on the value of the dimension of the problem and on the sample size. We proposed the representation (4) for quantiles of probability distribution, which approximate the distribution of the maximum of the natural logarithm of the complexity. We also showed that the normal distribution can serve as an approximation of the distribution of the maximum of the natural logarithm of complexity. In the paper, the values of the parameters of this approximating normal distribution are calculated on the basis of previously obtained results on the distribution of the natural logarithm of complexity and formulas (10).

The results obtained make it possible to give a prediction about the maximum complexity of the individual travelling salesman problem, depending on the dimension of the problem. To estimate the highest possible value of the maximum of complexity in the sample it is advisable to use $\mu * +4\sigma *$ or quantiles of 95% or more, and for a lower estimate one can use $\mu * -3\sigma *$ or a quantile of 5% or less (in accordance with formula (11)). Since the value $\mu * +4\sigma *$, as well as the quantile values, are used for the estimation of the maximum of the natural logarithm of complexity, it is obviously necessary to exponentiate these values for the prediction of the complexity itself.

Since the complexity of the individual salesman problem and the time necessary for executing the program implementation of the branch and boundary method for the travelling salesman problem are correlated [9], the results obtained can be useful in practical terms, since they allow estimating the maximum possible time costs for solving travelling salesman problem instances. Our present results in combination with those previously obtained in [2–6] are useful for estimating the running time of the program implementation of the branch and boundary method for solving the travelling salesman problem.

As the results of the experiments and their analysis show in this paper, the maximum complexity for a fixed dimension of the problem exceeds the average by about two orders of magnitude (for example, according to 10^5 computational experiments, when the dimension of the travelling salesman problem is $n = 49$ then the maximum complexity of the travelling salesman problem is 136 times greater than the average). Therefore, the authors see the continuation of research in this direction in the search for such characteristics of the initial matrices of individual problems that would allow predicting the complexity directly from the initial cost matrix of the asymmetric travelling salesman problem or allow the individual travelling salesman problem to be classified as belonging to a cluster of "bad" problems, i.e. having a complexity close to the maximum.

Acknowledgements. The authors are grateful to the student of the Master's program of the Higher School of Economics Fomichev Mikhail for carrying out a computational experiment.

The work was supported by the RFBR grant № 16-07-160.

References

1. Knuth, D.E.: Estimating the efficiency of backtrack programs. Math. Comput. **29**(129), 121–136 (1975). https://doi.org/10.2307/2005469
2. Goloveshkin, V.A., Zhukova, G.N., Ulyanov, M.V., Fomichev, M.I.: The estimations of the parameters of the distribution of the logarithm of the complexity of TSP. Mod. Inf. Technol. IT-Educ. **13**(1), 19–24 (2017). https://elibrary.ru/item.asp?id=29334525. (in Russian)
3. Goloveshkin, V.A., Zhukova, G.N., Ulyanov, M.V., Fomichev, M.I.: The estimation of the complexity of solving a particular travelling salesman problem by quantile-based measures for skewness and kurtosis. Int. J. Open Inf. Technol. **4**(12), 7–12 (2016). https://elibrary.ru/item.asp?id=27543353. (in Russian)
4. Goloveshkin, V.A., Zhukova, G.N., Ulyanov, M.V., Fomichev, M.I.: Probability distribution of the complexity of the individual traveling salesman problem (fixed number of nodes). Mod. Inf. Technol. IT-Educ. **12**(3–2), 131–137 (2016). https://elibrary.ru/item.asp?id=27705967. (in Russian)
5. Goloveshkin, V.A., Zhukova, G.N., Ulyanov, M.V., Fomichev, M.I.: Comparison of resource characteristics of traditional and modified branch and boundary method for TSP. Mod.

Inf. Technol. IT-Educ. **11**(2), 151–159 (2015). https://elibrary.ru/item.asp?id=26167483. (in Russian)

6. Ulyanov, M.V., Fomichev, M.I.: Resource characteristics of ways to organize a decision tree in the branch-and-bound method for the traveling salesmen problem. Bus. Inform. (4), 38–46 (2015). https://doi.org/10.17323/1998-0663.2015.4.38.46

7. Ulyanov, M.V.: Resource-efficiency Computer Algorithms. Development and Analysis. Fizmatlit, Moscow (2008). https://elibrary.ru/item.asp?id=20246208. (in Russian)

8. Cramér, H.: Mathematical Methods of Statistics. Princeton Mathematical Series, vol. 9, Princeton University Press, Princeton (1999)

9. Goloveshkin, V.A., Zhukova, G.N., Ulyanov, M.V., Fomichev, M.I.: Correlation of complexity and time of TSP solution. In: Proceedings of the XVIII Conference on Systems of Computer Mathematics and Their Applications, no. 18, pp. 136–138. SmogGU Publ., Smolensk (2017). https://elibrary.ru/item.asp?id=30469432. (in Russian)

Mathematical Modeling of Behavior of Complex Dynamical Systems Under Changing Conditions

Liliya Ibragimova[ID] and Marat Yumagulov[(✉)][ID]

Bashkir State University, Zaki Validi Str. 32, 450076 Ufa, Republic of Bashkortostan, Russia

Abstract. In the paper we consider some issues on using non-autonomous discrete models for describing the dynamics of the behavior of complex technical and natural systems. We discuss the questions on determining the coefficients of the model in the case, when these coefficients are time dependent. We propose an approach allowing one to determine these parameters so that their values reflect real data on external and internal conditions. We propose also a corresponding discrete mathematical model allowing to predict the dynamics of the behavior of the system under varying in time external and internal factors. We develop algorithms for solving this problem as well as corresponding programs in MatLab and MathCad. We provide some numerical and graphical results of the study of the proposed model.

Keywords: Mathematical model · Discrete model · Dynamics of a system · Non-autonomous equation · Parameters of a model

1 Introduction

Mathematical models of complex processes in natural, technical, biological and other systems often (see, for instance, [1–3]) involve differential equations of the form

$$x' = f(x, \mu), \tag{1}$$

or difference equations of the form

$$x_{n+1} = f(x_n, \mu), \quad n = 0, 1, 2, \ldots. \tag{2}$$

Here μ are the parameters in the model depending on external or internal factors, while $f(x, \mu)$ is chosen among some set of standard functions or their modifications. In particular, the Malthusian growth model, the logistic model, the Ricker model are widely used as well as their various modifications. Despite a relative simplicity of these models, under a proper (in a natural sense) choice of a model, they allow one to obtain useful results of qualitative and quantitative nature on the dynamics of a process.

At the same time, we should pay an attention to the following facts. First, while solving particular problems, one usually includes one or two parameters in Eqs. (1) or (2) since otherwise the analysis becomes too complicated, while in the reality, the

© Springer Nature Switzerland AG 2021
V. Sukhomlin and E. Zubareva (Eds.): SITITO 2017, CCIS 1204, pp. 271–277, 2021.
https://doi.org/10.1007/978-3-030-78273-3_26

processes depend on essentially greater number of characteristics each influencing the dynamics of the process. This is why, in modeling, one has to restrict himself by one or two most essential (in some sense) parameters or to include in the model some averaged parameter aimed to reflect the influence of many important characteristics of the system.

Second, Eqs. (1) and (2) are autonomous in the sense that the function $f(x, \mu)$ and the parameter are time independent, while in the reality this is not always the case. In particular, the autonomous property of Eq. (2) implies that the value of a solution as $t \geq n + 1$ is completely determined by its value at the moment $t = n$ only. Such assumption is natural once the external and internal factors are constant in time.

In the reality, these parameters can vary and as a result, influence essentially the dynamics of the system. In this case, it is more natural to replace (1) by a non-autonomous differential equation

$$x' = f(x, \mu(t)), \tag{3}$$

where $\mu(t)$ are the coefficients in the model varying in time. Similarly, instead of (2), it is natural to employ a non-autonomous difference equation

$$x_{n+1} = f(x_n, \mu(n)), \quad n = 0, 1, 2, \dots. \tag{4}$$

where $\mu(n)$ is some function.

In many works on mathematical modeling of complex processes in natural and technical processes, external and internal factors are assumed to be constant and as a result, autonomous models are employed. This also leads to disagreement between the modeling and the observed data, which is first of all due to the influence of the external and internal varying factors. At the same time, the problems on studying the dynamics of systems under varying condition are poor studied, although a series of non-trivial results was obtained.

To increase the exactness of the modeling, one has to take into consideration all given information. This information can concern different time intervals and taking this information into consideration, one is lead to the need to specify the parameters of the system and respectively, to reconstruct the model during observing a real object. In particular, while constructing models (3) and (4), one of the main problems is to determine the nature of the time dependence for the coefficients μ. As a rule, this problem is accompanied by serious mathematical difficulties.

To resolve the above problems, it is natural to employ modern computer mathematical software. Together with a theoretical study, such approach allows one to obtain an essentially better model taking into consideration the influence of varying external and internal factors on the process. This allows one to find not only a more adequate model, but also, for instance, to solve the problem on system's behavior prediction.

In the present work we study the issue on determining the coefficients in the models of form (2) and (4) under varying external and internal conditions. We propose algorithms for determining these coefficients. These algorithms are realized as programs for numerical calculations in MatLab and MathCad.

2 Problem on Determining the Coefficients in a Model Under Changing Conditions

For the sake of definiteness, in what follows, we consider only difference Eqs. (2) and (4). Similar results can be also obtained for the models described by differential Eqs. (1) and (3).

The dynamics of autonomous system (2) is determined by the function $f(x, \mu)$. In problems of mathematical modeling various processes in nature, engineering, economics, etc., the functions of various kind can be used. In particular, very popular models are those, where the function $f(x, \mu)$ reads as $f(x, \mu) = \mu x$ (the Malthusian growth model), $f(x, \mu) = \mu x(1 - x)$ (the logistic model), $f(x, \mu) = x \, \exp\left(r\left(1 - \frac{x}{K}\right)\right)$ (the Ricker model); here μ, r, K are some coefficients.

To employ these models and their modifications for the description of the dynamics of a system, one has to determine the corresponding coefficients. Usually, these coefficients are determined by selecting characteristics in a real system making the main influence on the dynamics of the system. If there are too many of such characteristics, various ways of averaging and similar operations are employed to reduce the number of basic parameters in the model. To determine numerically these coefficients or their ranges, usually, the methods of parametric identifications are employed, see, for instance, [4, 5]; here experimental data play an important role.

Let us consider non-autonomous system (4). The behavior of solutions of this system is determined not only by the properties of the function $f(x, \mu)$, but also by the structure of the dependence on n of the coefficient μ. The more complicated this dependence, the more complicated behavior is demonstrated by the solutions of system (4).

An important particular case is when the coefficient $\mu(n)$ is a periodic function of the time n. The models with a periodically varying parameter are often employed for solving many rich in content problems, for instance, for studying the influence of periodic actions on the system's dynamics.

In the case, when the coefficient μ is non-periodic function, the problem on studying system (4) becomes essentially more complicated. Here we have to select to basically different situations. The first relates with an assumption that the dependence of the coefficient μ on n is known for all n. In this case, one can carry out a qualitative and approximate study of the system's dynamics for model (4) and, in particular, to predict the behavior of this system.

The second situation concerns the case, when the values of the coefficient μ are known only for a given time moment n or up to a given time moment n. In this situation, model (4) allows one to determine the solution only at the next time moment $n + 1$. Nevertheless, in this situation model (4) is also useful since it allows to consider various scenarios of the dynamics of the system depending on possible options of variation of external and internal condition.

As in the case of autonomous models, to employ non-autonomous model of form (4) for describing the dynamics of a real system, one has to determine the corresponding coefficients and in addition, the nature of the dependence of these coefficients on the time. Here the coefficients are also determined by selecting the characteristics in the real system making the main influence on the dynamics of the system. Since the coefficients in the non-autonomous system vary in time, to determine such characteristics one can use the methods of regression and correlation analysis, see, for instance, [6], the least squares method, etc. To determine numerically the coefficients or their ranges, the methods of parametric identification are also quite effective; the use of such methods needs the presence of a rather big base of experimental data.

We consider the problem on determining the coefficients μ in model (4) with a given function $f(x, \mu)$ in the following formulation. Let the coefficient μ be a scalar or vector function of the time n. We need to find the value of the function $\mu(n)$ at the moment n_0 so that this value to reflect real data on external and internal conditions up to the moment n_0. Since these conditions vary with the time, probably, with some cyclicity, the function $\mu(n)$ turns out to be non-constant and we obtain a non-autonomous equation of form (4).

3 Description of Proposed Algorithm

Given a function $f(x, \mu)$, and respectively, model (4), we propose to solve the problem by the following scheme.

1. At the first step, among all real data on changing external and internal conditions, we select data $\Delta_1, \Delta_2, \ldots, \Delta_m$ making the most essential influence on the dynamics of the system.
2. The value of the function $\mu = \mu(n)$ at the time moment $n = n_0$ is determined as a linear combination $\mu(n_0) = \alpha_1 \Delta_1(n_0) + \alpha_2 \Delta_2(n_0) + \ldots + \alpha_m \Delta_m(n_0)$, where $\alpha_1, \alpha_2, \ldots, \alpha_m$ are some coefficients constructed in a special way, which can be found by the given information on values of $\Delta_1, \Delta_2, \ldots, \Delta_m$ at the previous time moments.

It is natural to test the obtained model, for instance, by the methods of regression and correlation analysis. The model depends also on the choice of the function $f(x, \mu)$ in (4) and this is why it is natural to analyze the properties of the model taking into consideration various options of choosing the function $f(x, \mu)$.

Let us provide an algorithm for determining the coefficients μ in model (4) in the following formulation. For the definiteness we assume that Eq. (4) describes the population dynamics for some biological system and μ is a scalar parameter. This dynamics is often rather complicated and features both the time intervals of fast growth and decay of the population and the time intervals of a relatively stable population. The population is strongly influenced by external and internal factors, first of all, the weather and climatic conditions, which are not stable for a year to year. This is why to describe the dynamics of the population, it is natural to employ non-autonomous equation of form (4).

Assume that we know the following information:

- values $x_1, x_2, \ldots, x_k$ of population in years indexed as $n = 1, 2, \ldots, k$. The values x_n are determined at the beginning of the year n.
- climate and weather parameters $\Delta_1, \Delta_2, \ldots, \Delta_m$ in the years $n = 1, 2, \ldots, k$.

For instance, this can the averaged monthly temperature and precipitation, the year average temperature, etc.

By this information we need to find the population x_n in the year with the index $n = k + 1$.

We propose the following algorithm for solving this problem.

1. Employing data $\Delta_1, \Delta_2, \ldots, \Delta_m$, $(n = 1, 2, \ldots, k - 1)$ and $x_1, x_2, \ldots, x_k$, we find the coefficients $\alpha_1, \alpha_2, \ldots, \alpha_m$. At that, the coefficients $\alpha_1, \alpha_2, \ldots, \alpha_m$ can be found, for instance, by the least squares method.
1. We find the value of the parameter μ at the moment $n = k$ by means of the identity:
$$\mu(k) = \alpha_1 \Delta_1(k) + \alpha_2 \Delta_2(k) + \ldots + \alpha_m \Delta_m(k).$$
2. By formula (4) we find the needed population at the time moment $n = k + 1$:
$$x_{k+1} = f(x_k, \mu(k)).$$

The proposed scheme is realized in MatLab and MathCad. The developed programs allow one to solve a wide range of problems on determining the coefficients μ in model (4) with a given function $f(x, \mu)$. By means of these programs, we can predict the behavior of complex natural, technical, biological and other systems depending on many characteristics.

In work [7], the described approach was applied for modeling the dynamics of the population of Burzayan hollow bee (Apis mellifera mellifera) inhabiting on the area of reserve "Shulgan-Tash" (see [8]). To describe the bee population, the Ricker model serves as a basic one [9]:

$$x_{n+1} = x_n e^{r\left(1-\frac{x_n}{K}\right)}. \tag{5}$$

In this model, the positive coefficient r characterizes the growth rate of the population with no limiting, while the parameter K represents the capacity of the environmental niche of this population; in [7], it was adopted that $K = 167$.

Equation (5) does not take into consideration the fact that in the reality, the external and internal conditions vary in time and often in an unpredictable way and they can change essentially the dynamics of the system. In order to describe the dynamics of the bee populations with varying external and internal conditions, we propose to replace autonomous system (5) by an non-autonomous one of form

$$x_{n+1} = x_n e^{r_n\left(1-\frac{x_n}{K}\right)}, \quad n = 0, 1, 2, \ldots. \tag{6}$$

in which the coefficient r_n depends on the time n.

To determine the dependence of the coefficient r_n on n in model (6), we employ the known (see [8]) observations in the period from 1960 to 2012 of a series of climate and natural parameters, which can influence the dynamics of the bee population.

On Fig. 1 we provide the results of calculations via the proposed model.

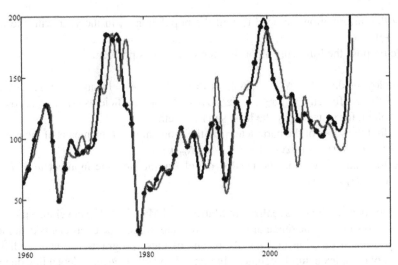

Fig. 1. Dynamics of bee families populations in the period 1960–2012. The red graph represents the population dynamics obtained via the proposed model, the black color indicates a real data.

4 Conclusion

In the paper we considered some issues on employing non-autonomous difference models of form (4) for describing the dynamics of complex natural, technical, biological systems depending on many characteristics influenced by time dependent external and internal factors. The main problem was to determine the coefficients μ in model (4) with a given function $f(x, \mu)$. We proposed an approach allowing one to determine these parameters so that their values reflect real data on external and internal conditions. We also developed algorithms for solving this problem as well as corresponding programs in MatLab and MathCad. We provided some numerical and graphical results of the study of the proposed model.

The proposed model can be employed not only for determining the parameters in a model, but also for studying the problem on predicting the dynamics of the system's behavior. It can be also used to studying the issue on possible scenarios of the behavior of a dynamical system depending on variation options for external and internal factors.

References

1. Bratus, A.S., Novozhilov, A.S., Platonov, A.P.: Dynamical Systems and Models in Biology. Fizmatlit, Moscow (2010).(in Russian)
2. Riznichenko, G.Yu.: Lectures on mathematical models in biology. In: Part 1. RC "Regular and Chaotic Dynamics", Izhevsk (2002). (in Russian)
3. Yumagulov, M.G.: Introduction into the Theory of Dynamical Systems. Lan, St.-Petersburg (2015). (in Russian)
4. Dejch, A.M.: Methods of Identification of Dynamic Objects. Energiya, Moscow (1979).(in Russian)

5. Ljung, L.: System identification. In: Procházka, A., Uhlíř, J., Rayner, P.W.J., Kingsbury, N.G. (eds.) Signal Analysis and Prediction. Applied and Numerical Harmonic Analysis. Birkhäuser, Boston (1998). https://doi.org/10.1007/978-1-4612-1768-8_11

6. Draper, N., Smith, H.: Applied Regression Analysis. Wiley, New York (1966). https://doi.org/10.1002/bimj.19690110613

7. Ibragimova, L.S., Yumagulov, M.G., Ishbirdin, A.R., Ishmuratova, M.M.: Mathematical modeling of dynamics of the number of specimens in a biological population under changing external conditions on the example of the Burzyan wild-hive honeybee (Apismellifera L., 1758). Math. Biol. Bioinform. **12**(1), 224–236 (2017). https://doi.org/10.17537/2017.12.224. (in Russian)

8. Sharipov, A.Ya., Ishbirdin, A.R.: Population dynamics of wild-hive bee (Apis mellifera mellifera L.) in the reserve "Shulgan-Tash" for half a century of observations. In: Rosenberg, G.S. (ed.) Problems of Population Ecology. Proceedings of All-Russia Seminar "Homeostatic Mechanisms of Biology Systems". Kassandra, Tolyatti, pp. 336–341 (2015). https://elibrary.ru/item.asp?id=26403653. (in Russian)

9. Ricker, W.E.: Stock and recruitment. J. Fish. Res. Board Canada **11**(5), 559–623 (1954). https://doi.org/10.1139/f54-039

Directed Fluidized Bed in Vortex Granulators: Optimization Calculation of Hydrodynamic Characteristics

Artem Artyukhov[✉]

Sumy State University, Rymskogo-Korsakova Str. 2, Sumy 40007, Ukraine
a.artyukhov@pohnp.sumdu.edu.ua

Abstract. The article deals with the study of main hydrodynamic characteristics of the directed fluidized bed in vortex granulators. The algorithm to calculate hydrodynamic characteristics of the directed vortex fluidized bed in the granulator's workspace is described. Every block of algorithm has theoretical model of calculation. Principles of granules' motion in various areas in the vortex granulator with variable heightwise workspace area are established. The software realization of author's mathematic model to calculate granules' motion trajectory in free and constrained regime, granule's residence time in the granulator's workspace, polydisperse systems classification is proposed in the study. Calculations of granule's motion hydrodynamic characteristics using the software product ANSYS CFX, based on the author's mathematic model, are presented in the article. The software product enables to automatize calculation simultaneously by several optimization criteria and to visualize calculation results in the form of 3D images. The fields of the granules' vortex flows velocity are obtained, principles of wide fraction granules' distribution in the workspace of the vortex granulator are fixed. The way to define granule's residence time in the workspace of the vortex granulator in free (without consideration of cooperation with other granules and granulator's elements) and constrained motion regimes is proposed in the research. The calculation results make a base for optimal choice of the granulator's working chamber sizes.

Keywords: Vortex granulator · Directed fluidized bed · Software · Hydrodynamics · Motion trajectory · Residence time · Free and constrained motion

1 Introduction

Creation of the fluidized bed directed motion thanks to the selection of workspace optimal configuration in the device and implementation of the gas flow accelerating elements (swirlers) enable to form disperse phase motion, controlled in time. The workspace rational construction, optimum flow of heat transfer agent and its temperature-humidity characteristics in every block of the granulation module are searched due to the optimization criterion "minimum "hydrodynamic" residence time of the disperse phase in the device's

© Springer Nature Switzerland AG 2021
V. Sukhomlin and E. Zubareva (Eds.): SITITO 2017, CCIS 1204, pp. 278–292, 2021.
https://doi.org/10.1007/978-3-030-78273-3_27

workspace". "Hydrodynamic" time has not to exceed "thermodynamic" time – that is time, by which temperature-humidity characteristics of the disperse phase must have normative value. The directed vortex fluidized bed enables to control "hydrodynamic" residence time of the disperse phase in the device's workspace.

The urgent scientific and practical tasks are to define principles of the twisted flows in the axysimmetrical channels when they are used in the granulation technology [1]. Ways to solve these tasks are to investigate new mathematic models, which will describe hydrodynamic characteristics of the flows motion, to create software computer modeling of the flows motion hydrodynamics, and to implement author's mathematic models in hydrodynamic processes modeling in the modern software products.

Today scientists from Sumy State University continue to work on theoretical description and experimental investigation of the vortex flows motion hydrodynamics and granulation process kinetics in the devices with disperse phase twisting [2–6]. Therefore, the main attention in further studies is paid to creation of the vortex granulators' automated optimization calculation, based on the theoretical base, developed earlier [7–9].

Aim of the work is to create mathematic tool, which will describe two-phase flow hydrodynamics in the vortex granulator's workspace, and software implementation of the created mathematic model.

Methodology. The demonstrated results are obtained through computer modeling on the model, formed in accordance with an experimental-industrial sample of the vortex granulator, based on the analytical model of the two-phase flows motion hydrodynamics.

Results. The hydrodynamic characteristics of two-phase flows, based on the software implementation of the hydrodynamics analytical model are obtained. The model is implemented in the software product ANSYS via author's mathematic model for calculations.

Scientific novelty. It is demonstrated that analytical models implementation to calculate hydrodynamics of two-phase flows in the software products, enables to perform optimization constructive calculation of the vortex granulator with heightwise variable cross sectional area.

Practical significance. The presented results of computer modeling together with theoretical investigations, carried out earlier, regarding flows motion hydrodynamics and experimental data give base to develop the vortex granulator's engineering calculation technique.

This article continues the work [10], where fundamentals of two-phase vortex flow modeling are observed. In this research a new approach to study hydrodynamics of the granules' constrained vortex motion is proposed and the author's approach to define granule's residence time in the device under conditions of their cooperation with other particles and vortex granulator's elements is developed.

2 Theoretical Bases of Modeling

In order to model two-phase flows, in which granules compose a disperse phase, Lagrange approach is used. Based on this approach, disperse phase motion, influenced by continuous phase is observed. Unlike the gas flow description models (in this case one may disregard mass force as a result of phase's small density), it is obligatory to analyze active forces, which influence the disperse phase, in granule's motion description [3]. Besides, under conditions of the granules' constrained motion, it is necessary to take into account changing of the disperse phase trajectory and its residence time in the vortex granulator's workspace, depending on relative ratio of granules in the device [6].

The continuous phase flow, streaming of which is modeled by Navier-Stokes equations and by continuity equation (as it is shown in [2]), gives the disperse flow part of the motion quantity moment. When the disperse phase appears in the working volume of the device, it is drawn into the circular motion thanks to the gas flow energy. Therefore, input of the disperse phase into the continuous phase flow will cause great changes in the circumferential component of the gas flow velocity V_φ.

Thus, author proposes the following algorithm of the calculation, block-scheme of which is demonstrated in Fig. 1.

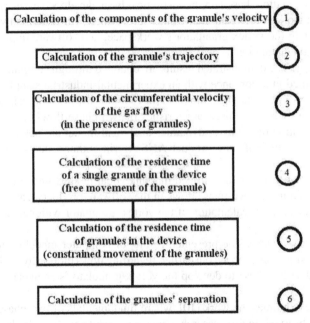

Fig. 1. Block-scheme of the algorithm of vortex granulator's hydrodynamic characteristics calculation.

Blocks 1
Equations system of the granule's motion:

$$\left.\begin{aligned}
\frac{dW_r}{d\tau} &= \frac{W_\varphi^2}{r} + \psi \cdot \frac{\pi \cdot \mu_g \cdot d_{gr}}{8 \cdot m}(V_r - W_r), \\
\frac{dW_\varphi}{d\tau} &= -\frac{W_r W_\varphi}{r} + \psi \cdot \frac{\pi \cdot \mu_g \cdot d_{gr}}{8 \cdot m}(V_\varphi - W_\varphi), \\
\frac{dW_z}{d\tau} &= -g + \psi \cdot \frac{\pi \cdot \mu_g \cdot d_{gr}}{8 \cdot m}(V_z - W_z),
\end{aligned}\right\}
\tag{1}$$

where W_r, W_φ, W_z – radial, circumferential and axial (vertical, rate) components of the granule's motion; m – mass of the granule; τ – time; r – current radius of the vortex granulator's workspace; g – gravity acceleration; ψ – linear coefficient of the granule's resistance to the gas flow; μ_g – gas flow viscosity; d_{gr} – diameter of the granule.

Blocks 2
In order to find the granule's motion trajectory, we will write the equations system (1) taking into account the fact that granule during time τ passes some way in the radial S_r, circumferential S_φ and vertical S_z directions:

$$\left.\begin{aligned}
m\frac{d^2 S_r}{d\tau^2} &= \frac{W_\varphi^2}{r} + \psi \cdot \frac{\pi \cdot \mu_g \cdot d_{gr}}{8 \cdot m}(V_r - W_r), \\
m\frac{d^2 S_\varphi}{d\tau^2} &= -\frac{W_r W_\varphi}{r} + \psi \cdot \frac{\pi \cdot \mu_g \cdot d_{gr}}{8 \cdot m}(V_\varphi - W_\varphi), \\
m\frac{d^2 S_z}{d\tau^2} &= -g + \psi \cdot \frac{\pi \cdot \mu_g \cdot d_{gr}}{8 \cdot m}(V_z - W_z),
\end{aligned}\right\}
\tag{2}$$

The equations system solving (2) towards variable S in each direction is carried out for definite time of the granule's motion inside the granulator's case.

Blocks 3
Moment of the gas phase motion quantity with absence of disperse phase in the working volume

$$M_g = 2 \cdot \pi \cdot \rho_g \cdot V_\varphi \cdot r_{gr}^2 drdz, \tag{3}$$

where ρ_g – gas flow density, r_{gr} - radius of the granule.

Moment of the gas phase motion quantity after cooperation with disperse phase in the working volume

$$M_g' = 2 \cdot \pi \cdot \rho_g \cdot V_\varphi' \cdot r_{gr}^2 drdz, \tag{4}$$

where V_φ' – circumferential velocity of the gas flow after cooperation with disperse phase.

Moment of the gas phase motion quantity, which is gained after cooperation with gas flow

$$M_d = m \cdot W_\varphi \cdot r_{gr}. \tag{5}$$

Due to the ratio between disperse phase and gas flows rates Q_{gr}/Q_g, Eq. (5) will be

$$M_d = 2 \cdot \pi \cdot \rho_{gr} \cdot \left(\frac{Q_{gr}}{Q_g}\right) W_\varphi \cdot r_{gr}^2 dr dz, \tag{6}$$

where ρ_{gr} – the granule's density.

According to [3] we write down equality

$$M_g = M_g' + M_d, \tag{7}$$

or

$$\rho_g \cdot V_\varphi = \rho_g \cdot V_\varphi' + \rho_{gr} \cdot \left(\frac{Q_{gr}}{Q_g}\right) W_\varphi. \tag{8}$$

In this case the circumferential velocity of the gas flow after cooperation with disperse phase is

$$V_\varphi' = V_\varphi - \frac{\rho_{gr}}{\rho_g} \cdot \left(\frac{Q_{gr}}{Q_g}\right) W_\varphi. \tag{9}$$

Blocks 4, 5

In case of the granule's free motion its residence time in the granulator's working area is determined by solving of the third differential equation of the system (1) regarding granule's motion in the vertical direction.

The free motion of granule is observed only with small volume content of the disperse phase in two-phase system ($\phi < 0.1$). In this case distance between granules enables to avoid crashes and mutual impact on each other. If $\phi > 0.1$ distance between surfaces of granules (size of pass) become smaller than their diameter, granule cannot easy jump between two others. In this case it is necessary to consider granules' crash effect between each other. The granules' crash in two-phase system can appear when disperse phase consists of polydisperse granules (that relates to the observed process). Besides, the granule's motion in the surrounding gas environment forms velocity and pressure fields. Other granules, which compose the so called assembly, and granulator's walls, have hydrodynamic impact on the granule.

Consideration of such hydrodynamic situation and calculation of the granule's motion velocity (or its residence time in the device) in the constrained motion regime is an important factor in description of two-phase vortex flow hydrodynamics.

This study proposes to take into account terms of the constrained motion in calculation of the granules' residence time in the workspace of the device in the following way

$$\tau_{st} = \tau f_{et}(\phi), \tag{10}$$

where τ_{st} – the granule's residence time in the workspace of the device under conditions of granule's constrained motion; τ – residence time of the single granule in the workspace of the device; $f_{et}(\phi)$ – empiric function of the constraint impact on the granule's residence time in the workspace of the device.

Function $f_{et}(\phi)$ is:

$$f_{et}(\phi) = (1 - \phi)^{-m}, \tag{11}$$

where m – empiric index (constraint coefficient for time calculation).

Results of investigations [7] show that it is necessary to distinguish three zones of the gas flow motion and of granules heightwise of the device in the vortex granulator's workspace (Fig. 2). In every zone intensity of gas flow and granules' motion is determined by the velocity's components and preferential direction of the total velocity.

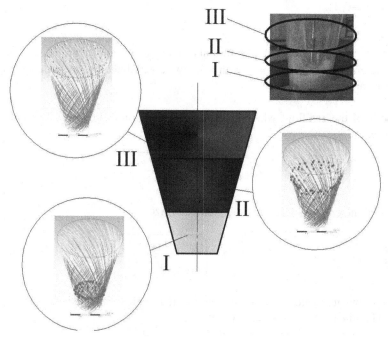

Fig. 2. Main zones of granules' motion in the vortex granulator [7]: I – zone of the granules' preferential vortex motion; II – zone of the granules' combined vortex and ascendant motion; III – zone of the granules' preferential ascendant motion.

Under conditions of the granule's constrained motion, constrain coefficient and granule's residence time is defined individually for zones I, II, III.

Results of investigations [8] let to determine values of the parameter m in every granulator's zone by formula (11): zone I – $m = 1.7$–1.74; zone II – $m = 1.46$–1.49; zone III – $m = 1.1$–1.13.

Thus, total residence time of granules in the constrained motion regime is calculated by formula

$$\sum \tau_{cm} = \tau_{cm}^{I} + \tau_{cm}^{II} + \tau_{cm}^{II} = \tau^{I}(1 - \phi^{I})^{-m^{I}} + \tau^{II}(1 - \phi^{II})^{-m^{II}} + \tau^{III}(1 - \phi^{III})^{-m^{III}}, \tag{12}$$

where an average value of ϕ in every zone depends on average porosity of the weighted layer ε [9] and is calculated by the formula

$$\phi_i = 1 - \varepsilon_i. \tag{13}$$

According to data of experimental studies to determine the optimal construction of the gas distributor device and its impact on the vortex weighted layer stability [10] one proposes the following diapasons of average values ϕ in every zone of vortex granulator, which will be implemented in computer modeling and in further engineering calculation of the medium-powered device: zone I $-\phi = 0.48$–0.53; zone II $- \phi = 0.35$–0.4; zone III $- \phi = 0.2$–0.24.

Blocks 6

Based on the force analysis (Fig. 3), formulas to find conditions of granules' classification in the granulator's workspace with heightwise variable cross sectional area of the workspace are received [6]:

– Velocity of the gas flow, which confirms the condition of granule's (with size r_{gr}) balance

$$V_{op} = 1,63 \cdot \sqrt{\frac{\rho_{gr} \cdot g \cdot r_{gr}}{\psi \cdot \rho_g}}. \tag{14}$$

– height of the current location of the granule in size r_{gr}

$$Z = 1,584 \sqrt{\frac{Q_g}{tg\varphi^2 \cdot \sqrt{\frac{\rho_{gr} \cdot g \cdot r_{gr}}{\psi \cdot \rho_g}}}}. \tag{15}$$

– radius of the granulator's lower cross section, if granules with maximum size r_{max} are located in the polydisperse system

$$R_0 = 0,442 \sqrt{\frac{Q_g}{\sqrt{\frac{\rho_{gr} \cdot g \cdot r_{max}}{\psi \cdot \rho_g}}}}. \tag{16}$$

– height in accordance with Fig. 3

$$Z_1 = Z - Z_0, \tag{17}$$

$$Z_0 = R_0 / tg\varphi. \tag{18}$$

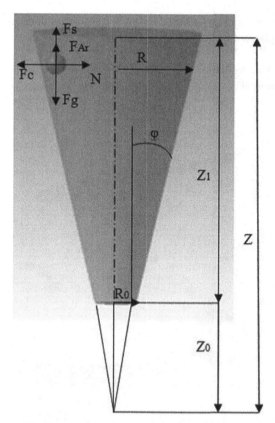

Fig. 3. Calculation model of the vortex granulator's workspace [6]: Z – total height of the cone; Z_0 – height of the gas distributor unit; Z_1 – height of the granulator's workspace; φ – half of the cone angle; R_0 – radius of the gas distributor; R – present radius of the workspace; F_g – gravity force; F_S – drag force; F_{Ar} – Archimedes force; F_C – centrifugal force; N – response of the wall.

3 Results of Studies, Analysis and Comparison of Theoretical and Experimental Data

Some results after calculation of granule velocity's components in the vortex granulator's workspace are shown in Fig. 4. Fields of the granule's velocities enable to find resultant velocity of the disperse phase. This velocity and its direction vector compose the base to calculate granules' motion trajectory and their "hydrodynamic" residence time in granulator.

Analysis of the previous works in the two-phase flows modeling sphere, consisting of gas (disperse phase) and disperse particles, shows that one of the most perspective ways to calculate particles' motion is the trajectory method [11]. Authors [12, 13] conclude that Lagrangian model of the particles' motion force analysis via motion differential equations, which was implemented to describe hydrodynamic conditions of the disperse phase motion in the vortex granulator's workspace can be the basis in the constrained motion modeling of particles with large diameter (0.5–5 mm) [14]. At the same time, implementation of the trajectory method for granules' motion in the vortex granulator's workspace is complicated by the following factors:

– polydispersity of the system;
– constrained motion of granules in the vortex granulator.

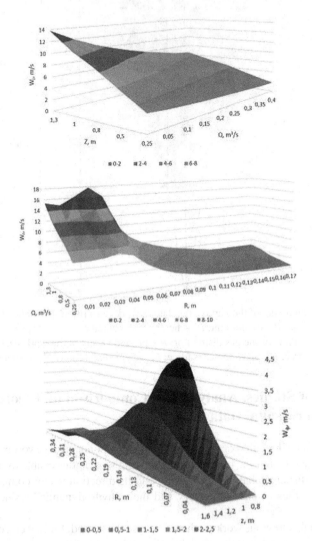

Fig. 4. Components of the granule's velocity in the vortex granulator's workspace.

Nevertheless, the trajectory method with accurate obtained results can be implemented only if there is the software, which enables to export theoretical model of singular particle's motion and to consider degree of the flow constraint.

In this research the software product ANSYS FLUENT is used to export an author's mathematic model, to calculate granules' motion trajectory and polydisperse system distribution law in the granulator's workspace considering granules concentration (degree of the flow constraint) [15].

The Fig. 5 demonstrates motion trajectory of the granules' polydisperse composition in the vortex granulator with different configuration of the workspace. Based on the computer modeling results, it is possible to observe division of granules into separate zones by fractions - large (or heavy) granules are concentrated in the lower cross section, small non-commodity fraction enters the separation zone. Besides, height of every fraction zone is changed in inverse proportion to the cone angle given steady parameters of the heat transfer agent.

The granulator's working regime starting process is demonstrated in this figure. The granules' separation and classification processes are clearly expressed – tiny particle get to the vortex granulator's separation zone, and large fraction is classified by size, is thrown away to walls and moves along the spiral trajectory.

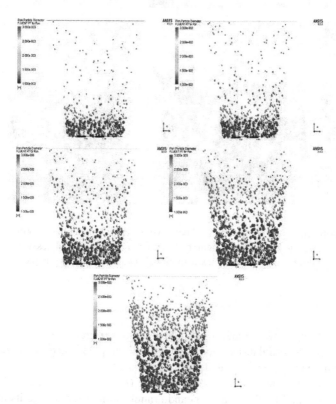

Fig. 5. The granulator's working regime starting process (demonstration of data on calculation by the theoretical model).

Theoretical calculations and computer modeling results are confirmed by experimental studies of the granulator's working regime starting process. Evolution of this process is shown in Fig. 6.

Fig. 6. Development of the vortex fluidized bed (evolution of the granules' motion trajectory): a - starting of the layer horizontal movement; b – combined motion of granules; c – vortex motion of granules; d – vortex motion of granules with partial separation of tiny granules.

Such trajectories analysis shows that:

– increase of the gas flow rate and cone angle of the vortex granulator's workspace leads to reduction of the spiral turns amount, growth of their pitch and decrease of granule's residence time in the vortex granulator's workspace;
– increase of the gas flow initial twisting degree (it is defined by the angle of tilt of swirler's vanes and by their number) and granule's diameter change its motion trajectory thanks to spiral turns number increase, reduction of their pitch, upper spiral turn diameter increase and increase of the granule's residence time in the vortex granulator's workspace.

Granules are moving along the wall of the vortex granulator and are not practically hold in its central zone. It is explained by the direction of total velocity vector action of their motion from center to periphery owing to the domination of granule's motion radial component up to two thirds of the device's radius. The radial component influence decreases close to the granulator's walls, granules are drawn into the rotating movement with vertical transfer.

In general, spiral trajectories of the granules' motion depending on its properties and vortex granulator's construction differ by number of turns and pitch between them, and also by the diameter of lower and upper spiral turn. It causes the fact that granule gets over different way in length in the vortex granulator's workspace that has an impact on its contact time with gas flow.

Analysis of the calculation results shows that as the granule moves from center to the wall, total velocity vector is changed in the direction depending on this or that component predominance. At the initial moment of time granule is moving from the axis of the device perpendicular to it owing to its velocity's radial component predominance. Granules are drawn into the vortex motion when they get closer to the vortex granulator's half radius, owing to its velocity's circumferential component predominance. At the granulator's wall granules move along spiral trajectories with gradual movement in vertical direction thanks to the impact increase of its velocity's rate component; motion trajectory is not changed till reaching of the vortex granulator's upper cross section.

The clearly demonstrated granules' motion trajectory in the developed vortex layer regime (Fig. 6c) and clear division of the polydisperse system into fractions (Fig. 7) give ground to confirm the appropriateness of the modeling results.

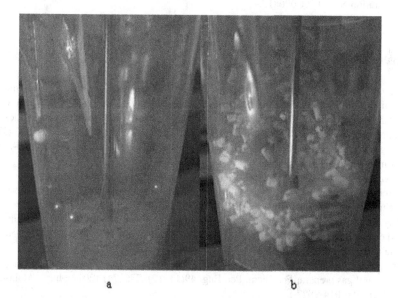

a   b

Fig. 7. Distribution of granules in the vortex granulator's workspace [6]: a – wide fraction composition of the polydisperse system; b – narrow fraction composition of the polydisperse system.

4 Conclusion and Recommendations

The algorithm to calculate hydrodynamic characteristics of two-phase flow in the vortex granulator's workspace, proposed in the article, enables to perform optimization projecting by the criterion of minimum required time of granules' contact with high-temperature heat transfer agent. The received results of the computer modeling based on the proposed algorithm let to predict granule's behavior with various physical and chemical properties in the working volume of the device. Therefore, it is important to observe conditions, under which the granule's "hydrodynamic" residence time in the workspace of the device must not be less than "thermodynamic" time (this parameter is defined by kinetics of the granule's dehydration process) [16–20]. The optimal construction of the vortex granulator, which satisfies optimization criterion requirements, is achieved by the regulation of hydrodynamic characteristics of the flows motion.

The aim of further studies is to model the vortex granulator's work under conditions of different constraint flow degree and to create "hybrid" calculation model, which will include both author's software products and present tools for calculation of thermodynamics and heat and mass transfer in devices with active hydrodynamic regimes.

Acknowledgments. The authors thank researchers of department Processes and Equipment of Chemical and Petroleum Refinery Department, Sumy State University, for their valuable comments during the article preparation.

This work was carried out under the project «Improving the efficiency of granulators and dryers with active hydrodynamic regimes for obtaining, modification and encapsulation of fertilizers», state registration No. 0116U006812.

References

1. Artyukhova, N.A., Shandyba, A.B., Artyukhov, A.E.: Energy efficiency assessment of multi-stage convective drying of concentrates and mineral raw materials. Naukovyi Visnyk Natsionalnoho Hirnychoho Universytetu. (1), 92–98 (2014). http://nv.nmu.org.ua/index.php/en/archive/on-the-issues/887-2014/contents-no-1-2014/power-supply-technologies/2472-energy-efficiency-assessment-of-multi-stage-convective-drying-of-concentrates-and-mineral-raw-materials. (in Russian)
2. Artyukhov, A., Sklabinskyi, V.: Theoretical analysis of granules movement hydrodynamics in the vortex granulators of ammonium nitrate and carbamide production. Chem. Chem. Technol. **9**(2), 175–180 (2015). https://doi.org/10.23939/chcht09.02.175
3. Artyukhov, A., Sklabinskyi, V.: Hydrodynamics of gas flow in small-sized vortex granulators in the production of nitrogen fertilizers. Chem. Chem. Technol. **9**(3), 337–342 (2015). https://doi.org/10.23939/chcht09.03.337
4. Artyukhov, A.E.: Optimization of mass transfer separation elements of columnar equipment for natural gas preparation. Chem. Pet. Eng. **49**(11–12), 736–741 (2014). https://doi.org/10.1007/s10556-014-9827-8
5. Prokopov, M.G., Levchenko, D.A., Artyukhov, A.E.: Investigation of liquid-steam stream compressor. Appl. Mech. Mater. **630**, 109–116 (2014). https://doi.org/10.4028/www.scientific.net/AMM.630.109

6. Artyukhov, A.E., Fursa, A.S., Moskalenko, K.V.: Classification and separation of granules in vortex granulators. Chem. Pet. Eng. **51**(5–6), 311–318 (2015). https://doi.org/10.1007/s10 556-015-0044-x

7. Artyukhov, A.: Application software products for calculation trajectories of granules movement in vortex granulator. In: CEUR Workshop Proceedings, Selected Papers of the XI International Scientific-Practical Conference Modern Information Technologies and IT-Education (SITITO 2016), Moscow, Russia, 25–26 November 2016, vol. 1761, pp. 363–373 (2016). http://ceur-ws.org/Vol-1761/paper47.pdf

8. Artyukhov, A., Sklabinskiy, V., Ivaniia, A., Moskalenko, K.: Software for calculation of vortex type granulation devices. In: CEUR Workshop Proceedings, Selected Papers of the XI International Scientific-Practical Conference Modern Information Technologies and IT-Education (SITITO 2016), Moscow, Russia, 25–26 November 2016, vol. 1761, pp. 374–385 (2016). http://ceur-ws.org/Vol-1761/paper48.pdf

9. Artyukhov, A.E., Obodiak, V.K., Boiko, P.G., Rossi, P.C.: Computer modeling of hydrodynamic and heat-mass transfer processes in the vortex type granulation devices. In: CEUR Workshop Proceedings, Proceedings of the 13th International Conference on ICT in Education, Research and Industrial Applications. Integration, Harmonization and Knowledge Transfer, Kyiv, Ukraine, 15–18 May 2017, vol. 1844, pp. 33–47 (2017). http://ceur-ws.org/Vol-1844/10000033.pdf

10. Artyukhov, A.E.: Calculation of hydrodynamic indicators of vortex granulators working: program implementation of the mathematical model. Mod. Inf. Technol. IT-Educ. **13**(2), 215–222 (2017). https://doi.org/10.25559/SITITO.2017.2.246

11. Polyanin, A.D., Kutopov, A.M., Vyazmin, A.V., Kazenin, D.A.: Hydrodynamics, Mass and Heat Transfer in Chemical Engineering. Taylor and Francis, London (2001). https://doi.org/10.1201/9781420024517

12. Bowman, K.P., et al.: Input data requirements for Lagrangian trajectory models. Bull. Am. Meteorol. Soc. **94**(7), 1051–1058 (2013). https://doi.org/10.1175/BAMS-D-12-00076.1

13. Chen, X.Q., Pereira, J.C.F.: Computation of particle dispersion in turbulent liquid flows using an efficient Lagrangian trajectory model. Int. J. Numer. Methods Fluids **26**(3), 345–364 (1998). https://doi.org/10.1002/(SICI)1097-0363(19980215)26:3%3c345:: AID-FLD636%3e3.0.CO;2-G

14. Reynolds, A.M., LoIacono, G.: On the simulation of particle trajectories in turbulent flows. Phys. Fluids **16**(12), 4353–4361 (2004). https://doi.org/10.1063/1.1804551

15. Rybalko, M., Loth, E., Lankford, D.: A Lagrangian particle random walk model for hybrid RANS/LES turbulent flows. Pow. Technol. **221**, 105–113 (2012). https://doi.org/10.1016/j.powtec.2011.12.042

16. Artyukhov, A.E., Sklabinskyi, V.I.: Experimental and industrial implementation of porous ammonium nitrate producing process in vortex granulators. Naukovyi Visnyk Natsionalnoho Hirnychoho Universytetu. (6), 42–48 (2013). http://nvngu.in.ua/index.php/en/monographs/862-engcat/archive/2013/contents-no-6-2013/geotechnical-and-mining-mechanical-engine ering-machine-building/2398-experimental-and-industrial-implementation-of-porous-amm onium-nitrate-producing-process-in-vortex-granulators. (in Russian)

17. Artyukhov, A.E., Sklabinskyi, V.I.: 3D nanostructured porous layer of ammonium nitrate: influence of the moisturizing method on the layer's structure. J. Nano- Electron. Phys. **8**(4), 04051 (2016). https://doi.org/10.21272/jnep.8(4(1)).04051

18. Artyukhov, A.E., Voznyi, A.A.: Thermodynamics of the vortex granulator's workspace: the impact on the structure of porous ammonium nitrate. In: 2016 International Conference on Nanomaterials: Application & Properties (NAP), Lviv, pp. 02NEA01-1–02NEA01-4 (2016). https://doi.org/10.1109/NAP.2016.7757296

19. Artyukhov, A.E.: Kinetics of heating and drying of porous ammonium nitrate granules in the vortex granulator. In: 2016 International Conference on Nanomaterials: Application & Properties (NAP), Lviv, pp. 02NEA02---02NEA02-3 (2016). https://doi.org/10.1109/NAP.2016.7757297
20. Artyukhov, A.E., Sklabinskyi, V.I.: Thermodynamic conditions for obtaining 3D nanostructured porous surface layer on the granules of ammonium nitrate. J. Nano- Electron. Phys. **8**(4), 04083-1–04083-4 (2016). https://doi.org/10.21272/jnep.8(4(2)).04083

Economic Informatics

Industrial Policy and the Technological Revolution: The Case of Russian Digitalization Program

Mikhail Lugachev(✉) [iD] and Kirill Skripkin [iD]

Moscow State University, Leninskie gory 1, 119991 Moscow, Russia
{mil,skripkin}@econ.msu.ru

Abstract. Industrial policy was an object of intense discussions for the three recent decades. Now the information revolution raises new challenges. Spread of Artificial Intelligence, which is a general purpose technology (GPT), increases dramatically the uncertainty of technology development. Ubiquitous global IT platforms like Amazon or Google require achieving balance between their interests, on the one hand, and the interests of local consumers and producers, on the other. New class of peer-to-peer networks arising in the last decade challenge both platform markets and modern corporations. This situation leads to a number of tradeoffs to be solved in modern industrial policy. The paper discusses these tradeoffs by example of the Information Society Strategy and Digitalization Program in Russia and draws consequences influencing industrial policy in general.

Keywords: Digitalization · Information revolution · Industrial policy

1 Introduction

Industrial policy is one of the most controversial fields in economic research and the Great Recession empowered new round of discussion. Currently theoretical discussion came to a sort of consensus in the form of 'moderate' neoclassical approach. This viewpoint accepts that market may fail and so the government intervention can (but not necessary will) have positive effects [2, 28]. On the ground of practical policy, the spectrum of opinions is much wider, starting from the classical doctrine of so-called infant industries protection [17] to the position of informed skepticism, described in [22], which tends to deny the usefulness of industrial policy in most practical situations.

In this paper we discuss an industrial policy in the narrow sense, that is government policies directed at affecting the economic structure of the economy [26], leaving aside antitrust and other spheres, not related directly to structural change. The paper is focused on the government role in the interaction between the emerging industries arising within the current information revolution and the "old" industries, consuming the products and serviced of the former.

Contemporary status and further development of the industrial policy theory and practice is shaped by three drivers:

© Springer Nature Switzerland AG 2021
V. Sukhomlin and E. Zubareva (Eds.): SITITO 2017, CCIS 1204, pp. 295–309, 2021.
https://doi.org/10.1007/978-3-030-78273-3_28

- Globalization, that is internationalization of supply chains, improving flexibility and decreasing costs [1];
- Servitization, that is offering industrial goods together with the services [1];
- Value chain reconfiguration (so-called "smile curve"), that is concentration of added value on the initial (concept, R&D, commercialization etc.) and final stages of the value chain, while intermediate stages (mainly manufacturing) receive only small part of it [2].

We argue that recently the fourth driver came into the stage, that is new information revolution, based on the artificial intelligence (AI) and other AI-complementary technologies. In this paper we show that this revolution changes the environment of industrial policy, substantially raising uncertainty of future technology, future business models and as a result the uncertainty of the desired outcome for the economy. The effect of this new driver is complemented by the rise of platform economics, which presents another challenge to the traditional view of industrial policy. Finally, Industry 4.0 concept may relate not only to the diffusion of cyber-physical systems, but also to the new kind of peer-to-peer networks, which sometimes complements more common platform markets and sometimes compete with them. This kind of networks reveals its own specific demands for industrial policy.

To understand the effect of this new set of drivers we will study the case of Russian digitalization program, adopted in 2016–2017. The analysis rests on the approach developed in [27]. According to this approach a researcher can never know for sure the vision of a "good economy" which policymakers follow and thus cannot give well-proven recommendations on the industrial policy itself[1]. The most fruitful in this case is the research, demonstrating the most likely consequences of the actual variant of the industrial policy. From our point of view such analysis of Russian digitalization program is a typical example of discrepancies between classic-style "infant industry protection" industrial police and the effects of informational revolution. Consequently, we consider this case study somewhat typical and useful for shaping new industrial policy.

The paper is structured as follows. Next section describes the general purpose technology (GPT) approach towards understanding a technology revolution and discusses if artificial intelligence suits GPT criteria. Section 3 deals with the effects of new GPT on the environment, goals and methods of the industrial policy. Section 4 analyses Russian digitalization program and its probable outcomes from the point of view of these effects. Section 5 is devoted to the generalization of this case study. Final section contains concluding remarks.

2   GPT Diffusion as the Economic Model of Technology Revolution

The concept of General purpose technology (GPT) was introduced in late 1980s – early 1990s in [8, 10] and other papers. According to this concept, GPT's (or General Purpose Engines in [10]) "are characterized by pervasiveness (they are used as inputs by many downstream sectors), inherent potential for technical improvements, and innovational complementarities', meaning that the productivity of R&D in downstream sectors

---

[1] The reasoning for this conclusion is described in detail in [27].

increases as a consequence of innovation in the GPT" [8]. In line with this argument is the thesis that GPT is a technology that supports a broad range of applied technologies, and require heavy investment in new business models, business processes, new professional knowledge and skills, and, finally, new institutions on the macro level [10]. This process of technology and business process mutual adaptation was later named co-invention [6].

In later works [7, 11] the key features of GPT were made more specific.

1. Wide scope for improvement and elaboration.
2. Applicability across the broad range of uses.
3. Potential for use in a wide variety of products and processes.
4. Strong complementarities with existing or potential new technologies.
5. Mutual adaptation between business process and technology.
6. Tight correlation between co-invention intensity and stimuli to adopt the given GPT.
7. High levels of demand uncertainty in case of new products and services.

For example, when IBM introduced IBM PC it forecasted sales of only 25000 units, while actual sales peaked 2 million units for the first 2 years [20].

Now let us turn back to information revolution. First, we will check if the artificial intelligence (AI) suits properties of GPT. AI has already shown its potential in industry, banking and financial services, agriculture, health care, transportation, different services etc. It is also complementary to a broad range of applied technologies (see Table 1).

Table 1. Complementary relations between AI and other advanced technologies.

Technology	Complementary relations with AI
Internet of things (IoT)	IoT sensors provide data for AI analysis, IoT smart devices execute AI commands
Cloud computing	Cloud platform is a natural form of matching AI with IoT, medical data, industrial applications, etc.
3D printing and other additive technologies	AI provides personalized digital model of the object even in most complex situations
Quantum computing	Provides new powerful algorithms for intelligent data processing and information security
Nanorobotics	AI (built-in, centralized or distributed) processes data collected by nanorobots and controls their work
Blockchain	AI is useful in blockchain pruning (purging out excess data from blocks), secure blockchain application deployment, homomorphic encryption to improve blockchain privacy, improving trustworthy of AI itself, etc.

AI also demonstrates vast area for further improvement. Current list of key AI problems includes [25]:

- Understanding meaning (semantics) of words, so-called barrier of meaning;
- Robots ability to act in complex real-world situations, so-called reality gap;
- AI information security and guard against hacking;
- Ability to go beyond the game with transparent and known by both players situations like chess, go, etc.
- Ability of AI and robots to keep within safe and ethical bounds.

When we turn to co-invention process, we can see a broad range of new business models, supported by new business processes. In [15] several business models for manufacturing are described, based on so-called smart products and smart services. Both imply ability to monitor the environment and performance of product or service and optimizing the latter in automatic mode or in contact with the customer. [21] describes new business model in telemedicine and depicts its innovative features: enablement (creating a platform for expert communication), support (delivery of medical infrastructure) and empowerment (providing additional valuable data directly to the patient). In financial sector digitalization leads, for example, to peer-to-peer lending [19] and so on. To summarize, new business models arise in different industries including manufacturing and services.

Finally, we should examine stimuli to implement AI and its applications. AI is now widely adopted by a broad range of firms in different industries including IT, financial services, manufacturing, agriculture etc. AI already provides dramatic increase in the effectiveness, (numerous examples are provided in [13] and other sources), Signals from financial markets are important either. In 2013 there was coined a term "unicorn" to denote a startup, which achieved capitalization one billion dollars or higher within 7 years [16]. At the time of writing her paper the author thought that such a firm can be met as easily as a unicorn. Now there are 227 unicorns throughout the world, most in USA (113) and China (61) [9].

So, we can conclude that AI matches all the criteria of the general purpose technology. This means that next 20–30 years we will see multitude of new applied technologies, business models and business processes. Most of them will have one feature in common – we do not anticipate them right now. This does not necessary mean than nobody anticipates, but these guesses are at least controversial. As a result, we will likely see many errors of the first and the second kind in forecasting new technologies, business processes and business models.

3   Information Revolution and Industrial Policy

In the previous section we discussed the nature of contemporary information revolution, that is global diffusion of AI (which turned to be a GPT) and complementary applied technologies. Before turning towards the policy implications of this thesis, let us briefly discuss another less fundamental yet important feature of this revolution.

This feature is rapid rise of two-sided and multi-sided platforms around the world. If in previous decades platforms (like Amazon, Google, iTunes/Google Play, eBay, PayPal,

Uber) were hosted in developed countries primarily in USA, today successful platform operators may grow at emerging market as well. Among the most striking examples we can name Alibaba, WeChat[2], Snapdeal[3], Paytm[4], Coupang[5] and others.

In this paper we use the following definition of platform: "The 'platform' encompasses the set of components and rules employed in common in most user transactions" [5] cited in [12]. The distinguishing features of such platforms embrace:

- Significant economies of scale on supply side, especially for the platform operator [20–23];
- Strong positive network externalities for both consumers and complementors [23, 173–225];
- Market segmentation in the form of multitude of niches (so-called "long tail") [3]
- Spread of the business models based on giving a product or a service away for free [23] (advertising-based models), [4] (freemium business model).

One of the most important characteristics of the platform is the degree of its openness. This degree may be different for different roles within the network: end users, complementors, platform providers and platform sponsors [12]. The platforms listed earlier in the section usually are more or less open for sponsors and complementors (less for platforms operated by Apple Inc.) but closed in terms of provider and sponsor. Yet in recent years we saw the rise of platforms open for providers and sponsors as well. Among the most famous examples are Bitcoin and Etherium, cryptocurrency platforms successfully operating as peer-to-peer networks. Within this paper we will call the first type of platforms "closed" and the second type of platforms "open".

Less famous but maybe even more important example is Industry 4.0. The central idea of Industry 4.0 concept is a complex of cyber-physical systems and appropriate standards, supporting real-time interaction between the physical objects in production process and their digital twins, that is single consistent digital representation of the object on all stages of its lifecycle. This leads to the production integration model flexible enough to allow integration with any new participant supporting the same set of standards. As a result, Industrie 4.0 is a powerful instrument of creation peer-to-peer networks in manufacturing.

So, in recent years we see the development of both open and closed models of platform integration. Though they exploit the same positive network effects and the same economies on scale and scope, their economic mechanisms are different. The closed platform is usually a marketplace where buyer and seller meet each other. Any firm may use such platform as a complementor until it follows the rules established by platform operator and sponsor (which usually are the same in case of close platforms). Peer-to-peer network may possibly be useful for a much broader spectrum of tasks (e.g. manufacturing), but in exchange it requires rebuild of the firm's processes. The latter

---

[2] Chinese social network operated ty Tencent.

[3] Largest E-Commerce platform in India.

[4] Largest Fintech platform in India, operated by One97 Communicatios.

[5] Korean E-commerce platform.

must become fully digital, highly automated on the basis of intelligent self-optimizing components and open for collaboration with the suppliers and consumers.

The most important impact of these new factors is uncertainty. We already have the new GPT in place, yet many business models, business properties, government policies and human skills are still to be invented or acquired. The same is true for applied technology, implemented it these models, processes and skills. As a result, almost any possible vision of the "good economy" may be challenged by further technology development and entrepreneurial activity. Facing this challenge, the effective industrial policy should turn to be "Bayesian", that is it should include new activities, executed in real-time:

- Developing validity tests for built-in view of "good economy";
- Developing information strategy for such a test;
- Implement the monitoring system for testing this validity;
- Introduce the "gates", where the validity of the "good economy" will be reviewed and appropriate testing procedure:
- Develop and implement the procedure of correction both the vision itself and policy measures resulting from it.

This reviewing process should influence the legislation in the field of industrial policy. If a policy itself is subject to review and changes, the laws and other regulations should avoid excess details. If these details are fixed in laws, any change in the policy will cause a dilemma of either obsolete law or too frequent changes in legislation. The only way to avoid this dilemma is to is to treat legislation as a framework leaving details to self-regulated associations and other private or collective actors.

This demand of flexible industrial policy is in line with the idea of embedded industrial policy in [22]. D.Rodrik shows that industrial policy requires complex multidimensional information flow between the government and the private sector ("a thicker bandwidth is needed"). So industrial policy must be constructed as a system of discovery about all sources of uncertainty. This in turn requires close collaboration between all the actors involved, that is "embeddedness". This "embedded" industrial policy contrasts sharply with the usual top-down approach to the industrial policy.

To finalize, it should be stressed that this "embedded" approach is a question of effectiveness for any given policy, not a question of choosing one policy option or the other. So, implementing this reviewing process is important for achieving any goal, no matter what the goal is.

Another consequence of GPT diffusion is extreme importance of demand side. The co-invention process where new products, business models and services are created goes in collaboration of producers and consumers. Meanwhile most of protection measures implemented within industrial policy protect producer in expense of consumer. In case of GPT it deteriorates stimuli to implement new GPT and thus co-invention process. It in turn leads to lack of new entrepreneurial, commercial and organizational knowledge creation and to faded adaptation of business and government to the opportunities and risks of new GPT. This demand protection approach is in line with "carrots and sticks" problem in [22], which means that degree of protection should correspond to export performance of the firm.

Platform economy introduces yet another challenge. The major platforms like Amazon, Google, Alibaba, etc., aggregate the demand of hundreds of millions if not of billions of people and enjoy tremendous economies on both scale and scope. If a government tries to block the activity of global platforms or make it costlier and riskier, the economy will suffer much higher transaction costs either due to price increase or trying to substitute missing platforms. The only exception can occur at extremely large national markets which is a case for China and India. As a result, a number of new platforms like Alibaba/Ali Express, WeChat, Snapdeal, Paytm originate from these two countries.

This challenge has three implications. First, cooperation is important for both governments and global platforms while the regulation wars create a loose-loose situation for both. Second, governments should cooperate to increase their bargaining power against global platforms. Third, to create and protect platforms of its own as opposed to global ones, the government should control the market of one billion consumers or higher. Currently only China and India fit this requirement, but cooperation of the governments may change the situation. Another less risky option is support (and in some cases protection) of the complementors for global platforms. The "long tail" model decreases entry barriers for complementors and in case of success applications, games, messengers or services can create serious value. At the same time complementor business helps local firms to integrate in the global economy due to the low transaction costs provided by platform-mediating business. Global complementary products can help to maintain export discipline in case of government support[6] which is another bonus for the industrial policy.

Finally, let us consider implications of the rise of Industry 4.0 and other open peer-to-peer platforms. They imply quite different challenge: the firms themselves should become open to the peers yet maintaining their information security on a due level. This in turn demands dramatic changes in processes, internal organization and culture of the firms involved. The scope of these changes can be compared only with the transition from relatively entrepreneurial firms of the 19th century to the large often global organizations like American trusts in late 1890-s – early 1900-s. Yet the direction of these changes may be different: recently we saw several cases[7] when a network of relatively small firms outperforms large bureaucratic organizations.

In this situation what government does not do may be even more important than what it does. Protection of "too-big-to-fail" firms may slow this transition and make it much costlier for the economy as a whole. On the contrary, thorough enforcement of anti-trust legislation may help this transition.

To summarize, effective industrial policy should resolve several rather complicated tradeoffs.

1. To maintain consistency of the overall industrial policy yet review it at some gates to achieve adequate view of the "good economy".

---

[6] On the importance of export discipline see [17, 29] and other sources.

[7] Some cases of this kind are provided in the Guardian article "How can SMEs compete with big businesses?", https://www.theguardian.com/small-business-network/2013/jan/10/sme-compete-big-business.

2. To protect local producers in the "infant industries" yet avoiding deterioration of the co-invention process.
3. To introduce laws and other regulations in the new digital markets yet avoiding excess details which may either make the regulation obsolete or induce instability of legislation.
4. To protect the interests of consumers and local firms facing the global platforms yet avoiding sufficient increase in transaction costs for economic actors.
5. To breed large scale complementors for the global platform markets yet maintaining enough stimuli for creating local jobs.
6. To support transition from large-scale bureaucratic organizations to relatively small firms yet harnessing negative impact for labor market.

The resolution of these tradeoffs will vary depending on the view of the "good economy" and the resulting policy measures. Yet effective industrial policy like any policy should be consistent, so the authorities should formulate all the five tradeoffs at least for themselves and find for all of them solutions that fit together.

The question whether the resolution of these tradeoffs should be described explicitly is still open. Main reason in favor of explicitness is the facilitation of coordination of the government and business, main reason against is that very uncertainty of "good economy" that was demonstrated in this section. Possible answer is that the degree of explicitness should depend on national culture.

4   Industrial Policy and/or Information Revolution: The Case of Russian Digitalization Program

In 2017 Russian Government adopted two key documents in the field of digital economy development: Strategy of Information Society Development for 2017–2030[8], further referred to as the Strategy-2030 or simply the Strategy and the Program "Digital Economy of the Russian Federation"[9], further referred to as the Digitalization Program. The former document is aimed at creating the framework for the development of the information society and the digital economy while the latter provides specific policy instruments. Although there is a lot of other laws and regulations influencing information markets, it is broadly accepted that these documents govern the process of digital economy development. Following top-down approach, we will start with the Strategy-2030.

The Strategy-2030 is a high-level document, details of policy measures are to be delivered in the Digitalization Program. Still it has some specific features:

1. The incremental approach towards development of information society and digital economy. According to the Strategy current trends in the development of information

---

[8] Strategy of the Information Society Development for the 2017-2030, adopted by the Decree of the President on May 9 2017, http://www.kremlin.ru/acts/bank/41919 (in Russian).

[9] Program "Digital Economy of Russian Federation", adopted by the Распоряжение of the Government on July 28, 2017, http://static.government.ru/media/files/9gFM4FHj4PsB79I5v7 yLVuPgu4bvR7M0.pdf (in Russian).

society and digital economy in general has not changed since late 2000-s when the first strategy of information society development was adopted. New technologies provide some improvements and require some additional regulation.

2. In the sphere of industrial policy, the key task is substitution of imports. Export promotion is mentioned only twice without any specific tasks or measurable goals.

3. The information and cyber security in a broad sense (starting with the availability of key infrastructure elements and ending with problems of trust and information quality), are treated as key risks[10]. Risks in the economic or social sphere, like job losses, digital inequality and so on are not considered at all.

4. The Strategy is focused on production of digital goods and services, not on their consumption in Russian economy. In particular, the problem of the global platforms presence and resulting tradeoffs is not posed at all. Meanwhile the Strategy set protection of traditional technologies, organizations and markets as one of explicit goals (paragraph 42).

5. The Strategy does not deal with "soft" factors of the digital technologies utilization like organization, processes and culture. This relates to the Industry 4.0 and its managerial and cultural issues as well.

So, we can say that the Strategy-2030 does not deal with the vision of the future in general and the view of the "good economy" in particular. In place of both we see the extrapolation of the trends, which existed in 2000-s. As a result, the Strategy does not deal with the information revolution. Yet the advance of this document is an important distinction between mission-critical services and infrastructure elements, where substitution of import is treated as an important task, and other elements where this problem is not treated as urgent. In the current situation of economic sanctions this

Now let us turn to the Digitalization Program. This document is much more specific, it enlists different policy instruments, so it can give us the answers we seek.

Generally, the program includes five key areas: regulations and norms, human capital and education, building research and technology capacities, information infrastructure and information security. Its goals are stated as follows:

- Creating in Russia ecosystem of digital economy;
- Creating necessary and sufficient infrastructure and institutional conditions for development of high-tech business (including prevention of new restrictions emergence);
- Raising global competitiveness of several industries and Russian economy as a whole.

The program is structured in two parts, general description and roadmaps for all the key areas. General description consists of introduction (Sect. 1), "as is" analysis (Sects. 2, 3), key areas of a program (Sect. 4), organization of governance and management (Sect. 5), indicators and their values (Sect. 6). The second part contains five detailed roadmaps, one for each key area. One should note that three areas out of five relate to "soft" factors, that is norms, human capital and research capacities. This feature is in line with the common sense of industrial policy design, as well as roadmap approach.

---

[10] For example, the word "security" is mentioned 26 times.

In solving the problem of "embeddedness" the impression of the Program is twofold. On the one hand, the program provides both for the changes of basic technologies array (Sect. 1) and the roadmaps in key areas, though does not define mechanisms of such changes. On the other hand, the roadmap follows top-down approach and is rather detailed, so it would be difficult to change this map in a consistent manner. Top-down here means the step-by-step specification of each roadmap position. The problem of reviewing and changing the framework formed on the previous steps of the roadmap realization is not dealt with. Last but not least issue is rather vague description of the mechanisms of interaction between the government and the business. So, it does not protect either from excess centralization or against one-sided concentration of power in the hands of government bodies.

The tradeoff between the local producers' protection and co-invention process is solved in favor of protection. The Program prescribes preferential usage of local hardware and software in most of areas. Exports is encouraged as well, especially in the fields of information infrastructure and information security. Yet, there is no sign of direct linking export performance to the amounts of assistance provided by the government authorities. Section 6 also lacks even indicative target values for exports of digital goods, services and technologies. This problem is extremely important for the information technology field due to the extreme economies of scale in this sphere. If an economy is relatively small compared with the leaders, exports is an important factor of achieving necessary economies of scale. So, the problem of "carrots and sticks" is solved in favor of carrots.

This problem has one more dimension. Finance in Russia are a scarce resource. For example, in 2017 the whole venture market in Russia estimated as $125 mln[11]. If we compare this figure with the investment of top world players [18, Exhibit 2], we can see, that American and Chinese venture investment in any of 9 leading technologies (fintech, virtual reality, autonomous driving, wearables, education technology, robotics and drones, 3d printing, big data, AI and machine learning) is far greater than overall venture investment in Russia. The import substitution without stick of export discipline produces good profits without serious risks, so it may channel this scarce amount of money into creating local operation systems, office suits, databases and other similar areas, reinventing technologies of 1980-s–1990-s. This would be convenient for the business, but of little value for advances in digitalization.

The solutions in the field of legislation are twofold like in some other tradeoffs. The Program states decreasing of regulative barriers for the digital economy in general and innovative business in this field. Still, it does not establish barriers against excess details in the legislation and too intensive changes in legislation. The latter is a real problem for Russian business, for example, the law of information, IT and information security was changed 27 times within 11 years, while the law of advertising was changed 52 times within 11 years[12]. This once again can be compared with Chinese experience where the interval between the rise of new technology and mandatory legislation in this field

---

[11] Russian Association of Electronic Communications (RAEC), https://ria.ru/economy/20180419/1518953367.html.

[12] Calculations of the authors based on the sources, http://www.consultant.ru/document/cons_doc_LAW_61798/ and http://www.consultant.ru/document/cons_doc_LAW_58968/ respectively (in Russian).

varied from 5 to 11 years [18, Exhibit 7]. Meanwhile the Program does not tell us how the legislation approach will be changed towards more cooperative one.

The Digitalization program approach towards platforms is focused on creating the local platforms in Russia. Section 4 states as a goal achieving technological independence in all the key technology areas (p. 11). This goal should be achieved by the platforms, presumably local. In roadmaps we can see details of this plan: at least one local platform for each of the key technology area (p. 19), totally not less than 10 platforms. Here we again see the problem of financing, described above. The goal of interaction with the global platforms like Alibaba, Amazon, Google, Facebook, LinkedIn and others is not even stated.

The current practice of Russian authorities towards the global platforms like mandatory storage of personal data on the Russian territory[13], blocking LinkedIn[14] and Telegram[15], the claims towards Facebook[16] can be characterized as "not a single inch to the enemy". It may be a good slogan for the war time (though even at war it can cause unnecessary losses), but in the economy this approach usually creates "loose – loose" situation. Currently the losses are decreased with mass usage of anonymizers, VPNs by consumers and usage of elastic cloud resources by platform operators, but the Digitalization program sets the goal of creating mechanisms to effectively block all illegal content (Item 5.8 of the Roadmap 5 "Information security").

Meanwhile, the key obstacle to the rise of Russian-based platforms is relatively small number of users and resulting lack of economies of scale. While Google, for example, enjoys 1 billion of active users monthly[17], the monthly number of active Internet users in Russia is only 87 million people[18]. As most of them will not use all the local platforms at once, the number of users for each platform will be even smaller. This results in higher tariffs for the users or advertisers, less functionality due to the lack of money and less network effects. The latter problem is especially important for export activities and other forms of international cooperation, as we cannot expect lots of foreign users on such platforms. As a result, the problem of cooperation with global platforms is probably one of the weakest points in the whole Program.

In the case of scarce resources, the possible way out may be focus strategy, that is achieving competitiveness in a relatively small niches of the global market. The current structure of platform markets which is sometimes called "Long Tail" (Anderson [3]) favors such a strategy. Yet it requires close cooperation with the operators of at least some global platforms which is impossible under "not a single inch to the enemy" approach. As a result, this way out is also blocked in the Digitalization Program.

Maybe the most important problem of Digitalization Program is involvement of major Russian firms. Russian economy is highly concentrated: 400 major firms produce

---

13 Law of July 21 2014 #242-FZ, http://base.garant.ru/70700506/ (in Russian).

14 See "LinkedIn is Blocked", https://lenta.ru/news/2016/11/17/linkedin_block/ (in Russian).

15 See "Blocking Telegram in Russia", https://ria.ru/trend/russia-block-telegram-13042018/ (in Russian).

16 See "Roscomnadzor warned Facebook of possible blocking", https://lenta.ru/news/2018/04/18/facebook/ (in Russian).

17 See Statista data on Google, https://www.statista.com/statistics/432390/active-gmail-users/.

18 Data of Russian Internet Forum, http://2017.russianinternetforum.ru/news/1298/ (in Russian).

43% of gross product [30], so they are the most important consumers of the digital products and services. Their role in the co-invention process is also important, as they control the major part of the investment resources in Russia. As a result, the successful digital transformation of these companies is a key factor of the overall Program success. Somewhat paradoxically this problem matches none of the key areas and thus none of the roadmaps.

The paradox lies in the fact that state is a key shareholder of 40% of the 400 major firms [30] and respectively has effective means of influence on their policy in general and their investment and innovation policy in particular. The state ownership means not only the right to set goals, but also the opportunity to test different organizational forms of embeddedness. The successful ones may be rolled out as standards of the interaction between business and government authorities throughout the whole Russia.

This opportunity is tricky to exploit within current arrangements of the Program. As we saw, it is designed on the base of so-called "horizontal" paradigm, aimed at improvement of institutions, human capital and infrastructure. Meanwhile, to ignite co-invention process the industrial policy should become more selective, that is aimed at solving problems and removing roadblocks for particular industries. To be more specific, there could be one more key area of learning by doing, based on goals of improving performance, primarily, export performance, which is much easier subject to control than other performance indicators.

To summarize, the Russian Digitalization program results from two conflicting trends. One trend is the horizontal approach towards industrial policy which was viewed as best practice in two recent decades and implemented in the industrial policy of European Union and other countries. It is grounded in costly failures of selective industrial policy in Latin America and some other regions in 1970-s–1980-s and overall shift towards less interventionists policy in 1990-s (so-called Washington Consensus). The second one is trend for "sovereignty", which can be described as an attempt to control all the aspects of information technology and information flows. It is grounded in sanction war, started in 2014.

At first glance, the key problem is incompatibility of these approaches. To some extent this answer is right, as attempts to achieve sovereignty lead to dispersion of scarce resources. Yet it is only a fraction of a real problem. On the one hand, the "sovereignty" strategy solves a real problem of Russian economy vulnerability to Western sanctions. On the other hand, "horizontal policy" itself does not solve a number of crucial problems, that is relations with global platforms, creating niches for complementors or ignition of co-invention process. All the three problems require the specific measures based on the analysis of specific situation which is hardly compatible with "horizontal policy". With jobs moving from humans to robots, both industrial and informational, the large-scale control system of the modern corporation loses the object of control and thus turns to be unnecessary. At the same time lowering of transaction costs blurs the borders of the firm in the forms of outsourcing, servitization, freelancing and so on. These are the signs of new forms of organizations yet to be discovered.

5 Conclusion

From our point of view, Russian digitalization policy should be treated as an example of problems, arising in many industrial policy case studies. Surely, most countries do not face sanctions as Russia faces. Yet they face trade wars[19], cancellation of global trade blocks, like TPP[20], calls for control of cyberspace. All these new phenomena create stimuli for regionalization if not for campaigns for national sovereignty. Maybe for many countries the difference from Russia is more quantitative than qualitative. In other words, Russia may be just an extreme example of the problems facing many countries.

The problems of "horizontal policy" are even more typical. This approach towards industrial policy does not deal with almost all tradeoffs to be faced in modern industrial policy. Spread of new GPT raises dramatically the uncertainty of technology progress thus challenging common sense of the roadmap. The co-invention process demands stimuli for consumers, which are inconsistent with most instruments of "infant industries protection". The problem of legislation flexibility looks less challenging as delay of mandatory legislation solves the problem in many cases. Yet one needs either outstanding intuition or good monitoring system to know right moment for putting legislation in place.

The tradeoffs concerning the balance of interests with the global platform operators are much more difficult. Global platform has enormous potential to lower transaction costs, yet its presence is a serious challenge for competition due to network effects. At the same time, blocking activities of global platforms in favor of building local ones is a question of extreme risk due to loss of economy of scale and network effects. We state a hypothesis that such a policy is a privilege for the most populated nations like China and India. In other case the government has to choose between two other alternatives: either create a regional platform on the basis of agreement between several different states or focus on complementary activities. The latter option is the least sensitive to the economy of scale due to "Long tail" market structure.

It is highly probable that the informational revolution challenges the current model of the corporation as well. The bureaucratic model of the corporations was aimed at control of masses of employees performing standardized and formalized functions. Many functions of such kind are already automated, and many will be automated in the near future.

References

1. Ambroziak, A.A.: Review of the literature on the theory of industrial policy. In: Ambroziak, A.A. (ed.) The New Industrial Policy of the European Union. CE, pp. 3–38. Springer, Cham (2017). https://doi.org/10.1007/978-3-319-39070-3_1
2. Ambroziak, A.A.: A theoretical concept of a modern industrial policy. In: Ambroziak, A.A. (ed.) The New Industrial Policy of the European Union. CE, pp. 173–186. Springer, Cham (2017). https://doi.org/10.1007/978-3-319-39070-3_7

---

[19] See, for example, White House to Impose Metal Tariffs on E.U., Canada and Mexico, https://www.nytimes.com/2018/05/31/us/politics/trump-aluminum-steel-tariffs.html.

[20] Trump executive order pulls out of TPP trade deal, https://www.bbc.com/news/world-us-canada-38721056.

3. Anderson, C.: The Long Tail: Why the Future of Business Is Selling Less of More. Hachette Books, Revised edition (2008)
4. Anderson, C.: Free: The Future of a Radical Price. Random House Business (2010)
5. Boudreau, K.: Opening the Platform vs. Opening the Complementary Good? The Effect on Product Innovation in Handheld Computing (2008). http://dx.doi.org/10.2139/ssrn.1251167
6. Bresnahan, T.F., Greenstein, S.: Technical progress and co-invention in computing and in the uses of computers. Brookings Papers: Microeconomics, vol. 1996, pp. 1–83 (1996). https://www.brookings.edu/wp-content/uploads/1996/01/1996_bpeamicro_bresnahan.pdf
7. Bresnahan, T.F., Greenstein, S.: The economic contribution of information technology: towards comparative and user studies. J. Evol. Econ. **11**(1), 95–118 (2001). https://doi.org/10.1007/PL00003859
8. Bresnahan, T.F., Trajtenberg, M.: General purpose technologies: "engines of growth"? NBER Working Paper, no. 4148 (1992). https://www.nber.org/papers/w4148.pdf
9. The Global Unicorn Club, CBInsights (2017). https://www.cbinsights.com/research-unicorn-companies
10. David, P.A.: The dynamo and the computer: an historical perspective on the modern productivity paradox. Am. Econ. Rev. **80**(2), 355–361 (1990). www.jstor.org/stable/2006600
11. David, P.A., Wright, G.: General purpose technologies and surges in productivity: historical reflections on the future of the ICT revolution. In: David, P.A., Thomas, M. (eds.) The Economic Future in Historical Perspective. British Academy Scholarship Online (2003). https://doi.org/10.5871/bacad/9780197263471.003.0005
12. Eisenmann, T.R., Parker, G., Van Alstyne, M.: Opening platforms: how, when and why?. In: Annabelle, G. (ed.) Platforms, Markets and Innovation, Chapter 6. Edward Elgar Publishing (2009). https://doi.org/10.4337/9781849803311.00013
13. Gilchrist, A.: Industry 4.0: The Industrial Internet of Things. Apress, Berkeley, CA (2016). https://doi.org/10.1007/978-1-4842-2047-4
14. Pohjola, M.: The new economy: facts, impacts and policies. Inform. Econ. Policy **14**(2), 133–144 (2002). https://doi.org/10.1016/S0167-6245(01)00063-4
15. Ibarra, D., Ganzarain, J., Igartua, J.I.: Business model innovation through industry 4.0: a review. Procedia Manuf. **22**, 4–10 (2018). https://doi.org/10.1016/j.promfg.2018.03.002
16. Lee, A.: Welcome To The Unicorn Club: Learning From Billion-Dollar Startups. http://techcrunch.com/2013/11/02/welcome-to-the-unicorn-club
17. Lin, J.Y., Chang, H.J.: Should industrial policy in developing countries conform to comparative advantage or defy it? A debate between Justin Lin and Ha-Joon Chang. Dev. Policy Rev. **27**(5), 483–502 (2009). https://doi.org/10.1111/j.1467-7679.2009.00456.x
18. China's Digital Economy: A Leading Global Force. Discussion Paper. McKinsey Global Institute (2017)
19. Niţescu, D.C.: New pillars of the banking business model or a new model of doing banking? Theor. Appl. Econ. **XXIII**(4), 143–152 (2016). http://store.ectap.ro/articole/1229.pdf
20. O'Reilly, E.: Milestones in Computer Science and Information Technology. Greenwood Publishing Group (2003)
21. Peters, C., Blohm, I., Leimeister, J,M.: Anatomy of successful business models for complex services: insights from the telemedicine field. J. Manage. Inform. Syst. **32**(3), 75–104 (2015). https://doi.org/10.1080/07421222.2015.1095034
22. Rodrik, D.: Normalizing Industrial Policy. Commission of Growth and Development, Working Paper no. 3 (2008). https://j.mp/2o6K6Ye
23. Shapiro, C., Varian, H.: Information Rules: A Strategic Guide to the Network Economy. Harvard Business School Press, Boston, Massachusetts (1998)
24. Shuh, G., Potente, T., Wech-Potente, C., Weber, A.R., Prote, J.-P.: Collaboration mechanisms to increase productivity in the context of industrie 4.0. Procedia CIRP. **19**, 51–56 (2014). https://doi.org/10.1016/j.procir.2014.05.016

25. Simonite, T.: As Artificial Intelligence Advances, Here Are Five Tough Projects for 2018. Wired (2017). https://www.wired.com/story/as-artificial-intelligence-advances-here-are-five-projects-for-2018
26. Stiglitz, J.E., Lin, J.Y., Monga, C.: The rejuvenation of industrial policy. World Bank Policy Research Working Paper (2013). https://doi.org/10.1596/1813-9450-6628
27. Tambovtsev, V.L.: Industrial policy: towards new interpretation. Izvestiya Uralskogo gosudarstvennogo ekonomicheskogo universiteta. J. Ural State Univ. Econ. (5), 55–67 (2017). https://doi.org/10.29141/2073-1019-2017-17-5-5. (in Russian)
28. Warwick, K.: Beyond industrial policy: emerging issues and new trends. OECD Science, Technology and Industry Policy Papers, no. 2 (2013). https://doi.org/10.1787/5k4869clw0xp-en
29. Westphal, L.E.: Industrial policy in an export propelled economy: lessons from south korea's experience. J. Econ. Persp. **4**(3), 41–59 (1990). https://doi.org/10.1257/jep.4.3.41
30. Zhogha, G.: Inventory of the first echelon. Expert, no. 43(1049). 23 Oct 2017. https://expert.ru/expert/2017/43/opis-pervogo-eshelona. (in Russian)

Using Graph Theory to Solve One Pricing Problem

Tatiana Makarovskikh$^{(\boxtimes)}$, Egor Savitskiy , and Ruslan Yakupov

South Ural State University, Lenin Ave. 76, 454080 Chelyabinsk, Russia
Makarovskikh.T.A@susu.ru

Abstract. The paper is devoted to the application of graph theory as one of the most effective tools for assessing various economic indicators. A graph model of an enterprise distribution system based on the classic Dijkstra and Floyd-Warshall algorithms is presented. With the help of the model used, it is possible to calculate the gross profit of an enterprise from trade in a distributed territory. The developed algorithms allow performing calculations taking into account the so-called product flows and determining the maximum profit of a reseller. We show that the average price when the "flow" of products arises depends on the level of dispersion of final prices. In particular, we show that for enterprises with a high average price, the risk of "product flows" is high even for a small dispersion of prices and enterprises with a higher cost of production are recommended to use non-price methods of combating these "product flows".

Keywords: Dijkstra algorithm · Floyd-Warsell algorithm · Pricing problems · Optimization

1 Introduction

Nowadays, the problem of goods delivery and supply chain optimization is one of the most important ones for the successful functioning of any manufacturer [1–4]. Hence, manufacturers face the challenge of the competent distribution system identifying and determining the optimal prices for their goods and services [2]. The main goal is in profit maximization, and one of the main factors impacting the profit is the product price. Setting any products price in the distribution system may bring any volume of losses and profits. One of the losses reasons is imperfect logistics dealing with so called "product flows".

Let the product flow be a case when a reseller delivers and sells the goods between two distribution points. Obviously, if the distance between two neighboring cities (or cities the distance between which is short in comparison with width of the distribution market) is small and the difference of prices is great then the path between these cities is problematic as soon as reseller may get the greater profit after reselling from one distributer to another. As a result a consumer needs to buy the goods at the other regions because of these goods shortage at his native region.

The main objective in the goods distribution across a distributed territory is to minimize the goods transporting costs. Therefore, regardless of the expected demand for

© Springer Nature Switzerland AG 2021
V. Sukhomlin and E. Zubareva (Eds.): SITITO 2017, CCIS 1204, pp. 310–324, 2021.
https://doi.org/10.1007/978-3-030-78273-3_29

goods in specific regions, the enterprise needs to set such prices for its products that maximize gross profit.

One of the effective modeling methods for manufacturers distribution systems and defining the problematic regions is graph theory the usage of which nowadays is rather wide [5–7]. With the help of shortest paths algorithms and the possibility of big graphs representation, it is possible to use computer technologies for obtaining the exact results characterizing the distribution model. The reduction of the problem to graph-theoretic structures requires certain efforts; nevertheless, it substantially simplifies the problem statement due to the reasonable allocation of the minimum number of necessary structural or numerical characteristics for actually existing processes or systems [8]. So, graph-theoretic statement allows to get the qualitative solution of complex problems using effective algorithms of polynomial complexity.

Let the non-oriented weighted graph $G(V, E)$ and a set of variables defining the whole system status are used as a model of territorial distribution of goods. Let graph vertices $V(G)$ be the large logistics centers, and edges $E(G)$ be the roads of transporting network between them. Hence, the edge $e = \{u, v\} \in E(G)$ weight $w(e)$ be the distance between the corresponding logistics complexes u and v.

The following weights correspond to any vertex $v \in V(G)$:

- $p(v)$ be a price of the goods on the territory adjacent to the complex;
- $d(v)$ be projected average monthly sales volume in the adjacent territory (ton).

Moreover, this model has variables determining the state of the whole system:

- C_t be the cost of one ton of products transportation for 1 km,
- a be the value of coverage the market by a reseller,
- $v_0 \in V(G)$ be the graph vertex satisfying the complex from which delivery to the other regions is carried out.

Besides we need the following supplementary data for calculations:
- the average cost of ton of products;
- dispersion of products price;
- the average demand for products.

2 The Statement of the Problem of Enterprise and Reseller Profit Calculation

2.1 Problem of Enterprise Gross Profit of Trading Calculation

Nowadays the heads of enterprises control lots of factors affecting on the success of enterprise operations. The market price of production set up by the manufacturer is among of these factors. While distributing the production to some territories the enterprise has to build such a pricing policy that the summary profit of selling the products be higher than summary logistics expenses.

However, not all enterprise representatives take into account these expenses and make the wrong calculations of price. As a result the existing pricing policy leads to losses or unexpected low profit what means the unscheduled claims of enterprise resources.

According to this we may state the following problem – to create the graph model of the enterprise distribution system allowing calculate the gross profit of selling. In the other words, we need two stages:

– to define the common weight of graph edges representing profits and losses of an enterprise;
– to calculate of difference between them.

Using the above graph model of goods distribution the businessmen may estimate the probable gross profit after using the planned pricing policy.

2.2   Problem of Calculating the Maximal Profit of Reseller After Resale the Goods Between Regions of Distribution

For the successful operation of the manufacturing enterprises the distributors of their products should be perfectly manageable and carry out selling within the regions without any influence on sales of similar products in neighboring regions.

In modern conditions, the distributors of goods of the same producer have a negative impact on each other by setting a highly differentiated price of the goods. When launching sales of goods in one of the regions by setting low prices on it leads to product flows to other regions. As a result, there are:

– a deterioration in the manageability of the goods distribution system;
– discrepancy of the available quantity of sales to real demand;
– decreasing of total profit of sales;
– the non-left spending of the company's budgets.

According to this, we can formulate the following problem – to search for the maximum weight path in the graph model of the enterprise distribution system. Successive solution of this problem allows to find such a pair of vertices $v_0, v_n \in V(G)$ and the path $P = v_0 e_1 v_1 e_2 \ldots e_n v_n$ between them which corresponds to the most problematic route in terms of possible products flow.

2.3   Problem of Dependency Recognition Between Maximal Possible Profit After Products Flow and Parameters of Pricing Policy

Nowadays one of the goals of any enterprise is production and sales risk avoidance. One of the risk types is artificial changing of quantitative goods structure at the end-points of distribution system. The main reason of these risks is activity of the resellers.

The problem is that the choice of pricing policy parameters is not obvious and the producer needs know in advance which pricing policy parameters are acceptable for him. According to this we may formulate a problem of dependency recognition between maximal reseller profit (and, correspondingly, the probability of products flow appearance) and such pricing policy parameters as

– average price of goods;

– deviation of the price.

In other words it is necessary to hold multiple modeling of data describing the distribution system of an enterprise with different weights for the vertices $v \in V(G)$ (corresponding to distribution complexes) and to search for the maximum weight path $P = v_0 e_1 v_1 e_2 \ldots e_n v_n$. After getting statistics on the data listed above and calculating the values of the resellers' profits it is necessary to analyze and determine the optimal levels of pricing policy parameters that do not lead to product flow.

3 The Example of Using the Graph Model of Product Distribution on a Set of Territories

Let us use the graph discussed above (see Sect. 1) to represent the map of a real world. Let a manufacturer is situated in the Central Federal District of Russian Federation. The logistics centers are situated in the following 17 cities – Moscow, Yaroslavl, Tver, Smolensk, Kaluga, Bryansk, Kostroma, Ivanovo, Vladimir, Ryazan, Tula, Oriel, Kursk, Belgorod, Lipetsk, Tambov, and Voronezh (see Fig. 1).

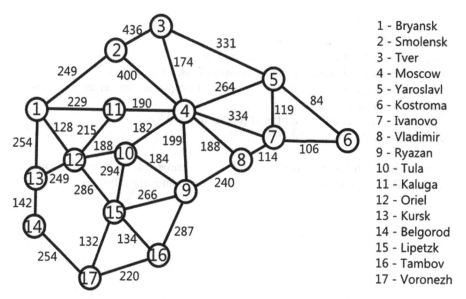

1 - Bryansk
2 - Smolensk
3 - Tver
4 - Moscow
5 - Yaroslavl
6 - Kostroma
7 - Ivanovo
8 - Vladimir
9 - Ryazan
10 - Tula
11 - Kaluga
12 - Oriel
13 - Kursk
14 - Belgorod
15 - Lipetzk
16 - Tambov
17 - Voronezh

Fig. 1. The example of graph for products distribution model with use of zonal pricing strategy.

To solve the stated problems one needs to construct the distribution model for production and represent the road-map as non-oriented weighted graph $G(V, E)$. For each $e \in E(G)$ the weight $w(e)$ be the distance between corresponding logistics centers according to Google maps service. For each $v \in V(G)$ the weight $w(v)$ be represented by two numbers: the unit price; demand at each logistics center.

4 Solving a Problem of Gross Profit Using the Model Constructed and Dijkstra Algorithm

The solution of gross profit calculation problem allows to estimate the value of potential enterprise profit after setting the different prices in different logistics centers in a moment. Estimation of potential profit for each pricing system may clarify to a company chef what prices should be set at each center. Lack of profit loss may allow the company to distribute funds according to the plan and avoid force majeure situations.

The common formula for calculating the profit of any activity is the following:

$$P = I - E,$$

where I be a profit of activity, and E be a loss.

Let us use this formula for the distribution graph model. In the terms of this model the profit be a sum of proceed of goods selling at each city; the losses be a transportation cost to each city. According to this, formula of calculation a profit is the following:

$$P = \sum \left(p(v) - C_t w(v) - C_p \right) \cdot d(v) N = 1,$$

where

- N be a number of logistics complexes;
- $p(v)$ be the products cost at the adjacent regions;
- $d(v)$ be a forecasted average monthly volume of sales at region v;
- $w(v)$ be the length of the shortest path between the production center and logistics complex at region v;
- C_t be the transportation cost for ton of production on 1 km;
- C_p be expenses to produce the ton of goods.

The length of the shortest path to any logistics center can be defined by Dijkstra algorithm. Thus, algorithm for calculating the gross profit is the following.

Algorithm Gross_Profit

Input data: Graph $G\ (V,\ E)$ representing the distribution model. The following functions are defined for it:

- $p(v)$ is the price of ton of goods at city v (monetary unit),
- $d(v)$ is the demand of goods at city v (ton),
- $l(e)$ is the length of a route between two points;
- C_t is expenses for one kilometer transportation of ton of production;
- C_p is expenses for producing the ton of production;
- $v_0 \in V(G)$ is the graph vertex where production complex is situated.

Output data: P is awaited profit.

Supplementary variables:

- $I(v)$ is a profit of selling at city v;
- $E(v)$ is loss for distribution at city v;
- $w(v)$ is the length of the shortest path from v_0 to v;
- I is common profit, E is common loss.

BEGIN

Step 1. Foe each $v \in V$ calculate $I(v) = p(v) \cdot d(v)$.

Step 2. Initiate $I = \sum I(v)$.

Step 3. For each $v \in V$ define $w(v) = \sum l(e)$ using Dijkstra algorithm.

Step 4. For each $v \in V$ define $E(v) = w(v) \cdot C_t \cdot d(v)$.

Step 5. Initiate $E = \sum E(v)$.

Step 6. $E = E + C_p \cdot \sum d(v)$.

Step 7. $P = I - E$.

Step 8. Output P.

END

The complexity of this algorithm is comparable to the complexity of Dijkstra algorithm as soon as it is the most time- and resource consuming for this algorithm. As soon as complexity of Dijkstra algorithm is less than $O(|V|^2)$ (if a graph is presented by adjacency matrix [9]) then the computing complexity of algorithm Gross_Profit is $O(|V|^2)$. The results of running of Step 3 for algorithm Gross_Profit do not depend on input data – there we define all distances from v_0 to all others.

5 The Problem of Maximal Resellers' Profit

The solution the problem of calculation the maximal resellers' profit yields increasing of accuracy of enterprise pricing policy management for a distributed territory. Using this problem solution one may estimate the probable profit of a reseller for resale the goods using the enterprise distribution system and define the routes between points of sale affected by product flow process. As a result one may correct the prices at towns of problem route and avoid changing the amount of goods at storehouses.

According to the constructed model the reason of product flows appearing may lay in possibility of getting the profit after resale the goods to neighboring regions. This opportunity appears only when the profit after resale of goods to neighboring regions is higher than expenses to transportation and sale of the goods. As far as this type of activity is peculiar to businessmen with formed client base we may exclude the expenses for organizing the sale.

Let so called reseller carry and sale the goods. Then probability of product flow appearance in distribution system be the maximal probability of product flow appearance between two regions.

The main aim of a reseller is to get the maximal profit after resale and transporting of goods, that is why the probability of product flow appearance between two regions be defined by supposed profit of a reseller. Surely, the reseller cannot take all the market but his profit directly depends on percent of market coverage (let it be designated as a).

Thus, the formula for calculation of resellers' supposed profit according to product flow amount between two regions is the following:

$$b = \max\{a \cdot d(v_1) \cdot (p(v_1) - p(v_2)) - C_t \cdot l(v_1, v_2)); a \cdot d(v_2) \cdot (p(v_2) - p(v_1)) - C_t \cdot l(v_1, v_2))\};$$

where

- a is a percent of market coverage;
- $p(v_1)$ be a price of goods at the first region;
- $p(v_2)$ be a price of goods at the second region;
- $d(v_1)$ be a forecasted average monthly sales volume at the first region;
- $d(v_2)$ be a forecasted average monthly sales volume at the second region;
- C_t be the expenses for 1 km transportation of ton of goods;
- $l(v_1, v_2)$ be a length of the shortest path between regions.

We may consider two types of product flows in distribution system:

- product flow between neighboring regions;
- product flow between any regions.

In the second case we mean that reseller may buy some goods at one region and sell it somewhere far away.

Let us consider two algorithms of estimation the supposed profit of resale according to segmentation of problems to these two types. Obviously if a problem claims to estimate the supposed profit of resale between two neighboring cities (incident vertices of graph) then $l(v_1, v_2) = l(e)$.

Algorithm of the supposed resale profit between two neighboring regions estimation is following.

Algorithm Maximal_Product_Flow

Input data:

Graph $G\ (V, E)$ as a model of goods distribution with defined functions:

- d_i^1 be demand for goods at the first vertex of each edge $e \in E(G)$;
- d_i^2 be demand for goods in the second vertex of each edge $e \in E(G)$;
- p_i^1 be goods cost at the first vertex of each edge $e \in E(G)$;
- p_i^2 be goods cost at the second vertex of each edge $e \in E(G)$;
- $l(e)$ be the path length between two incident vertices;
- C_t be expenses for one kilometer transportation of ton of the goods.

Output data: b_i be vector of profits from product flows between two neighboring regions.

BEGIN

Step 1. For each $e \in E(G)$ initiate $b(e)$.

Step 2. For each $e \in E(G)$ calculate:

$$b(e) = a \cdot d_i^2 \left(p_i^1 - p_i^2 - C_t \cdot l(e) \right) \text{ if } p_i^1 > p_i^2;$$

$$b(e) = a \cdot d_i^1 \left(p_i^2 - p_i^1 - C_t \cdot l(e) \right) \text{ if } p_i^1 \leq p_i^2.$$

Step 3. For each $e \in E(G)$ output $b(e)$.

Step 4. Output the maximal $b(e)$.

END

Let us consider the algorithm of estimation the supposed profit after reselling between all regions. If we need to estimate the reselling profit between remote regions then the shortest way length $l(v_1, v_2)$ between them is defined by Floyd-Warshell algorithm. Hence, algorithm of resale profit calculation between a pair of remote regions is following

Algorithm Maximal_Remote_Product_Flow

Input: Graph $G(V, E)$ be a goods distribution model with defined functions:

- d_i be demand for goods at the first vertex of each pair of vertices;
- d_j be demand for goods at the second vertex of each pair of vertices;
- p_i be goods cost at the first vertex of each pair of vertices;
- p_j be goods cost at the second vertex of each pair of vertices;
- $l(e)$ be the path length between two incident vertices;
- C_t be expenses for one kilometer transportation of ton of the goods.
- a be the share of market coverage by a reseller.

Output: $b(v_i, v_j)$ maximal value of resellers' profit due to product flow between all pairs of regions.

BEGIN

Step 1. Initiate $b(v_i, v_j)$ for each pair of vertices $(v_i, v_j) \in V$, $i \neq j$.

Step 2. Initiate $l(e)$ for each pair of adjacent vertices $(v_i, v_j) \in V$.

Step 3. For each pair of non-adjacent vertices $(v_i, v_j) \in V$ calculate $l(v_i, v_j)$ using Floyd-Warshell algorithm as $\sum l(e)$ of vertices between v_i and v_j.

Step 4. For each pair of vertices $(v_i, v_j) \in V$, $i \neq j$ calculate

$$b(v_i, v_j) = a \cdot d_j \left(p_i - p_j - C_t \cdot l(v_i, v_j) \right) \text{ if } p_i > p_j;$$

$$b(v_i, v_j) = a \cdot d_i \left(p_j - p_i - C_t \cdot l(v_i, v_j) \right) \text{ if } p_i \leq p_j.$$

Step 5. For each pair v_i, v_j output $b(v_i, v_j)$;

Step 6. Choose the maximal value $b(v_i, v_j)$.

END

The complexity of algorithm Maximal_Remote_Product_Flow is comparable with complexity of Floyd-Warshell algorithm as soon as step 3 running it claims maximal time in compare with the other steps. As soon as Floyd-Warshell algorithm contains three embedded cycles on the number of vertices then it has cubic complexity [10]. Hence, computing complexity of algorithm Maximal_Remote_Product_Flow is $O(|V|^3)$.

6 Computation Experiment

To hold the computational experiment we developed two C++ programs solving two problems of negative influence of product flows. They are:

- the estimation of the existing distribution system;
- identification of optimal parameters of the planned distribution system.

During solving the first problem the maximal gross profit of an enterprise and maximal possible resellers' profit for a fixed distribution system were defined.

Let us present the dependency of reseller's profit on the average production price by a dot chart in Fig. 2.

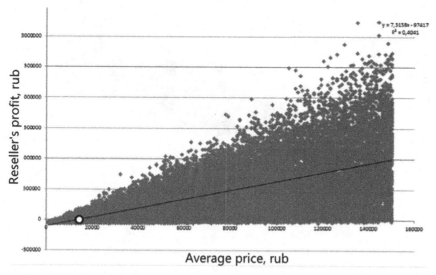

Fig. 2. The dependency of reseller's profit on average production price.

Then we display the trend equation using all the data. Proceeding from it, we may find the point of intersection of the trend equation with the abscissa axis, thus we find the average price of production from which a risk of product flow arises.

Let us construct the dependency of reseller's profit on dispersion of prices in different regions using the dot chart in Fig. 3.

It is easy to see that the rise of price dispersion yields the rise of reseller's profit. This is due to the fact that depending on the distribution of final prices on the sales territory the possible profit of a reseller may be significantly different.

Let us consider the same dependency if price dispersion is less than 5000 rubles (see Fig. 4) and define for this dot chart the trend line and its equation.

The dot chart in Fig. 4 allows seeing that different price dispersion may correspond to absolutely different values of resellers profit. For example, dispersion of the final prices of 500 rubles may give some profit to the reseller with a certain distribution of prices values in the cities of the distribution system. At the same time there are some cases when dispersion of prices equal to 2500 rubles brings reseller no profit. These situations are fixed in Fig. 4 by dots.

Let us define the value of prices dispersion when the probability of product flows is essential. Let us consider the trend equation for the given dependency and find its point of intersection with X-axis. Thus, we define the average value of prices dispersion when product flows begin to appear. The trend equation of dependency in Fig. 3 is $y = 80.614x - 72551$.

Hence, $y = 0$ if $x = 72551/80.614 = 899.98$. Respectively, for distribution systems with price dispersion less than 5000 rubles the probability of product flow emergence

Fig. 3. The dot chart of dependency of reseller's profit on the price dispersion.

Fig. 4. Dot chart of dependency of reseller's profit on dispersion of a price less or equal to 5000 rubles.

is high when the price dispersion is greater than 899.98 rubles, so, such a dispersion is undesirable for their establishment.

Obviously, at different average product prices, product flows behave differently. It depends on prices dispersion which is a certain percentage of the average price. To determine the moments of product flows occurrence we construct the dependence of the reseller's profit on the average products price for different percentages of prices dispersion. Figure 5 shows the diagram of the dependence of the reseller's profit on the products price with a price dispersion equal to 1% of the average price.

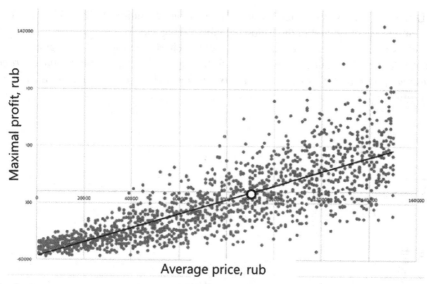

Fig. 5. Dependence of the reseller's profit on the average price of the goods with a price spread equal to 1% of the average.

The point in dot chart (see Fig. 5) shows the intersection of trend line with X-axis. This point corresponds to the average product price when the reseller gets some profit. Trend equation for dependency in Fig. 5 is $y = 0.6164 - 56320$. Hence, $y = 0$ if $x = 56320/0.6164 = 91369.24$. Accordingly, for such a system of prices when the final prices vary within 1% of the average price, product flows arise when the average price is greater than 91369.24 rubles.

Table 1. The levels of percentage deviation.

Percentage of price variation from the average price, %	Average price for the product flow appearing, rubles
1	91369.24
2	43281.40
3	30261.78
4	23749.21
5	19145.99
6	16621.17
7	15072.71
8	13891.66
9	13214.00
10	11897.71

Let us analyze some other levels of percentage deviation of 2%, 3%, etc. The calculations are presented in the following table (Table 1).

Let us represent the obtained data as a graph chart (see Fig. 6). This graph chart allows to conclude about existence of the following tendency: *the greater the average deviation of final prices from the average is, the lower the average price of the product when product flows arise.*

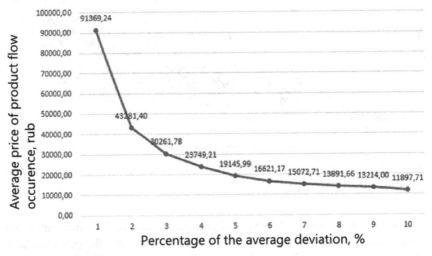

Fig. 6. The graph of the dependence of the product flow occurrence average price from the average dispersion of prices in the distribution system.

Obviously, the reseller's profit and, correspondingly, the probability of product flows occurrence do not depend on the average product price and depend only on the difference of prices at the neighboring regions or regions situated not too far away one from another.

It may seem that for an enterprise selling its products on a large territory it is unprofitable to set final prices of wide range in different cities. However, analyzing the diagram shown in Fig. 4 we can conclude that this statement is true only if the prices for products when moving from territory to territory have large differences.

For example, the probability of product flows occurrence for the distribution system which model is presented in Fig. 7 is rather higher than one in Fig. 8.

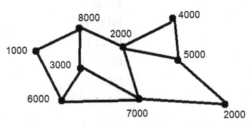

Fig. 7. The model of distribution system with high probability of product flow occurrence.

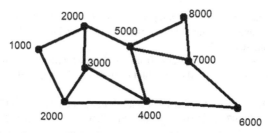

Fig. 8. The model of distribution system with low probability of product flow occurrence.

7 Conclusion

Graph theory may be used as one of the effective tools for calculating various economic indicators and results. The paper considers the way of using graph theory for modeling the distribution system of an enterprise. To calculate the shortest paths between the vertices of the graph the shortest path algorithms (Dijkstra algorithm and Floyd-Worshall algorithm) are used. In turn they are called up by algorithms developed by the authors to calculate the gross profit and the maximum profit of a reseller.

We showed that the average price when the product flow begins depends on the level of final prices dispersion. For example, for enterprises that have standard prices deviation equal to 1% product flows may occur at an average price greater than 91369.24 rubles, and for enterprises that have deviation of prices of 5% product flows occur at an average price of 19145.99 rubles. Accordingly, for enterprises that have a large average price, the risk of product flows is high even for a small prices deviation and enterprises with a higher cost of production are recommended to use non-price methods of combating product flows.

The probability of product flows occurrence for the distribution system determined by the reseller's profit is greater for those enterprises that have a more uneven distribution of final prices when moving from one sale area to another.

Acknowledgements. The work was supported by Act 211 Government of the Russian Federation, contract № 02.A03.21.0011.

References

1. Agarwal, P., Sahai, M., Mishra, V., Bag, M., Singh, V.: A review of multi-criteria decision making techniques for supplier evaluation and selection. Int. J. Indust. Eng. Comput. **2**(4), 801–810 (2011). https://doi.org/10.5267/j.ijiec.2010.06.004
2. Terrada, L., Bakkoury, J., El Khaili, M., Khiat, A.: Collaborative and communicative logistics flows management using the internet of things. In: Mizera-Pietraszko, J., Pichappan, P., Mohamed, L. (eds.) RTIS 2017. AISC, vol. 756, pp. 216–224. Springer, Cham (2019). https://doi.org/10.1007/978-3-319-91337-7_21

3. Kouvelis, P., Turcic, D., Zhao, W.: Supply chain contracting in environments with volatile input prices and frictions. Manuf. Serv. Oper. Manage. **20**(1), 130–146 (2018). https://doi.org/10.1287/msom.2017.0660

4. Tang, C.S., Yang, S.A., Wu, J.: Sourcing from suppliers with financial constraints and performance risk. Manuf. Serv. Oper. Manage. **20**(1), 70–84 (2018). https://doi.org/10.1287/msom.2017.0638

5. Teng, W., Mao, B., Cao, J.: A multi-level traceability system based on GraphLab. Procedia Comput. Sci. **91**, 971–977 (2016). https://doi.org/10.1016/j.procs.2016.07.126

6. Zhang, X., Chen, Y., Li, T.: Optimization of logistics route based on Dijkstra. In: 2015 6th IEEE International Conference on Software Engineering and Service Science (ICSESS), pp. 313–316. Beijing (2015). https://doi.org/10.1109/ICSESS.2015.7339063

7. Huber, S.: Strategic decision support for the bi-objective location-arc routing problem. In: 2016 49th Hawaii International Conference on System Sciences (HICSS), pp. 1407–1416. Koloa, HI (2016). https://doi.org/10.1109/HICSS.2016.178

8. Makarovskikh, T.A.: Combinatorics and Graph Theory, 3rd edn. Librocom, Moscow (2017). (in Russian)

9. Levitin, A.V.: Introduction to the Design and Analysis of Algorithms, 3rd edn. Pearson (2011)

10. Cormen, T.H., Leiserson, C.E., Rivest, R.L., Stein, C.: Introduction to Algorithms, 3rd edn. The MIT Press (2009)

Objective Determination of the Graduating Students' Competencies Level

Kirill Roshkovan(✉) ⓘ, Ivan Chaley ⓘ, and Olga Latypova ⓘ

OJSC "Surgutneftegas", Grigoriya Kukuevickogo Str., 1, k. 1, 628415 Surgut, Russia
roshkovan_ks@surgutneftegas.ru

Abstract. The use of the competency-based approach in the educational process results in the need to formulate a quantification and objective evaluation of students' competencies that they mastered in the course of their studies.

The article proposes a methodology and algorithm for calculating the achieved competencies level formed during training of university graduates. The methodology is based on a structural description of competencies through the results of training in individual disciplines and the number of credits allocated for the subject mastery.

To display the links between disciplines and learning outcomes, an index designation system is introduced. Connected sets are a mathematical representation of a curriculum. Learning outcomes are evaluated through controls, each of which is characterized by a specific labor intensity. The use of labor intensity as weighting factors enables an objective assessment of learning outcomes and the competencies level.

The results can be used to justify the objectivity of using a point-rating system both within the individual disciplines, and the curriculum as a whole.

Keywords: Competencies · Assessment model · Learning outcomes · Mathematical models

1 Introduction and Problematique

Federal State Educational Standards of the third generation plus (FSES 3+) have fixed a competency-based approach to assessing the results of the education outcomes. A graduate, as a product of higher education, is assessed in accordance with the totality of general cultural, general professional and professional competencies [1].

The requirements for these competencies are established by the educational standard. They are the goal of an educational program that meets the needs of the modern labor market (professional standards as a guide) and satisfies the needs of the individual. They are formulated as the ability of a graduate to apply the acquired knowledge, skills, experience and social and personal qualities to carry out professional activities [2].

In the practice of higher education, quite a lot of experience has been gained in implementing the requirements of the competency-based approach. However, many problems remain unresolved. This is due to the following factors:

V. Sukhomlin and E. Zubareva (Eds.): SITITO 2017, CCIS 1204, pp. 325–329, 2021.
https://doi.org/10.1007/978-3-030-78273-3_30

- weak capacity for formalizing competencies and related concepts;
- inconsistency between the requirements of educational and professional standards;
- lack of a clear meaningful description of competencies;
- interdisciplinary, continuous and cyclical nature of the competencies development.

In the context of the practical implementation of the competency-based approach, methodological developments of its application are still in demand.

As a result, today there is no single methodological basis for assessing the formed level of competencies [3]. This leads to the fact that each educational institution develops one or more point-rating systems with a significant proportion of subjectivity.

The purpose of this study is to develop a model that allows you to determine the objective level of competencies through the learning outcomes (Fig. 1) of a student and a high school graduate.

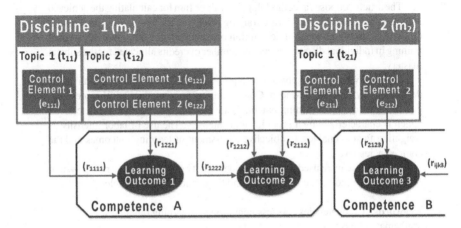

Fig. 1. Schematic representation of the model.

2 Software

Let's introduce an index system to display the relationship between disciplines and learning outcomes r_{ijks}, where:

- index i is the sequence number of the discipline in the core curricula;
- index j is the sequence number of the topic in the discipline i;
- index k is the serial number of the control in the topic i of the discipline j;
- index s is the serial number of the learning outcome.

Thus, the notation system reflects the semantics of the general education curriculum.

Let us introduce the basic mathematical definitions for the derivation of the final evaluation formulas.

The set of disciplines forms a training program and it is referred to as:

$$M = \{m_1 \ldots m_{1 < i < |M|} \ldots m_{|M|}\}, \tag{1}$$

where $|M|$ – total number of disciplines.

The set of all topics:

$$T = T_1 \cup T_{1 < i < |M|} \cup T_{|M|}. \tag{2}$$

The set T_i of topics of the i-th academic discipline reflects the syllabuses of the discipline and is defined as follows:

$$\forall m_i \in M \; \exists t_{i,j} \in T_i : \; 1 \le i \le |M|, \; 1 \le j \le |T_i|, \tag{3}$$

where $|T_i|$ – number of topics of i-discipline.

The set of all controls:

$$E = E_{11} \cup E_{1 < i < |M| \; 1 \le j \le |T_i|} \cup E_{|M| \, |T_i|}. \tag{4}$$

The set E_{ij} set of control elements of the j-th topic of the i-th discipline makes up the fund of evaluative tools of the discipline and is determined as follows:

$$\forall m_i \in M \; \forall t_{i,j} \in T_i \exists e_{ijk} \in E_{ij} : \; 1 \le i \le |M|, \; 1 \le j \le |T_i|, 1 \le k \le |E_{ij}|, \tag{5}$$

where $|E_{ij}|$ – the number of controls in the j-th topic of the i-th discipline.

Controls are characterized by the numerical value $o_{ijk} = \{0, 2, 3, 4, 5\}$ and the norm of time n_{ijk} (in hours, fractional values are permitted). The ratio of the time norm for the implementation of the control element to the total hour norm for all control elements aimed at assessing the learning outcome is the weight coefficient of the contribution of this element to the overall assessment of the learning outcome.

Example of the designation of the norm of time: $n_{231} = 7.5$ – in the second discipline in the third topic, the norm of 7.5 h is established for the first control element.

The set of all learning outcomes:

$$R = R_{111} \cup R_{1 < i < |M| \; 1 \le j \le |T_i| \; 1 < k < |E_{ij}|} \cup R_{|M| \, |T_i| |E_{ij}|}. \tag{6}$$

The set R_{ijk} of the all learning outcomes, the k-th control element of the j-th topic of the i-th discipline is aimed at assessing their achievement, is determined as follows:

$$\forall m_i \in M \; \forall t_{i,j} \in T_i \forall e_{ijk} \in E_{ij} \; \exists r_{ijks} \in R_{ijk} :$$
$$1 \le i \le |M|, \; 1 \le j \le |T_i|, 1 \le k \le |E_{ij}|, \; 1 \le s \le |R|, \tag{7}$$

where $|R|$ – the number of learning outcomes.

The index definitions given above exclude the possibility of the presence of empty sets, which is justified from the point of view of the educational process: $M \ne \emptyset$ (curriculum), $T_i \ne \emptyset$ (the syllabus of the training course), $E_{ij} \ne \emptyset$ (valuation fund).

If a separate topic forms and evaluates the achievement of several learning outcomes through an element of control, then this fact s displayed by the presence of several elements in the set R_{ijk} For example, a record of the type $R_{234} = \{r_{2343}, r_{2347}\}$ indicates that in the second discipline in the third topic, the fourth control element is aimed at assessing the achievement of results 3 and 7.

It should be especially emphasized that in the adopted notation system there is no dependence of the learning outcome index on discipline indices, topics and control elements (Formula 7). This is due to the fact that the same competence can be formed in several disciplines (topics). In this regard, records of the form indicate the same learning outcome, however, it is achieved in different disciplines (topics).

3 Assessment of Learning Outcomes

The assessment of learning outcomes is carried out according to the following formula:

$$
RO_s = \sum_{i=1}^{|M|} \sum_{j=1}^{|T_i|} \sum_{k=1}^{|E_{ij}|} \left(\frac{o_{ijk} \times n_{ijk}}{\sum_k n_{ijk}} \right), \tag{8}
$$

where M – a set of disciplines by which the topics of disciplines from the set T_i are distributed; T_i – the set of topics of disciplines, which include elements of control from the set E_{ij}; E_{ij} – a set of control elements in which the considered result s is evaluated.

The denominator of the formula is the total laboriousness of the implementation of all control elements aimed at assessing the achievement of the learning outcome in question (Table 1).

Table 1. The calculation example of the assessment of learning s.

Discipline i	Topic j	Control k	Time norm n_{ijks}	Assessment per item o_{ijks}
1	1	1	2.0	4
		2	4.0	3
		3	6.0	5
	2	1	10.0	4
2	1	1	5.0	4
	2	2	7.0	5
M^j	T_i^k	E_{ij}^s	34.0	4.27

$$
RO_s = \left(\left(\frac{2 \times 4}{34} + \frac{4 \times 3}{34} + \frac{6 \times 5}{34} \right) + \frac{10 \times 4}{34} \right) + \left(\frac{5 \times 4}{34} + \frac{7 \times 5}{34} \right) = 4.27
$$

The described method for calculating the assessment of learning outcomes can be performed at any time during the implementation of the educational program. The time of the assessment is established by the choice of one or another set of control elements.

The resulting assessment is compared with the level of competence development (Table 2):

Table 2. The resulting assessment is compared with the level of competence development.

The assessment of learning outcomes RO_s		Competency mastery
Lower bound	Upper bound	
0	2	Not mastered
2	3	Basic
3	4	Advanced
4	5	Creative

4 Conclusion

Despite the widespread use of a point-rating system in many universities, the proposed model as input involves the use of a traditional assessment system. In most cases, point-rating systems are of author's origin, they are also conditional in nature and often turn into a tool for legalizing of students' "purchases" of an examination scores.

The proposed assessment, together with weights based on the physical quantity - hours (in accordance with the syllabuses of the disciplines), reflect the true complexity of didactic units. The flexibility of the proposed model makes it possible to use it to assess the formation of competencies at any stage of the educational process.

References

1. Federal State Educational Standards of Higher Education in the Areas of IT-magistracy. Portal of Federal State Educational Standards. http://fgosvo.ru/fgosvo/93/91/5/31. (in Russian)
2. Latypova, O. (ed.): Lifecycle Management of Information Business Systems. Competencies. Enterprise Architecture, pp. 27–32. Neft Priobya Publ., Surgut (2014). (in Russian)
3. Ibragimov, G.I., Ibragimova, E.M.: Competence assessment: challenges and solutions. High. Educ. Russia (1), 43–52 (2016). https://elibrary.ru/item.asp?id=24993105. (in Russian)

Author Index

Printed in the United States
by Baker & Taylor Publisher Services